Digital Image Processing: Technologies and Applications

Digital Image Processing: Technologies and Applications

Guest Editors

Héctor Manuel Pérez-Meana
Mariko Nakano-Miyatake

MDPI

Basel • Beijing • Wuhan • Barcelona • Belgrade • Novi Sad • Cluj • Manchester

Guest Editors

Héctor Manuel Pérez-Meana
Escuela Superior de Ingeniería Mecánica y Eléctrica
Instituto Politécnico Nacional
Mexico City
Mexico

Mariko Nakano-Miyatake
Escuela Superior de Ingeniería Mecánica y Eléctrica
Instituto Politécnico Nacional
Mexico City
Mexico

Editorial Office
MDPI AG
Grosspeteranlage 5
4052 Basel, Switzerland

This is a reprint of the Special Issue, published open access by the journal *Applied Sciences* (ISSN 2076-3417), freely accessible at: https://www.mdpi.com/journal/applsci/special_issues/BGU6JYZI97.

For citation purposes, cite each article independently as indicated on the article page online and as indicated below:

Lastname, A.A.; Lastname, B.B. Article Title. *Journal Name* **Year**, *Volume Number*, Page Range.

ISBN 978-3-7258-6454-6 (Hbk)
ISBN 978-3-7258-6455-3 (PDF)
https://doi.org/10.3390/books978-3-7258-6455-3

Contents

About the Editors

Héctor Manuel Pérez-Meana

Héctor Manuel Pérez-Meana received an M.S. degree from the University of Electro-Communications and a Dr. Eng. Degree from Tokyo Institute of Technology in 1989. He was a visiting researcher at the Fujitsu Laboratories from April 1989 to July 1991. From July 1991 to February 1997, he was a Professor at the Electrical Engineering Department of the Metropolitan University of Mexico. In February 1997, he became a professor in the Mechanical and Electrical Engineering Department at the National Polytechnic Institute of Mexico (IPN), where he was the Dean of the Graduate and Research Section from 2006 to 2010, as well as from 2016 to 2019. He was Chair of the ISITA in 1998, the IEEE MWSCAS in 2009, the IEEE-IWBF in 2018, the SOMET in 2021, and the SOMET in 2024. He is also an Associate Editor of Elsevier's *Applied Intelligence* journal. He received the IEICE Best Paper in 1991, the IPN Research Award in 1999, and the IPN Research Diploma in 2000. He is a Life Senior Member of the IEEE, a member of the IEICE, and a member of the Mexican Academy of Science, as well as a member of the National Researchers System of Mexico (Level III). He has published about 290 indexed international journal papers. He has been the director of more than 40 Ph.D. theses and 51 M.Sc theses. His research interests include adaptive systems, signal and image processing, artificial intelligence, and related fields.

Mariko Nakano-Miyatake

Mariko Nakano-Miyatake obtained her bachelor's and master's degrees from the University of Electro-Communications, Tokyo, Japan, in 1983 and 1985, respectively, and her doctorate from the Metropolitan Autonomous University in 1998. Currently, she is a Research Professor at the Mechanical and Electronic Engineering (ESIME) School, Culhuacán Campus, Instituto Politécnico Nacional (IPN), and she is a member of the National System of Researchers (SNII) at Level III. She has published approximately 90 research articles in JCR-indexed journals and has over 400 publications in national and international conference proceedings. To date, she has supervised 23 doctoral dissertations and 77 master's theses. Her main research areas are machine learning, deep learning, artificial intelligence, image and signal processing, and computer security.

applied sciences

MDPI

Editorial

Digital Image Processing: Technologies and Applications

Hector Perez-Meana * and Mariko Nakano-Miyatake

Mechanical and Electrical Engineering School, Instituto Politécnico Nacional, Ciudad de Mexico 04450, Mexico; marikonakano2@gmail.com
* Correspondence: hmperezm@ipn.mx

1. Introduction

Image processing has been an active research topic since the mid-1970s, during which time schemes for filtering noise reduction, enhancement, compression, and spectral analysis, among others, have been developed [1,2]. Subsequently, with the advancement of digital technology, the number of digital processing applications has increased, becoming an essential tool in the development of biometric identification systems, schemes that enhance security in transportation, video surveillance, early tumor detection and other medical applications, security schemes, pattern recognition, information protection and authentication, and remote sensing, among others [3–7].

The above prompted the publication of this Special Issue, which addresses topics related to image filtering in both grayscale and color as well as hidden information transmission and lossless recovery of the carrier image [4,8]. In many cases, the important thing is the recovery of the hidden information without paying attention to the carrier image [8]; however, in many cases, it is also necessary to recover the carrier with the least possible distortion. Regarding information hiding, the insertion of digital watermarks for authentication has been another important aspect [9] in applications such as copyright protection. In terms of medical applications, segmentation is a topic of great interest since it allows separating the background from the objects of interest as well as applications related to viral detections that enable the development of treatments for various diseases [10]. Finally, another aspect that has received considerable attention is the authentication of images whose content is intentionally modified to alter their meaning [11–13]. The next section presents a description of the articles included in this Special Issue.

2. Overview of Published Articles

Information hiding mechanisms, which can be divided into watermarking and steganography, have found applications in various fields such as the storage of relevant information in medical images as well as the transmission of hidden information embedded in various carrier images, image authentication, etc. In many cases, it is necessary to recover hidden information without considering the quality of the carrier image. However, there are applications in which the carrier image must be recovered without distortion. To this end, mechanisms that allow reversible data hiding have been a topic of recent development interest. This has led to the development of various reversible data hiding (RDH) methods that aim to prioritize the exact recovery of the original carrier image. However, this limits both the embedding capacity and the flexibility of the system design. One of the articles in this Special Issue presents a partially reversible data hiding (PRDH) scheme that differs from conventional standards by allowing relative reversibility to an estimated covered image instead of the original one. The proposed system leverages a structure that enhances the (7,4) HC Hamming code to synthesize virtual pixels, enabling efficient coding. The proposed system achieved embedding rates up to 1.5 bpp with PSNR values above 48 dB while avoiding the use of auxiliary data; however, its reliability depends on the availability of paired images, which could be a limitation in real-world situations. The demonstrated resilience to RS-based steganographic analysis suggests its feasibility in sensitive domains. However, further evaluation with a wider variety of image types is required. Further details can be found in the article included in this Special Issue.

Entropy-based thresholding is a widely used technique for medical image segmentation. The basic principle is to determine the optimal threshold by maximizing or minimizing the image entropy, dividing the image into different regions or categories. In many cases, the intensity distributions of objects and backgrounds often overlap and consequently contain many outliers, making segmentation extremely difficult. This Special Issue includes a paper that presents a new thresholding method that incorporates the Cauchy distribution into a Tsallis entropy-based Bayesian estimation framework. By introducing Bayesian a priori probability estimation to address the overlap in intensity distributions between the two classes, the estimation of the probability of a pixel belonging to either class is improved. Additionally, the Cauchy distribution is used to adjust gray levels during optimal multilateral estimation for medical brain images based on Tsallis entropy, incorporating both Bayesian estimation and Cauchy distribution. The optimal threshold is derived by optimizing an information measure formulated using Tsallis entropy. Experimental results demonstrated that the proposed method, called Cauchy-TB, achieved significant superiority compared with existing approaches.

Digital watermarking is a technique used to solve or reduce problems associated with the widespread use of the Internet for sharing digital information such as copyright protection, tamper detection, and information authentication, among others. However, in most cases, watermarking negatively affects the quality of the original image. To address this problem, a digital watermarking optimization process is presented that utilizes the double-tree complex wavelet transform (DTCWT) in conjunction with a particle swarm optimization (PSO) algorithm. The presented approach attempts to maintain the highest possible quality of the watermarked image while minimizing any perceptible changes. In the proposed scheme, during the embedding phase, the original image is decomposed using the technique called double-tree complex wavelet transform (DTCWT) in conjunction with the particle swarm optimization method (PSO), which allows for the selection of appropriate coefficients. The bits of a binary logo are then embedded into the least significant bits of the selected coefficients, creating the watermarked image. Watermark extraction is performed by reversing the embedding process, first decomposing the input image using DTCWT and subsequently extracting the same coefficients to recover the bits corresponding to the watermark. Experimental results using a dataset commonly used by other researchers demonstrated the functionality of the proposed system through metrics such as signal-to-noise ratio (PSNR) and normalized cross-correlation (NCC), yielding PSNR and NCC values of 80.50% and 92.51%, respectively.

The spread of the chikungunya virus, a member of the Alphavirus genus, is a major health problem. It continues to pose a global health challenge due to its widespread presence and the lack of specific antiviral therapies. Accurate detection of viral infections, such as that caused by the chikungunya virus, is crucial for antiviral research; however, traditional methods are time-consuming and error prone. This Special Issue presents the development and validation of an image-processing-based algorithm that improves the accuracy and speed of virus detection, which will contribute to the development of potential anti-chikungunya compounds. The proposed system used MvTec Halcon software (version 22.11) to develop an algorithm for detecting and classifying infected and uninfected cells in viral assays. Its performance was validated using manual counts performed by virology experts, showing promising results with Pearson coefficients of 0.9807 for cell detection and 0.9886 for virus detection. This indicates a high correlation between the values obtained by the algorithm and manual counts performed by three virology experts, demonstrating that the algorithm's accuracy closely matched the experts' manual assessments. Following statistical validation, the algorithm was applied to screen antiviral compounds, demonstrating its effectiveness in improving the throughput and accuracy of drug discovery workflows. This technology represents a scalable and efficient tool that contributes to accelerating drug development and improving the diagnosis of vector-borne and emerging viral diseases.

Another proposal presented in this Special Issue consists of a new edge-oriented sliding-window filter that computes output pixels using a cross-correlation-like equation derived from fractional calculus (FC); we will call this the "fractional cross-correlation filter" (FCCF). The performance of this filter is evaluated exclusively using edge-preserving metrics such as gradient driving mean square error (GCMSE), edge-based structural similarity (EBSSIM), and multi-scale structural similarity (MS-SSIM). The filter's performance was evaluated using statistical techniques based on the Berkeley segmentation dataset as a test corpus. Experimental data showed that based on the considered metrics, the proposed approach achieved an improved performance compared with conventional edge filters. The experimental results underscore the potential of FCCF to significantly contribute to the advancement of image processing techniques in many practical applications such as medical imaging, image enhancement, and computer vision, which rely heavily on the edge detection filters employed.

Grayscale image processing is of utmost importance in computer vision and image analysis, where image quality and visualization effects can be severely affected by high-density impulse noise. Typically, a traditional median filter is used to reduce this noise, which can result in poor performance by distorting details under high amounts of noise, resulting in weak robustness. To reduce the effects of high-density impulse noise on image quality by processing high-noise grayscale versions of images, a median filter using the enhanced two-dimensional Shannon maximum entropy filter (TSETMF) was proposed for adaptive threshold selection. This improved the filter performance while stably and effectively retaining the image details. This paper presented an improved TSETMF algorithm, which filters the noise in images by automatically partitioning the window size, whose threshold value is adaptively calculated using the two-dimensional maximum Shannon entropy. The theoretical model was verified and analyzed through comparative experiments using three types of classical grayscale images. The experimental results demonstrate that the proposed improved TSETMF algorithm exhibited a better processing performance than that of the traditional filter, with superior high-density noise suppression and denoising stability. The experimental results showed a peak signal-to-noise ratio (PSNR) greater than 24.97 dB when the noise density was 95% located on the classical grayscale image of Lena.

Image filtering is a very important task in image processing. To this end, this Special Issue presents a new filter for removing impulse noise in digital color images. The proposed filter uses a detection stage to correct only noisy pixels, performing their detection using a binary classification model generated using genetic programming. The classification training scheme considers three impulse noise models in color images: impulsive, uniform, and correlated. The correction stage consists of a vector median filter that modifies the color channel values if any of them are noisy. The proposed filter was compared with other state-of-the-art filters related to noise removal in color images using PSNR, MAE, SSIM, and FSIM metrics. The experimental results showed substantial variation in the performance of the filters depending on the noise model under analysis and the image characteristics. The experimental results also indicate that, on average, the proposed filter exhibited highly efficient performance for all three impulse noise models, surpassed only by a deep learning-based filter. However, unlike the deep learning-based filters, the proposed filter exhibited high interpretability with a performance close to the break-even point for all images and noise models used in the experiment.

Image forgery using the copy-move scheme is a simple and common manipulation technique. To mitigate the problems related to the high time complexity of most copy-move forgery detection algorithms and the difficulty in detecting forgeries in smooth regions, a paper in this Special Issue proposes a copy-move forgery detection algorithm based on fused features and density clustering. The proposed algorithm combines two detection methods: accelerated robust features (SURF) and accelerated KAZE (A-KAZE), to extract descriptive features by setting a low contrast threshold. Subsequently, the density-based spatial clustering of applications with noise (DBSCAN) algorithm is employed to eliminate mismatched pairs and reduce false positives. The algorithm uses the original image and the image transformed by the affine matrix to compare similarities at the same position and locate the counterfeit region, thereby improving counterfeit detection. Experimental results showed that the method effectively improved counterfeit detection accuracy in smooth regions and reduced computational complexity, demonstrating high robustness to post-processing operations such as rotation, scaling, and noise addition.

3. Conclusions

This Special Issue presents a series of articles related to the technological development and applications of image processing in solving various existing problems in different fields. These applications involve the treatment, analysis, verification, and modification of images, ranging from schemes aimed at improving image quality through noise reduction via filtering and enhancement, to image segmentation that allows separating objects of interest from their background as well as schemes to improve people's quality of life by enabling the development of new antiviral drugs and facilitating the early detection of tumors. Likewise, schemes are presented that will contribute to advances in the development of security systems through reversible recovery of the cover image used in information hiding, watermarking, and image authentication schemes. All of the developments presented will surely impact the development of technology associated with image processing and its use in solving problems that still exist in various fields of science and technology.

Author Contributions: H.P.-M.: Writing—original draft preparation; M.N.-M.: Writing—review and editing. All authors have read and agreed to the published version of the manuscript.

Funding: This research received no external funding.

Conflicts of Interest: The authors declare no conflicts of interest.

References

1. Gonzalez, R.; Woods, R. *Digital Image Processing*; Pearson: Upper Saddle River, NJ, USA, 2008.
2. Dougherty, E. *Digital Image Processing Methods*; Dekker: New York, NY, USA, 1994.
3. Sencar, H.T.; Menon, N. *Digital Image Forensics*; Springer: New York, NY, USA, 2013.
4. Janhe, B. *Digital Image Processing and Image Acquisition*; Springer: Cham, Switzerland, 2025.
5. Pimenov, D.Y.; da Silva, L.R.R.; Ercetin, A.; Der, O.; Mikolajczyk, T.; Giasin, K. State-of-the-art review of applications of image processing techniques for tool condition monitoring on conventional machining processes. *Int. J. Adv. Manuf. Technol.* **2024**, *130*, 57–85. [CrossRef]
6. Myslicka1, R.M.; Kawala-Sterniuk, A.; Bryniarska, A.; Sudol, A.; Podpora, M.; Gasz, R.; Martinek, R.; Vilimkova, R.; Vilimek, D.; Pelc, M.; et al. Review of the application of the most current sophisticated image processing methods for the skin cancer diagnostics purposes. *Arch. Dermatol. Res.* **2024**, *316*, 99. [CrossRef] [PubMed]

7. Aggarwal, A.; Bharadwaj, S.; Corredor, G.; Pathak, T.; Badve, S.; Madabhushi, A. Artificial intelligence in digital pathology—time for a reality check. *Nat. Rev. Clin. Oncol.* **2025**, *22*, 283–291. [CrossRef] [PubMed]
8. Kirthiga, R.; Elavenil, S. A survey on crack detection in concrete surface using image processing and machine learning. *J. Build. Pathol. Rehabil.* **2024**, *9*, 15. [CrossRef]
9. Kadian, P.; Arora, S.M.; Arora, N. Robust Digital Watermarking Techniques for Copyright Protection of Digital Data: A Survey. *Wirel. Pers. Commun.* **2021**, *118*, 3225–3249. [CrossRef]
10. Shah, O.I.; Rizvi, D.R.; Mir, A.N. Transformer-Based Innovations in Medical Image Segmentation: A Mini Review. *SN Comput. Sci.* **2025**, *6*, 375. [CrossRef]
11. Sandhya; Kashyap, A. A comprehensive analysis of digital video forensics techniques and challenges. *Iran J. Comput. Sci.* **2024**, *7*, 359–380. [CrossRef]
12. Chaitra, B.; Reddy, P.V.B. Digital image forgery: Taxonomy, techniques, and tools–a comprehensive study. *Int. J. Syst. Assur. Eng. Manag.* **2023**, *14* (Suppl. S1), 18–33. [CrossRef]
13. Kaur, N.; Jindal, N.; Singh, K. Passive Image Forgery Detection Techniques: A Review, Challenges, and Future Directions. *Wirel. Pers. Commun.* **2024**, *134*, 1491–1529. [CrossRef]

applied sciences

MDPI

Article

Dual Partial Reversible Data Hiding Using Enhanced Hamming Code

Cheonshik Kim [1,*], Ching-Nung Yang [2] and Lu Leng [3,*]

1 Department of Computer Engineering, Sejong University, Seoul 05006, Republic of Korea
2 Department of Computer Science and Information Engineering, National Dong Hwa University, Hualien 97401, Taiwan; cnyang@gms.ndhu.edu.tw
3 School of Software, Nanchang Hangkong University, Nanchang 330063, China
* Correspondence: mipsan@sejong.ac.kr (C.K.); leng@nchu.edu.cn (L.L.)

Abstract

Traditional reversible data hiding (RDH) methods prioritize the exact recovery of the original cover image; however, this rigidity often hinders both capacity and design flexibility. This study introduces a partial reversible data hiding (PRDH) framework that departs from conventional standards by allowing reversibility relative to a generated cover image rather than the original. The proposed system leverages a dual-image structure and an enhanced HC(7,4) Hamming code to synthesize virtual pixels, enabling efficient and low-distortion syndrome-based encoding. Notably, it achieves embedding rates up to 1.5 bpp with PSNR values exceeding 48 dB. While the proposed method avoids auxiliary data, its reliability hinges on paired image availability, which is a consideration for real-world deployment. Demonstrated resilience to RS-based steganalysis suggests viability in sensitive domains such as embedding structured metadata in diagnostic medical imagery. Nonetheless, further evaluation across more diverse image types and attack scenarios is necessary in order to confirm its generalizability.

Keywords: data hiding (DH); reversible DH (RDH); dual RDH; Hamming coding; exploiting modification direction (EMD)

1. Introduction

Although the internet facilitates global communication, it cannot always be regarded as a fully secure channel, especially when handling sensitive information. Therefore, appropriate security protocols must be employed to ensure that confidential information is exchanged safely. A common approach to defending internet communications is to encrypt messages during transmission. However, because encrypted messages are often easy to recognize, they may themselves become targets of attack. An alternative method known as data hiding (DH) [1–4] involves embedding information within digital media. Because this process can appear the same as ordinary data transmission, it tends to draw less attention from potential attackers. Leveraging this characteristic can further strengthen the security of data exchanges.

DH can be broadly classified into reversible (RDH) and non-reversible (N-RDH) methods. RDH techniques have the characteristic that the original cover image can be fully restored after extracting the hidden data from the stego image. Several representative RDH algorithms have been proposed to date, including difference expansion (DE)-based methods [5–7], histogram shifting (HS) techniques [8–10], and prediction error expansion (PEE) [11].

First introduced by Tian in [5], the DE approach has demonstrated excellent performance in terms of embedding capacity. The histogram shifting (HS) method [8], first introduced in 2006, is regarded as an improvement over previous techniques due to the relatively lower distortion it causes to the cover medium. However, RDH schemes require a location map to embed data and recover the original cover image. While this method achieves good visual quality and reasonable embedding capacity, it has the drawback of requiring the transmission of two peak points and a zero-point pair to the receiver. PEE [11] involves obtaining prediction errors from the neighborhood of each pixel and embedding information bits into the expanded errors. If the difference between the original and predicted pixels is large, the embedding process can cause significant distortion to the cover image. DH methods based on ordered prediction can reduce distortion at low embedding rates.

On the other hand, secret sharing [12] has the feature that while n participants create n shadows using the same cover image to share data, the data can only be reconstructed when there are shadows of $k(k \leq n)$ participants. If the number of participants is less than k, then data reconstruction will fail. In terms of data confidentiality, secret sharing is very powerful and can be used in various applications.

Dual image-based RDH [13–26] adopts some features of secret sharing, utilizing $n(= k = 2)$ cover images. Thus, two shadow images are required to recover the original image. Chang et al. (2007) [13] introduced a dual-image RDH method using the exploitation modification direction (EMD). In their approach, two quinary secret data points are used to form a pair of stego pixels, with cover pixel pairs referenced according to the main and secondary diagonals of the EMD matrix. Later, Chang et al. (2013) [14] proposed an improved method for enhancing the visual quality of the stego images.

Lee and Huang (2013) [15] enhanced the visual quality of stego images by limiting modifications during the data hiding process to at most plus or minus one. Qin et al. [16] proposed an asymmetric dual-image RDH method in which the first stego image is generated using the EMD technique and the second is created based on three rule analyses applied to the first image. As a result, the first stego image experiences greater distortion compared to the second.

Lu et al. (2015) [17] discovered that the LSB-matching technique, originally used in N-RDH, could be adapted for dual-image schemes. However, because direct application was not feasible, they devised seven new rules for pixel recovery and applied them to the dual-image restoration process. They then demonstrated the effectiveness of their proposed method through experiments. In a separate work, Lu et al. (2015) [18] introduced a dual-image-based data hiding strategy utilizing a center folding technique. In this approach, secret data values are first compressed using the folding strategy, allowing more data to be embedded. The folded secret data are then hidden across two stego image pixels. Building on this, Yao et al. (2017) [19] focused on improving the visual quality of stego images by identifying and enhancing areas where Lu's [18] method could be further optimized.

Jana et al. (2018) [21] proposed a method that extracts seven-pixel blocks from the original image and duplicates them into two arrays. The least significant bits (LSBs) of each array are adjusted using odd parity, increasing error resilience during transmission. Secret message bits are embedded into specific positions within these arrays while deliberately excluding certain predesignated positions reserved for integrity checks. During the embedding phase, bit modifications may introduce errors, which are subsequently detected and corrected by the receiver using Hamming (7,4) error correction codes. While this method demonstrates innovative integration of error-correcting codes, its low embedding capacity (0.21 bpp) limits its suitability for applications requiring high payloads.

Chen and Hong (2021) [23] introduced a dual-image RDH scheme utilizing the exploiting modification direction (EMD) method, achieving reversibility without additional overhead. While their method represents an improvement in eliminating auxiliary data, it falls short of surpassing earlier EMD-based methods such as that of Chang et al. (2013) [14]. In addition, it involves complex orientation combinations, which increase implementation complexity and make optimization difficult.

Lee and Chan (2024) [26] proposed a novel dual-image RDH method based on vector coordinates with triangular order coding (TOC), achieving superior embedding capacity and image quality without requiring additional side information. Their method focuses on position-based embedding, allowing for flexible adjustment of capacity via the *k* parameter. Wan et al.(2025) [27] proposed a multi-party RDH framework for medical information that utilizes texture-guided hierarchical quantization coding (TGHQC) to enhance embedding capacity and security. Additionally, both image owners and data providers perform data embedding through a dual embedding mechanism, allowing for role-specific data access. This method maintains data reversibility and security, thereby improving the efficiency of medical information management. Zhan et al. (2024) [28] proposed a reversible fragile watermarking scheme based on the insect matrix reversible embedding algorithm to enable full recovery of untampered cover images. Upon tampering, adaptive dual recovery schemes are employed to restore corrupted data while maintaining high image quality. Moreover, image-rendering techniques are introduced to enhance the accuracy of tampering detection, particularly in cases of tampering coincidence.

This study proposes an enhanced dual-image RDH method based on the HC(7,4) Hamming code to overcome limitations in prior methods. By applying this Hamming code to pixel groups across two cover images, our method significantly increases embedding capacity, reaching 1.5 bpp, which is over seven times greater than in Jana et al. (2018) [21]. In addition, our method ensures high visual quality with PSNR values between 48 and 49 dB, outperforming methods such as that of Chang et al. (2013) [14]. Compared to complex EMD-based design of Chen and Hong (2021) [23], our scheme offers a simpler and more efficient solution. Unlike halftone-based methods [25], it supports general grayscale images while guaranteeing full reconstructability, making it suitable for secure high-capacity RDH applications.

The key contributions of this paper are summarized as follows: (1) The proposed scheme achieves a high embedding capacity of up to 1.5 bpp by applying enhanced Hamming codes to virtual pixels constructed from two cover images, offering a significant improvement over prior dual-image RDH methods. (2) Despite the high embedding rate, our method maintains excellent stego image quality with PSNR values of 48–49 dB, demonstrating a balanced tradeoff between capacity and imperceptibility. (3) The proposed method's robustness against statistical steganalysis is validated through RS analysis, confirming its resistance to detection and ensuring security in data hiding applications. (4) The reversibility of both cover images is guaranteed without additional side information, making the proposed scheme applicable to sensitive fields such as medical imaging and secure communications. (5) The proposed method is computationally efficient, relying on simple bitwise operations and lookup tables, enabling practical implementation in real-time systems.

The rest of this paper is organized as follows: Section 2 reviews the Hamming code used as a single error-correcting code along with the RDH method; Section 3 presents the proposed partial RDH method based on dual images; Section 4 presents the experimental results; and Section 5 presents the conclusions.

2. Preliminaries

2.1. Hamming Code

Error detection and correction are fundamental techniques for ensuring the reliability of data transmission. These processes are based on the principle of redundancy, wherein additional bits are appended to a message y according to predefined mathematical rules to enable error detection and correction at the receiver. Among various error control coding schemes, Hamming Code (HC) [29] has been widely adopted due to its simplicity and effectiveness in correcting single-bit errors. As a single-error-correcting linear block code with a minimum Hamming distance of three, HC remains a prevalent choice for many practical applications in digital communication.

In the notation $HC(n,k)$, n denotes the total length of a codeword, k represents the number of information bits, and $(n-k)$ corresponds to the number of parity bits. Given a k-bit information vector x, the corresponding n-bit codeword y is generated through the relation $y = xG$, where G is the $k \times n$ generator matrix. Errors may occur during transmission, resulting in a received vector $\tilde{y}$. The error vector is defined as $e = y - \tilde{y}$. If $e = 0$, this implies that no error has occurred and that $\tilde{y} = y$.

To detect and correct errors, a parity-check matrix H of size $(n-k) \times n$ is employed, satisfying the relation $GH = 0$. Applying the parity check matrix to the received word yields the syndrome $S = \tilde{y}H$. The syndrome S corresponds to a specific row of H, with its index indicating the position of the erroneous bit.

This relationship can be further elaborated as follows:

$$\tilde{y} \cdot H^T = (e \oplus y) \cdot H^T = e \cdot H^T + y \cdot H^T = e \cdot H^T \tag{1}$$

where $y \cdot H^T = 0$ by construction; consequently, the syndrome directly reflects the error pattern, enabling accurate and efficient error correction. Consider the example of HC(7,4) with the following parity check matrix **H** (Equation (2)):

$$H = \begin{bmatrix} 1 & 0 & 1 & 1 & 1 & 0 & 0 \\ 1 & 1 & 1 & 0 & 0 & 1 & 0 \\ 0 & 1 & 1 & 1 & 0 & 0 & 1 \end{bmatrix}. \tag{2}$$

Example: Suppose that the received string is $\tilde{y} = (1110111)$. The syndrome is computed as $\tilde{y}H = [101]$. This syndrome corresponds to the 4th row of **H**, indicating an error in the 4th bit position. Therefore, the corrected string is (1111111). If $\tilde{y}H = (000)$, this implies that no errors occurred.

2.2. Sun et al.'s RDH

Sun et al. [25] proposed an embedding procedure based on dual images utilizing the Hamming Code (7,4). Given a cover image $\mathbf{I}$, two identical copies $\mathbf{I}_1$ and $\mathbf{I}_2$ are generated. For the first cover image $\mathbf{I}_1$, a block B_{1j} of size 1×7 is selected and transformed into a codeword y_j. Binary hidden bits δ_j are embedded into y_j by flipping its syndrome, computed using Equation (1) with δ_j.

To apply changes to y_j, the new syndrome is calculated as $\tilde{s}_j = s_j \oplus \delta_j$. The new syndrome $\tilde{s}_j$ is then converted into a decimal value $D(\tilde{s}_j)$, with y_j modified as follows (Equation (3)):

$$y_{j,i} = \begin{cases} y_{j,i}, & \text{if } i \neq D(\tilde{s}_j) \\ 1 - y_{j,i}, & \text{if } i = D(\tilde{s}_j) \end{cases} \tag{3}$$

where $i = 1, 2, \ldots, 7$. For example, if $D(\tilde{s}_j) = 3$, then the least significant bit (LSB) of the third pixel in the block y_j is flipped. The resulting new block B'_{1j} updates the corresponding block B_{1j} in the image $\mathbf{I}_1$.

To construct the second stego image $\mathbf{I}_2$, the embedding process involves modifying B_{2j} based on the hidden bits δ_j. First, the block B_{2j} is converted into t_j, representing the LSBs of the first three pixels of B_{2j}. The hidden bit δ_j is embedded into t_j by applying $t_j = t_j \oplus \delta_j$. The modified blocks B'_{2j} are then used to reconstruct the stego image $\mathbf{I}'_2$.

Based on this background knowledge, the following section provides a detailed explanation of the proposed dual PRDH method.

2.3. Definition of Partial Reversible Data Hiding

In conventional reversible data hiding (RDH) schemes, the cover image is identical to the original image, making complete recovery of the original content possible after data extraction. In contrast, the proposed method deliberately modifies the original image to generate two cover images by applying HC(7,4) Hamming code transformations to selected pixel groups. This controlled transformation enables efficient data embedding while preserving image quality and reversibility with respect to the generated cover images.

As a result, the recovery process yields the cover images rather than the original image itself. A cover image differs slightly from the original due to the deterministic bit-level modifications applied during the encoding phase. This characteristic underlies the terminology of partially reversible data hiding (PRDH); while the embedding and extraction processes are fully reversible with respect to the cover images, the transformation from the original to the cover images is not reversible without additional information, which by design is not retained.

In this dual-image PRDH framework, both cover images are constructed with pixel-wise modifications that preserve high fidelity to the original (PSNR exceeding 48 dB in our experiments), and both can be precisely recovered from the corresponding stego images. In this way, the proposed scheme achieves strong perceptual quality and operational reversibility while intentionally sacrificing full recovery of the unmodified original image in favor of increased embedding capacity and structural simplicity.

3. Proposed Scheme

In this section, we propose an improved HC(7,4)-based dual-image reversible data hiding (RDH) technique. The overall conceptual workflow is illustrated in Figure 1, which briefly outlines the transition from the original image through the structurally correlated cover image generation to the subsequent embedding process. Figure 1 provides a high-level overview; in turn, Figure 2 shows the internal architecture, clearly detailing the module interactions, data flow, and role of each component.

Unlike conventional dual-image RDH techniques that simply replicate the original image into two identical cover images $\mathbf{I}_1$ and $\mathbf{I}_2$, our method performs a controlled bit-level transformation using an enhanced HC(7,4) Hamming code. This transformation introduces fine-grained structural modifications in the bit-plane, enabling error correction while preserving visual fidelity. Initially, $\mathbf{I}_1$ and $\mathbf{I}_2$ are generated by duplicating the original image. Then, for each pair of corresponding pixels from $\mathbf{I}_1$ and $\mathbf{I}_2$, a virtual 7-bit vector y is constructed by selecting specific bits from both pixels.

If the virtual vector y fails to satisfy the Hamming code condition $yH^T = 0$, a precomputed lookup table (LUT) is used to identify the closest codeword in the zero-syndrome coset. The selected codeword is then split and reassigned to the two pixels in such a way that structural similarity with the original is maintained. This process is applied iteratively across all pixels, resulting in two modified cover images that remain visually close to the original while ensuring compatibility with reversible data embedding in the following stage.

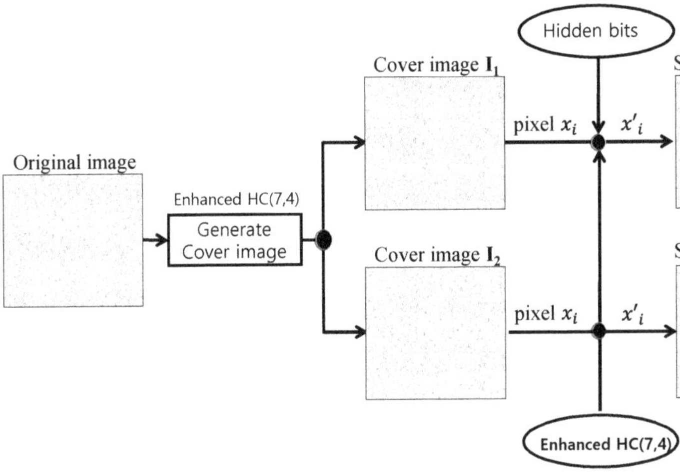

Figure 1. High-level schematic diagram of the proposed dual-image RDH system.

Figure 2 presents a more comprehensive block-level system architecture comprising three functional modules: the *cover image generator*, the *data embedder*, and the *data extractor*. These modules respectively correspond to Algorithms 1–3, and are designed for modular independence and engineering clarity.

Algorithm 1 Generation of Cover Images

Require: Original image O (grayscale, 8-bit)
Ensure: Cover images $\mathbf{I}_1$ and $\mathbf{I}_2$ satisfying HC(7,4) constraints
$\mathbf{I}_1 \leftarrow O$; $\mathbf{I}_2 \leftarrow O$
for $j = 1$ to $size(O)$ **do**
  Read pixel x_j from O ▷ Original pixel
  Extract x_j^1 and x_j^2 from x_j ▷ Bit vectors from pixel
  Construct virtual pixel y ▷ Selected bits from x_j^1 and x_j^2
  $\tilde{\alpha} \leftarrow b2d(a_4\, a_3\, a_2\, a_1)$ ▷ Decimal from x_j^1
  $\tilde{\beta} \leftarrow b2d(b_3\, b_2\, b_1)$ ▷ Decimal from x_j^2
  if $yH^T \neq 0$ **then** ▷ Coset condition check
    Initialize $\varepsilon_{min} \leftarrow \infty$, $h_{opt} \leftarrow \emptyset$
    for each codeword h in LUT **do** ▷ Candidate codeword
      $\alpha \leftarrow b2d(h_7\, h_6\, h_5\, h_4)$ ▷ Decimal upper bits
      $\beta \leftarrow b2d(h_3\, h_2\, h_1)$ ▷ Decimal lower bits
      $\varepsilon \leftarrow (\alpha - \tilde{\alpha})^2 + (\beta - \tilde{\beta})^2$ ▷ Similarity measure
      if $\varepsilon < \varepsilon_{min}$ **then**
        $\varepsilon_{min} \leftarrow \varepsilon$
        $h_{opt} \leftarrow h$ ▷ Update best codeword
      end if
    end for
    Update x_j^1 and x_j^2 with h_{opt}
  end if
  Save x_j^1 to $\mathbf{I}_1(j)$, x_j^2 to $\mathbf{I}_2(j)$
end for

Algorithm 2 Embedding Procedure

Require: Two cover images $\mathbf{I}_1, \mathbf{I}_2$; secret bits $M = (m_1, m_2, \ldots, m_n)$
Ensure: Two stego images $\Delta\mathbf{I}_1, \Delta\mathbf{I}_2$
$\Delta\mathbf{I}_1 \leftarrow \mathbf{I}_1$; $\Delta\mathbf{I}_2 \leftarrow \mathbf{I}_2$
$k \leftarrow 1$ ▷ Secret bit index
for $j = 1$ to $size(\mathbf{I}_1)$ **do**
  Access pixel x_j from $\mathbf{I}_1$ and $\mathbf{I}_2$
  Construct virtual pixel y according to Equation (4)
  $\tilde{\alpha} \leftarrow b2d(a_4\, a_3\, a_2\, a_1)$
  $\tilde{\beta} \leftarrow b2d(b_3\, b_2\, b_1)$
  Extract secret bits m_k^{k+2} (3 bits)
  if coset(y) $\neq$ target coset leader derived from m_k^{k+2} **then**
    Initialize $\varepsilon_{min} \leftarrow \infty$, $h_{opt} \leftarrow \emptyset$
    for each codeword h in LUT **do**
      $\alpha \leftarrow b2d(h_7\, h_6\, h_5\, h_4)$
      $\beta \leftarrow b2d(h_3\, h_2\, h_1)$
      $\varepsilon \leftarrow (\alpha - \tilde{\alpha})^2 + (\beta - \tilde{\beta})^2$
      if $\varepsilon < \varepsilon_{min}$ **then**
        $\varepsilon_{min} \leftarrow \varepsilon$
        $h_{opt} \leftarrow h$
      end if
    end for
    Update x_j^1 and x_j^2 according to Equation (6)
  end if
  Save updated x_j^1 to $\Delta\mathbf{I}_1(j)$; x_j^2 to $\Delta\mathbf{I}_2(j)$
  $k \leftarrow k + 3$ ▷ Move to next 3 secret bits
end for

Algorithm 3 Extraction and Recovery Procedure

Require: Two stego images $\Delta\mathbf{I}_1, \Delta\mathbf{I}_2$
Ensure: Recovered cover images $\mathbf{I}_1, \mathbf{I}_2$, and extracted secret bits m
Initialize: $k \leftarrow 1$
for $j = 1$ to $size(\Delta\mathbf{I}_1)$ **do**
  Access pixel data from $\Delta\mathbf{I}_1$ and $\Delta\mathbf{I}_2$
  Reconstruct virtual pixel y using selected bits
  Calculate syndrome $S \leftarrow yH^T$ ▷ Extract hidden bits
  Store S into $m(k : k+2)$; $k \leftarrow k + 3$
  $\tilde{\alpha} \leftarrow b2d(a_4\, a_3\, a_2\, a_1)$; $\tilde{\beta} \leftarrow b2d(b_3\, b_2\, b_1)$
  Initialize $\varepsilon_{min} \leftarrow \infty$, $h_{opt} \leftarrow \emptyset$
  for each codeword h in LUT **do**
    $\alpha \leftarrow b2d(h_7\, h_6\, h_5\, h_4)$; $\beta \leftarrow b2d(h_3\, h_2\, h_1)$
    $\varepsilon \leftarrow (\alpha - \tilde{\alpha})^2 + (\beta - \tilde{\beta})^2$
    if $\varepsilon < \varepsilon_{min}$ **then**
      $\varepsilon_{min} \leftarrow \varepsilon$; $h_{opt} \leftarrow h$
    end if
  end for
  Update x_j^1 and x_j^2 based on h_{opt} ▷ Recover cover pixels
  Save x_j^1 into $\mathbf{I}_1(j)$; x_j^2 into $\mathbf{I}_2(j)$
end for

The process begins with the **Cover Image Generator**, which takes the original image O and produces two structurally optimized cover images $\mathbf{I}_1$ and $\mathbf{I}_2$ using HC(7,4)-based syndrome modulation. These images are generated to support reliable and low-distortion embedding.

Next, the **Data Embedder** receives the cover images and a payload bitstream, then embeds the payload through a syndrome-modulated mapping strategy using a preconstructed lookup table. This process results in two stego images $\mathbf{I}'_1$ and $\mathbf{I}'_2$ containing the hidden information while preserving high image fidelity.

Finally, the **Data Extractor** takes the stego images as input, reconstructs the original message by performing parity-check-based extraction, and reverses the embedding steps to accurately restore the original image. This module ensures lossless recovery of both the hidden data and the original content.

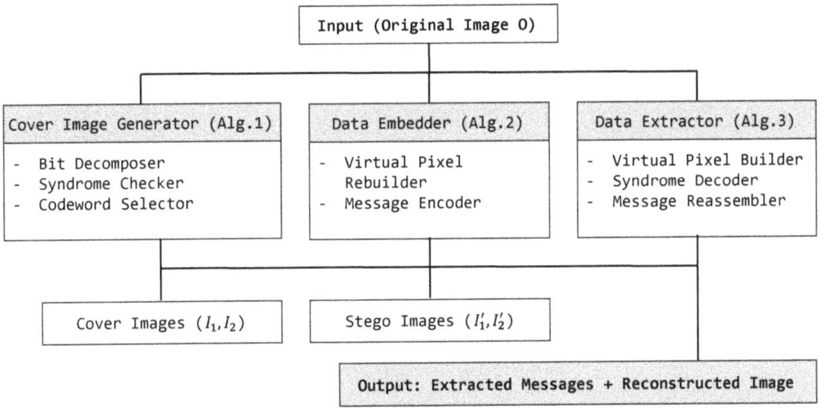

Figure 2. Modular architecture of the proposed RDH system: (1) cover image generator, (2) data embedder, and (3) data extractor.

3.1. Generation of Cover Images

In this subsection, we present the process for generating two cover images using the improved HC(7,4) scheme. The detailed procedure is summarized in Algorithm 1.

Initially, two copies of the original image are created, denoted by $\mathbf{I}_1$ and $\mathbf{I}_2$. For each pixel x_j in the original image O, the same value is assigned to the corresponding pixels in $\mathbf{I}_1$ and $\mathbf{I}_2$, denoted as x_j^1 and x_j^2, respectively. Each of these pixel values is represented in 8-bit binary format as

$$x_j^1 = (a_8\, a_7\, a_6\, a_5\, a_4\, a_3\, a_2\, a_1),$$
$$x_j^2 = (b_8\, b_7\, b_6\, b_5\, b_4\, b_3\, b_2\, b_1),$$

where a_i and b_i represent individual bits of x_j^1 and x_j^2.

A virtual 7-bit pixel y is then constructed by concatenating selected bits from x_j^1 and x_j^2:

$$y = (a_4\, a_3\, a_2\, a_1 || b_3\, b_2\, b_1) \tag{4}$$

where $||$ denotes bit-wise concatenation. Here, a_4 corresponds to the most significant bit (MSB) of y and b_1 to the least significant bit (LSB) of y.

To ensure that y satisfies the Hamming code constraint $yH^T = 0$, a syndrome check is performed. If the condition is not satisfied, the closest valid codeword is selected from a preconstructed lookup table (LUT) derived from the standard array of HC(7,4) codewords, as shown in Figure 3. This enables efficient correction by identifying the nearest codeword within the corresponding coset. The following algorithm corresponds to the Cover Image Generator module described in Figure 2, and performs syndrome-based modifications to construct cover images I_1 and I_2.

Standard array of a (7,4) Hamming code for DH								
Coset leader								
0000000	(0001101)	(0011010)	(0010111)	(0110100)	(0111001)	(0101110)	(1000011)	(1101000)
	(1100101)	(1110010)	(1111111)	(1011100)	(1010001)	(1000110)	(1001011)	
0000001	(0001100)	(0011011)	(0010110)	(0110101)	(0111000)	(0101111)	(0100010)	(1101001)
	(1100100)	(1110011)	(1111110)	(1011101)	(1010000)	(1000111)	(1001010)	
0000010	(0001111)	(0011000)	(0010101)	(0110110)	(0111011)	(0101100)	(0100001)	(1101010)
	(1100111)	(1110000)	(1111101)	(1011110)	(1010011)	(1000100)	(1001001)	
0000011	(0001110)	(0011001)	(0010100)	(0110111)	(0111010)	(0101101)	(0100000),	(1101011)
	(1100110)	(1110001)	(1111100)	(1011111)	(1010010)	(1000101)	(1001000)	
0000100	(0001001)	(0011110)	(0010011)	(0110000)	(0111101)	(0101010)	(0100111)	(1101100)
	(1100001)	(1110110)	(1111011)	(1011000)	(1010101)	(1000010)	(1001111)	
0000101	(0001000)	(0011111)	(0010010)	(0110001)	(0111100)	(0101011)	(0100110)	(1101101)
	(1100000)	(1110111)	(1111010)	(1011001)	(1010100)	(1000011)	(1001110)	
0000110	(0001011)	(0011100)	(0010001)	(0110010)	(0111111)	(0101000)	(0100101)	(1101110)
	(1100011)	(1110100)	(1111001)	(1011010)	(1010111)	(1000000)	(1001101)	
0000111	(0001010)	(0011101)	(0010000)	(0110011)	(0111110)	(0101001)	(0100100)	(1101111)
	(1100010)	(1110101)	(1111000)	(1011011)	(1010110)	(1000001)	(1001100)	

(a)

Standard array of a (7,4) Hamming code for DH								
Coset leader	MSB 4-BIT to DECIMAL NUMBER, LSB 3 -BIT to DECIMAL NUMBER Ex) ($a_1 = 1, b_1 = 5$) ∈ {(1 5) in coset leader 0}							
0	(1 5)	(3 2)	(2 7)	(6 4)	(7 1)	(5 6)	(8 3)	(13 0)
	(12 5)	(14 2)	(15 7)	(11 4)	(10 1)	(8 6)	(9 3)	
1	(1 4)	(3 3)	(2 6)	(6 5)	(7 0)	(5 7)	(4 2)	(13 1)
	(12 4)	(14 3)	(15 6)	(11 5)	(10 0)	(8 7)	(9 2)	
2	(1 7)	(3 0)	(2 5)	(6 6)	(7 3)	(10 4)	(4 1)	(13 2)
	(12 7)	(14 0)	(15 5)	(11 6)	(10 3)	(8 4)	(9 1)	
3	(1 6)	(3 1)	(2 4)	(6 7)	(7 2)	(10 5)	(4 0),	(13 3)
	(12 6)	(14 1)	(15 4)	(11 7)	(10 2)	(8 5)	(9 0)	
4	(1 1)	(3 6)	(2 3)	(6 0)	(7 5)	(5 2)	(4 7)	(13 4)
	(12 1)	(14 6)	(15 3)	(11 0)	(10 5)	(8 2)	(9 7)	
5	(9 0)	(3 7)	(2 2)	(6 1)	(7 4)	(5 3)	(4 6)	(13 5)
	(12 0)	(14 7)	(15 2)	(13 1)	(10 4)	(8 3)	(9 6)	
6	(1 3)	(3 4)	(2 1)	(6 2)	(7 7)	(5 0)	(4 5)	(13 6)
	(12 3)	(14 4)	(15 1)	(11 2)	(10 7)	(8 0)	(9 5)	
7	(1 2)	(3 5)	(2 0)	(6 3)	(7 6)	(5 1)	(4 4)	(13 7)
	(12 2)	(14 5)	(15 0)	(11 3)	(10 6)	(8 1)	(8 4)	

(b)

Figure 3. Standard array of the HC(7,4) code for coset-based data embedding and extraction [2]: (**a**) binary representation and (**b**) decimal representation.

To formalize this process, the selection of the most suitable codeword h is defined as a distortion minimization problem over the zero-syndrome coset $\mathcal{C}_0$:

$$\min_{h \in \mathcal{C}_0} \varepsilon(h) = (\alpha - \tilde{\alpha})^2 + (\beta - \tilde{\beta})^2 \tag{5}$$

where h is a candidate codeword from the LUT and $\tilde{\alpha}, \tilde{\beta}$ are derived from the original bits of x_j^1 and x_j^2, respectively. This formulation explicitly expresses the objective of minimizing perceptual distortion while satisfying HC(7,4) compliance.

Here, ε quantifies the difference between the original and candidate virtual pixel representations. The codeword $h = (h_7, h_6, h_5, h_4, h_3, h_2, h_1)$ that minimizes ε is selected as the best match. Among these bits, the first four (h_7, h_6, h_5, h_4) are written into the least significant bits of x_j^1 in $\mathbf{I}_1$ and the last three (h_3, h_2, h_1) are written into the least significant bits of x_j^2 in $\mathbf{I}_2$.

This process is repeated for every pixel in the original image. As a result, two structurally correlated cover images $\mathbf{I}_1$ and $\mathbf{I}_2$ are generated, both of which are optimized for low-distortion reversible data embedding.

3.2. Data Embedding

In this subsection, we describe the detailed procedure for embedding secret data into two cover images by applying the improved HC(7,4) scheme. The overall process is summarized in Algorithm 2.

In HC(7,4) codes, coset leaders correspond to eight distinct patterns, which can be naturally represented by 3-bit binary numbers ranging from 000 to 111. Thus, in the proposed embedding scheme, each group of three secret bits is directly mapped to a target coset leader. This mapping forms the basis for aligning the virtual pixel structure with the intended secret message. For each pixel location, the corresponding values from $\mathbf{I}_1$ and $\mathbf{I}_2$ are accessed to reconstruct the virtual pixel y by selecting and concatenating specific bits, as defined in Equation (4).

To embed secret data, a group of three consecutive secret bits m_k^{k+2} is selected. The three bits are interpreted as the target coset leader corresponding to the intended secret message. Thus, the *coset leader pattern* is defined as a 3-bit sequence indicating the desired coset class for the constructed virtual pixel.

Although the same error minimization formula presented in Equation (5) is employed, its purpose in this phase differs from that in cover image generation (Section 3.1). While the previous minimization aimed solely at ensuring codeword validity, here it is driven by the secret bits to align the virtual pixel with the target coset leader while minimizing visual distortion.

If the current virtual pixel y does not belong to the desired coset (i.e., the syndrome of y does not match the target coset leader pattern), then the closest matching codeword h is selected from the lookup table (LUT) by minimizing the error ε as defined in Equation (5).

After selecting the optimal codeword h, the cover pixel bits are updated according to

$$\begin{cases} x_j^1 = (a_8\, a_7\, a_6\, a_5 || h_7\, h_6\, h_5\, h_4), \\ x_j^2 = (b_8\, b_7\, b_6\, b_5\, b_4 || h_3\, h_2\, h_1). \end{cases} \tag{6}$$

Finally, the modified pixels are stored into the stego images $\Delta\mathbf{I}_1$ and $\Delta\mathbf{I}_2$. The full embedding process is outlined in Algorithm 2.

3.3. Data Extraction And Recovery Procedure

In this subsection, we describe the procedure for extracting the hidden information and recovering the original cover images from the two stego images $\Delta\mathbf{I}_1$ and $\Delta\mathbf{I}_2$ generated during the embedding process (Section 3.3). Based on the virtual pixel construction method described in Section 3.1 and the syndrome computation process defined in Section 3.3, the extraction and recovery are performed sequentially for each pixel pair in the stego images.

For data extraction, the virtual pixel y is reconstructed at each pixel position and the syndrome S is recalculated using the previously defined parity-check matrix H. Each extracted syndrome directly corresponds to a group of three secret bits, which are sequentially collected to form the hidden message vector m.

Following extraction, the recovery of the original cover images proceeds by leveraging the property that all virtual pixels belonged to the zero-syndrome coset prior to embedding. In this way, the codeword associated with the zero syndrome that minimizes the discrepancy from the current stego pixel is identified for each virtual pixel. The optimal codeword is determined by minimizing the Euclidean error between the extracted bits and the candidate codewords, following the error metric introduced in Section 3.1.

After the nearest codeword is found, the cover pixel values are reconstructed accordingly, restoring the two original cover images $\mathbf{I}_1$ and $\mathbf{I}_2$.

The overall extraction and recovery process is summarized in Algorithm 3.

3.4. Numerical Examples

3.4.1. Generating Two Cover Images

Suppose that a pixel in the original image is provided by

$$x_j = [1\,0\,0\,1\,1\,1\,0]^T.$$

Following the generation procedure described in Section 3.1, two cover pixels are derived as follows:

(1) Initialization: Copy the original pixel to create two initial cover pixels

$$x_j^1 = [1\,0\,0\,1\,1\,1\,0],$$
$$x_j^2 = [1\,0\,0\,1\,1\,1\,0].$$

(2) Virtual Pixel Construction: A virtual pixel y is constructed by selecting four LSB bits from x_j^1 and three LSB bits from x_j^2, as defined in Equation (4):

$$y = [1\,1\,1\,0\,1\,1\,1].$$

This process compresses the essential information of two pixels into a compact 7-bit structure, facilitating efficient error management.

(3) Decimal Conversion: The selected bits are separated into two groups and converted into decimal:

$$\tilde{\alpha} = b2d([1\,1\,1\,0]) = 14,$$
$$\tilde{\beta} = b2d([1\,1\,1]) = 7.$$

(4) Codeword Selection: To ensure that the virtual pixel belongs to a valid codeword set, the closest matching codeword is identified by minimizing the error defined in Equation (5):

$$\begin{aligned} \varepsilon &= \min\Big((\alpha_i - \tilde{\alpha})^2 + (\beta_i - \tilde{\beta})^2\Big) \\ &= \min\Big((15-14)^2 + (7-7)^2\Big) = 1. \end{aligned}$$

Thus, the optimal codeword h is determined as:

$$h = [1\,1\,1\,1\,1\,1\,1].$$

(5) Cover Pixel Reconstruction: Using the selected codeword h, the two cover pixels are reconstructed according to Equation (6):

$$x_j^1 = [1\,0\,0\,1\,1\,1\,1],$$
$$x_j^2 = [1\,0\,0\,1\,1\,1\,1].$$

(6) Assignment: The updated pixels x_j^1 and x_j^2 are assigned to their respective positions within the cover images $\mathbf{I}_1$ and $\mathbf{I}_2$.

(7) Iteration: The above process is repeated for each pixel of the original image to complete the construction of the two cover images.

3.4.2. Data Embedding Phase

Assume that the secret bits to be embedded are

$$m = [1\,0\,1].$$

The two cover pixels prepared for embedding are

$$x_j^1 = [1\,0\,0\,1\,1\,1\,1], \quad x_j^2 = [1\,0\,0\,1\,1\,1\,1].$$

The embedding process proceeds as follows:

(1) Virtual Pixel Reconstruction: A virtual pixel is formed:

$$y = [1\,1\,1\,1\,1\,1\,1].$$

(2) Target Coset Leader Mapping: The secret bits $m = [1\,0\,1]$ correspond to a coset leader index of 5.

(3) Optimal Codeword Identification: Among the codewords associated with coset leader 5, the optimal codeword minimizing the error is selected:

$$\varepsilon = \min\left((14-15)^2 + (7-7)^2\right) = 1,$$
$$h = [1\,1\,1\,0\,1\,1\,1].$$

(4) Stego Pixel Reconstruction: The cover pixels are updated as follows:

$$x_j^1 = [1\,0\,0\,1\,1\,1\,0],$$
$$x_j^2 = [1\,0\,0\,1\,1\,1\,1].$$

These updated pixels are stored in the stego images $\Delta\mathbf{I}_1$ and $\Delta\mathbf{I}_2$ respectively.

3.4.3. Data Extraction and Recover Phase

Given two stego pixels

$$x_j^1 = [1\,0\,0\,1\,1\,1\,0], \quad x_j^2 = [1\,0\,0\,1\,1\,1\,1],$$

extraction and recovery are performed as follows:

(1) Virtual Pixel Reconstruction: Reconstruct the virtual pixel

$$y = [1\,1\,1\,0\,1\,1\,1].$$

(2) Syndrome Computation: Compute the syndrome to extract the embedded bits:

$$S = yH^T = [1\,0\,1] = 5,$$

recovering the secret bits $m = [1\,0\,1]$.

(3) Cover Pixel Recovery: To restore the original cover images, the closest codeword associated with zero syndrome is selected:

$$\varepsilon = \min\left((15-14)^2 + (7-7)^2\right) = 1,$$
$$h = [1\,1\,1\,1\,1\,1\,1].$$

The recovered cover pixels are

$$x_j^1 = [1\,0\,0\,1\,1\,1\,1],$$
$$x_j^2 = [1\,0\,0\,1\,1\,1\,1].$$

Thus, both the hidden secret data and the cover images are perfectly restored.

4. Experimental Results and Discussions

In this section, we present the experimental evaluation of the proposed partial reversible data hiding (PRHB) method based on the enhanced HC(7,4) Hamming code. The primary objective of the experiments is to demonstrate the feasibility and advantages of the proposed technique through comprehensive simulations. All experiments were conducted on a system equipped with a Core i5-8250U processor (1.60 GHz) and 8 GB of RAM, utilizing Matlab R2019b as the simulation platform. This study aims to improve both embedding capacity and image quality through a dual-image RDH scheme. The proposed approach addresses prior limitations by incorporating structured virtual pixel construction and optimized codeword selection.

Unlike conventional RDH, our design avoids side-information overhead and achieves near-constant embedding performance across all tested images. The improvements introduced in the data embedding process can be summarized as follows:

- Optimized Virtual Pixel Construction: Virtual pixels are generated from two cover images to enhance error correction performance.
- Complete Data Recovery Without Auxiliary Information: The embedded data can be perfectly extracted without the need for any additional side information.
- Adaptive Tradeoff Between Embedding Capacity and Visual Distortion: The method employs an adaptive adjustment strategy to maintain a balance between data embedding rate and image quality.
- High Stego Image Quality: The visual quality of the stego images is preserved, as quantitatively measured by the peak signal-to-noise ratio (PSNR) [2].

To objectively evaluate the performance of the proposed method, extensive experiments were carried out using nine standard 512 × 512 grayscale images from the USC-SIPI dataset [30] (Figure 4). The evaluation metrics included embedding capacity (EC), embedding rate (ER, measured in bits per pixel, bpp, Equation (7)), and PSNR.

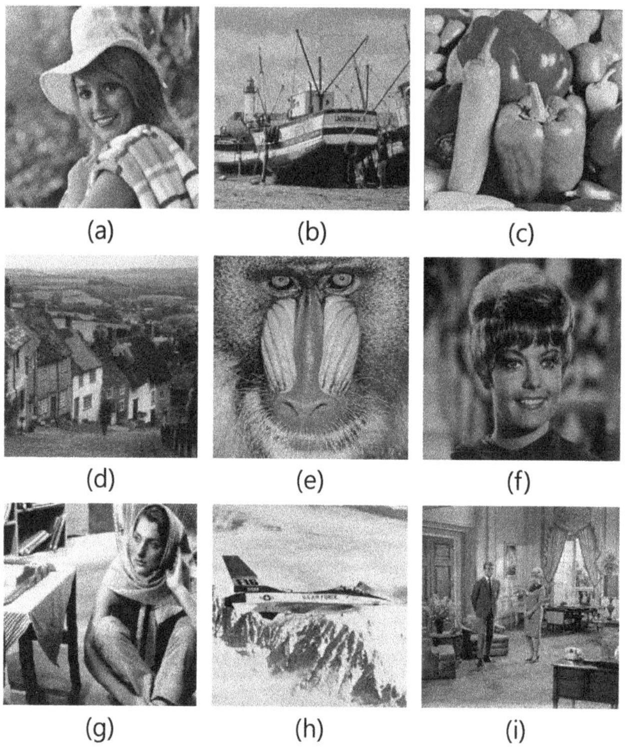

Figure 4. Test images: (**a**) Elaine, (**b**) Boat, (**c**) Peppers, (**d**) Goldhill, (**e**) Baboon, (**f**) Zelda, (**g**) Barbara, (**h**) Airplane, and (**i**) Couple (512 × 512).

By comparing these metrics with those achieved by conventional dual-image-based RDH methods, the superiority of the proposed scheme in terms of both capacity and visual quality is clearly demonstrated. The embedding rate (ER) is defined by Equation (7):

$$ER = \frac{C}{2 \times N \times N}(bpp). \quad (7)$$

The PSNR [2] is widely employed as an objective metric to evaluate the quality of marked images. It quantifies the difference between the reference image and the distorted (or marked) image in a logarithmic scale. The PSNR is defined by Equation (8):

$$PSNR = 10\log_{10}\left(\frac{255^2}{MSE}\right) \quad (8)$$

where 255^2 represents the square of the maximum possible pixel value in an 8-bit image. The mean squared error (MSE), provided by Equation (9), measures the average squared intensity difference between corresponding pixels of the original and marked images:

$$MSE = \frac{1}{N \times N}\sum_{i=1}^{N \times N}(x_i - x_i')^2. \quad (9)$$

In this expression, x_i and x_i' denote the pixel values of the original and marked images at position i, respectively. The error term $e = (x_i - x_i')^2$ reflects the squared deviation at each pixel. A lower MSE value indicates smaller distortion, leading to a higher PSNR value, which implies better perceived image quality. Typically, for 8-bit images, PSNR values for acceptable lossy compression range from 30 dB to 50 dB. A higher PSNR generally correlates with improved visual fidelity.

Table 1 presents a comparative analysis of PSNR values for cover images (#1 and #2) and stego images (#1 and #2) when embedding 10,000 bits using the enhanced HC(7,4) PRDH method. The evaluation focuses on three key PSNR measurements:

- PSNR(CI−OI): The PSNR between the original image (OI) and the cover image (CI), indicating the degree of modification introduced by the cover image generation process.
- PSNR(SI−CI): The PSNR between the cover image and the stego image (SI), measuring the level of distortion caused by data embedding.
- PSNR(SI−OI): The PSNR between the stego image and the original image, providing an overall assessment of image quality after data embedding.

Table 1. Comparison of PSNR for all enhanced HC(7,4) PRDH when embedding bits is 10,000 bits.

Images	PSNR(CI–OI)	PSNR(CI–OI)	PSNR(SI–CI)	PSNR(SI–CI)	PSNR(SI–OI)	PSNR(SI–OI)
	#1	#2	#1	#2	#1	#2
Elaine	47.0974	48.6768	67.1575	68.0772	47.0974	48.6768
Peppers	47.1624	48.7094	67.1219	67.7983	47.1326	48.6648
Airplane	47.2557	48.7013	67.1827	68.1199	47.2268	48.6643
Boat	47.3741	48.7739	67.2000	68.0625	47.345	48.7325
Goldhill	47.1820	48.7160	67.3303	68.1748	47.1572	48.6749
Couple	46.9334	48.5882	67.2376	68.0349	46.9039	48.5485
Baboon	47.2004	48.7209	67.2417	67.8930	47.1744	48.6777
Zelda	47.2009	48.7249	67.1814	67.9371	47.1751	48.6850
Barbara	47.3593	48.6522	67.3372	68.1084	47.3307	48.6082
Average	47.1962	48.696	67.2211	68.0229	47.1715	48.6592

Across all test images, PSNR(CI−OI) exhibits stable values around 47 dB for cover image #1 and 48 dB for cover image #2, indicating that the initial cover image generation introduces minimal distortion. Notably, PSNR(SI−CI) reaches approximately 67 dB for stego image #1 and 68 dB for stego image #2, demonstrating that the data embedding process maintains high image quality with minimal impact on the cover image. The final PSNR(SI−OI) values, which range between 47 dB and 48.7 dB, further confirm that the proposed method effectively preserves the original image quality. Given these results,

PSNR(SI−CI) was selected as the primary metric for evaluating stego image quality in this study, as it directly reflects the influence of the embedding process while isolating any distortions introduced during cover image generation. These findings validate the efficiency of our enhanced HC(7,4) PRDH method in achieving high embedding capacity while maintaining superior image fidelity.

Table 2 presents a comparative analysis of the maximum embedding ratio (ER) across various reversible data hiding methods, including those proposed by Lee et al. (2013) [15], Liu et al. (2018) [20], Lin et al. (2019) [24], Chen et al. (2020) [22], Chen et al. (2021) [23], and Jana et al. (2018) [21], alongside our proposed method.

Among the evaluated techniques, the highest embedding ratio is achieved by the method of Chen et al. (2021) [23], which reaches a maximum ER of 1.56, demonstrating its superior capacity for data embedding. Our proposed method achieves an ER of 1.50, which is the second-highest among the compared methods and only 0.06 lower than Chen et al. (2021) [23]. Despite this slight reduction in embedding capacity, our approach maintains a balance between embedding efficiency and computational complexity, offering a simpler and more efficient process for data hiding, extraction, and restoration.

Table 2. Comparison of maximum embedding ratio with different methods.

Images	Lee et al. [15]	Liu et al. [20]	Lin et al. [24]	Chen et al. [22]	Chen et al. [23]	Jana et al. [21]	Proposed
Elaine	1.09	1.00	1.07	1.14	1.56	0.21	1.50
Pepper	1.09	1.00	1.07	1.14	1.56	0.21	1.50
Airplane	1.09	1.00	1.07	1.14	1.56	0.21	1.50
Boat	1.09	1.00	1.07	1.14	1.56	0.21	1.50
Goldhill	1.09	1.00	1.07	1.14	1.56	0.21	1.50
Couple	1.09	1.00	1.07	1.14	1.56	0.21	1.50
Baboon	1.09	1.00	1.07	1.14	1.56	0.21	1.50
Zelda	1.09	1.00	1.07	1.14	1.56	0.21	1.50
Barbara	1.09	1.00	1.07	1.14	1.56	0.21	1.50
Average	1.09	1.00	1.07	1.14	1.56	0.21	1.50

Other methods, such as those presented by Lee et al. (2013) [15], Liu et al. (2018) [20], and Lin et al. (2019) [24], which exhibit embedding ratios ranging from 1.00 to 1.14. In comparison, our proposed method offers a significant improvement in data hiding capacity. Notably, the method presented by Jana et al. (2018) [21] has the lowest embedding ratio of 0.21, indicating a strong tradeoff between image quality preservation and data embedding capacity. Overall, our proposed method provides a near-optimal embedding ratio while maintaining computational efficiency, making it a strong candidate for practical reversible data hiding applications where both high capacity and low complexity are required.

Note: The embedding ratio (ER) is constant at 1.50 across all tested images. This is a deterministic result of the proposed scheme, with a standard deviation of 0.00. This consistency reflects the deterministic nature of the proposed embedding mechanism and demonstrates its robustness across diverse image contents.

Table 3 presents a comparative analysis of the embedding capacity (bpp) and peak signal-to-noise ratio (PSNR) across existing reversible data hiding methods, including those proposed by Chang et al. (2007) [13], Chang et al. (2013) [14], Lee & Huang (2013) [15], Qin et al. (2015) [16], Lu et al. (2015) [17], and Jana et al. (2018) [21], alongside our proposed approach.

Table 3. Comparison of maximum bpp and PSNR of existing methods and our proposed method.

Method	Measure	Elaine	Peppers	Barbara	Goldhill
Chang et al. (2007) [13]	bpp	1.00	1.00	1.00	1.00
	PSNR#1	45.12	45.14	45.13	45.13
	PSNR#2	45.13	45.15	45.11	45.14
Chang et al. (2013) [14]	bpp	1.53	1.53	1.53	1.53
	PSNR#1	39.89	39.94	39.89	39.9
	PSNR#2	39.89	39.94	39.89	39.9
Lee & Huang (2013) [15]	bpp	1.07	1.07	1.07	1.07
	PSNR#1	49.76	49.75	49.75	49.77
	PSNR#2	50.42	50.34	50.44	50.54
Qin et al. (2015) [16]	bpp	1.00	1.00	1.00	1.00
	PSNR#1	52.11	51.25	52.12	52.12
	PSNR#2	41.58	41.52	41.58	41.58
Lu et al. (2015) [17]	bpp	1.00	1.00	1.00	1.00
	PSNR#1	51.13	51.15	49.22	49.23
	PSNR#2	51.15	51.14	49.2	49.18
Jana et al. (2018) [21]	bpp	0.21	0.21	0.21	0.21
	PSNR#1	52.71	52.67	52.7	52.73
	PSNR#2	52.81	52.72	52.76	52.78
Proposed scheme	bpp	1.50	1.50	1.50	1.50
	PSNR#1	48.19	48.2	48.22	48.2
	PSNR#2	49.01	49.02	48.96	49.06

Among the evaluated methods, the highest embedding rate is achieved by Chang et al. (2013) [14] with 1.53 bpp, followed closely by our proposed method, which attains 1.50 bpp. In contrast, the method by Jana et al. (2018) [21] exhibits the lowest embedding rate, limited to 0.21 bpp. Notably, Qin et al. (2015) [16] and Jana et al. (2018) [21] achieve the highest PSNR values, exceeding 52 dB, albeit at the cost of significantly lower embedding rates. This trend suggests an inherent tradeoff between embedding capacity and image quality, where methods optimizing for PSNR often exhibit lower data-hiding capability.

Our proposed scheme effectively balances embedding capacity and image quality, achieving a competitive 48–49 dB PSNR while maintaining a high embedding rate. Compared to other methods with similar embedding rates, such as that of Chang et al. (2013) [14], our approach demonstrates superior PSNR performance, indicating reduced distortion in the stego images. This suggests that the proposed method offers an optimal tradeoff between embedding rate and visual fidelity, making it a strong candidate for practical reversible data hiding applications.

The proposed method shows a fixed embedding rate of 1.50 bpp across all images, resulting in a standard deviation of 0.00. In addition, the PSNR values exhibit only minor variations (standard deviation $\leq$ 0.06 dB), confirming our method's consistent visual quality across different images.

Figure 5a presents a comparative analysis of the average PSNR of stego image #1 across different reversible data hiding methods. The embedding rate (ER) of the proposed method is measured at 1.5 bpp. Among the evaluated techniques, the method proposed by Chen et al. (2021) [23] is also capable of embedding up to 1.5 bpp, although achieving a PSNR approximately 1–2 dB higher than the proposed method. Overall, except for the method of Chen et al. (2019) [22], all evaluated techniques maintain a marked image quality above 48 dB even at embedding rates exceeding 1.5 bpp, demonstrating a balance between high embedding capacity and imperceptibility.

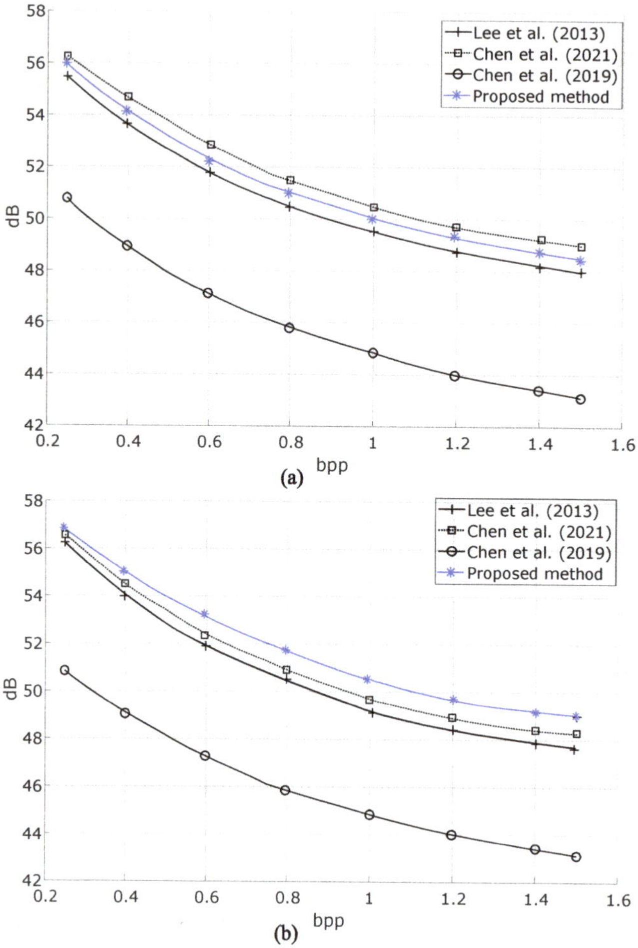

Figure 5. Comparative average PSNR of #1 (**a**) and #2 (**b**) with different ERs for all test images in different schemes, based on the methods in [15,22,23].

In Figure 5b, the relationship between PSNR and bpp for stego image #2 is illustrated. At an embedding rate of 0.2 bpp, the proposed method achieves a PSNR of 56.83 dB, marking the highest recorded value among all evaluated approaches. Furthermore, the proposed method consistently maintains the highest PSNR across the entire embedding range up to 1.5 bpp, ensuring superior image quality preservation. On the other hand, the method of Chen et al. (2021) [23] achieves the second-highest PSNR performance among the evaluated techniques, further demonstrating its effectiveness in maintaining image quality.

Overall, our proposed method effectively balances high embedding capacity and PSNR, making it a competitive solution for reversible data hiding. The ability to sustain high PSNR values across a broad embedding range highlights its robustness in preserving image quality while embedding a substantial amount of data.

The RS analysis results in Figure 6 illustrate the resistance of the proposed method against regular–singular (RS) analysis attacks. RS analysis is a commonly used statistical attack technique that helps detect the presence of hidden information in an image by analyzing local pixel patterns. In this method, each shadow image is divided into three distinct categories:

- **Regular Group (RM or R-M)**—Represents smooth pixel regions that follow predictable patterns.
- **Singular Group (SM or S-M)**—Represents highly textured or noisy pixel regions.
- **Unchanged Group (U)**—Represents pixels that remain stable and are not affected by the embedding process.

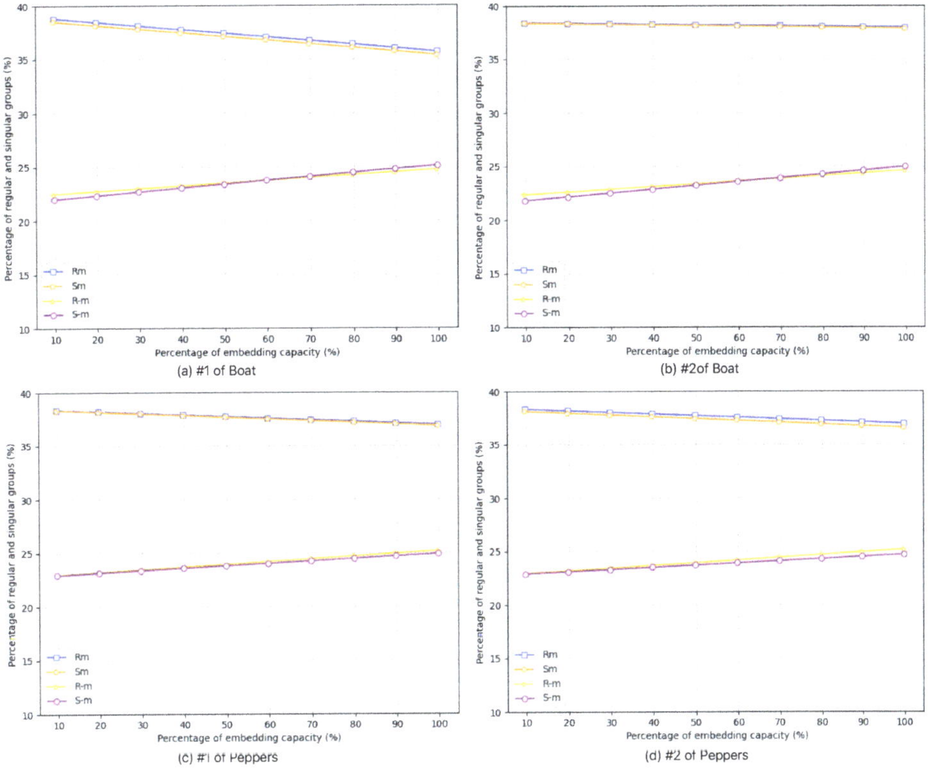

Figure 6. RS analysis for each shadow of Boat.

The RM and SM (or R-M and S-M) values indicate the proportion of regular and singular pixels, respectively, under different masks (M or -M). In our experiments, four consecutive pixels were grouped together, with the applied mask M is defined as [0,1,1,0].

The statistical relationship between the regular and singular groups must satisfy the following conditions:

$$RM + SM \leq 1, \quad R - M + S - M \leq 1, \tag{10}$$

$$RM \approx R - M, \quad SM \approx S - M. \tag{11}$$

From Figure 6, it can be observed that both shadow images (number 1 and number 2) conform to the constraints defined in Equations (10) and (11), ensuring that the statistical integrity of the stego images is preserved. This indicates that the proposed method effectively maintains a balanced distribution of regular and singular groups, making it resilient against RS analysis attacks.

Furthermore, the similarity between RM and R-M as well as SM and S-M, across different shadow images suggests that the embedding operation does not introduce significant statistical anomalies that could be exploited by steganalysis techniques. This highlights the robustness of the proposed scheme in preserving the natural statistical properties of the host image while embedding data.

In conclusion, the RS analysis results confirm that the proposed method maintains imperceptibility and structural consistency, reducing the likelihood of detection by statistical steganalysis techniques. The ability to resist RS analysis ensures that the hidden information remains undetectable, making the method a strong candidate for secure reversible data hiding applications.

Furthermore, a deeper analysis of the comparative results reveals the underlying reasons for the differences in performance among existing methods. For instance, the scheme proposed by Chang et al. (2013) [14] achieves a relatively high embedding capacity of 1.53 bpp; however, this comes at the cost of significantly reduced image quality, with PSNR values falling below 40 dB. This degradation can be attributed to their approach of embedding two bits per pixel pair, which introduces substantial pixel distortion and consequently lowers visual fidelity.

In contrast, the EMD-based method by Chen and Hong (2021) [23] demonstrates more balanced performance, offering reversibility without overhead and maintaining stable PSNR values for the first stego image. Nonetheless, their results indicate that the second stego image tends to exhibit slightly inferior image quality. This disparity is likely due to the nature of EMD-based embedding, where error adjustments are not evenly distributed and one image inevitably bears a greater share of modification, leading to perceptible quality differences.

The proposed method effectively addresses these issues by employing enhanced HC(7,4) codes in combination with virtual pixel grouping and error pattern optimization, resulting in a more uniform distribution of distortion across both stego images. Consequently, the experimental results demonstrate that the proposed method achieves a balance between embedding capacity and perceptual quality, maintaining PSNR values between 48 and 49 dB and outperforming several existing techniques.

The proposed method is also computationally efficient. Unlike matrix embedding or EMD-based techniques, which often require complex orientation checks and iterative optimization, the proposed scheme relies on simple bitwise operations, Hamming code lookups, and XOR computations. This design not only reduces computational overhead but also enables straightforward hardware or software implementation. Thus, the proposed method is well suited for real-time applications and resource-constrained environments. For example, it can be applied in medical imaging systems or secure communication platforms that require high performance and low computational overhead.

In addition to these performance advantages, the computational efficiency of the proposed method is noteworthy. Unlike matrix embedding or EMD-based techniques, which often require complex orientation checks and iterative optimization, the proposed scheme relies on simple bitwise operations, Hamming code lookups, and XOR computations. This design not only reduces computational overhead but also enables straightforward hardware or software implementation. Thus, the proposed method is well suited for real-time applications or resource-constrained environments where both high performance and low computational complexity are critical, such as medical imaging systems and secure communication platforms.

To further support this claim, we analyzed the algorithm's complexity and conducted runtime evaluations. The core procedures in both the embedding and extraction phases involve selecting an optimal codeword from a fixed-size lookup table containing sixteen valid HC(7,4) codewords. For each pixel, this search requires only basic integer operations and a minimal comparison loop. As such, the algorithm runs in constant time per pixel, resulting in an overall time complexity of $\mathcal{O}(N)$ for an image with N pixels.

To empirically validate this efficiency, we measured the execution time of the full embedding and extraction process on a 512 × 512 grayscale image using Matlab R2019b on a system equipped with an Intel Core i5-8250U processor (1.60 GHz) and 8 GB RAM. The total runtime including all encoding, decoding, and pixel reconstruction steps was approximately 0.97 s. These results demonstrate that the proposed method is computationally lightweight and suitable for low-latency applications. However, we acknowledge that strict real-time constraints in high-resolution or embedded systems may require additional platform-specific optimization, which is a topic for future research.

Although the proposed method provides excellent performance in terms of embedding capacity and image quality, it inherits the common limitation of LSB-based RDH schemes in that it is not robust against lossy image compression such as JPEG. Because the embedded data reside in the least significant bits, such transformations tend to remove or distort the hidden content. This tradeoff reflects a key difference between RDH and robust watermarking, and points toward a promising future research direction in transform-domain RDH.

5. Conclusions

In this paper, we proposed a dual partial reversible data hiding (PRDH) method based on an enhanced Hamming Code (HC(7,4)) to improve embedding capacity while maintaining high image quality. By constructing virtual pixels from two cover images and applying optimized error correction, our method achieves full reversibility with respect to the cover images and significantly increases embedding capacity. Experimental results demonstrate that the proposed approach achieves an embedding rate of up to 1.5 bpp with PSNR values consistently exceeding 48 dB, outperforming existing dual-image RDH techniques. While the proposed scheme guarantees accurate recovery of the generated cover images after data extraction, it does not support reconstruction of the original image itself. This limitation results from the intentional omission of auxiliary data during the cover image generation phase. Transformation from the original image to the cover image is deterministic but not reversible; as such, the proposed method offers partial reversibility. This tradeoff enables a more efficient embedding process but limits the applicability of the scheme in domains that require exact preservation of the original image, such as legal evidence processing or lossless medical archiving. In addition, we evaluated the computational complexity and runtime of the proposed method. The algorithm runs in linear time with respect to image size and achieves embedding and extraction within approximately one second for a 512 × 512 image on a standard laptop, demonstrating its lightweight design and practical applicability to latency-sensitive environments. Future work will explore the extension of the proposed framework to color images and video sequences as well as the integration of adaptive error correction and cryptographic mechanisms to further enhance robustness. The application of this approach to compressed image formats and its performance under advanced steganalysis attacks also remain promising directions. As with typical LSB-based RDH techniques, the proposed method is inherently fragile under lossy transformations such as JPEG compression. Because the embedded data reside in the least significant bits, such operations can distort or remove the hidden information. Therefore, the proposed scheme is best suited for uncompressed or lightly compressed domains where exact data reversibility is required. Future research will explore transform-domain extensions and robustness-enhancing strategies to improve resilience against compression and modern steganalysis attacks, including those based on neural networks. Although the proposed method is theoretical in scope, its efficient encoding structure and high visual fidelity suggest potential utility in practical domains such as medical image management and secure communications. Future research will explore its integration into application-specific frameworks, addressing requirements such as compatibility with standardized formats (e.g., DICOM) and clinical distortion tolerances.

While the proposed method shows promise for secure communication and metadata-preserving archiving, its applicability to clinical or forensic systems requiring perfect image reconstruction remains limited, and integration into existing pipelines is suggested as future work.

Author Contributions: Each author discussed the details of the manuscript. C.K. designed and wrote the manuscript. C.K. implemented the proposed technique and provided the experimental results. C.-N.Y. and L.L. reviewed and revised the article. C.K. drafted and revised the manuscript. All authors have read and agreed to the published version of the manuscript.

Funding: This research was supported in part by National Science and Technology Council (NSTC) under Grant No. 112-2221-E-259-007-MY2 (C.Y.) and by the National Natural Science Foundation of China (No. 62466038), the Technology Innovation Guidance Program Project (Special Project of Technology Cooperation, Science, and Technology Department of Jiangxi Province) (No. 20212BDH81003), and the Open Foundation of Jiangxi Provincial Key Laboratory of Image Processing and Pattern Recognition (ET202404437) (L.L.).

Institutional Review Board Statement: Not applicable.

Informed Consent Statement: Not applicable.

Data Availability Statement: The test images used in this study are publicly available from [26].

Acknowledgments: We thank the anonymous reviewers for their valuable suggestions that improved the quality of this article.

Conflicts of Interest: The authors declare no conflicts of interest.

Abbreviations

The following abbreviations are used in this manuscript:

DH	Data Hiding
RDH	Reversible Data Hiding
PRDH	Partial Reversible Data Hiding
HC	Hamming Code
OI	Original Image
$\mathbf{I}$	Cover Image
$\Delta\mathbf{I}$	Stego Image
x	pixel of grayscale image
y	virtual pixel
a and b	bits composed of a pixel
α	decimal number of 4 MSB of the virtual pixel y
β	decimal number of 3 LSB of the virtual pixel y
$\tilde{\alpha}$	decimal number of 4 LSB of a pixel x_j^1 belonging to cover image $\mathbf{I}_1$
$\tilde{\beta}$	decimal number of 3 LSB of a pixel x_j^2 belonging to cover image $\mathbf{I}_2$
min	function to find the minimum
ε	$min((\alpha - \tilde{\alpha}^2) + (\beta - \tilde{\beta}^2))$
h	codeword from the standard array of HC(7,4) in Figure 2
S	syndrome value of HC(7,4)
ER	Embedding Rate
EC	Embedding Capacity
PSNR	Peak Signal-to-Noise Ratio
MSE	Mean Squared Error
DE	Difference Expansion
HS	Histogram Shift

References

1. Bender, W.; Gruhl, D.; Morimote, N.; Lu, A. Techniques for data hiding. *IBM Syst. J.* **1996**, *35*, 313–336. [CrossRef]
2. Kim, C.; Shin, D.-K.; Yang, C.-N.; Leng, L. Hybrid Data Hiding Based on AMBTC Using Enhanced Hamming Code. *Appl. Sci.* **2020**, *10*, 5336. [CrossRef]
3. Yang, C.N.; Wu, S.Y.; Chou, Y.S.; Kim, C. Enhanced stego-image quality and embedding capacity for the partial reversible data hiding scheme. *Multimed. Tools Appl.* **2019**, *78*, 18595–18616. [CrossRef]
4. Kim, C.; Shin, D.; Leng, L.; Yang, C.N. Separable reversible data hiding in encrypted halftone image. *Displays* **2018**, *55*, 71–79. [CrossRef]
5. Tian, J. Reversible data embedding using a difference expansion. *IEEE Trans. Circuits Syst. Video Technol.* **2003**, *13*, 890–896. [CrossRef]
6. Wu, D.C.; Tsai, W.H. A steganographic method for images by pixel-value differencing. *Pattern Recognit. Lett.* **2013**, *24*, 1613–1626. [CrossRef]
7. Alattar, A.M. Reversible watermark using the difference expansion of a generalized integer transform. *IEEE Trans. Image Process.* **2004**, *13*, 1147–1156. [CrossRef]
8. Ni, Z.; Shi, Y.Q.; Ansari, N.; Su, W. Reversible data hiding. *IEEE Trans. Circuits Syst. Video Technol.* **2006**, *16*, 354–362.
9. Tsai, P.Y.; Hu, Y.C.; Yeh, H.L. Reversible image hiding scheme using predictive coding and histogram shifting. *Signal Process.* **2009**, *89*, 1129–1143. [CrossRef]
10. Chang, I.C.; Hu, Y.C.; Chen, W.L.; Lo, C.C. High capacity reversible data hiding scheme based on residual histogram shifting for block truncation coding. *Signal Process.* **2015**, *108*, 376–388. [CrossRef]
11. Ou, B.; Li, X.; Zhao, Y.; Ni, R.; Shi, Y.-Q. Pairwise Prediction-Error Expansion for Efficient Reversible Data Hiding. *IEEE Trans. Image Process.* **2013**, *22*, 5010–5021. [CrossRef] [PubMed]
12. Shamir, A. How to share a secret. *Commun. Assoc. Comput. Mach.* **1979**, *22*, 612–613. [CrossRef]
13. Chang, C.C.; Kieu, T.D.; Chou, Y.C. Reversible data hiding scheme using two steganographic images. In Proceedings of the IEEE Region 10 International Conference (TENCON), Taipei, Taiwan, 30 October–2 November 2007; pp. 1–4.
14. Chang, C.C.; Lu, T.C.; Horng, G.; Huang, Y.H.; Hsu, Y.M. A high payload data embedding scheme using dual stego-images with reversibility. In Proceedings of the Third International Conference on Information, Communications and Signal Processing, Tainan, Taiwan, 10–13 December 2013; pp. 1–5.
15. Lee, C.F.; Huang, Y.L. Reversible data hiding scheme based on dual stegano-images using orientation combinations. *Telecommun. Syst.* **2013**, *52*, 2237–2247. [CrossRef]
16. Qin, C.; Chang, C.C.; Hsu, T.J. Reversible data hiding scheme based on exploiting modification direction with two steganographic images. *Multimed. Tools Appl.* **2015**, *74*, 5861–5872. [CrossRef]
17. Lu, T.C.; Tseng, C.Y.; Wu, J.H. Dual imaging-based reversible hiding technique using LSB matching. *Signal Process.* **2015**, *108*, 77–89. [CrossRef]
18. Lu, T.C.; Wu, J.H.; Huang, C.C. Dual-image-based reversible data hiding method using center folding strategy. *Signal Process.* **2015**, *115*, 195–213. [CrossRef]
19. Yao, H.; Qin, C.; Tang, Z.; Tian, Y. Improved dual-image reversible data hiding method using the selection strategy of shiftable pixels' coordinates with minimum distortion. *Signal Process.* **2017**, *135*, 26–35. [CrossRef]
20. Liu, Y.; Chang, C.C. A Turtle Shell-based Visual Secret Sharing Scheme with Reversibility and Authentication. *Multimed. Tools Appl.* **2018**, *77*, 25295–25310. [CrossRef]
21. Jana, B.; Giri, D.; Mondal, S.K. Dual image based reversible data hiding scheme using (7,4) hamming code. *Multimed. Tools Appl.* **2018**, *77*, 763–785. [CrossRef]
22. Chen, X.F.; Guo, W.L. Reversible Data Hiding Scheme Based on Fully Exploiting the Orientation Combinations of Dual Stego-images. *Int. J. Netw. Secur.* **2019**, *22*, 126–135.
23. Chen, X.; Hong, C. An Efficient Dual image Reversible Data Hiding Scheme Based on Exploiting Modification Direction. *J. Inf. Secur. Appl.* **2021**, *58*, 102702 [CrossRef]
24. Lin, J.Y.; Chen, Y.; Chang, C.C.; Hu, Y.C. Dual-image with integrity verification using exploiting modification direction. *Multimed. Tools Appl.* **2019**, *78*, 25855–25872. [CrossRef]
25. Sun, Y.X.; Li, Q.; Yan, B.; Pan, J.S.; Yang, H.M. Reversible data hiding in dual encrypted halftone image using matrix embedding. *Multimed. Tools Appl.* **2020**, *79*, 27659–27682. [CrossRef]
26. Lee, C.-F.; Chan, K.-C. A Novel Dual Image Reversible Data Hiding Scheme Based on Vector Coordinate With Triangular Order Coding. *IEEE Access* **2024**, *12*, 90794–90814. [CrossRef]
27. Wan, W.; Wang, H.; Gu, L.; Ren, Y.; Li, J.; Meng, L.; Sun, J. Multi-party reversible data hiding in shared medical images based on texture-guided hierarchical quantization coding. *J. King Saud Univ. Comput. Inf. Sci.* **2025**, *37*, 29. [CrossRef]
28. Zhan, C.; Leng, L.; Chang, C.-C.; Horng, J.-H. Reversible Image Fragile Watermarking with Dual Tampering Detection. *Electronics* **2024**, *13*, 1884. [CrossRef]

29. Moon, T. K. *Error Correction Coding—Mathematical Methods and Algorithms*; John Wiley and Sons: Hoboken, NJ, USA, 2005; pp. 2001–2006.
30. Image Databases. Available online: https://www.imageprocessingplace.com/root_files_V3/image_databases.htm (accessed on 30 January 2025).

applied sciences

MDPI

Article

Optimizing Image Watermarking with Dual-Tree Complex Wavelet Transform and Particle Swarm Intelligence for Secure and High-Quality Protection

Abed Al Raoof Bsoul [1,*] and Alaa Bani Ismail [2]

[1] Information Systems Department, Yarmouk University, Irbid 21163, Jordan
[2] Computer Science Department, Yarmouk University, Irbid 21163, Jordan; ambaniismaeel@just.edu.jo
* Correspondence: raoofbsoul@yu.edu.jo

Abstract

Watermarking is a technique used to address issues related to the widespread use of the internet, such as copyright protection, tamper localization, and authentication. However, most watermarking approaches negatively affect the quality of the original image. In this research, we propose an optimized image watermarking approach that utilizes the dual-tree complex wavelet transform and particle swarm optimization algorithm. Our approach focuses on maintaining the highest possible quality of the watermarked image by minimizing any noticeable changes. During the embedding phase, we break down the original image using a technique called dual-tree complex wavelet transform (DTCWT) and then use particle swarm optimization (PSO) to choose specific coefficients. We embed the bits of a binary logo into the least significant bits of these selected coefficients, creating the watermarked image. To extract the watermark, we reverse the embedding process by first decomposing both versions of the input image using DTCWT and extracting the same coefficients to retrieve those corresponding bits (watermark). In our experiments, we used a common dataset from watermarking research to demonstrate the functionality against various watermarked copies and peak signal-to-noise ratio (PSNR) and normalized cross-correlation (NCC) metrics. The PSNR is a measure of how well the watermarked image maintains its original quality, and the NCC reflects how accurately the watermark can be extracted. Our method gives mean PSNR and NCC of 80.50% and 92.51%, respectively.

Keywords: watermarking; dual-tree complex wavelet transform; particle swarm optimization algorithm; imperceptibility

1. Introduction

Online piracy has caused significant financial losses and job displacement in some countries, amounting to over USD 12 billion annually and 70,000 lost jobs according to the Recording Industry Association of America (RIAA) [1]. The increased use of the internet positively correlates with rising privacy concerns for digital media usage. To alleviate the effects of pirating of such media, digital watermarking is one solution. Digital watermarking is a form of data-hiding technology [2] that involves masking pre-designed information into digital media such as images, videos, or audio. There are various types of digital watermarking schemes, including those based on spatial and frequency domains, and they are classified as robust, semi-fragile, and fragile methods [3]. Of course, a given technique has its own advantages and disadvantages. However, the use of a specific method depends on the application itself.

The internet's widespread use has made it quick and effortless to distribute digital media such as audio, video, and images. However, this convenience has also resulted in critical issues involving copyright infringement and authentication. Watermarking is one of the most effective and widely used techniques to address these concerns. Typically, image watermarking techniques follow a general set of steps that include a watermark embedder and a watermark detector, as depicted in Figure 1.

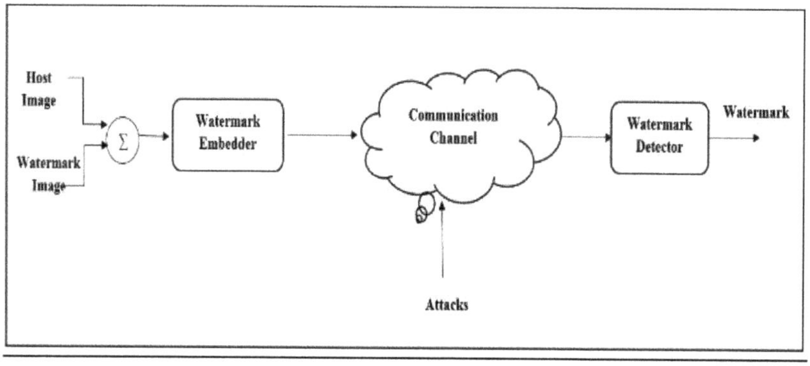

Figure 1. The architecture of a digital image watermarking system.

Watermarking systems need to have specific properties tailored to their intended applications, and as such there is no standard set of properties that all watermarking systems must meet. However, one of the most critical requirements is imperceptibility [4]. Image watermarking involves embedding secret data into a host image without degrading the quality of the watermarked image (imperceptibility). Imperceptibility requires that the quality of the original image is preserved even after inserting the watermark, such that it remains invisible to human eyes [5]. A watermarking approach is considered imperceptible if the host and watermarked images are visually indistinguishable. A robust watermarking scheme should not introduce artifacts into the images, and to assess imperceptibility, objective methods such as the peak signal-to-noise ratio (PSNR) are commonly used [6,7].

In addition to immanence, the watermarking method must also meet robustness requirements. A robust watermark is one that can largely survive variations in the host image (maintaining content with a level of computer independence) whilst other non-domain attack vectors are in play, i.e., cropping, resizing (scaling), contrast adjustment, and JPEG compression [4]. Balancing these numbers to find the watermark's secret formula, one that is strong enough but which does not cause severe degradation of the image, can be difficult. Thus, we should evaluate watermarking algorithms that are good enough to resist attacks with caution, and also aim to prevent significant changes in the quality of the embedded image.

The methods of watermarking that are best suited for proof of copyright and ownership in digital images are robust watermarking techniques. These are intended to withstand several image processing attacks that would either tamper with or erase the watermark. Therefore, robust watermarking techniques are employed to support intellectual property rights, including but not limited to digital image copyright, content authentication, and ownership proof [3]. Sensitive watermark-enabled methods are useful when one requires copyright protection, whilst fragile watermarking methods provide image authentication to confirm the integrity of an image without manipulation or modification. Semi-fragile watermarking is effective and strong, but it is also sensitive to higher image processing operations, and it can be employed for several tamper-detecting schemes [3].

Frequency domain watermarking schemes are generally preferred over the spatial domain watermarking approaches due to their inherent resistance against image processing attacks [8]. Also, as an embedding capacity extension is achieved, the frequency domain can provide more space while still achieving full imperceptibility [4]. However, the use of frequency domain techniques would incorporate some noise in the watermarked image which may be perceivable [9]. This has been countered by some researchers who came up with the idea of using optimization methods to select the best coefficients to embed watermarks, like particle swarm optimization (PSO) [10,11] and genetic algorithms (GAs) [12,13]. An alternative solution to increase the invisibility of watermarks is based on multiresolution decomposition techniques, such as dual-tree complex wavelet transform (DTCWT) [14,15].

In recent years, GAs have been successfully applied, in particular for optimization problems in watermarking. GA-based wavelet-based image watermarking schemes are given in [9]. The embedding energy of a DWT-based watermarking scheme has also been optimized by means of an artificial neural network. A fuzzy clustering technique was used in [16] to determine the optimal embedding locations for a DCT-based watermarking scheme. These AI techniques enhance the performance of watermarking schemes and their parameters (capacity, strength, or location).

In 2017, Liu et al. [17] proposed an image watermarking scheme in the contourlet transform domain, in connection with a probabilistic neural network. They distilled the watermark extraction to a great degree of robustness. Hamamoto and Kawamura [18] proposed an approach using an autoencoder to train two distinct neural networks (embedder and extractor) with a digital image using DCT coefficients. In [19], Ding et al. proposed a generalized approach of using deep neural networks in digital watermarking. They presented a method that obtained great robustness under common image processing attacks, such as filtering, compression, and geometric transformations.

Since the selection of transformation coefficients for embedding affects any watermarking method, researchers have exploited evolutionary algorithms to optimize the selection criteria. Researchers have used genetic algorithms widely in the watermarking of images in the last few years, and it has become an important research branch for many researchers [12,20–22]. Moreover, PSO has been proven to give promising accuracies in terms of robustness and impeccability. As such, many studies have exploited this fact in the literature, with particular highlights being outstanding approaches such as the work carried out in [11,23,24]. Other interesting approaches can be found in the literature, incorporating nature-inspired optimization algorithms such as artificial bee colony optimization [25,26], the bat algorithm [27], and gray wolf optimization [28].

Despite the advances in digital watermarking techniques, significant challenges remain in balancing imperceptibility and robustness. Conventional methods like DWT, DCT, or DFT usually leave visible artifacts on images or fail in preserving the integrity of the watermark under common malicious attacks (e.g., cropping, compression, and scaling). Although optimization algorithms have been applied in watermarking, their integration with newer wavelet-based transforms, like DTCWT, has not been fully explored. This study will address these gaps by exploring the following research questions:

- How can the use of DTCWT and PSO be incorporated to improve the imperceptibility of watermarked images while retaining high robustness?
- How well does the proposed method compare with traditional techniques like DWT and DCT in terms of PSNR (peak signal-to-noise ratio) and NCC (normalized cross-correlation) under standard image-processing manipulations such as compression, cropping, and scaling?

- What are the practical challenges involved in this watermarking scheme when applying it to real-world digital media applications, and how can these limitation be addressed?

The motivation underlying this work is to contribute to the domain of image watermarking and to propose an invisible and fragile method using DTCWT along with PSO algorithms. The main theoretical contribution of this work is the exploitation of shift invariance, redundancy, and directionality selection properties of DTCWT, which when applied in image applications give better results than traditional transform techniques such as DWT, DCT or DFT. These features make the watermark more robust against a number of image processing attacks, while preserving exceptional image quality. In order to improve the method and reduce any distortion of the watermarked images, PSO is used as an optimization algorithm. The proposed application of PSO has been integrated very well in research, and in this work, it is used to determine better coefficient embedding with optimal performance that will lead to good robustness and less visual distortion in the watermarked image. Additionally, DTCWT has a parallel dual-tree structure that enables efficient computation and is perfectly reconstructable, and therefore, it is well suited for real-world applications requiring both quality and security [29]. However, the proposed method faces limitations in computational complexity, applicability to color images, and resistance to advanced attacks.

2. Methodology

2.1. Overall Research Design

The proposed watermarking system is composed of two main phases: watermark embedding and watermark extraction. The system works as follows: The watermark image and the host image are first pre-processed and then input into the watermarking system. In the embedding phase, the host image is transformed into the frequency domain by applying DTCWT. The embedding process is optimized to choose the most suitable coefficients for watermark insertion. The watermark is then inserted into the least significant bit (LSB) of the selected coefficients. In the extraction phase, the watermark image is extracted by reversing the embedding process. To evaluate the proposed approach, the similarity between the watermark image and the extracted watermark is measured by computing the normalized cross-correlation (NCC). Additionally, the imperceptibility of the proposed approach is evaluated by calculating the peak signal-to-noise ratio (PSNR) of the watermarked images. Figure 2 illustrates the framework of the proposed approach.

2.2. Dataset

In this study, we used a standard dataset commonly employed in watermarking research. The experiments were performed on seventeen standard testing images: Lena, Cameraman, Baboon, Airplane, Boat, House1, House2, House3, Barbara, Elaine, Pirate, Zelda, Living room, Kiel, Lighthouse, Lake, and Pepper. All images were 512 $\times$ 512 in size, grayscale, and had an 8-bit depth.

The watermark image used in the experiments is the black and white logo for Yarmouk University, with a size of 100 $\times$ 109 bits. The logo of Yarmouk University is illustrated in Figure 3.

To ensure the reproducibility of the experiments, all images are publicly available and widely accepted in digital watermarking research. Further details about the dataset source can be provided upon request.

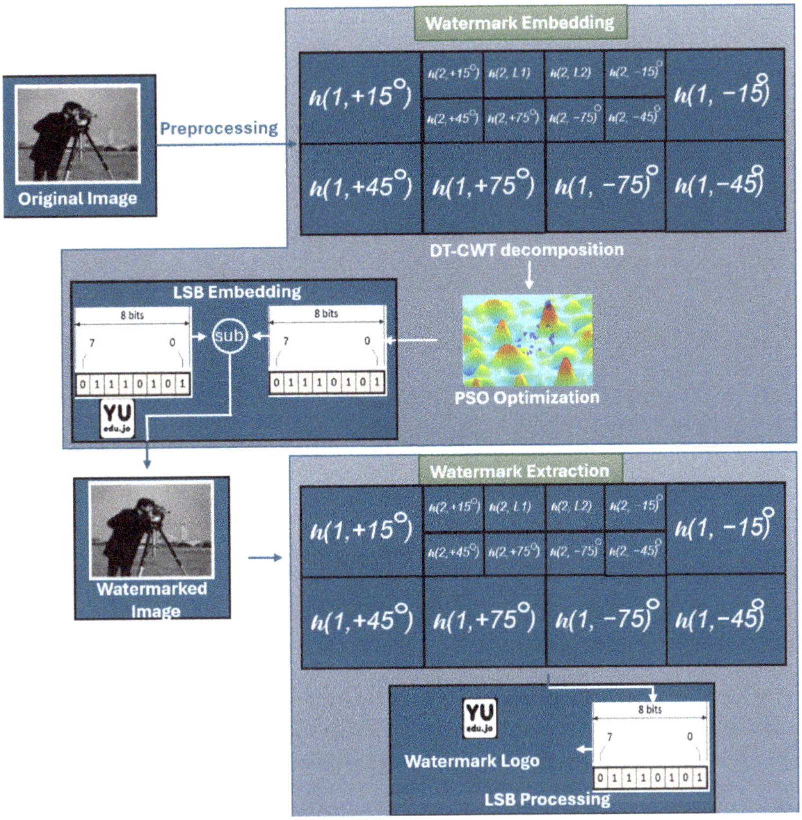

Figure 2. The overall design of the proposed method.

Figure 3. The logo used for embedding in this research. The actual logo size is 100 × 112, and the logo is black and white.

2.3. *Watermark Embedding*

Watermark embedding is the process of inserting the watermark image into the host image. In this research, this step can be split into three main sub-steps.

2.3.1. Frequency Domain Transformation

The insertion of the watermark image is performed in the frequency domain, and this involves converting the host image to the frequency domain using DTCWT. This transformation technique has gained attention due to its advantageous properties over DWT. The most notable properties are approximate shift invariance, directionally selective filters, and perfect reconstruction [29]. DTCWT utilizes two real DWT trees to produce the real and imaginary parts of the transformed image. After applying DTCWT, the image is decomposed into eight sub-bands, including Low–Low (LL), Low–High (LH), High–

Low (HL), and High–High (HH), for both the real and imaginary parts of a one-level decomposition. Figure 4 illustrates a multi-level decomposition for the LL sub-band. The coefficients from the LL sub-band are selected for embedding the watermark image.

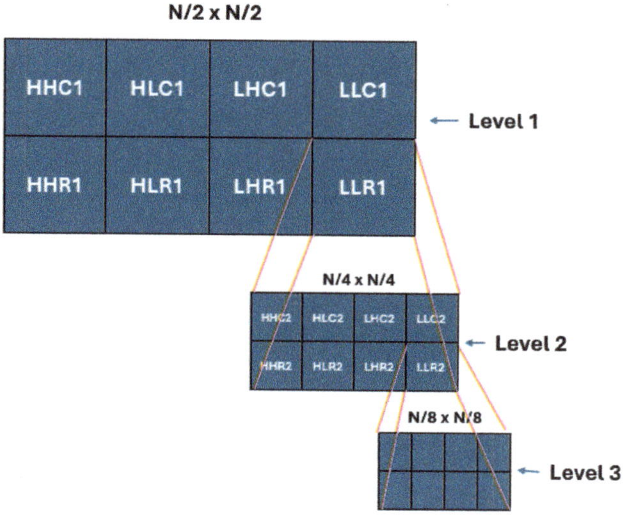

Figure 4. DTCWT sub-bands using multi-level decomposition.

The dual-tree complex wavelet transform differs from DWT in that it uses two orthogonal parallel transforms of the real wavelet, with the first DWT tree producing the real part and the second tree producing the imaginary part. Each tree contains a unique set of orthogonal filters. This results in DTCWT being able to obtain coefficients of six directions, namely $\pm 15^\circ$, $\pm 45^\circ$, and $\pm 75^\circ$, which solves the problem of poor directionality. At each level of decomposition, DTCWT produces two complex low-frequency sub-bands and six high-frequency complex detailed sub-bands, which are oriented by these angles. This property provides superior perceptual characteristics compared to DWT and enables the development of a watermarking approach with high imperceptibility. In mathematical terms, the low-frequency coefficients can be expressed as shown in Equation (1) [29].

$$x\,(\lambda, L, u, v) = \mathrm{Re}\,(x\,(\lambda, L, u, v)) + j\mathrm{Im}\,(x\,(\lambda, L, u, v)) \quad (1)$$

where λ is the scaling factor (wavelength), L is the decomposition level, Re is the real part of the tree, Im is the imaginary part of the tree, u and v indicate the location of the coefficient in each sub-band, and j represents the square root of -1.

In this equation, the image is factorized using both real and imaginary parts to preserve information during processing.

The high-frequency coefficients can be written as in Equation (2).

$$\begin{gathered} x\,(\hat{}, \theta, u, v) = \mathrm{Re}\,(x\,(\hat{}, \theta, u, v)) + j\mathrm{Im}\,(x\,(\hat{}, \theta, u, v)) \\ \theta \in \{-75, -45, -15, +15, +45, +75\} \end{gathered} \quad (2)$$

In the embedding process, the frequency component at locations u and v in the decomposition is represented by the complex coefficient after applying the DTCWT. Therefore, by modifying the least significant bits of these coefficients, the watermark data can be embedded without significantly altering the image's appearance.

2.3.2. Optimizing the Embedding Process

To embed a watermark in an image, we should first select frequency domain coefficients from the decomposed host image. Usually, this process is applied sequentially on the coefficients. However, in this research, we will use the particle swarm intelligence algorithm to optimize the selection of the coefficients. The optimization algorithm fitness function is used for minimizing degradation in the watermarked image.

PSO is a type of stochastic optimization algorithm and its process is inspired by the social interaction behavior of flocking birds or schooling fish, which differs significantly from traditional individual cognitive elements. This algorithm consists of a population of candidate solutions (particles) which exist in the search space and are given a fitness value for the maximization function. The PSO algorithm focuses on the purpose of minimizing or maximizing the objective function. All particles update their position based on their own experience (cognitive behavior) and development, as well as the best location reached so far by all other particles (social behavior).

For a brief overview of the PSO algorithm, the methodology was introduced in [30]. Each particle in the swarm consists of three 3-dimensional vectors, the current position (x_i), the best position reached by that particle ($pbest_i$), and the velocity (v_i), as shown in Equation (3). The velocity vector (v_i) controls the optimization process and enables information exchange between particles as well as utilizing the historical knowledge of each particle, as given in Equation (4). By adding the velocity coordinates (v_i) to the current position (x_i), the updated position of each particle (x'_i) is calculated.

$$v_i = \omega\, v_i + C_1\varphi_1\,(p_{besti} - x_i) + C_2\varphi_2(g_{best} - x_i) \tag{3}$$

$$x'_i = x_i + v_i \tag{4}$$

where inertia weight (ω) is a constant that determines the balance between global and local search, while $\varphi 1$ and $\varphi 2$ represent uniformly distributed random values within [0, 1]. Additionally, positive acceleration constants C1 and C2 are used to scale the contribution of cognitive and social components, respectively, in the particle's movement.

As an example, suppose that a particle's current velocity is $v_i = 2$, its personal best is at position 5, and the global best is at position 8. If the inertia weight is $\omega = 0.7$ and C_1 and C_2 are both set to 1.5, with random values $\varphi_1 = 0.9$ and $\varphi_2 = 0.7$, the updated velocity would be

$$v_i = 0.7\,(2) + 1.5\,(0.9)\,(5 - x_i) + 1.5\,(0.7)\,(8 - x_i)$$

This gives the new velocity based on how far the particle is from its personal best and the global best, allowing it to move closer to an optimal solution.

PSO is applied to the coefficients obtained from the decomposition step. The pseudocode for finding the optmal set of coefficients using PSO is shown in Algorithm A1 (Appendix A).

As the algorithm shows, the coefficients are divided into *m* swarms, where each swarm has several particles. Each coefficient in a swarm is considered as a particle. The objective function is calculated over each particle in each swarm, and the best value in swarm *i* is denoted as $pbest_i$, while the best objective function over all swarms is considered as *gbest*. The inertia is calculated for each iteration and used as a weight contribution of the previous velocity. The updated velocity is computed from the weighted velocity in the previous iteration, along with the distance of particle *i* from the *pbesti* and the distance of particle *i* from *gbest*.

After finding out the velocity of particle *i*, we can generate a random number from [0, 1] and compare the obtained number with the sigmoid value of the new velocity. If the random number is less than the sigmoid value, we will choose that particle (coefficient) as an embeddable particle by setting it to 1. Then, the *pbest* and *gbest* are updated and the iteration continues.

After optimizing the selected coefficients in the transformed image using PSO, we calculated their mean, variance, skewness, and kurtosis, as well as the entropy and the energy of the selected coefficients. We found that the selected coefficients exhibit a non-Gaussian distribution. As a result, this fact will help in identifying the embeddable coefficients during the reconstruction of the stego-image.

2.3.3. Optimizing PSO Parameters for Computational Efficiency

Particle swarm optimization (PSO) plays a critical role in determining the coefficients used for watermark embedding in the proposed method. However, the choice of PSO parameters significantly impacts not only the quality of the watermarking results but also the computational efficiency of the optimization process. To address this, we conducted a focused analysis of the key parameters involved in PSO: inertia weight (ω), cognitive component (C1), social component (C2), swarm size, and the number of iterations.

The optimization of PSO parameters was approached with the dual objectives of minimizing computational time while maintaining high performance in terms of imperceptibility and robustness. The following parameter ranges and configurations were examined based on insights from the existing literature and empirical observations:

- Inertia Weight (ω): Tested within the range [0.4, 0.9] to balance exploration and exploitation.
- Cognitive Component (C1): Varied between 0.5 and 2.0 to evaluate the effect of individual particle learning.
- Social Component (C2): Varied between 0.5 and 2.0 to assess the influence of swarm-wide cooperation.
- Swarm Size: Analyzed for sizes ranging from 20 to 50 particles to explore trade-offs between computational cost and optimization performance.
- Number of Iterations: Evaluated over a range of 50 to 200 iterations to identify the point of convergence for the objective function.

2.3.4. Insertion in the Least Significant Bit (LSB)

A digital image is composed of small dots called pixels, and each pixel is a series of zeros and ones that represent a given color. When masking the least significant bits of the color value with message bits, embedding takes place. This process is called the least significant bit (LSB) technique, and it is a widely used method in image manipulation. The more bits used in masking, the more noticeable the distortion in the image. On the other hand, using more bits in the masking process provides more embeddable data. As a result, a compromise should be made to balance the quality of the resulting watermarked image and the amount of data embedded. The process of LSB is repeated in the given manner until the whole message has been embedded. Although it has been used in various applications, such as information hiding, copyright protection, and authentication, LSB has some limitations, especially when implemented in a time domain. For example, the use of advanced steganalysis techniques may result in the whole method becoming corrupted. Therefore, to overcome these limitations, researchers have developed more complex steganography techniques that provide better security and greater capacity for hiding data while maintaining imperceptibility.

One such technique is the transformation of the image to the frequency domain and the application of LSB on selected coefficients of the transformation. By utilizing other image domains, larger amounts of data can be hidden while still maintaining excellent transparency. As more steganalysis techniques are introduced, the acquisition of more advanced and secure steganography techniques becomes of paramount importance.

2.3.5. Watermarking Evaluation

According to the applied method for watermarking, the performance can change dramatically. To find out the performance of a given watermark method, one can measure the method's transparency. As artifacts are introduced during the watermarking process, the host image's quality is affected. Transparency is defined as the amount of information disclosed after the watermark operation. In practice, transparency is usually measured by evaluating the imperceptibility of the algorithm, which in turn is measured by an objective image quality metric called peak signal-to-noise ratio (PSNR). Measuring the PSNR of a method is straightforward and simple, and as a result, PSNR has become a widely used metric for watermarking methods. The PSNR is evaluated by comparing the host image I of size $N \times M$, with the watermarked image K, as follows [6]:

$$\text{PSNR} = 10 \cdot \log_{10}\left(\frac{\text{Max}^2}{\frac{1}{M \cdot N}\sum_{i=1}^{M}\sum_{j=1}^{N}(I(i,j) - K(i,j))^2}\right) \quad (5)$$

where

- Max: Maximum possible pixel value (e.g., 255 for 8-bit images).
- M and N: Dimensions of the image (rows and columns).
- I(i,j) Pixel value at position (i,j) in the original image.
- K(i,j): Pixel value at position (i,j) in the distorted or compressed image.

Alongside transparency, the degree of similarity between the watermarked image and the original image is also crucial in assessing the performance of a watermarking technique. Evaluating and measuring the similarity between the extracted watermark and the original one is essential in determining the level of distortion introduced by the method. Normalized cross-correlation (NCC) is used to measure image similarity between the original and extracted images in watermarking.

NCC is computed as follows: W, W′ are the original watermark image and the extracted watermark, respectively, while $\mu_W . \mu_{W'}$ represent the means of the original and extracted watermark.

$$NC\,(W.W') = \frac{\sum_{i=1}^{M}\sum_{j=1}^{N}[W(i\,.\,j) - \mu_W][W\prime(i\,.\,j) - \mu_{W\prime}]}{\sqrt{\sum_{i=1}^{M}\sum_{j=1}^{N}\left[W'^{(i\,.\,j)} - \mu_{W'}\right]^2}\sqrt{\sum_{i=1}^{M}\sum_{j=1}^{N}[W(i\,.\,j) - \mu_W]^2}} \quad (6)$$

NCC is particularly useful in evaluating the accuracy of the watermark extraction process.

3. Results

The proposed scheme was evaluated using the dataset described in Section 2.2, and the validation of the proposed scheme was performed as described in Section 2.3.5, by calculating the PSNR between the host and watermarked images and the NCC between the embedded logo image and the extracted image logo.

The implementation of the approach was carried out in Python on a laptop computer equipped with an Intel Core i7 processor, with 32 GB RAM, and running on the Windows 10 operating system.

To embed the watermark logo into the host image, the host image was decomposed using DTCWT. The filters "near_sym_b" and "qshift_b" were empirically found to produce the best coefficients, and a decomposition level of four was chosen. The PSO algorithm described in Section 2.3.2 was utilized to select the best embeddable coefficients from the LL sub-band.

The parameters of the PSO algorithm were optimized for computational efficiency using empirical settings. Specifically, the cognitive component (C1) and social component (C2) were both tested for a value which varied between 0.5 and 2.0. The inertia weight (ω), which controls the search direction, was tested in the range of a maximum weight (W_{max} = 0.9) and a minimum weight (W_{min} = 0.4). Additionally, φ1 and φ2 were assigned uniformly distributed random values within [0, 1]. The number of swarms was analyzed in sizes ranging from 20 to 50, and the number of iterations was evaluated in the range of 50 to 200 iterations in order to discover the convergence point of our objective function.

The findings of the PSO parameters' optimization underscore the importance of carefully selecting PSO parameters to enhance computational efficiency. Figure 5 demonstrates that $\omega = 0.7$ is the optimal inertia weight, achieving the best balance between computational efficiency and performance quality. At this ω value, PSNR reaches its peak while computational cost is at its minimum, highlighting it as the ideal value. The red dashed line effectively emphasizes this point. Figure 6 shows that $C1 = 1.5$ is the optimal cognitive component, achieving the highest PSNR while maintaining a decreasing computational cost. The red dashed line emphasizes this ideal balance between performance and efficiency.

The optimization results identified $C2 = 1.5$ as the optimal value, as illustrated in Figure 7. This value achieved the highest PSNR, while the computational cost increased gradually. The optimization process was also applied to the swarm size and number of iterations of PSO parameters to determine the optimal values that minimized the computational cost. The results of these optimization processes are presented in Figures 8 and 9.

It should be noted that this insertion process may introduce artifacts and distortion into the watermarked image. To evaluate the impact of these distortions, the PSNR was measured for the watermarked image. A visual comparison between some standard cover images before and after the watermark was applied, along with the PSNR between the two images, is provided in Table 1.

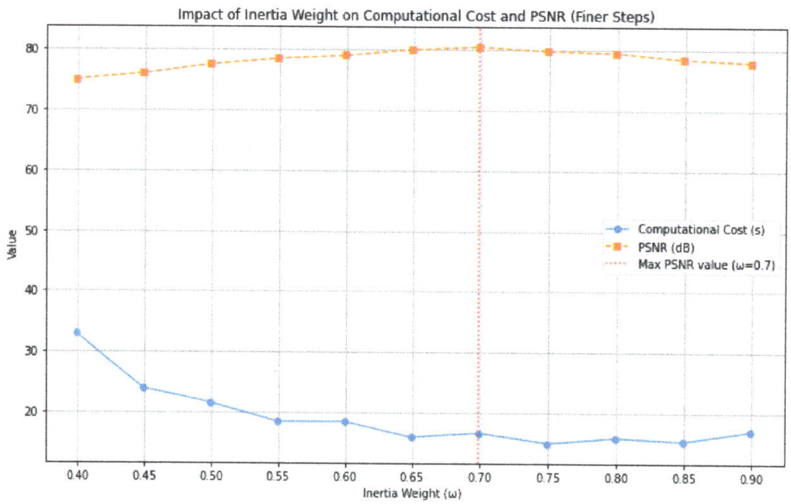

Figure 5. Impact of inertia weight (ω) on computational cost and PSNR.

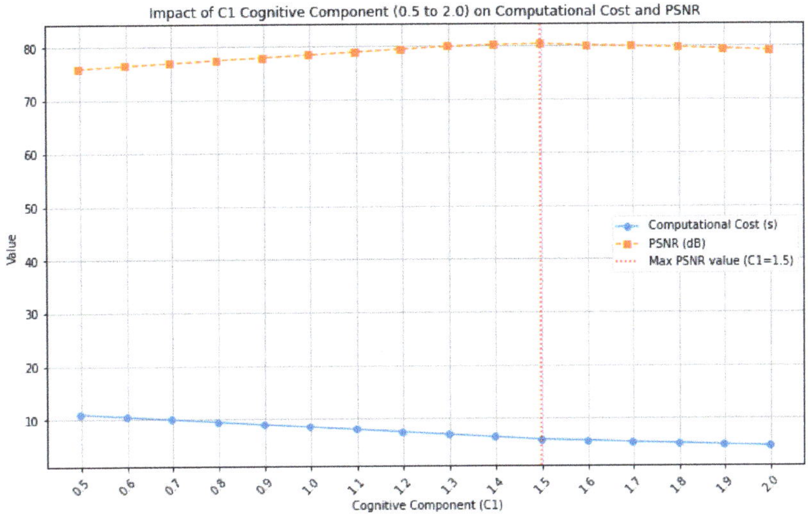

Figure 6. Impact of cognitive component (C1) on computational cost and PSNR.

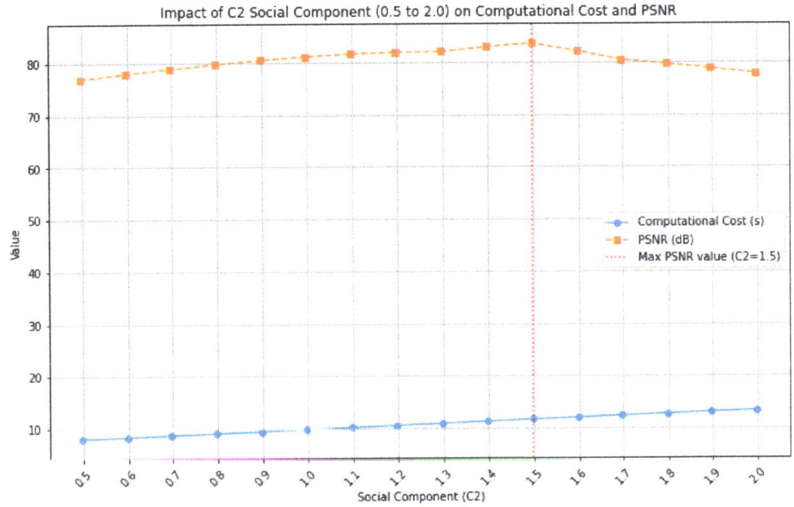

Figure 7. Impact of social component (C2) on computational cost and PSNR.

As shown in Table 1, the proposed method achieved a high PSNR between the host and watermarked images, indicating that the watermark was embedded effectively. The shift-invariant properties of DTCWT were found to be crucial in achieving this high PSNR. These properties allow for robust watermark embedding while preserving the quality of the host image.

To verify the embedding algorithm, we performed an extraction of the logo embedded in the images and measured the NCC between the original image logo and the extracted logo image. The results are provided in Table 2.

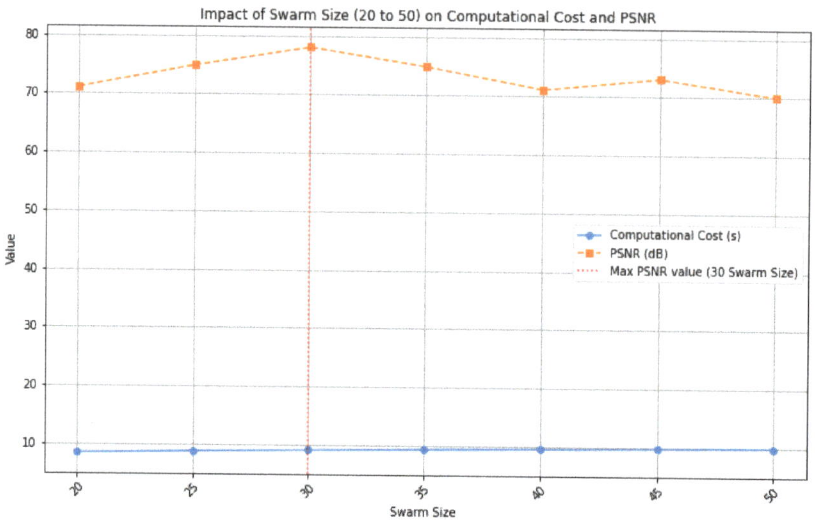

Figure 8. Impact of swarm size on computational cost and PSNR.

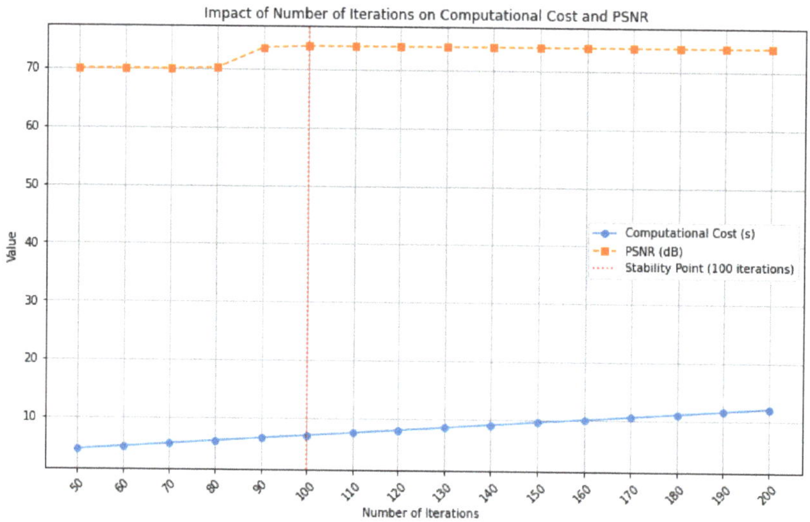

Figure 9. Impact of number of iterations on computational cost and PSNR.

Table 1. The original host images along with the watermarked image for visual comparison; filters used are near_sym_b and qshift_b, while the decomposition level is four.

(**a**) PSNR = 80.65.		(**b**) PSNR = 81.17.	

Table 1. *Cont.*

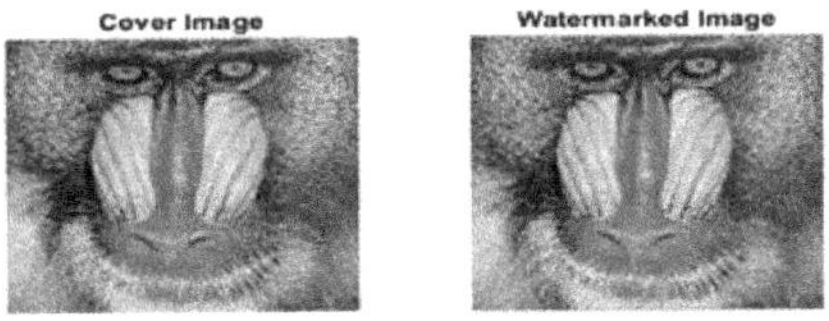 (**c**) PSNR = 80.14.	 (**d**) PSNR = 80.4.
 (**e**) PSNR = 80.42.	 (**f**) PSNR = 80.46.
 (**g**) PSNR = 80.2.	 (**h**) PSNR = 80.1.

Table 2. NCC values for extracted watermarks.

Image	Extracted Logo	NCC
Leena		93.3%
Cameraman		94.9%
Mandrill		89.2%

Table 2. *Cont.*

Image	Extracted Logo	NCC
Homecar		91.1%
House		96.1%
Airplane		90.7%
Lighthouse		91.3%
Bedroom		93.5%

Table 2 examines the robustness of our watermarking method through various images. The high NCC values indicate that the watermarking technique is effective at embedding and extracting the watermark even after possible distortions or manipulations to the image. The consistency in NCC values across different images means that the method is functionally robust for image content or complexity.

To assess the performance of the proposed PSO-based watermarking method, a comparative analysis was conducted against other classical optimization approaches commonly used in watermark optimization. The comparison highlights the strengths and trade-offs of the proposed method. The evaluation focused on three primary metrics, PSNR, NCC, and computational cost, which collectively reflect the efficiency and effectiveness of the optimization process. The findings are summarized in Table 3.

Table 3. Comparison of the proposed PSO–DTCWT method and classical approaches.

Method	PSNR (dB)	NCC	Computational Cost
GA-Based Method [12]	47.81	97.84%	High (requires DCNN-SVR correction)
DE-Based Method [31]	69.25	93.30%	High (due to embedding additional data)
ACO + LGBA Method [32]	46.4–49.8	99% for most attacks	Significantly improved with LGBA
Proposed PSO–DTCWT	80.5	92.51%	Lower (due to parameter optimization)

The results in Table 3 highlight the superior performance of the proposed PSO–DTCWT method compared to the GA-based, differential evolution (DE)-based, and ant colony optimization with light gradient boosting algorithm (ACO + LGBA) methods. The proposed method achieves the highest imperceptibility, with a PSNR of 80.5 dB.

The PSNR significantly surpasses that of the other methods, whose values range from 46.4 to 69.25 dB. Although the PSO–DTCWT method's robustness (NCC of 92.51%) is slightly lower than that of the ACO + LGBA method (99%) and the GA-based method (97.84%), it remains competitive and sufficient for reliable watermark extraction. Furthermore, the PSO–DTCWT method demonstrates a clear advantage in computational efficiency due to parameter optimization, unlike the GA- and DE-based methods, which incur higher costs from additional processes such as DCNN-SVR correction and the embedding of extra data. These findings indicate that the PSO–DTCWT method achieves the best balance between imperceptibility, robustness, and computational cost, making it a practical and efficient solution for real-world applications.

4. Discussion and Conclusions

Using dual-tree complex wavelet transform (DTCWT) and particle swarm optimization (PSO), the watermarking method proposed revealed drastic improvements in terms of imperceptibility and resilience against attack, with a high capacity to embed large bits of messages into target images. Higher PSNR values indicate less degradation in the quality of host images due to watermarking operation. The technique shows good performance in preserving the image's quality up to a mean PSNR value of 80.50% across the dataset.

Moreover, the average NCC value of 92.51% indicates high accuracy in extracting watermarks from an original image compared to its corresponding retrieved version (Table 2). This highlights the robustness of the proposed method in authenticating and verifying forgeries performed on watermarked images.

Utilizing DTCWT for frequency domain transformation confers benefits such as shift invariance and directional selectivity, which are pivotal in obtaining high imperceptibility. The PSO algorithm's optimization of coefficient selection augmented the watermark's robustness against frequent image manipulation attacks. Overall, combining DTCWT and PSO in the proposed watermarking method delivers a highly effective solution for secure and superior image watermarking.

To assess the performance of the proposed PSO-based watermarking method, a comparative analysis was conducted against other classical optimization approaches commonly used in watermark optimization. The comparison highlights that the proposed PSO-based watermarking method achieves the highest imperceptibility (PSNR of 80.5 dB) compared to the GA-based, DE-based, and ACO + LGBA methods. While its robustness (NCC of 92.51%) is slightly lower than the GA-based (97.84%) and ACO + LGBA methods (99%), it remains competitive. The PSO-based method also demonstrates significantly lower computational cost due to parameter optimization, making it an efficient and practical solution for watermarking applications.

By leveraging PSO's ability to find optimal solutions in uncertain environments and DTCWT's capacity for multi-dimensional data analysis, the proposed approach can effectively address uncertainties, improve efficiency, and provide robust solutions across various industrial applications.

The proposed watermarking method has limitations in terms of computational complexity, applicability to color images and advanced attack resistance. Future work must be considered to minimize the effect of these limitations and widen the use of the algorithm in other domains. Future research can be applied to improve such limitations in 3D gray scale and color images, optimize PSO parameters, and apply the method in real-time and IoT environments.

Author Contributions: Conceptualization, A.A.R.B.; methodology, A.A.R.B. and A.B.I.; software, A.B.I.; validation, A.A.R.B.; formal analysis, A.A.R.B. and A.B.I.; investigation, A.A.R.B. and A.B.I.; resources, A.A.R.B.; data curation, A.B.I. and A.A.R.B.; writing—original draft, A.B.I.; writing—review and editing, A.A.R.B.; data visualization, A.B.I.; supervision, A.A.R.B. All authors have read and agreed to the published version of the manuscript.

Funding: This research received no external funding.

Institutional Review Board Statement: Not applicable.

Informed Consent Statement: Not applicable.

Data Availability Statement: The raw data supporting the conclusions of this article will be made available by the authors on request.

Conflicts of Interest: The authors declare no conflicts of interest.

Appendix A

Algorithm A1: PSO to find the best coefficients for watermark embedding

```
Input:  sub band coefficients <c1, c2, ... cm>.
Output:  Particles matrix where row i and column j of the matrix is set
to 1 if the corresponding coefficient is selected by the optimization.

// Initialize algorithm variables
pbest = array of size num_swarms x num_of_watermark_bits, initialized to
all zeros
gbest = array of size 1 x num_of_watermark_bits, initialized to all
zeros
pbest_fitness = array of size num_swarms, initialized to all zeros
gbest_fitness = 0
max_iterations = user-defined maximum number of iterations
num_swarms = user-defined number of swarms
Wmax = user-defined maximum weight factor
Wmin = user-defined minimum weight factor
K = user-defined number of selected particles
iteration = 1
```

```
// Evaluate initial fitness values
For i = 1 to m
     F_i = calculate objective function of particle c_i
     If F_i is better than F(pbest_i) then
          pbest_i = c_i
          pbest_fitness(i) = F_i
     EndIf
     If F_i is better than gbest_fitness then
          gbest = c_i
          gbest_fitness = F_i
     EndIf
EndFor

// Particle Swarm Optimization loop
while iteration <= max_iterations do
      For i = 1 to num_swarms do
          // Calculate new particle velocities
          W = Wmax - (Wmax - Wmin) * iteration / max_iterations
          For j = 1 to num_of_watermark_bits do
               r1 = random number between 0 and 1
               r2 = random number between 0 and 1
               velocity_i_j = W * velocity_i_j + C1 * r1 * (pbest_i_j -
particles_i_j) + C2 * r2 * (gbest_j - particles_i_j)
               // Update particle position based on sigmoid function
               if rand() < 1 / (1 + exp(-velocity_i_j)) then
        particles_i_j = 1
               else
        particles_i_j = 0
               EndIf
          EndFor

          // Select subset of particles based on K
          M = sum(particles_i)
          if M > K then
               index = find(particles_i == 1)
               index_to_remove = index(randperm(length(index), M - K))
               particles_i(index_to_remove) = 0
          else if M < K then
               index = find(particles_i == 0)
               index_to_add = index(randperm(length(index), K - M))
               particles_i(index_to_add) = 1
          EndIf
```

```
            // Update personal best and global best particles
            fitness_i = calculate objective function of particle i
            if fitness_i > pbest_fitness(i) then
                pbest_fitness(i) = fitness_i
                pbest_i = particles_i
            EndIf
            if fitness_i > gbest_fitness then
                gbest_fitness = fitness_i
                gbest = particles_i
            EndIf
        EndFor
        iteration = iteration + 1
EndWhile

// Output selected particles
Output particles
```

References

1. Siwek, S.E. *The True Cost of Sound Recording Piracy to the US Economy*; Institute for Policy Innovation Lewisville: Lewisville, TX, USA, 2007.
2. Rizzi, M.; D'Aloia, M.; Longo, A. Digital watermarking for healthcare: A survey of ECG watermarking methods in telemedicine. *Int. J. Comput. Sci. Eng.* **2020**, *23*, 235–249. [CrossRef]
3. Kumar, R.; Singh, P.K.; Yadav, J. Digital image watermarking technique based on adaptive median filter and HL sub-band of two-stage DWT. *Int. J. Comput. Aided Eng. Technol.* **2023**, *18*, 290–310. [CrossRef]
4. Begum, M.; Uddin, M.S. Digital image watermarking techniques: A review. *Information* **2020**, *11*, 110. [CrossRef]
5. Garg, P.; Kishore, R.R. Performance comparison of various watermarking techniques. *Multimed. Tools Appl.* **2020**, *79*, 25921–25967. [CrossRef]
6. Setiadi, D.R.I.M. PSNR vs SSIM: Imperceptibility quality assessment for image steganography. *Multimed. Tools Appl.* **2021**, *80*, 8423–8444. [CrossRef]
7. Rustad, S.; Andono, P.N.; Shidik, G.F. Digital image steganography survey and investigation (goal, assessment, method, development, and dataset). *Signal Process.* **2023**, *206*, 108908.
8. Evsutin, O.; Dzhanashia, K. Watermarking schemes for digital images: Robustness overview. *Signal Process. Image Commun.* **2022**, *100*, 116523. [CrossRef]
9. Yuan, Z.; Su, Q.; Liu, D.; Zhang, X. A blind image watermarking scheme combining spatial domain and frequency domain. *Vis. Comput.* **2021**, *37*, 1867–1881. [CrossRef]
10. Garg, P.; Kishore, R.R. Optimized color image watermarking through watermark strength optimization using particle swarm optimization technique. *J. Inf. Optim. Sci.* **2020**, *41*, 1499–1512. [CrossRef]
11. Husain, A.; Mishra, A.D.; Jena, S.K. A robust approach for digital watermarking of satellite imagery dataset. *Int. J. Swarm Intell.* **2022**, *7*, 82–93. [CrossRef]
12. Barlaskar, S.A.; Singh, S.V.; Monsley, K.A.; Laskar, R.H. Genetic algorithm based optimized watermarking technique using hybrid DCNN-SVR and statistical approach for watermark extraction. *Multimed. Tools Appl.* **2022**, *81*, 7461–7500. [CrossRef]
13. Zhu, T.; Qu, W.; Cao, W. An optimized image watermarking algorithm based on SVD and IWT. *J. Supercomput.* **2022**, *78*, 222–237. [CrossRef]
14. Huang, T.; Xu, J.; Yang, Y.; Han, B. Robust zero-watermarking algorithm for medical images using double-tree complex wavelet transform and Hessenberg decomposition. *Mathematics* **2022**, *10*, 1154. [CrossRef]
15. Nouioua, N.; Seddiki, A.; Ghaz, A. Blind Digital Watermarking Framework Based on DTCWT and NSCT for Telemedicine Application. *Trait. Du Signal* **2020**, *37*, 955–964. [CrossRef]
16. Balasamy, K.; Suganyadevi, S. A fuzzy based ROI selection for encryption and watermarking in medical image using DWT and SVD. *Multimed. Tools Appl.* **2021**, *80*, 7167–7186.
17. Liu, J.-X.; Wen, X.; Yuan, L.-M.; Xu, H.-X. A robust approach of watermarking in contourlet domain based on probabilistic neural network. *Multimed. Tools Appl.* **2017**, *76*, 24009–24026. [CrossRef]
18. Hamamoto, I.; Kawamura, M. Digital watermarking method by encoder using neural network. *IEICE Tech. Rep.* **2017**, *117*, 17–22.

19. Ding, W.; Ming, Y.; Cao, Z.; Lin, C.-T. A generalized deep neural network approach for digital watermarking analysis. *IEEE Trans. Emerg. Top Comput. Intell.* **2021**, *6*, 613–627. [CrossRef]
20. Kumsawat, P.; Attakitmongcol, K.; Srikaew, A. A new approach for optimization in image watermarking by using genetic algorithms. *IEEE Trans. Signal Process.* **2005**, *53*, 4707–4719. [CrossRef]
21. Wu, Q.; Qu, A.; Huang, D.; Ma, L. Robust and blind audio watermarking scheme based on genetic algorithm in dual transform domain. *Math. Probl. Eng.* **2021**, *2021*, 3378683. [CrossRef]
22. Thanki, R. Genetic algorithm-based intelligent watermarking for security of medical images in telemedicine applications. In *Intelligent Data Security Solutions for e-Health Applications*; Elsevier: Amsterdam, The Netherlands, 2020; pp. 185–204.
23. Laxmanika; Singh, P.K. Robust and imperceptible image watermarking technique based on SVD, DCT, BEMD and PSO in wavelet domain. *Multimed. Tools Appl.* **2022**, *81*, 22001–22026.
24. Awasthi, D.; Srivastava, V.K. Performance enhancement of SVD based dual image watermarking in wavelet domain using PSO and JAYA optimization and their comparison under hybrid attacks. *Multimed. Tools Appl.* **2023**, *82*, 35685–35717. [CrossRef]
25. Sharma, S.; Sharma, H.; Sharma, J.B. Artificial intelligence based watermarking in hybrid DDS domain for security of colour images. *Int. J. Intell. Eng. Inform.* **2020**, *8*, 331–345. [CrossRef]
26. Garg, P.; Kishore, R.R. An efficient and secured blind image watermarking using ABC optimization in DWT and DCT domain. *Multimed. Tools Appl.* **2022**, *81*, 36947–36964. [CrossRef]
27. Pourhadi, A.; Mahdavi-Nasab, H. A robust digital image watermarking scheme based on bat algorithm optimization and SURF detector in SWT domain. *Multimed. Tools Appl.* **2020**, *79*, 21653–21677. [CrossRef]
28. Gupta, M.; Saraswat, M. Grey wolf optimisation-based colour image watermarking. *World Rev. Entrep. Manag. Sustain. Dev.* **2020**, *16*, 648–664. [CrossRef]
29. Selesnick, I.W.; Baraniuk, R.G.; Kingsbury, N.C. The dual-tree complex wavelet transform. *IEEE Signal Process. Mag.* **2005**, *22*, 123–151. [CrossRef]
30. Wang, D.; Tan, D.; Liu, L. Particle swarm optimization algorithm: An overview. *Soft Comput.* **2018**, *22*, 387–408. [CrossRef]
31. Salimi, L.; Haghighi, A.; Fathi, A. A novel watermarking method based on differential evolutionary algorithm and wavelet transform. *Multimed. Tools Appl.* **2020**, *79*, 11357–11374. [CrossRef]
32. Sharma, V.K.; Mir, R.N. An enhanced time efficient technique for image watermarking using ant colony optimization and light gradient boosting algorithm. *J. King Saud Univ. Comput. Inf. Sci.* **2022**, *34*, 615–626. [CrossRef]

applied sciences

MDPI

Article

Image Copy-Move Forgery Detection Based on Fused Features and Density Clustering

Guiwei Fu, Yujin Zhang * and Yongqi Wang

School of Electronic and Electrical Engineering, Shanghai University of Engineering Science, Shanghai 201620, China; fgw9295@163.com (G.F.)
* Correspondence: yjzhang@sues.edu.cn

Abstract: Image copy-move forgery is a common simple tampering technique. To address issues such as high time complexity in most copy-move forgery detection algorithms and difficulty detecting forgeries in smooth regions, this paper proposes an image copy-move forgery detection algorithm based on fused features and density clustering. Firstly, the algorithm combines two detection methods, speeded up robust features (SURF) and accelerated KAZE (A-KAZE), to extract descriptive features by setting a low contrast threshold. Then, the density-based spatial clustering of applications with noise (DBSCAN) algorithm removes mismatched pairs and reduces false positives. To improve the accuracy of forgery localization, the algorithm uses the original image and the image transformed by the affine matrix to compare similarities in the same position in order to locate the forged region. The proposed method was tested on two datasets (Ardizzone and CoMoFoD). The experimental results show that the method effectively improved the accuracy of forgery detection in smooth regions, reduced computational complexity, and exhibited strong robustness against post-processing operations such as rotation, scaling, and noise addition.

Keywords: copy-move; A-KAZE; density clustering algorithm; affine matrix transformation; location similarity

1. Introduction

With the rapid development of information technology and the widespread adoption of new computer techniques, digital images have become an important means of obtaining information. People can access high-resolution images and videos through Internet technology, and can capture high-quality images or videos using mobile devices or cameras. Moreover, image processing and editing software such as Adobe Photoshop and Lightroom enable people to manipulate and edit images more easily and quickly. However, not only do these advanced software processing techniques bring convenience, but they also provide criminals with the opportunity to commit crimes. The issue of image tampering and manipulation is common and has caused serious problems in news dissemination, design, social media, and even digital forensic investigation [1]. The credibility and integrity of digital images are especially being questioned in areas such as medical records, scientific publications, celebrity magazines, news reports, political activities, and judicial appraisals. Image copy-move forgery is currently one of the most commonly used methods of tampering [2]. The technique involves copying and pasting a specific region of an image to other regions of the same image for the purpose of emphasizing certain visual information or concealing certain image content. Figure 1 provides an example of image copy-move forgery [3].

In image copy-move forgery, the tampered area may not be identical to the source area, as it often undergoes post-processing operations such as rotation, scaling, edge softening, blurring, noise addition, and JPEG compression. Therefore, the human eye can easily be deceived by tampered images, leading to misdirection [4].

(**a**) (**b**) (**c**)

Figure 1. Image copy-move forgery examples: (**a**) original images; (**b**) forged images; (**c**) binarized truth images.

Many researchers have explored image copy-move forgery detection in detail. Currently, there are two main types of methods to detect copy-move forgery: divide the image into image blocks or extract feature points from the image [5]. It was found that the block-based method, which requires matching a large number of overlapping blocks, is inefficient when it comes to geometric transformation attacks because block features are very sensitive to scale and rotation transformations, which ultimately results in high computational cost. Feature point-based methods are commonly used in copy-move forgery detection because they are unaffected by rotation and scaling, making them highly reliable.

This paper proposes a forgery detection method based on two detection approaches, speeded up robust features (SURF) and accelerated KAZE (A-KAZE), to reduce the computational cost and extract more feature points in smooth regions. The SURF detector has a lower-dimensional feature descriptor and is invariant to rotation and scaling, resulting in faster speed. On the other hand, A-KAZE can extract a large number of useful feature points in smooth regions, allowing for improved accuracy of forgery detection in these regions. After feature matching with g2NN for the two detectors, we adopted the DBSCAN algorithm to eliminate mismatched pairs and locate tampered areas by comparing similarities between the original image and the image transformed by the affine matrix. The experimental results demonstrate that the method proposed in this paper improved the accuracy of smooth region forgery detection by combining the two detection approaches and exhibited strong robustness to geometric transformations such as rotation and scaling.

The rest of this article is arranged as follows: Section 2 provides an overview of the latest research on image copy-move forgery. Section 3 describes SURF and A-KAZE in detail. In Section 4, the proposed image copy-move forgery detection method based on fused features and density clustering is described in detail. Section 5 analyzes the performance of the proposed method and compares it with other algorithms through experiments. Finally, Section 6 summarizes the method proposed in this article.

2. Related Works

At present, copy-move forgery detection (CMFD) is divided into image block-based and feature point-based methods. Using the method of image blocks, the image is typically segmented into overlapping rectangular or circular blocks, from which feature points are extracted, and then feature matching is conducted. Fridrich et al. [6] first proposed a block-based method that uses CMFD with discrete cosine transform (DCT) in this algorithm. Several features were proposed to describe these blocks. For example, Kumar et al. [7] proposed a method based on principal component analysis (PCA) for image CMFD. This method extracts image features using the Haar transform, simplifies the features through PCA to reduce computational complexity, and then detects, locates, and removes false boundaries. Additionally, the texture features of the input image are analyzed using the gray-level co-occurrence matrix (GLCM). Fattah et al. [8] applied a two-dimensional discrete wavelet transform (DWT) to tampered images, considering only the approximate DWT coefficients for block segmentation, and matching was carried out by computing the distance between pairs of blocks. The results showed that the algorithm was not suitable for forgery detection under geometric transformation attack. Finally, the features were matched using Euclidean distance, and non-matching feature points were identified. Sabeena et al. [9] proposed a method for image CMFD that utilizes local binary patterns (LBP) and Harlick features for feature extraction. In order to verify the authenticity of the image, various supervised machine learning classifiers, such as support vector machines (SVMs), random forest (RF), and gradient boosting classifiers, were used, and the forgery detection performance based on these classifiers was analyzed. In order to address the problem of tampering operations such as rotation and scaling in the tampered area, many local invariant features have been applied in the research of CMFD forensics, such as Zernike moments, Hu moments, and so on [10,11]. Lee et al. utilized statistical features based on a histogram of gradients (HOG) for CMFD [12]. As can be seen from the results, the algorithm's performance in detecting forgeries in the case of rotation and scaling of large regions needs improvement. A perceptual image hashing scheme based on block truncated coding is presented in [13]. In this paper, centrosymmetric local binary patterns are used as image feature descriptors. This method requires a small amount of calculation and is not sensitive to grayscale changes. Wang et al. [14] proposed a CMFD algorithm based on the polar complex exponential transform (PCET). In this algorithm, the suspicious image is first divided into overlapping circular blocks, and PCET is used to extract the geometric invariant features of each block. However, dividing the image into circular blocks results in some loss of image information, which may have a certain impact on the detection performance of the algorithm.

Due to the high computational complexity of block-based methods and their limitations in detecting scale displacement tampering, researchers have shown increasing interest in feature point-based methods for image CMFD to address these problems. These methods first extract feature points from high-entropy regions of the image, then calculate and match feature vectors corresponding to each point, and finally identify tampered regions. The advantage of these methods lies in the point extraction, point description, point matching, and positioning methods applied [15–20]. In order to enhance the sensitivity of copy-move detection algorithms to manipulations such as rotation and scaling, Pun et al. [21] proposed an early feature point-based CMFD method. This method utilizes scale-invariant feature transform (SIFT) [22,23] to extract feature points and applies the random sample consensus (RANSAC) algorithm [24] to remove mismatched pairs through affine transformations. However, the time complexity of this algorithm is relatively high, and it cannot detect multiple types of tampering operations. Subsequently, researchers conducted studies on various tampering operations. However, the location accuracy of this algorithm on pixel-level datasets is still slightly insufficient.

Currently, feature-point-based methods are not effective at detecting tampering in small or smooth areas. To address this issue, Liu et al. [25] proposed a detection method based on k-means clustering. This method divides the image into smooth and complex regions and uses SIFT and sector mask features to detect tampering in each region. However, the accuracy of this algorithm needs to be improved. When compared to methods based on blocks, methods based on feature points have numerous advantages [26]. For instance, the most representative key points in the target region can be retrieved using the feature point method, enabling more precise detection and positioning of the target region. Feature point extraction methods typically have a certain robustness and can withstand post-processing operations such as rotation and scaling [27].

Compared to block-matching methods, the time required for feature point extraction and matching is usually shorter, resulting in lower computational complexity. However, there are still some issues with feature point-based methods. For example, matching time increases accordingly when the extracted key points are dense, and tampering that occurs in smooth areas is difficult to detect accurately [28].

3. SURF and A-KAZE Descriptors

This section mainly summarizes the feature descriptors SURF and A-KAZE [29].

3.1. SURF Descriptor

At present, the image CMFD algorithms based on feature points are mainly the SIFT and SURF algorithms. The SURF algorithm uses the Hessian matrix for efficient calculations, which overcomes the shortcomings of SIFT in terms of too high feature dimension and long calculation time [30]. The SURF algorithm simplifies the Gaussian second-order differential template in the Hessian determinant, i.e., converts the convolution smoothing operation, to an addition and subtraction operation. Furthermore, the SURF algorithm has better robustness and lower time complexity compared to the SIFT algorithm. SURF cannot maintain the scale and rotation invariance of SIFT, but it has strong robustness to changes in lighting and affine distortion [31]. SURF determines the key points by computing the extreme points of the scale space through calculating the relevant Hessian matrix. The Hessian matrix $H(x,\sigma)$ can be represented as:

$$H(x,\sigma) = \begin{bmatrix} C_{xx}(x,\sigma) & C_{xy}(x,\sigma) \\ C_{xy}(x,\sigma) & C_{yy}(x,\sigma) \end{bmatrix} \tag{1}$$

In the formula, $x = (x,y)$, $C_{xx}(x,\sigma)$ is the convolution of the second-order partial derivative $\partial G(x,y,\sigma)/\partial x^2$ of the Gaussian function and the image at the pixel point. The determinant of matrix $H(x,\sigma)$ is expressed as:

$$\det(H) = C_{xx}(x,\sigma) \cdot C_{yy}(x,\sigma) - \left[C_{xy}(x,\sigma)\right]^2 \tag{2}$$

Due to the high time complexity of computing second-order partial derivatives of images, SURF uses rectangular box filters to approximate the second-order partial derivatives of Gaussian functions. The box filter is composed of a simple rectangular template, which speeds up the convolution calculation and reduces the time complexity. Filtering the image with the rectangular box filter can obtain $C_{xx}(x,\sigma)$, $C_{xy}(x,\sigma)$, and $C_{yy}(x,\sigma)$, and the Hessian matrix determinant for each coordinate point can be calculated to obtain the Hessian determinant image. By changing the size of the rectangular box-shaped filter and the scale of the Gaussian function σ, scale changes are achieved, thus generating multiple Hessian determinant images and constructing a pyramid image. Using non-maximum suppression to filter key points, we can compare each point with eight neighboring points in the same scale and 18 neighboring points in adjacent scales. If the value of the point is greater than the value of its 26 neighbors and the preset threshold T_S (subscript $_S$ indicates SURF), the point is determined as a key point.

The direction of SURF feature points depends on the response of a circular region with a radius of 6 centered on the key point. With the key point as the center, a sector region with an angle of $\pi/3$ is scanned within the circular region to calculate the total horizontal and vertical Harr feature points of all points in the sector region. The longest vector direction is selected as the main direction of the key point. After determining the direction of the key point, a SURF descriptor is generated. Specifically, a square region in the neighborhood with a side length of 20σ is selected around and aligned with the main direction of the key point. The square region is divided into 4 × 4 sub-regions, and 4-dimensional features are calculated for each of the $5\sigma \times 5\sigma$ grids, including the horizontal and vertical responses of the Harr wavelet in directions $\sum dx$ and $\sum dy$, as well as the absolute values of the responses in directions $\sum|dx|$ and $\sum|dy|$. Finally, the 4-dimensional features of each sub-region are accumulated into a 64-dimensional feature vector descriptor by dividing it into 16 sub-regions.

3.2. A-KAZE Descriptor

A-KAZE is a feature-based image matching algorithm used for tasks such as image feature detection, matching, and object tracking. The A-KAZE algorithm was developed from the KAZE algorithm and employs a new feature detection method called accelerated scale space extrema detection (ASSED), which can detect local extrema points in scale space faster [32]. ASSED searches for local extrema points by comparing the Laplacian of the Gaussian transformation at different scales. In smooth areas, the response of the Gaussian Laplacian transformation is small, so only local extrema points can be detected in larger scale spaces. The design of ASSED enables the A-KAZE algorithm to detect local extrema points in larger scale spaces quickly, thus extracting features in smooth regions. A-KAZE's feature descriptor includes multi-scale and multi-directional features. The feature descriptor, particularly for smooth regions, has distinct response values at different scales, making it robust at various scales and enabling it to extract features in smooth regions. At the same time, the feature descriptor can also calculate the main direction, making them invariant to orientation and allowing them to match the same feature points at multiple rotation angles, enhancing feature stability and discriminability.

In the A-KAZE feature detection method, a non-linear scale space is constructed using non-linear diffusion filtering. Non-linear diffusion filtering considers the changes in pixel intensity at different scales as the divergence of some form of flow function. The classical non-linear diffusion formula is defined as:

$$\frac{\partial L}{\partial t} = div[c(x,y,t)\cdot\nabla L] \tag{3}$$

In the formula, div represents the divergence operator, ∇ represents the gradient operator, L represents the brightness information of the image, and $c(x,y,t)$ represents the transfer function, which can be expressed as:

$$c(x,y,t) = g(|\nabla L_\sigma(x,y,t)|) \tag{4}$$

where ∇L_σ represents the gradient of image L_σ after Gaussian smoothing and time t is used as a scale parameter; the larger its value, the simpler the representation of the image. In this article, the conduction function used to extract key points with A-KAZE detector is [33]:

$$g_2 = \frac{1}{1+\frac{|\nabla L_\sigma|^2}{\lambda^2}} \tag{5}$$

In the formula, λ is the contrast factor that controls the level of diffusion; the larger its value, the less corresponding edge information will be retained. The fast explicit diffusion (FED) algorithm is used to build an image pyramid and obtain one group of images, each with two layers. Then, group O and layer S are mapped to scale σ through the corresponding formula:

$$\sigma_i(o,s) = 2^{o+\frac{s}{S}}, o = 0,1,\ldots,O-1, s = 0,1,\ldots,S-1, i = 0,1,\ldots,M-1 \tag{6}$$

where M is the number of images in the image pyramid, and $M = O \times S$. The unit of linear filtering is scale σ_i, and the unit of non-linear diffusion filtering is time. The transformation of $\sigma_i \rightarrow t_i$ is realized by the following formula:

$$t_i = \frac{1}{2}\sigma_i^2, i = 0, 1, \ldots, M-1 \quad (7)$$

where t_i is evolutionary time. A set of evolutionary time values is obtained through this mapping, and a non-linear scale space is constructed through these time values.

The key point detection of A-KAZE is similar to SURF; it calculates the Hessian determinant of image L^i in the non-linear scale space as follows:

$$L^i_{Hessian} = \sigma^2_{i.n}\left(L^i_{xx}L^i_{yy} - L^i_{xy}L^i_{xy}\right) \quad (8)$$

In the formula, $\sigma_{i.n}$ represents the scale-normalized scaling factor, and $\sigma_{i.n} = \sigma^i/2^{o^i}$. A-KAZE determines the key points in the same way as SURF.

However, unlike SURF, A-KAZE computes all first-order differentials within $\pi/3$ circular sectors and applies Gaussian weighting to make the response near the key points most useful and the response far from the key points contribute the least. The response values within the $\pi/3$ circular sectors are then vector-summed, and the angle of the maximum vector over the entire circular region is the main orientation. A-KAZE uses M-LDB as the descriptor of the key point. LDB divides a $q \times q$ square region centered on the key point into $p \times p$ sub-squares, extracts the mean and gradient information of pixel intensity (grayscale) within each sub-square, and performs binary testing, as follows:

$$\tau\left(F_{function}(i), F_{function}(j)\right) = \begin{cases} 1, \left(F_{function}(i) - F_{function}(j)\right) > 0, i \neq j \\ 0, other \end{cases} \quad (9)$$

where $F_{function}(\cdot)$ represents the function that extracts the mean and gradient information of pixel intensity, defined as:

$$F_{function}(\cdot) = \left\{F_{intensity}(\cdot), F_{dx}(\cdot), F_{dy}(\cdot)\right\} \quad (10)$$

$$F_{intensity}(i) = \frac{1}{m}\sum_{k=1}^{m} Intensity(k), F_{dx}(i) = Gradient_x(i), F_{dy}(i) = Gradient_y(i) \quad (11)$$

In the formula, $F_{intensity}(i)$ represents the average pixel intensity information of the ith sub-box, m represents the number of pixels in the ith sub-box, and $F_{dx}(i)$ and $F_{dy}(i)$ represent the gradient information of the ith sub-box in the x and y directions, respectively.

Later, we rotated the sub-boxes to the main direction and adaptively down-sampled them based on the scale space where the feature points were located in the sub-box. This greatly improved the robustness of M-LDB, because it is no longer necessary to calculate the mean of all pixel intensity information within the sub-box.

4. The Proposed Scheme

The general flow of the method proposed in this article is shown in Figure 2, which includes first using two detection methods, SURF and A-KAZE, to extract feature points from the input image. To solve the problem of insufficient feature point extraction in smooth areas, we lowered the contrast threshold and combined the two detection methods to extract feature points. Then, g2NN is used for feature matching to find similar feature vectors. To improve the accuracy of tampering localization, we used the DBSCAN algorithm to remove false matches. Finally, the tampered area is located by comparing the similarity between the original image and the image after affine transformation.

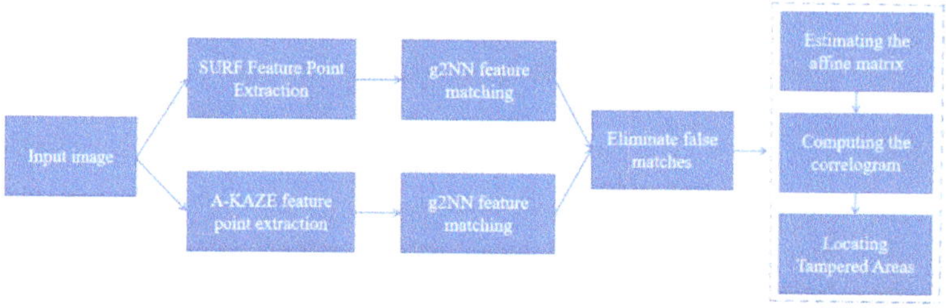

Figure 2. Flowchart of method proposed in this paper.

4.1. SURF and A-KAZE Feature Extraction

To address the issues of difficult detection and high computational complexity that occur in smooth regions with tampering at the present stage, we combined two detection methods, SURF and A-KAZE. Specifically, these methods are used to extract feature points from tampered images, and descriptions of them are provided in Section 3 [34].

When using SURF to extract feature points from an image, we set the contrast to P_s and store the extracted feature points in matrix $x_s = \{x_1, x_2, \ldots, x_n\}$. To better represent the coordinates of each feature point, the coordinates of the ith feature point are represented as $x_s^i = (x_x^i, y_s^i)$. When extracting feature points from an image using A-KAZE, the contrast threshold is set to P_A and the extracted feature points are stored in matrix $x_A = \{x_1, x_2, \ldots, x_m\}$. To better represent the coordinates of each feature point, the coordinates of the ith feature point are represented as $x_A^i = (x_x^i, y_s^i)$. Then, SURF feature matrix $f_s = \{f_1, f_2, \ldots, f_n\}$ and A-KAZE matrix $f_A = \{f_1, f_2, \ldots, f_m\}$ are calculated separately. In this article, contrast threshold P_s is set to 0.1 and contrast threshold P_A is set to 0.0001.

4.2. g2NN Feature Matching

After extracting feature points in the previous stage, g2NN is used to perform feature matching on SURF feature $f_s = \{f_1, f_2, \ldots, f_n\}$ and A-KAZE feature $f_A = \{f_1, f_2, \ldots, f_m\}$ to search for similar feature vectors [35]. Assuming there are n features, $f = \{f_1, f_2, \ldots, f_n\}$, the Euclidean distance is used to determine the similarity between two feature vectors. For the ith key point, its corresponding feature is represented by f_i, and the Euclidean distance between f_i and the remaining features $\{f_1, f_2, \ldots, f_{i-1}, f_{i+1}, \ldots, f_n\}$ is calculated. The results are sorted in ascending order to obtain $D = \{d_1, d_2, \ldots, d_{n-1}\}$. In D, the ratio of d_j and d_{j+1} is calculated and evaluated using threshold V_t, as shown in the following formula:

$$\frac{d_j}{d_{j+1}} < V_t, V_t \in (0,1), j = 1,2,\ldots,n-1 \tag{12}$$

When the iteration reaches step $k+1$, the process of this iteration will terminate, and key point k will be considered as a candidate similar point matching the ith key point. The value of V_t is 0.6. In the algorithm in this section, the k-d tree and nearest neighbor algorithm are used to search for the N_{kd} points closest to the key point. g2NN feature matching is then used on these points to find similar feature vectors to obtain the matching key point pair matrix x_w. However, there are still some mismatches in the obtained matrix x_w, which requires removing the mismatched pairs.

4.3. Removing Mismatched Pairs

Matching point pairs were obtained in the previous step, but many of them contain errors. At this point, an effective method is needed to eliminate the mismatched pairs in order to improve the accuracy of forgery detection and localization. Currently, the k-means clustering algorithm or the hierarchical clustering algorithm are commonly used to eliminate mismatches, but the problem is that they only consider the positional information of the matching point pairs and ignore the constraints between the point pairs. The number of clusters needs to be set before clustering. Ester et al. [36] proposed a density-based clustering algorithm, DBSCAN, which considers clusters as sets of maximum density-connected points and partitions the dense areas accordingly. DBSCAN does not require the extraction or setting of clustering parameters and can handle clusters of any shape even in the presence of noise. Therefore, in this paper, DBSCAN is used for feature clustering to eliminate mismatched pairs.

DBSCAN requires setting two important parameters, Eps and MinPts, respectively denoting the radius of density and the threshold of core points, which is the minimum number of points required to form a cluster. In this paper, Eps and MinPts are represented as τ and M, respectively. In DBSCAN, point sets are defined based on the following three categories, as shown in Figure 3:

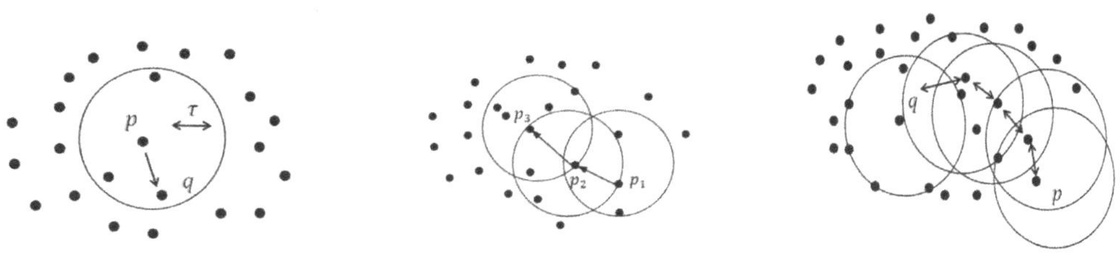

Figure 3. DBSCAN point-to-point relationship diagram: (**a**) density direct; (**b**) density reachable; (**c**) density connected.

1. Core point: If point X_i has at least M points in its neighborhood, then X_i is a core point. We can define the sets of all core points as P_c and the set of non-core points as P_{nc}.
2. Boundary point: If X_i satisfies $X_i \in P_{nc}$ and is in the τ neighborhood of a core point, then X_i is a boundary point. Boundary points can be located within the τ neighborhood of one or more core points at the same time.
3. Outlier: This is neither a core point nor a boundary point.

The relationships between points are classified into three types: density direct, density reachable, and density connected, as shown in Figure 3. The main process of the DBSCAN algorithm is to classify the input points into different categories, iteratively search for density-reachable objects of core points, form a new cluster, and then produce the final clustering result through density connectivity. Figure 3 illustrates the relationships between points, where density reachable is a transitive relationship but not symmetric. Two boundary points in the same cluster may not be density reachable to each other because the core point condition may not be satisfied for both of them. However, there must be at least one core point within a cluster from which all points are density reachable. In Figure 3c, both boundary points are density reachable. Therefore, we introduce the concept of density connectedness, which encompasses this relationship between boundary points. The steps to transition from density reachable to density connected are as follows: First, we calculate the density of each region and label them as density reachable based on a set density threshold. At this stage, we focus on the internal density of each region. Building upon density reachable, we further consider the adjacency relationships between regions. If two density reachable regions have sufficient neighboring regions that can be connected through density reachability, they are considered density connected. In this stage, we emphasize the connectivity between regions.

Specifically, the goal of the algorithm is to divide set P into k effective clusters (where k is obtained through the algorithm and does not need to be set in advance) and a cluster of outliers. The calculation of the clustering identification array m_i is as follows:

$$m_i = \begin{cases} j(j > 0), if\ X_i\ belongs\ to\ cluster\ j \\ -1, if\ X_i\ is\ an\ outlier \end{cases} \quad (13)$$

The goal of DBSCAN is transformed into generating clustering identification array m_i, where $i = 1, 2, \ldots, n$ and k is the number of all non-negative values in the $\{m_i\}_{i=1}^{n}$ types (negative values represent outliers). The outliers in clustering identification array m_i are mismatched points. Finally, removing outliers produces an accurate matching sequence.

4.4. Tampered Region Localization

To further improve the accuracy of tampered region localization, in this paper we compute the affine matrix of matching pairs and apply this transformation to the dense regions of the image at the pixel level. The final tampered region is located by comparing the similarity between the transformed image and the original image at the same unknown location.

Estimation of affine transformation: An affine transformation matrix can reveal geometric changes that occur between objects, such as rotation, scaling, and so on. Based on feature point matching, the affine transformation between original and tampered regions can be estimated using the coordinates of the matching pairs. Given two corresponding sets of matching pair coordinates $X = (x, y)$ and $\widetilde{X} = (\widetilde{x}, \widetilde{y})$, their relationship is shown as follows:

$$\begin{pmatrix} \widetilde{x} \\ \widetilde{y} \\ 1 \end{pmatrix} = \begin{pmatrix} a & b & t_x \\ c & d & t_y \\ 0 & 0 & 1 \end{pmatrix} \begin{pmatrix} x \\ y \\ 1 \end{pmatrix} = T \begin{pmatrix} x \\ y \\ 1 \end{pmatrix} \tag{14}$$

In the formula, t_x and t_y are translation parameters, while a, b, c, and d are scale and rotation transformation parameters. Matrix T can be calculated using at least three non-collinear matching pairs.

The set of matching pairs after removing the mismatched pairs is denoted as $\left\{\left(X_1, \widetilde{X_1}\right), \left(X_2, \widetilde{X_2}\right), \ldots, \left(X_n, \widetilde{X_n}\right)\right\}$. Three points are randomly selected from each cluster, their corresponding points are found in the matching list, and an affine transformation matrix T_i is estimated from the three pairs of points. All matrices are then computed, and an optimal matrix T is found that minimizes the error, as shown in the following formula:

$$\underset{T}{\operatorname{argmin}} \|\widetilde{X} - T_i X\|^2 \tag{15}$$

Using the obtained optimal affine matrix T, the transformation is applied to all pixels in the entire image. Then, the transformed image is overlaid with the original image, with the original region Y_O overlapping the tampered region Y_D. Similarly, the inverse transformation is applied to region T^{-1}, with the tampered region Y_D overlapping the original region Y_O in the same way.

$$Y_D = TY_O, Y_O = T^{-1} Y_D \tag{16}$$

To locate the tampered regions, we utilize the polar cosine transform (PCT) feature as the similarity measure and compute it for corresponding positions in both the original and transformed images. When the difference between the two features is less than a certain threshold, the location is marked to obtain a region-of-interest map. The PCT feature calculation of the n-order continuous image g for l consecutive times is as follows:

$$f = \{|M_{n,l}| such\ that\ n + l \leq 3, 0 \leq n, l < 3\} \tag{17}$$

In the formula:

$$M_{n,l} = \Omega_n \int_0^{2\pi} \int_0^1 [H_{n,l}(r, \theta)] \times g(r, \theta) r dr d\theta \tag{18}$$

$$\Omega_n = \begin{cases} 1/\pi n = 0 \\ 2/\pi\ n \neq 0 \end{cases}, \ H_{n,l}(r, \theta) = \cos\left(\pi n r^2\right) e^{jl\theta} \tag{19}$$

where $g(r, \theta)$ is the image representation in polar coordinates.

Using a threshold value t to compare the feature differences in the overlapping areas, the region is identified, and the final correlation map is obtained. Then, a Gaussian filter is applied with a window size of 7×7 and a standard deviation of 0.5 for denoising and detail processing. Finally, the closing operation is performed to obtain the final detection result.

5. Experimental Results

This section describes the experimental tests conducted on public image datasets, and the comparative analysis performed using evaluation indicators and detection effect diagrams. This section verifies the advantages of the proposed method in terms of accuracy and robustness against geometric transformations and shows that it is comparable to existing research methods.

5.1. Datasets

In our experiments, we used two challenging datasets for evaluation: Ardizzone [37] and CoMoFoD.

5.1.1. Ardizzone

This dataset is composed of medium-sized images, most of them with a size of either 1000×700 or 700×1000 pixels. The Ardizzone dataset is divided into several subsets: Subset D0 contains 50 images with simple tampering that only involves basic translation transformations; subsets D1 and D2 contain tampered images with additional rotations and scaling transformations; and subset D3 contains the corresponding original images of the tampered images in D0.

5.1.2. CoMoFoD

This dataset contains 200 original images with a size of 512×512 pixels that have undergone various geometric transformations, which are divided into five categories: scaling, rotation, translation, deformation, and combination. Each category contains 40 examples of tampered images, with different tampering methods applied to each category, including noise, blur, JPEG compression, rotation, and scaling. The CoMoFoD dataset contains a total of 10,400 images, in which the area of the replicated region ranges from 0.14 to 14.3% of the image area.

Figure 4 displays original images, tampered images, and corresponding binary ground truth maps from both datasets.

Figure 4. Examples of image copy-move forgery in the dataset. First row: original images; second row: forged images; third row: binarized truth images.

5.2. Evaluation Metrics

The three most commonly used evaluation metrics—precision, recall, and F_1 score—are used in this paper to comprehensively analyze the detection performance of the proposed method. These evaluation metrics are represented by P, R, and F_1, respectively, and their specific formulas are as follows:

$$P = \frac{N_{FF}}{N_{FF} + N_{AF}}, R = \frac{N_{FF}}{N_{FF} + N_{FA}}, F_1 = 2 \times \frac{P \times R}{P + R} \tag{20}$$

where N_{FF} represents the number of tampered images/pixels that are considered to be tampered; N_{AF} represents the number of real images/pixels that are considered to be tampered; and N_{FA} represents the number of tampered images/pixels that are determined to be real. On the basis of comparison with other relevant algorithms, the superiority of the proposed method can be objectively evaluated. This approach not only relies on intuitive detection results, it also enables a comprehensive evaluation of the proposed method through objective data.

5.3. Lab Environment

The experimental environment was Core i5-6200U CPU (2.30 GHz), 8 GB memory, and the software environment was Windows 10 + MATLAB R2019a.

5.4. Copy-Move Forgery Detection

This section presents the experimental detection results. The effectiveness of the algorithm was validated by comparing the detection results with the given binary ground truth image in the dataset. The first row of each detection result represents the tampered image, the second row represents the binary ground truth image in the dataset, which indicates the real tampered region, and the third row represents the experimental detection result of the method in this paper. The blue area represents the correctly detected tampered region, the red area represents the falsely detected region, the white area represents the missed detection region, the dark gray area represents the real tampered region, and the light gray area represents the tampered region after boundary post-processing. In order to verify the effectiveness of the algorithm, two comparison algorithms were used to comprehensively evaluate the detection performance of the proposed method. These were the feature point method combining SIFT and KAZE, proposed by Aydan et al. [38], followed by the feature extraction method using SURF proposed by Badr et al. [17]. The experimental comparison results are presented in tables or figures.

Compared with block-based methods, the feature point extraction stage is extremely important in feature point-based methods, especially the number of feature points extracted in smooth areas. In this experiment, we tested SIFT, SURF, A-KAZE, and BRISK. For traditional methods, a contrast threshold does not need to be set in advance during feature extraction, and feature matching can be completed using functions in the OpenCV database. After wrong matches have been eliminated, the set of matched pairs is then counted, as shown in Table 1. We selected photos from the dataset for testing; the images in the first and second columns came from the Ardizzone dataset, and those in the third and fourth columns came from the CoMoFoD dataset. Among them, the first and third columns show occlusion tampering on the original image, and the second and fourth columns show addition tampering on the original image. Specific test photos are shown in Figure 5.

Table 1 presents the experimental results for the four columns of images in Figure 5, clearly showing that the proposed SURF and A-KAZE feature points have significant advantages compared to other feature points. Compared to some traditional feature points that do not require setting a contrast threshold, a small contrast threshold was set in the method proposed in this paper and SURF and A-KAZE were fused to obtain more matching feature points in the feature extraction stage. Especially for the test image in the first column of Figure 5, where tampering occurs in the smooth area of the sky, only the proposed method detects the correct matching pairs, while other feature extraction methods do not detect any tampering. This leads to the tampering operations in the smooth area being ignored, resulting in reduced detection effectiveness.

Table 1. Number of matching points of different feature points in tampered area.

Feature \ Row	First Row	Second Row	Third Row	Fourth Row
SIFT	0	16	215	16
SURF	0	2	124	5
A-KAZE	0	23	175	5
BRISK	0	17	96	4
SURF + A-KAZE	98	145	325	18

Figure 5. Experimental photos for detecting the number of matching points of different key point features in the tampered area: (**a**) obscured images; (**b**) tampered images; (**c**) obscured images; (**d**) tampered images.

5.4.1. Geometric Transformation Forgery Detection

This paper mainly focuses on the experimentation and testing of geometric transformation forgery, including simple translation forgery detection, rotation forgery detection and scaling forgery detection. A certain number of photos were selected from the dataset for each type of tampering, and the experimental detection results are presented in the form of detection effect images.

Simple translation forgery detection: We conducted experimental tests on geometric transformation forgery, including simple translation forgery detection, rotation forgery detection, and scaling forgery detection. For each type of tampering, a certain number of photos were selected from the dataset for experiments, and the results of the experimental detection are displayed. Partial experimental results are given below, and are shown in Figure 6. The first row of images in the figure represent the original image, the second row comprises the binarized truth images provided in the dataset (used for comparison with the detection results), and the third row presents the effect images. The third row shows the detection results of the proposed algorithm, which was mainly used to test for simple translation forgery operations. From Figure 6, it can be intuitively seen that the experimental effect image of the proposed method almost coincides with the binary image given in the dataset, and there are no missed detection areas. For images that have not undergone complex tampering, the proposed method can more accurately locate tampered areas, and there is no occurrence of false detection or missed detection in simple tampering.

Figure 6. Experimental results of simple translational forgery detection. **First row**: original images; **second row**: binarized truth images; **third row**: effect images of forgery detection.

Rotation transform forgery detection: We conducted forgery detection experiments on images from two publicly available datasets, with the images subjected to rotation-based tampering at angles of $\pm 1^\circ$, $\pm 2^\circ$, $\pm 3^\circ$, $\pm 4^\circ$, $\pm 5^\circ$, and $\pm 10^\circ$. The images in Figure 7 demonstrate the detection results for rotation angles of 1°, 3°, 5°, and 10°. The first row of the figure shows the original images, the second row shows the binarized truth images provided in the dataset (used for comparison with the detection algorithm), and the third row shows the detection results of the method proposed in this paper; the detection results are shown at different rotation angles. The comparison with the binarized truth images from the dataset indicates that the proposed method maintains high detection accuracy even at different rotation angles. The comparison with the binarized truth images in the second row shows that there are almost no missed detections. This advantage is particularly evident in small-scale rotations, and the proposed method has good detection performance.

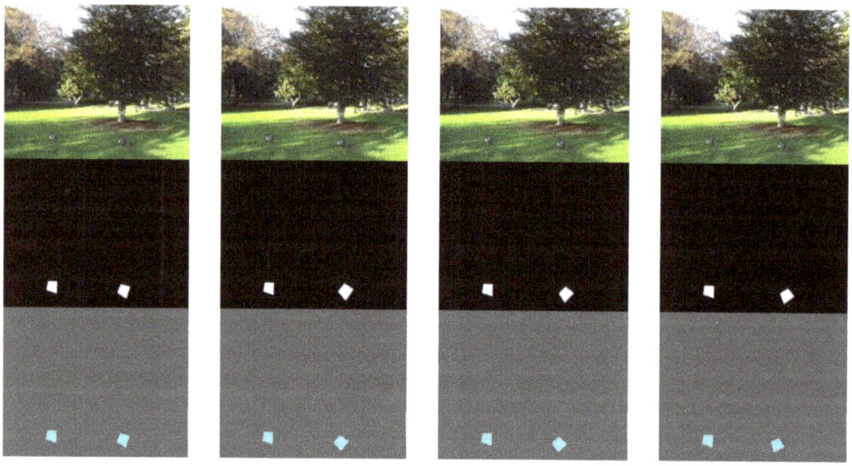

Figure 7. Rotation angle forgery detection experiment results. **First row**: original images; **second row**: binarized truth images; **third row**: effect images of forgery detection.

Scale transform forgery detection: We conducted scale manipulation experiments on images from two publicly available datasets. The scaling factors used were 0.9, 0.95, 1.05, 1.25, and 1.5. Figure 8 presents the experimental results for these scaling factors, from left to right. The first row represents the original image, the second row shows the binary ground truth provided in the dataset, and the third row displays the experimental results of the proposed method.

Figure 8. Different scaling factor transformations falsify experimental results. **First row**: original images; **second row**: binarized truth images; **third row**: effect images of forgery detection.

By comparing the detection results in the figure (third row) with the binary images provided in the dataset (second row), it is clear that the proposed method still has good detection performance in scaling forgery detection. Especially for small compression factors, the detection results almost have no missed detection areas. However, as the scaling factor increases, for example, at a scaling factor of 1.5, it can be observed that there are missed detection areas in the boundary of the detection results.

In summary, after conducting experiments on simple translation forgery, rotation forgery at different angles, and compression factor forgery, it can be seen by comparison with the binary images provided in the dataset that the method proposed in this paper is an effective detection algorithm. For geometric transformation forgery, the proposed method can accurately locate tampered regions, especially in smooth areas, where the detection performance still shows good results. In addition, it also performs well in small-scale rotation and compression tampering scenarios.

In addition to using intuitive effect diagrams to demonstrate the effectiveness of the proposed method, we also conducted experiments at the image level. All images from the Ardizzone and CoMoFoD datasets were tested to calculate the number of tampered images correctly identified as tampered, the number of tampered images incorrectly identified as real, and the number of real images incorrectly identified as tampered. In comparison with other methods in the literature, precision, recall, and F_1 were calculated, and the experimental results are listed in Tables 2 and 3. The standard deviations of the three evaluation metrics were also calculated, and the data are presented in Table 4.

Table 2. Experimental results of precision (P), recall (R), and F_1 evaluation metrics for images in the Ardizzone dataset.

Method	P (%)	R (%)	F_1 (%)
Badr et al. [17]	89.52	91.23	90.37
Aydin et al. [38]	90.23	90.56	90.39
Proposed method	92.75	92.43	92.89

Table 3. Experimental results of precision (P), recall (R), and F_1 evaluation metrics for images in the CoMoFoD dataset.

Method	P (%)	R (%)	F_1 (%)
Badr et al. [17]	88.56	90.54	89.58
Aydin et al. [38]	89.46	91.56	90.50
Proposed method	95.23	93.78	95.12

Table 4. Standard deviation of three evaluation indicators on the two datasets.

Image Dataset	Precision	Recall	F_1
Ardizzone	±0.14	±0.20	±0.21
CoMoFoD	±0.15	±0.24	±0.28

We comprehensively analyzed the performance of the proposed algorithm through three evaluation metrics and compared it with the algorithms proposed in [17,38]. Table 2 presents the experimental data obtained by testing the proposed method and the comparison algorithms on the Ardizzone dataset [37], where it can be clearly seen that the method has certain advantages. Compared with the other algorithms, the precision of our proposed algorithm is higher. Although the recall rate is slightly lower than that of the algorithm in [17], the F_1 value of the proposed algorithm indicates a significant advantage. This is mainly because in the feature extraction stage, we used two detection methods, and the A-KAZE detector extracted more features in smooth areas, resulting in better detection performance in the tampering localization stage.

Table 3 shows the results of experimental testing on the CoMoFoD dataset. The proposed algorithm has significant advantages in precision, which is higher than that of the two comparison algorithms. The proposed method also has significant advantages in recall and overall F_1 value. The main reason for this is that the method proposed in [17] only uses SURF for feature point extraction, determines suspicious areas by replacing matching feature points with corresponding superpixel blocks, and then merges adjacent blocks based on similar local color features. This method is less robust to rotation and scale invariance and does not perform well in geometric transformation forgery detection. In this paper, we combined SURF and A-KAZE in the feature extraction stage to obtain enough feature points in smooth areas, and removed mismatches through a density-based clustering method, thereby effectively and accurately locating tampered areas.

To further test the superiority of the proposed method in terms of time complexity, we conducted tests on images in the Ardizzone and CoMoFoD datasets, and recorded the time required for the proposed method and the comparison algorithms to detect a single image. Table 5 presents the data. The proposed method required an average of 2.54 s for feature extraction on the Ardizzone dataset, and 61.58 s on average for feature matching and detection of mismatched pairs. On the CoMoFoD dataset, the average time for feature extraction was 2.24 s, and the time required for other detections was 51.99 s. The method proposed in [38] required a longer time for feature extraction due to the greater number of iterations and redundant feature points extracted, resulting in longer detection time. The average detection time was 122.12 s on the Ardizzone dataset and 99.25 s on the CoMoFoD dataset. The method proposed in [17] segmented the image equally and without overlapping, and used a segmentation algorithm to divide the entire image into superpixel blocks, which undoubtedly increased the computational complexity of the algorithm. Consequently, the average time required for this method was 184.23 s on the Ardizzone dataset and 145.23 s on the CoMoFoD dataset. In summary, as a result of combining SURF and A-KAZE, which has the advantage of two detectors complementing one another, the proposed method outperformed the two comparison algorithms in terms of time complexity.

Table 5. Time complexity comparison.

Image Dataset	Badr et al. [17]	Aydin et al. [38]	Proposed Method
Ardizzone	184.23 s	122.12 s	65.12 s
CoMoFoD	145.23 s	99.25 s	54.23 s

5.4.2. Post-Processing Forgery Detection

This paper focuses primarily on post-processing operations for detecting tampering in images using two methods: noise and Gaussian blur. The detection results were compared and analyzed by comparing the visual detection effect with the binary image given in the dataset.

Gaussian blur forgery detection: To evaluate the detection performance of the proposed method on Gaussian blur forgery, we selected two blur factors, $\sigma = 0.5$ and $\sigma = 2$. The detection results are shown in Figure 9. The first row in the figure shows the original images, the second row shows the binarized truth images provided in the dataset, and the third row shows the detection results of the proposed method. When the Gaussian blur factor is set to $\sigma = 2$, it can be observed from the comparison between the detection results of the proposed method (Figure 9, third row) and the binary images from the dataset (Figure 9, second row) that there was no missed detection with the proposed method, and it accurately located the tampered regions in the dataset. This indicates that the proposed method has good detection performance on Gaussian blur forgery.

Figure 9. Rendering of Gaussian blur forgery detection. **First row**: original images; **second row**: binarized truth images; **third row**: effect images of forgery detection.

Gaussian white noise forgery detection: To verify the detection performance of the proposed method on Gaussian white noise tampering, we also tested the images in the dataset by adding Gaussian white noise with mean $m = 0$ and variance $v = 0.001$ and $v = 0.0005$. The detection results with Gaussian white noise forgery detection are shown in Figure 10. The first row shows the original images, the second row shows the binary images provided in the dataset, and the third row shows the experimental test results obtained in this study. It can be observed from the comparison between the experimental detection results (Figure 10, third row) and the binary images (Figure 10, second row) that the proposed method had no missed detection and accurately located the tampered regions with Gaussian white noise, demonstrating its effectiveness in detecting Gaussian white noise forgery.

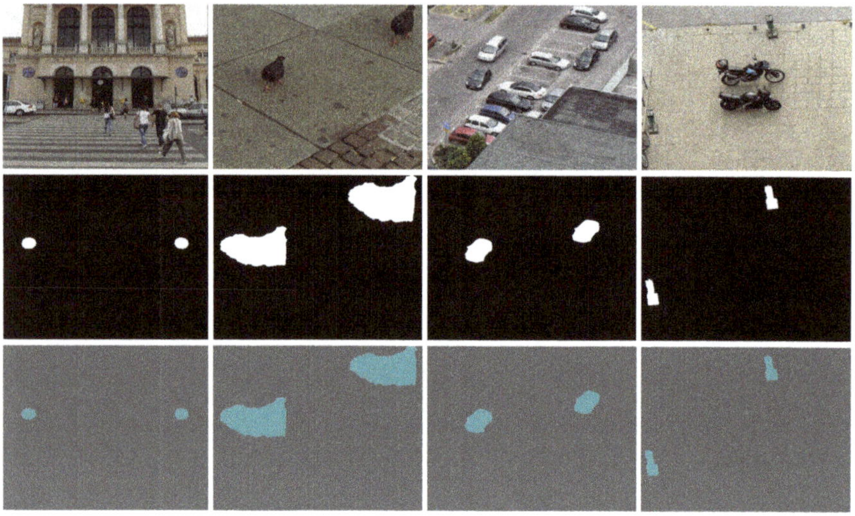

Figure 10. Effect images of Gaussian white noise forgery detection. **First row**: original images; **second row**: binarized truth images; **third row**: effect images of forgery detection.

The comparison between binarized truth images and detection results in Figures 9 and 10 shows that there are almost no missed detection regions with the proposed method. Whether in noise forgery or Gaussian blur forgery detection, the detection results of this paper are almost identical to the binary images provided in the dataset. This indicates that the proposed method demonstrates excellent performance in post-processing operations, such as Gaussian blur forgery and Gaussian white noise. Overall, the proposed method can accurately locate tampered regions, especially when the selected blur factor and noise variance are small, and the detection results are more accurate.

The results of the F_1 score for the proposed method and the two comparison algorithms are shown in Figure 11. From the figure, it can be observed that the proposed method has a significant advantage in detecting Gaussian noise and blur forgery.

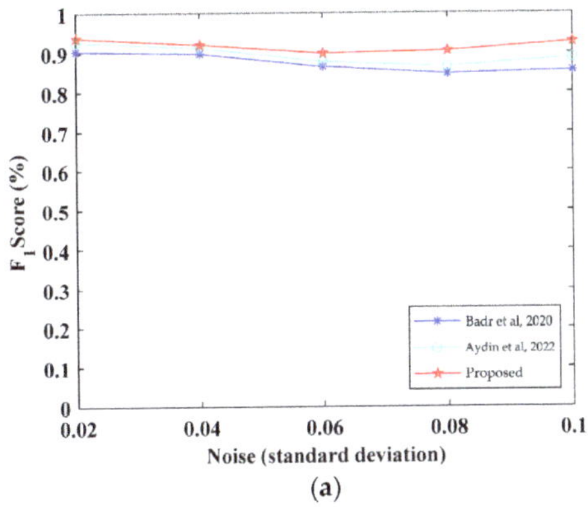

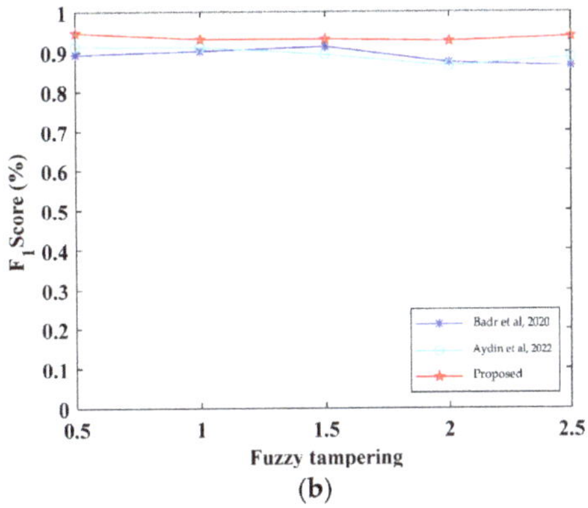

Figure 11. Score for different approaches against (**a**) noise addition attack and (**b**) fuzzy addition attack. Badr et al., 2020 [17]. Aydin et al., 2022 [38].

6. Conclusions

In this paper, we combined SURF and A-KAZE detectors and used g2NN for feature matching. To improve the localization accuracy, the DBSCAN algorithm was applied to remove erroneous matches and reduce false positives. The experimental results show that the proposed method has good detection performance. SURF and A-KAZE can extract effective feature points in smooth areas, and the DBSCAN algorithm can remove incorrect matchings, thus reducing false alarms. The proposed method demonstrates strong robustness against various tampering types such as rotation and scaling, and achieves improved detection accuracy in smooth areas. When small blur factors and noise variances are used in tampering operations, this method exhibits good detection performance.

Author Contributions: Conceptualization, G.F.; data curation, G.F.; investigation, Y.W.; methodology, G.F.; software, G.F.; validation, Y.W.; visualization, Y.Z.; writing—original draft, G.F.; writing—review and editing, Y.Z. All authors have read and agreed to the published version of the manuscript.

Funding: Industry-University-Research Innovation Fund of the Chinese Ministry of Education, Item Number: 2021ZYB01003; Shanghai Natural Science Foundation Project, Item Number: 17ZR1411900; Shanghai Science and Technology Commission Key Project, Item Number: 18511101600.

Conflicts of Interest: The authors declare no conflict of interest.

References

1. Bensaad, A.; Loukhaoukha, K.; Sadoudi, S. Keypoint-based copy-move forgery detection in digital images: A survey. In Proceedings of the 2022 7th International Conference on Image and Signal Processing and Their Applications (ISPA), Mostaganem, Algeria, 8–9 May 2022; IEEE: Piscataway, NJ, USA, 2022; pp. 1–6.
2. Paul, S.; Pal, A.K. A fast copy-move image forgery detection approach on a reduced search space. *Multimed. Tools Appl.* **2023**, *82*, 25917–25944. [CrossRef]
3. Anushree, R.; Vinay Kumar, S.B.; Sachin, B.M. A Survey on Copy Move Forgery Detection (CMFD) Technique. In Proceedings of the 2023 International Conference on Intelligent and Innovative Technologies in Computing, Electrical and Electronics (IITCEE), Bengaluru, India, 27–28 January 2023; IEEE: Piscataway, NJ, USA, 2023; pp. 439–443.
4. Venugopalan, A.K.; Gopakumar, G. Copy-Move Forgery Detection-A Study and the Survey. In Proceedings of the 2022 Third International Conference on Intelligent Computing Instrumentation and Control Technologies (ICICICT), Kannur, India, 11–12 August 2022; IEEE: Piscataway, NJ, USA, 2022; pp. 1327–1334.
5. Zhang, Z.; Wang, C.; Zhou, X. A survey on passive image copy-move forgery detection. *J. Inf. Process. Syst.* **2018**, *14*, 6–31.
6. Fridrich, J. Detection of copy-move forgery in digital images. In Proceedings of the Digital Forensic Research Workshop, Cleveland, OH, USA, 6–8 August 2003; pp. 19–23.
7. Kumar, A.; Singh, K.U.; Swarup, C.; Singh, T.; Raja, L.; Kumar, A. Detection of Copy-Move Forgery Using Euclidean Distance and Texture Features. *Traitement Signal* **2022**, *39*, 781–788. [CrossRef]

8. Fattah, S.A.; Ullah, M.M.I.; Ahmed, M.; Ahmmed, I.; Shahnaz, C. A scheme for copy-move forgery detection in digital images based on 2D-DWT. In Proceedings of the 2014 IEEE 57th International Midwest Symposium on Circuits and Systems (MWSCAS), Station, TX, USA, 3–6 August 2014; IEEE: Piscataway, NJ, USA, 2014; pp. 801–804.
9. Sabeena, M.; Abraham, L.; Varghese, A. Digital Image Forgery Detection Using Local Binary Pattern (LBP) and Harlick Transform with classification. In Proceedings of the 2021 IEEE International Power and Renewable Energy Conference (IPRECON), Kollam, India, 24–26 September 2021; IEEE: Piscataway, NJ, USA, 2021; pp. 1–6.
10. Rahma, F.I.; Utami, E.; Al-Fatta, H. Gaussian Pyramid Decomposition in Copy-Move Image Forgery Detection with SIFT and Zernike Moment Algorithms. *Telematika* **2022**, *15*, 1–13. [CrossRef]
11. Ye, W.; Zeng, Q.; Peng, Y.; Liu, Y.; Chang, C.C. A two-stage detection method of copy-move forgery based on parallel feature fusion. *EURASIP J. Wirel. Commun. Netw.* **2022**, *2022*, 30. [CrossRef]
12. Lee, J.C.; Chang, C.P.; Chen, W.K. Detection of copy–move image forgery using histogram of orientated gradients. *Inf. Sci.* **2015**, *321*, 250–262. [CrossRef]
13. Qin, C.; Chen, X.; Ye, D.; Wang, J.; Sun, X. A novel image hashing scheme with perceptual robustness using block truncation coding. *Inf. Sci.* **2016**, *361*, 84–99. [CrossRef]
14. Wang, C.; Huang, Z.; Qi, S.; Yu, Y.; Shen, G.; Zhang, Y. Shrinking the Semantic Gap: Spatial Pooling of Local Moment Invariants for Copy-Move Forgery Detection. *IEEE Trans. Inf. Forensics Secur.* **2023**, *18*, 1064–1079. [CrossRef]
15. Kumar, S.; Mukherjee, S.; Pal, A.K. An improved reduced feature-based copy-move forgery detection technique. *Multimed. Tools Appl.* **2023**, *82*, 1431–1456. [CrossRef]
16. Salman, M.; Uhl, A. Countering Anti-forensics of SIFT-based Copy-Move Detection. In Proceedings of the 2020 25th International Conference on Pattern Recognition (ICPR), Milan, Italy, 10–15 January 2021; IEEE: Piscataway, NJ, USA, 2021; pp. 2701–2707.
17. Badr, A.; Youssif, A.; Wafi, M. A robust copy-move forgery detection in digital image forensics using SURF. In Proceedings of the 2020 8th International Symposium on Digital Forensics and Security (ISDFS), Beirut, Lebanon, 1–2 June 2020; IEEE: Piscataway, NJ, USA, 2020; pp. 1–6.
18. Kumar, N.; Meenpal, T. Salient keypoint-based copy–move image forgery detection. *Aust. J. Forensic Sci.* **2023**, *55*, 331–354. [CrossRef]
19. Samel, M.; Reddy, A.M. An Empirical Study on Copy-Move Forgery Detection Techniques in Images. *Math. Stat. Eng. Appl.* **2022**, *71*, 183–193.
20. Benhamza, H.; Djeffal, A.; Cheddad, A. Image forgery detection review. In Proceedings of the 2021 International Conference on Information Systems and Advanced Technologies (ICISAT), Tebessa, Algeria, 27–28 December 2021; IEEE: Piscataway, NJ, USA, 2021; pp. 1–7.
21. Pan, X.; Lyu, S. Region duplication detection using image feature matching. *IEEE Trans. Inf. Forensics Secur.* **2010**, *5*, 857–867. [CrossRef]
22. Lowe, D.G. Distinctive image features from scale-invariant key points. *Int. J. Comput. Vis.* **2004**, *60*, 91–110. [CrossRef]
23. Zheng, J.; Zhang, K. Copy-Move Forgery Detection Algorithm based on Feature Point Clustering. In Proceedings of the 2022 IEEE 6th Information Technology and Mechatronics Engineering Conference (ITOEC), Chongqing, China, 4–6 March 2022; IEEE: Piscataway, NJ, USA, 2022; Volume 6, pp. 775–780.
24. Fischler, M.A.; Bolles, R.C. Random sample consensus: A paradigm for model fitting with applications to image analysis and automated cartography. *Commun. ACM* **1981**, *24*, 381–395. [CrossRef]
25. Liu, Y.; Wang, H.; Chen, Y.; Wu, H.; Wang, H. A passive forensic scheme for copy-move forgery based on superpixel segmentation and K-means clustering. *Multimed. Tools Appl.* **2020**, *79*, 477–500. [CrossRef]
26. Wang, X.Y.; Wang, C.; Wang, L.; Jiao, L.X.; Yang, H.Y.; Niu, P.P. A fast and high accurate image copy-move forgery detection approach. *Multidimens. Syst. Signal Process.* **2020**, *31*, 857–883. [CrossRef]
27. Wang, X.; Chen, W.; Niu, P.; Yang, H. Image copy-move forgery detection based on dynamic threshold with dense points. *J. Vis. Commun. Image Represent.* **2022**, *89*, 103658. [CrossRef]
28. Fatima, B.; Ghafoor, A.; Ali, S.S.; Riaz, M.M. FAST, BRIEF and SIFT based image copy-move forgery detection technique. *Multimed. Tools Appl.* **2022**, *81*, 43805–43819. [CrossRef]
29. Orhei, C.; Radu, L.; Mocofan, M.; Vert, S.; Vasiu, R. Urban landmark detection using A-KAZE features and vector of aggregated local descriptors. In Proceedings of the 2022 International Symposium on Electronics and Telecommunications (ISETC), Timisoara, Romania, 10–11 November 2022; IEEE: Piscataway, NJ, USA, 2022; pp. 1–4.
30. Ouyang, T.; Shen, X. Online structural clustering based on DBSCAN extension with granular descriptors. *Inf. Sci.* **2022**, *607*, 688–704. [CrossRef]
31. Sujin, J.S.; Sophia, S. Copy-Move Geometric Tampering Estimation Through Enhanced SIFT Detector Method. *Comput. Syst. Sci. Eng.* **2023**, *44*, 157–171. [CrossRef]
32. Bay, H.; Ess, A.; Tuytelaars, T.; Van Gool, L. Speeded-up robust features (SURF). *Comput. Vis. Image Underst.* **2008**, *110*, 346–359. [CrossRef]
33. Perona, P.; Malik, J. Scale-space and edge detection using anisotropic diffusion. *IEEE Trans. Pattern Anal. Mach. Intell.* **1990**, *12*, 629–639. [CrossRef]
34. Alcantarilla, P.F.; Solutions, T. Fast explicit diffusion for accelerated features in nonlinear scale spaces. *IEEE Trans. Patt. Anal. Mach. Intell.* **2011**, *34*, 1281–1298.

35. Amerini, I.; Ballan, L.; Caldelli, R.; Del Bimbo, A.; Serra, G. A sift-based forensic method for copy–move attack detection and transformation recovery. *IEEE Trans. Inf. Forensics Secur.* **2011**, *6*, 1099–1110. [CrossRef]
36. Borah, B.; Bhattacharyya, D.K. An improved sampling-based DBSCAN for large spatial databases. In Proceedings of the International Conference on Intelligent Sensing and Information Processing, Chennai, India, 4–7 January 2004; IEEE: Piscataway, NJ, USA, 2004; pp. 92–96.
37. Ardizzone, E.; Bruno, A.; Mazzola, G. Copy–move forgery detection by matching triangles of key points. *IEEE Trans. Inf. Forensics Secur.* **2015**, *10*, 2084–2094. [CrossRef]
38. Aydin, Y.I. Comparison of color features on copy-move forgery detection problem using HSV color space. *Aust. J. Forensic Sci.* **2022**, 1–17. [CrossRef]

applied sciences

MDPI

Article

A New Class of Edge Filter Based on a Cross-correlation-like Equation Derived from Fractional Calculus Principles

Mario Gonzalez-Lee [1,*], Hector Vazquez-Leal [2], Jose R. Garcia-Martinez [1], Eli G. Pale-Ramon [3], Luis J. Morales-Mendoza [1], Mariko Nakano-Miyatake [4] and Hector Perez-Meana [4]

[1] Facultad de Ingeniería en Electrónica y Comunicaciones, Universidad Veracruzana, Av. Venustiano Carranza S/N, Poza Rica Veracruz 93390, Mexico; romangarcia@uv.mx (J.R.G.-M.); javmorales@uv.mx (L.J.M.-M.)

[2] Facultad de Instrumentacion Electronica, Universidad Veracruzana, Cto. Gonzalo Aguirre Beltrán S/N, Xalapa 91000, Mexico; hvazquez@uv.mx

[3] Department of Electronics Engineering, Universidad de Guanajuato, Salamanca 36885, Mexico; eg.paleramon@ugto.mx

[4] Seccion de Estudios de Posgrado e Investigacion, Instituto Politécnico Nacional, Av. Santa Ana No. 1000, Del. Coyoacan, Ciudad de Mexico 04440, Mexico; mnakano@ipn.mx (M.N.-M.); hmperezm@ipn.mx (H.P.-M.)

* Correspondence: mgonzalez01@uv.mx

Abstract: In this paper, we propose a new sliding window edge-oriented filter that computes the output pixels using a cross-correlation-like equation derived from the principles of fractional calculus (FC); thus, we call it the "fractional cross-correlation filter" (FCCF). We assessed the performance of this filter utilizing exclusively edge-preservation-oriented metrics such as the gradient conduction mean square error (GCMSE), the edge-based structural similarity (EBSSIM), and the multi-scale structural similarity (MS-SSIM); we conducted a statistical assessment of the performance of the filter based on those metrics by using the Berkeley segmentation dataset benchmark as a test corpus. Experimental data reveal that our approach achieves higher performance compared to conventional edge filters for all the metrics considered in this study. This is supported by the statistical analysis we carried out; specifically, the FCCF demonstrates a consistent enhancement in edge detection. We also conducted additional experiments for determining the main filter parameters, which we found to be optimal for a broad spectrum of images. The results underscore the FCCF's potential to make significant contributions to the advancement of image processing techniques since many practical applications such as medical imaging, image enhancement, and computer vision rely heavily on edge detection filters.

Keywords: edge filter; fractional calculus; filtering model

1. Introduction

Edge detectors are a very important class of filters used for identifying sharp variations for different image processing applications, including but not limited to object recognition, motion analysis, pattern recognition, and medical image processing, among others. As a consequence, major technical computing software includes a module specifically intended for computing edge maps of images; for example, Matlab, OpenCV, Maple, Scilab, Skimage, and among others.

The edges play a crucial role in computer vision tasks, such as in the medical image analysis field, where edges are expected to convey relevant information about patients' health; the inaccurate distinction of the boundaries in medical images could lead to a false diagnosis; therefore, it is paramount to identify and highlight edges effectively so that analysts can learn any information the image was intended to convey. An example of such works is [1], where authors stress the importance of carrying on effective image segmentation based on edge detection for reaching an accurate diagnosis.

The conventional approach to edge detection involves convolving the image with a specifically designed 2D kernel that is responsive to significant gradients. However, current research is shifting towards techniques utilizing machine learning and deep-learning-based algorithms specifically tuned for detecting edges in images. For instance, Yunhong et al. [1] developed an edge detection algorithm based on an artificial neural network (ANN), expecting that the edges information the ANN computes might be useful for diagnosing illness from magnetic resonance images (MRI). Their algorithm was reported to be up to three times faster than traditional edge detection schemes; however, they noted that one drawback of the ANN-based approach they proposed is that it requires data preparation and cleaning, which imply a significant additional effort compared to approaches based on the Canny or Sobel operators.

On the computer vision applications to the industry realm, Ahmadian et al. [2] developed a deep-learning-based edge detection to improve building footprint extraction from satellite images. A common issue in these target applications is that the resulting edge maps are sensitive to noise; thus, this study focused on reducing noise in the edges computed from images of buildings that may affect boundary resolution. They addressed this problem by utilizing detected edge bands. Another example is the work of Chaduvula et al. [3], who introduced a neural network-based hybrid filter that combines neural edge enhancers and bilateral filters. In this study, the neural filter works as a fusion operator, effectively eliminating quantum noise from an input image. A common drawback of these approaches is the requirement for an extensive dataset to train effective models and the significant computational power needed to fit the model.

Scientists and engineers are making a transition towards machine learning and deep learning models to implement various image processing tasks; however, they must overcome the problems related to the construction of such models, especially for the late majority who prefer to work with more traditional approaches before they can adopt new trends in technology such as deep learning.

For these reasons, researchers are still working with the most well-known methods for edge detection, such as the Robert's filter, Prewitt filter, Sobel filter, Canny filter, and Laplacian filter. For instance, in Liu's [4] research, he developed an edge detection method based on an improved Canny operator to solve problems related to noise sensitivity, false edges, and the lack of self-adaptability on rebar thread heads. The filter we introduce in this paper resembles the traditional approaches, so it shares desirable characteristics, such as the advantage of exhibiting lower computational complexity because it relies on the linear convolution operator. In addition, these methods lead to a straightforward interpretation since they are based on well-understood mathematical principles while avoiding the burdens related to the development and deployment of machine learning models.

Another field that converges to the topic discussed in this paper is fractional calculus (FC); FC is a branch of mathematics that studies a general framework of calculus where derivatives and integrals have a fractional or even complex order. Scientists are interested in finding new applications of the FC theory to solving engineering problems; in this regard, we will discuss some edge map computing algorithms based on FC in Section 2.

Given the active research in the field of edge filters and their implementation using fractional calculus, and encouraged by the results achieved in our previous works [5,6], we are interested in applying these results to other signal processing tasks. The first work [5] presented a digital watermarking scheme that embeds a binary signal called the watermark into an image, resulting in a watermarked image; the watermark has to be detected later from the watermarked signal for copyright enforcing applications using a FC-based model the authors derived, which they called the fractional cross-correlation. The authors of [5] extended their research in [6] to the case of Gaussian watermarks, that is to say, for watermarks as sequences of numbers with Gaussian distribution. In both cases, the fractional cross-correlation watermarking scheme they proposed, exhibited a higher performance in almost all tests, whereas the few unfavorable tests indicate that the performance of the proposed scheme equals the performance of typical watermark detection schemes for the worst-case scenario.

We believe that this particular fractional model for watermark detection is applicable to other signal processing tasks, and thus, supported by evidence from our previous works, we are dedicated in this paper to developing an edge filter model based on the fractional cross-correlation equation.

The main contributions reported in this paper are:

- We introduce a new image filter designed for detecting edges in grayscale images using a model derived from the FC principles (Section 4).
- We detail the methodology to calculate the parameters of the filter (Section 6).
- We assess the performance of the proposed filter as an edge filter for grayscale images (Section 6).
- We compare the proposed system with de facto standard edge filters (Section 6).

Also, Section 2 covers a review of works closely related to our proposed scheme; Section 5 details the materials used for the experiments we conducted to evaluate the performance of the proposed filter and the validation criteria as well. We present our conclusions in Section 7; next to it, the references, and in the last part, relevant Appendices A–C.

2. Related Works

Fractional calculus has gained popularity in accomplishing several signal processing tasks as it serves to generalize some of the current system models that are based on integer-order derivatives. As a consequence, some scientists are working to incorporate FC into several engineering models, such as in digital controllers, digital filtering, and various image processing tasks, and then compare the performance of the resulting schemes to the previously achieved performance by conventional methods.

Numerous image processing techniques rely on derivatives to gain valuable insights into image structures. Fractional derivatives, in particular, introduce an additional dimension of flexibility, which proves advantageous in performing tasks like edge detection. One can find several studies that confirm the advantages of FC-based models; we will discuss a few examples that particularly fall within the scope of this paper.

Mekideche [7] proposed an algorithm based on a fractional-order mask, which was used as the convolution kernel for edge enhancement. This method is characterized by its noise immunity and ability to detect edges in satellite and medical imaging; furthermore, the authors proved that their algorithm is suitable for real-time applications. Li et al. [8] proposed a fractional order edge detection method where they used an integral filter and a differential mask simultaneously for edge detection, allowing the extraction of targets with precise edges and complete structures in both noisy and noise-free images.

Nandal et al. [9] proposed an algorithm to improve pixel contrast based on foreground and background gray levels by using the Riemann-Liouville fractional differential operator. Their proposed method controls the degree of contrast enhancement with the fractional differential order. Ghanbari et al. [10] proposed two general structures and a method for creating fractional masks; then, the components of these structures were evaluated using the fractional integral Atangana-Baleanu operator. Their results indicate that, with the proper choice of the fractional derivative order, this algorithm overcomes existing problems related to well-known masks such as Canny, Prewitt, and Sobel.

Another example is a comprehensive image quality assessment metric proposed by Varga [11], which evaluated both the overall alterations of an image by computing Grünwald-Letnikov derivatives and the localized alterations through image gradients. Additionally, they utilized visual saliency to prioritize changes in areas that are perceptually significant to the human visual system. To conclude the examples of the use of FC in image processing, Henriques et al. [12] reported extensive experiments on well-known benchmark image quality assessment databases; these results validate the effectiveness of their proposed approach. While existing research predominantly focuses on grayscale imagery, Henriques' paper diverges by implementing and evaluating six fractional derivative-based edge detection algorithms tailored for color images. These algorithms encompass familiar techniques such as Canny, Sobel, Roberts, Laplacian, and Gaussian, as well as less common approaches, like the fractional-order robust edge detector (Contour Robuste d'Ordre Non Entier: CRONE) and fractional derivatives, showcasing their comparative performance.

The following are a few examples that provide insight into the role and importance of edge filters in various practical scenarios that designers might find interest in.

Innovative edge filters are important for image processing task applications. For example, Harshavardhan and Anith [13] compared modified Canny edge and Prewitt edge detection methods to evaluate their effectiveness in identifying bone fractures. Their study aimed to enhance the accuracy and specificity of diagnosing bone fractures by utilizing edge detection techniques. The results revealed that the customized Canny edge detection method exhibited a higher accuracy rate of 95% and a specificity of 86%, surpassing the performance of the Prewitt edge detection method. Their findings underscore the importance of utilizing cutting-edge technologies to enhance the efficiency and precision of bone fracture detection, ultimately contributing to more effective healthcare practices.

Zhang et al. [14] discussed the significance of edge detection in image processing and analysis, focusing on its crucial role in human visual recognition and target identification. This paper underscored the importance of edge detection quality for successful target recognition and the practical value of signal and image edge detection research. The study that the authors conducted aimed to address the limitations of traditional edge detection algorithms; thus, they proposed an algorithm based on wavelet modulus maxima to improve edge detection. They focused on dislocation phenomena, threshold selection, and multi-scale edge fusion. To address these challenges, they tailored an enhanced self-adaptive layered threshold algorithm and a weighted multi-scale edge fusion algorithm. The influence of wavelet characteristics on image edge detection was explored, emphasizing the conditions for wavelet construction and evaluation criteria for edge detection methods.

Yang [15] focused on generating facial contours using a bidirectional algorithm to improve edge detection accuracy with applications to facial reconstruction and medical applications. He highlighted the importance of image segmentation and the 3D reconstruction of faces as relevant research areas in image processing, as it leads to identifying tissue edges. Also, he mentioned histogram equalization as a technique used to enhance contrast in medical computed tomography (CT) images as it contributes to enhanced visualization of anatomical details. He emphasised the relevance of edge detection in digital image processing, especially in medical and plastic surgery applications where precision in contour identification is paramount.

Begun et al. [16] developed a hybrid edge detection approach that combines the Canny and Sobel edge detection techniques and applied it to identify discontinuities in images of the Tocklai Vegetative Tea Clone Series TV1, TV9, and TV10 in Assam. This approach provides accurate information on the boundaries of TV1, TV9, and TV10 by using a dilation morphological operation to eliminate flaws and compute boundaries. They compared their approach with popular edge detection techniques like Sobel, Prewitt, Robert, Canny, Laplacian of Gaussian, and Gaussian based on noise level parameters including the mean square error (MSE), peak signal noise ratio (PSNR), and signal to noise ratio (SNR). Their results showed that the hybrid edge detection approach, combined with dilation using the morphological operation, is efficient and can be widely used for detecting the edges of the Tocklai Vegetative Tea Clone Series.

Ye et al. [17] applied the ant colony optimization (ACO) algorithm, Canny, and Gabor edge detection techniques to illustrate classical, dynamic, and intelligent edge detection schemes. This approach explored the complex skyline digital images as case studies and conducted a qualitative analysis to examine the visual appeals of detection outcomes based on red-blue-green (RGB) scales. In contrast, quantitative analysis compares edge detection outcomes based on gray and binary scales in the frequency and spatial domains. This study provided an extensive evaluation of the overall quality of edge detection schemes.

These works exemplify potential applications that might benefit from edge filters like the one proposed in this paper.

3. Background

The cross-correlation formula and its variations have been widely used for accomplishing many signal processing tasks, for example, pattern recognition and digital watermarking, to name just a few. Although there are various forms of this equation, one of the most useful for computing the cross correlation ($\tilde{x_k}$) between two signals $x = [x_1, x_2, \ldots, x_N]$ and $y = [y_1, y_2, \ldots, y_N]$ is as follows:

$$\tilde{x_k} = \frac{1}{N}\sum_{i=1}^{N} x_i y_i. \tag{1}$$

Despite the advances in the signal processing field, the cross-correlation formula continues to be used by many authors as a means to measure the similarity between two signals due to its remarkable performance; however, like many models, it has its weaknesses.

On the other hand, to overcome some of the weakness of that model, we deduced in our previous works [5,6] a fractional model of a correlation-like equation for watermarking derived using principles of FC. Recognizing the complexity of fractional calculus and to facilitate its implementation, we have provided comprehensive details on simplification and approximation techniques in Appendix A. This appendix offers a solid foundation, ensuring that readers can effectively navigate and apply the mathematical concepts involved.

In this paper, Equation (2) will be referred to as the "Fractional Cross-correlation"; this model outperforms Equation (1) in matching signals under adverse conditions; thus, we are interested in extending the use of this model to other related areas. The fractional cross-correlation is defined as follows:

$$\tilde{x_k} = -\operatorname{Im}\left[\frac{3}{4}\frac{1}{N}\sqrt{\left(\sum_{i=1}^{N} x_i y_i\right)^2 - \frac{2}{3}\sigma^2 N[2NH-1]} - \epsilon\right], \tag{2}$$

for signals x and y, where:

$$\epsilon = \frac{3}{4}\frac{1}{N}\sqrt{\frac{2}{3}\sigma^2 N[2NH-1]},$$

and $H = \ln(\sqrt{2\pi\sigma^2 e})$ for a signal with variance σ^2.

As we stated earlier in this section, this FC model performs remarkably well in matching signals under severe conditions, and now we present an example to clarify this. Let us examine Figure 1a–c. In this figure, we illustrate the case of a generic watermark detector based on Equation (1) for detecting watermarks. Such a device must output an almost zero value when no watermark is embedded in a presumably watermarked image and produce a much higher value when it detects a watermark in the tested image, as shown in Figure 1b. Usually, a watermarking system relies on a threshold for deciding whether a watermark is present or not. The main issue here is that, depending on several factors, the response of the system can be higher than expected for the case of no watermarks actually embedded in the image, leading to false positives.

Figure 1b exemplifies how Equation (1) is unable to resolve ownership on the watermarked image shown in Figure 1 since there are many false positives. Conversely, Figure 1c shows how the response of a system based on Equation (2) is able to overcome this particular scenario since there are no false positives. We also observed that the rate of the matching and the non matching responses is higher in the case of the fractional cross-correlation. This evidence motivated us to use this fractional model for other applications in the signal processing area; in the case of this paper, we focused on developing an image processing filter.

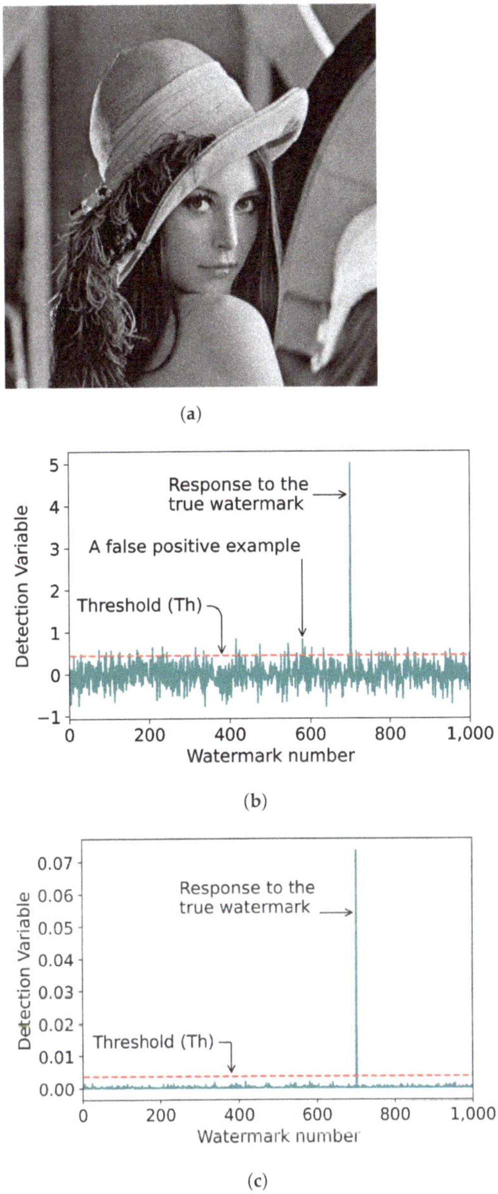

(c)

Figure 1. Comparison of the response of watermarking detection variables between the cross-correlation-based detector and the fractional-correlation-based detector. (**a**) The watermarked image. (**b**) Detection variable for the cross-correlation-based detector. (**c**) detection variable for the fractional-correlation-based detector.

4. The Main Idea

Equation (2) yields a non-linear response that is very high only for signals that match; in other words, there is a high fractional correlation; we exploited this characteristic to derive an edge filter for images, which will be described in the remainder of this paper. Since the core of the proposed filter is Equation (2), we have named our proposed method the "Fractional Cross-Correlation Filter" (FCCF), since the equation that computes the output image comes from the principles of fractional calculus.

We define the FCCF as a sliding window filter, whose input is a grayscale image and which outputs the corresponding edge map. The principle of operation is similar to other sliding window approaches, as described in Algorithm 1.

Algorithm 1: Computing the edge map of an image following the FCCF approach.

```
Data: Input image (I), Filter's Kernel (K), Parameter K_p.
// slide the window across rows and columns
for r in Rows do
    for c in Cols do
        Get the window x centered in (r,c);
        Compute x̃_{m,n} using Equation (3);
        Compute the decision threshold Th using Equation (8);
        if x̃_{m,n} ≥ Th then
        |   E(m,n) = 1        // the pixel at (m,n) belongs to an edge
        end
        else
        |   E(m,n) = 0        // otherwise
        end
    end
end
Result: Edge map of image (E)
```

One of the main components of the filter is its kernel, which we will develop and discuss in the next section.

4.1. The Filtering Equation and Kernel Design

We used Equation (2) to compute the pixel value at position (m,n) as Follows:

$$\tilde{x}_{m,n} = -\operatorname{Im}\left[\frac{3}{4}\frac{1}{MN}\sqrt{\left(\sum_m\sum_n x_{m,n}h_{m,n}\right)^2 - \frac{2}{3}\sigma_x^2 MN[2MNH-1] - \epsilon}\,\right], \tag{3}$$

where $x_{m,n}$ is the pixel within the window at position (m,n), $H = \ln(\sqrt{2\pi\sigma_x^2 e})$ for an image x with size $M \times N$ and variance σ_x^2. To filter, we propose to use the following well known kernel $K = [h_{m,n}]$ for enhancing edges [18].

$$K = \begin{bmatrix} -\frac{k}{8} & -\frac{k}{8} & -\frac{k}{8} \\ -\frac{k}{8} & k+1 & -\frac{k}{8} \\ -\frac{k}{8} & -\frac{k}{8} & -\frac{k}{8} \end{bmatrix}. \tag{4}$$

Given the symmetry of this kernel, the convolution associated with the filtering process is equivalent to the correlation between the filter window and the kernel.

Kernel Design

By letting $k = 1$, we get the kernel

$$K = \begin{bmatrix} -\frac{1}{8} & -\frac{1}{8} & -\frac{1}{8} \\ -\frac{1}{8} & 2 & -\frac{1}{8} \\ -\frac{1}{8} & -\frac{1}{8} & -\frac{1}{8} \end{bmatrix}. \tag{5}$$

Above is a well-known kernel used for edge enhancement. Now, let us recall the following term of Equation (3):

$$\sum_{m}\sum_{n} x_{m,n}h_{m,n} = x_{2,2}h_{2,2} - \sum_{m\neq 2}\sum_{n\neq 2} x_{m,n}h_{m,n}. \tag{6}$$

This form of the equation illustrates how edge enhancement depends on the difference between the center and its surroundings. Furthermore, we started our dissertation by establishing that our premise is that we should rely only on the signal-matching capabilities of the filtering equation and its non-linear nature. As a consequence, we propose maximizing the sum in (6). The straightforward way to achieve this is to discard the minus sign so the second term adds instead of subtracting. In other words, we propose to use all values as positive, leading to the following kernel:

$$K = \begin{bmatrix} \frac{1}{8} & \frac{1}{8} & \frac{1}{8} \\ \frac{1}{8} & 2 & \frac{1}{8} \\ \frac{1}{8} & \frac{1}{8} & \frac{1}{8} \end{bmatrix}. \tag{7}$$

To support the hypothesis that maximizing Equation (6) yields a better approach to edge detection, we present an example in Figure 2.

(a) (b)

Figure 2. Comparison of the edge maps output by the proposed FCCF. (**a**) Using the kernel defined by Equation (5). (**b**) Using the kernel defined by Equation (7). This figures illustrates how the edge map exhibits edges more defined as the sum (6) maximizes.

4.2. Calculating the Decision Threshold of the Filter (Th)

Equation (8) was utilized in [5,6] to ascertain whether the signal matched or not, and thus, we applied it to determine whether the data within the filter's window indicates an edge. Given that H, ϵ, and σ_x^2 are inherent characteristics of the signal x, the sole parameter remaining for the designer's discretion is K_p. The value assigned to K_p for our experiments will be detailed in Section 6.

The threshold is computed using the following equation:

$$Th = K_p \sigma_x^2 \sqrt{\frac{H}{\epsilon}}. \quad (8)$$

4.3. Computing the Resulting Edge Map

We compute the resulting edge map using Equations (1) and (8) as follows:

$$E(m,n) = \begin{cases} 1 & x_{m,n} \geq Th \\ 0 & \text{Otherwise.} \end{cases} \quad (9)$$

In the following section, we discuss the materials used, the methodology followed, and the experimental setup to assess the performance of the proposed filter.

5. Materials, Methods, and Experiment Setup

We designed three experiments to validate the FCCF: the first one aimed at establishing a relationship between the parameter K_p and the resulting edge map, a second experiment for determining the best value for parameter K_p for filtering images, and finally, a third experiment with the goal of assessing the performance of the filter and comparing it to other popular approaches.

In the remaining portion of this section, we will discuss the materials we utilized and the metrics we considered, and then we will describe the experiments we conducted.

5.1. Materials

We utilized the Berkeley Segmentation Dataset 500 (BSDS500) [19], which is publicly available. This is a standard benchmark for contour detection aimed at evaluating edge detection in images. This dataset includes images featuring both object interior and background boundaries. It consists of 500 color images with dimensions of either 321 × 481 or 481 × 321 pixels, which we converted into grayscale images during our test.

5.2. Objective Edge-Oriented Metrics

We omitted commonly used metrics such as MSE, SNR, PSNR, and median absolute error (MAE), which, as argued in [20], have been proven to be insufficient for assessing performance in scenarios where edge preservation is paramount. Instead, we followed the authors' recommendation to employ metrics that specifically measure edge detection capabilities.

Therefore, we considered the following edge-focused metrics: the Edge-Based Structural Similarity (ESSIM) [21], which compares the information edges of distorted image blocks to the corresponding of the original image and uses this result for computing the Structural Similarity Measure (SSIM); an ESSIM evaluation leads to results similar to the Mean Opinion Score (MOS); the Multi-Scale Structural Similarity (MS-SSIM) [22], this approach replaced the Sobel filter involved in the process by a dyadic wavelet transform, and thus, the assessment spawns several decomposition levels of the wavelet transform. The Gradient Conduction Mean Square Error (GCMSE) can be thought of as an edge-aware version of the Mean Square Error (MSE). This algorithm computes the average of the weighted sum of gradients for four directions for computing a MSE-based estimate of the GCMSE [23] for this experiment.

5.3. Parameter Optimization Methodology

This is the first experiment we conducted. We investigated the relationship between the parameter K_p of Equation (8) and the resulting edge map. To compare the edge maps dependent on parameter K_p, we filtered each image in the dataset, setting various values for K_p, and then we observed whether parameter K_p influences the resulting edge map.

Subsequently, we undertook a second experiment to ascertain a value for K_p that maximizes the edge preservation metrics considered in this study. To achieve this goal, we measured the corresponding edge-preservation metrics to determine which value of parameter K_p maximizes each metric.

5.4. Methodology for the Statistical Assessment of the Performance of the FCCF

In the third experiment we conducted, we evaluated the filter's efficacy as an edge detector. We filtered the images in the dataset and calculated pertinent metrics. This enabled us to compare the edge maps generated by our proposed filter to those corresponding to established filters such as the Sobel and Roberts filters.

We opted to compare our results solely with the Sobel and Roberts methods, as they represent the most prevalent techniques in image processing applications. While numerous other methods have been proposed, they have not yet gained widespread acceptance within the scientific community, whereas the Roberts and Sobel filters were implemented in major software projects around the world.

6. Experimental Results and Discussion

As we previously mentioned, through the first experiment we designed, we examined the relationship between K_p and the resultant edge map. To achieve this objective, we observed the output of the filter over the entire BSD500 dataset for values of K_p ranging from 0.1 to 1. For clarity, we display here only selected results for the standard test image "Lena" in Figure 3. Additional edge maps for this example are detailed in Appendix B, and additional examples of images drawn from the BSD500 are included in Appendix C, which provides a more comprehensive insight into the relationship between K_p and the resultant edge maps. Figure 3 reveals a relationship between the number of edges in the filter outputs and the parameter K_p; although this is a subjective assessment, we confirmed this relationship with the second experiment we proposed using metrics oriented towards edge preservation.

With the second experiment, we aimed to determine a K_p value that would result in the highest edge preservation. We calculated the metrics discussed in the last paragraph of Section 5 using a grid of 10 equally spaced values within the interval $\frac{1}{10} \leq K_p \leq \frac{1}{2}$; subsequently, we computed the edge-oriented metrics and presented the distribution of this data in the box plot shown in Figure 4, which depicts the distribution of K_p values that maximize each metric. This figure indicates that the median K_p value for maximizing the metrics MSSSIM and GCMSE is $\frac{1}{2}$ for nearly all images in the BSDS500; in contrast, the median for ESSIM is 0.4. Moreover, these results imply that finding a fixed K_p value that ensures high edge preservation for the ESSIM metric is challenging in most cases. Using this premise, we evaluated the performance of the proposed filter, letting $K_p = \frac{1}{2}$, and then we compared the resultant metrics with those computed using the Sobel and Roberts filters.

Figure 5a–c displays the evaluation metrics from the output edge map computed using the FCCF, the Sobel filter, and the Roberts filter. As observed in Figure 5a, the proposed filter achieves higher performance compared to the Sobel and Roberts filters, as evidenced by attaining the lowest GCMSE. Additionally, Figure 5b illustrates the superior performance of the filter when assessed using ESSIM, indicated by a higher median value of ESSIM, and consequently, the FCCF exhibits a distribution skewed towards higher values in comparison to the Sobel and Roberts methods. Furthermore, the evaluation from the MSSSIM perspective also substantiates the enhanced performance of the FCCF, as Figure 5c clearly demonstrates.

We observed that for this test, the metrics for the Sobel and Roberts filters are nearly identical; thus, we focused our comparison on the FCCF versus the Sobel filter. To facilitate this, we constructed a violin plot to depict the distributions of the edge-preservation metrics and positioned them side by side for an easier comparison in Figure 6. This comparative analysis reveals that the proposed filter surpasses the performance across all metrics considered in this study.

(a) Original Lena Image.

(b) $K_p = 0.1$

(c) $K_p = 0.5$

(d) $K_p = 0.7$

Figure 3. The effects of varying the value of the parameter K_p on the edge map.

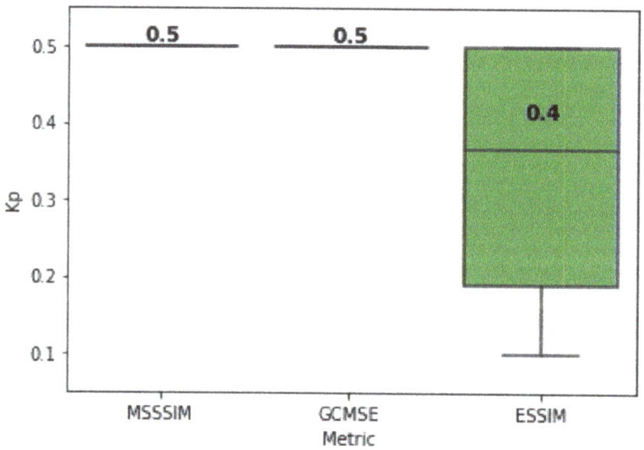

Figure 4. The search of a value for maximizing each metric led us to letting $K_p = \frac{1}{2}$.

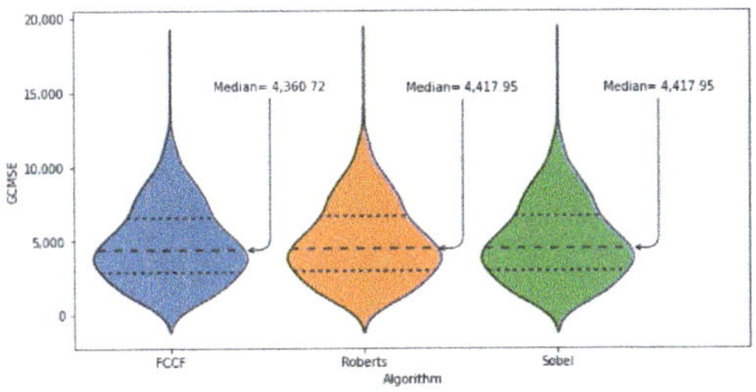

(a)

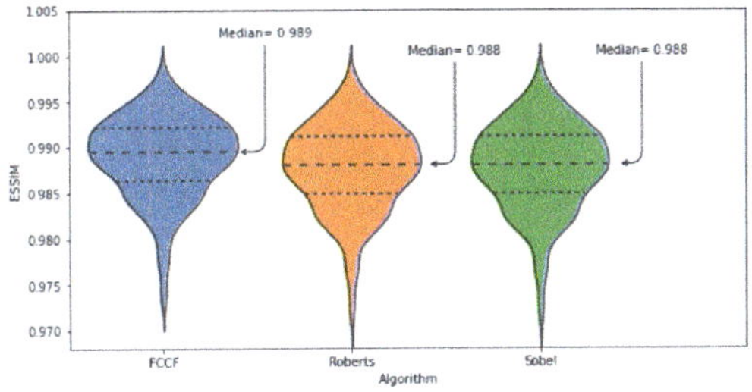

(b)

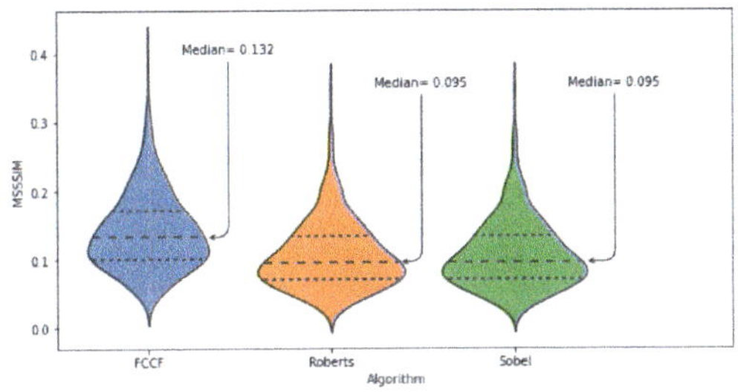

(c)

Figure 5. Frequency of K_p values expressed as a percentage. (**a**) GCMSE, (**b**) ESSIM, (**c**) MSSSIM.

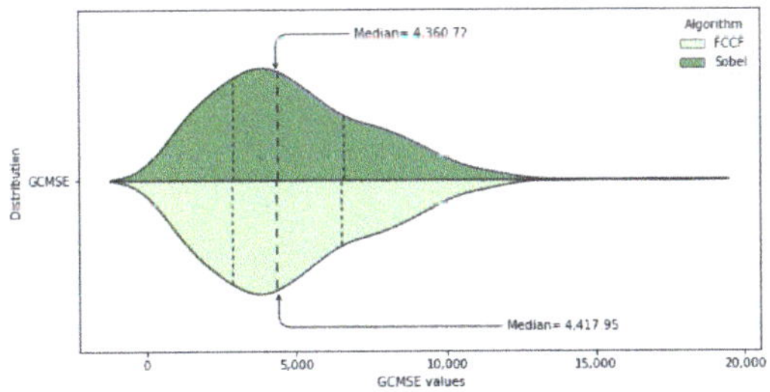

(a)

Figure 6. *Cont.*

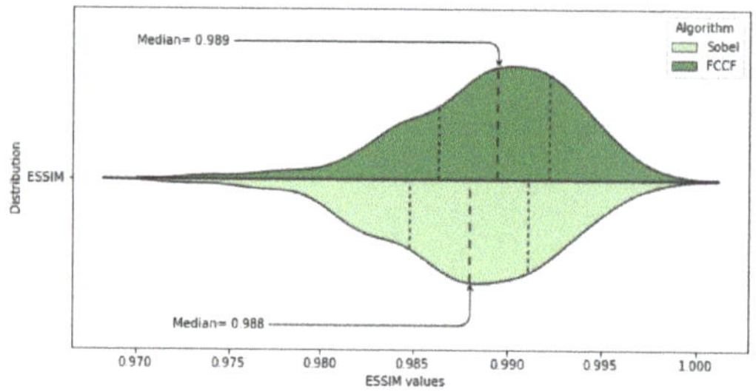

(**b**)

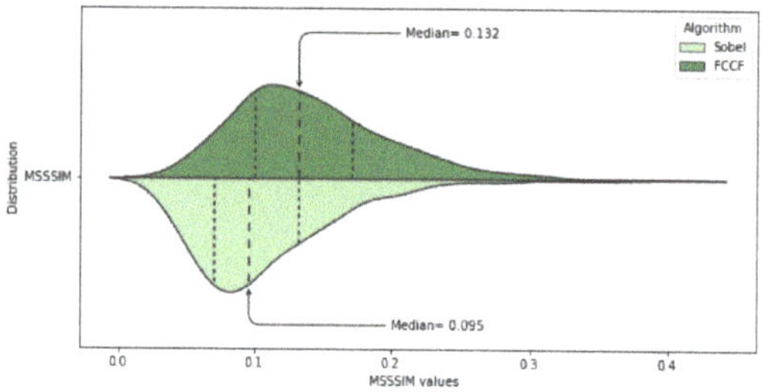

(**c**)

Figure 6. Frequency of K_p values expressed as a percentage. (**a**) GCMSE, (**b**) ESSIM, (**c**) MSSSIM.

Deviant Filter Performance Conditions

We found that the filter is unable to find edges for some binary images. Figure 7 shows an example that illustrates this.

We expected that the FCCF would generate a cross-like shape; however, it was not the case. This sets a constraint in achievable applications of the FCCF.

(**a**)

(**b**)

Figure 7. Output of the proposed FCCF for binary images. (**a**) Input binary image. (**b**) Output binary image. These figures illustrate how the FCCF fails in finding the edge map of a binary images.

For this reason, we do not recommend using the FCCF for computing edge maps of binary images.

7. Conclusions

In this paper, we proposed a new class of edge-oriented filters for grayscale images, determined the filter's parameters, conducted a series of experiments to assess both its performance as an edge filter and the influence of parameters on its overall behavior, and compared the proposed system to standard edge filters.

We determined that parameter K_p influences the edge map of the filter outputs; experimentation revealed that values within the interval $\frac{1}{10} \leq K_p \leq \frac{1}{2}$ are suitable for edge filtering according to the criteria of maximizing the MSSSIM and GCMSE metrics. On the other hand, we explored the possibility that the output edge map would be related to some statistics of the image; however, we did not ascertain a definitive relationship between the image's statistics and the value of K_p that would lead to a model for calculating an optimal K_p for maximizing the ESSIM metric. The investigation on this subject involved exploring whether K_p correlates with some image statistics such as the mean, variance, kurtosis, skewness, and entropy, which at first we hypothesized might relate to edge content in an image; however, our experimental results did not support this hypothesis, suggesting that these metrics and K_p are unrelated. Therefore, this parameter must be determined by the user. From our experiments, we concluded that a $K_p \leq \frac{1}{2}$ value is adequate for most images. We recommend setting K_p at smaller values for images that contain textures such as grass or thick animal hair, such as the second illustrative example in Appendix C.

The evidence indicates that by using this value of K_p, the FCCF computes an edge map with higher quality than the well-established filters we considered in this study.

The main drawback we identified is that the FCCF is unable to find edge maps in binary images, and thus, we do not recommend the FCCF for applications where binary images need to be processed; however, the FCCF preserved the edges well, thus it leads to a study focused on adapting the FCCF for filtering binary images; this research direction was not followed here since it requires a re-design of the filter, and we think this new design will be incompatible with the theory presented in this paper, and as a consequence, we believe such a study will lead to another class of filters.

Future works include assessing the performance under challenging scenarios common in real-world applications, such as noise, variable light conditions, and real-time image processing. Another research direction is to explore the potential improvements in image processing algorithms resulting from replacing the corresponding edge filter with the FCCF approach, which envisions promising perspectives given the wide variety of topics that make use of edge filters to accomplish various computer vision tasks. Yet, another research direction is to assess the performance of the FCCF for filtering medical images, and finally, another work is tuning the filter for finding edges of binary images, which is currently a limitation as discussed above.

Based on the experimental results, we believe that target applications might include machine inspection, object recognition, and pattern recognition, among others, in cases where designers prefer to avoid solutions based on machine learning models or deep learning models.

Author Contributions: Conceptualization, M.G.-L. and H.V.-L.; methodology, M.G.-L., H.V.-L. and M.N.-M.; formal analysis, J.R.G.-M.; software, L.J.M.-M. and E.G.P.-R.; investigation, J.R.G.-M.; validation, M.N.-M. and H.P.-M. All authors have read and agreed to the published version of the manuscript.

Funding: This research received no external funding.

Institutional Review Board Statement: Not applicable.

Informed Consent Statement: Not applicable.

Data Availability Statement: The dataset utilized in this study is the The Berkeley Segmentation Dataset and Benchmark available at https://www2.eecs.berkeley.edu/Research/Projects/CS/vision/bsds/ (accessed on 12 February 2024) [19].

Acknowledgments: The authors thank the Universidad Veracruzana for their support in this work. Also, we want to thank Darin Lovaas for helping to proofread this manuscript.

Conflicts of Interest: The authors declare no conflicts of interest.

Appendix A. The Fractional Model of the Cross-Correlation Equation

In this appendix, we present the key concepts for deriving the Fractional Cross-correlation model for matching signals defined by Equation (2). To reach this goal, firstly, we will comment briefly the fractional calculus derivation formula, and then the fractional model itself.

Appendix A.1. Fractional Calculus Basics

Recalling the derivative of order α has the form:

$$\frac{d^{\alpha}}{dx^{\alpha}}f(x), \tag{A1}$$

where scientists consider the derivative order α as an integer; unlike this perspective on derivatives, fractional calculus studies the implications of α being a fractional number instead of an integer, and furthermore, this theory also covers the cases when the derivative order is a complex number.

One of the most essential formulas for derivatives is the corresponding to functions of the type $f(x) = x^k$; the Riemman-Liouville derivative is a formula intended for calculating fractional derivatives of order α for functions of the type $f(x) = x^k$ and is defined as follows:

$$\frac{d^{\alpha}}{dx^{\alpha}}x^k = \frac{\Gamma(k+1)}{\Gamma(k-\alpha+1)}x^{k-\alpha}, \tag{A2}$$

for any value of derivative order α and $\Gamma(z)$ is the Gamma function. A useful extension of this result is:

$$\frac{d^{\alpha}}{dx^{\alpha}}(x+a)^k = \frac{\Gamma(k+1)}{\Gamma(k-\alpha+1)}(x+a)^{k-\alpha}, \tag{A3}$$

with a being an arbitrary constant.

Appendix A.2. Signal Matching Model

The fractional Cross-correlation model we discuss in this paper was developed originally for detecting digital watermarks embedded using the following rule:

$$y_i = x_i + gw_i \tag{A4}$$

From the embedding rule defined by (A4), we get for Gaussian channels $x_i = y_i - gw_i \in N(\mu, \sigma)$, so, the likelihood function is:

$$L(\theta) = \prod_{i=1}^{N} \frac{1}{\sqrt{2\pi\sigma^2}} \exp\left[-\frac{1}{2}\left(\frac{y_i - gw_i - \mu}{\sigma}\right)^2\right] = \frac{1}{(2\pi\sigma^2)^{\frac{N}{2}}} \exp\left[-\frac{1}{2}\sum_{i=1}^{N}\left(\frac{y_i - gw_i - \mu}{\sigma}\right)^2\right] \tag{A5}$$

To simplify, logarithm is taken to get:

$$L = -\frac{N}{2}\ln(2\pi\sigma^2) - \frac{1}{2}\sum_{i=1}^{N}\left(\frac{y_i - gw_i - \mu}{\sigma}\right)^2 \tag{A6}$$

Now, using algebraic manipulations, we reduce (A6) to:

$$L = -\frac{N\ln(2\pi\sigma^2) + N - 1}{2} + \frac{g}{\sigma^2}\sum_{i=1}^{N} y_i w_i - \frac{Ng^2}{2\sigma^2} \tag{A7}$$

Unlike classical approaches which take the derivative to maximize the last likelihood function, a fractional derivative is computed instead using (A2) to get:

$$\frac{\partial^\alpha L}{\partial g^\alpha} = -\frac{N\ln(2\pi\sigma^2)+N-1}{2\Gamma(1-\alpha)}g^{-\alpha} + \frac{g^{1-\alpha}}{\Gamma(2-\alpha)\sigma^2}\sum_{i=1}^{N} y_i w_i - \frac{Ng^{2-\alpha}}{\Gamma(3-\alpha)\sigma^2} \quad \text{(A8)}$$

Now, to advance in computing the maximum of (A8), we let it be zero, in addition, we multiply by g^α and get the following equation:

$$0 = -\frac{N\ln(2\pi\sigma^2)+N-1}{2\Gamma(1-\alpha)} + \frac{g}{\Gamma(2-\alpha)\sigma^2}\sum_{i=1}^{N} y_i w_i - \frac{Ng^2}{\Gamma(3-\alpha)\sigma^2} \quad \text{(A9)}$$

It is a quadratic equation for g, and thus, the estimator for the embedding gain is:

$$\hat{g} = \frac{\Gamma(3-\alpha)}{2\Gamma(2-\alpha)}\frac{1}{N}\sum_{i=1}^{N} y_i^* w_i + \frac{\Gamma(3-\alpha)\sigma^2}{2N}\sqrt{\frac{1}{\Gamma^2(2-\alpha)\sigma^4}\left(\sum_{i=1}^{N} y_i^* w_i\right)^2 - \frac{2N[2NH-1]}{\Gamma(3-\alpha)\Gamma(1-\alpha)\sigma^2}} \quad \text{(A10)}$$

where $H = \ln(\sqrt{2\pi\sigma^2}\mathrm{e})$.

This fractional model generalizes the cross-correlation formula as one gets Equation (1) by letting $\alpha = 1$ which is the derivative of order 1, or in other words, the classical approach to compute a first order derivative.

Gonzalez-Lee et al. [5] determined that the minimum variance of this equation is reached for $\alpha = \frac{1}{2}$; thus, using this value, we get $\Gamma(2-\alpha) = \frac{\sqrt{\pi}}{2}$, $\Gamma(1-\alpha) = \sqrt{\pi}$, and $\Gamma(3-\alpha) = \frac{3}{4}\sqrt{\pi}$, leading to the following equation:

$$\hat{g} = \frac{3}{4}\frac{1}{N}\sum_{i=1}^{N} y_i^* w_i + \frac{3}{4}\frac{1}{N}\sqrt{\left(\sum_{i=1}^{N} y_i^* w_i\right)^2 - \frac{2}{3}\sigma^2 N[2NH-1]} \quad \text{(A11)}$$

Through experimentation, it was noted that (A11) is complex-valued when y and w are matching signals. The first term of this equation was observed to provide a coarse approximation to the correlation where as, the second term exhibits an almost ideal behavior, that is to say, a close to zero response for non-matching signals and a higher response for matching signals; as a consequence, only the complex part of the equation will be used as signal matcher as follows:

$$d = -\,\mathrm{Im}\left(\frac{3}{4}\frac{1}{N}\sqrt{\left(\sum_{i-1}^{N} y_i^* w_i\right)^2 - \frac{2}{3}\sigma^2 N[2NH-1]}\right) \quad \text{(A12)}$$

Also, it was observed that this detector is highly biased, to remove the bias, we consider y and w be orthogonal and as a consequence, the sum equal zero, so we eliminate the bias in this way:

$$d = -\,\mathrm{Im}\left(\frac{3}{4}\frac{1}{N}\sqrt{\left(\sum_{i=1}^{N} y_i^* w_i\right)^2 - \frac{2}{3}\sigma^2 N[2NH-1]} - \theta\right) \quad \text{(A13)}$$

where:

$$\theta = \frac{3}{4}\frac{1}{N}\sqrt{\frac{2}{3}\sigma^2 N[2NH-1]} \quad \text{(A14)}$$

Finally, The threshold equation proposed in [5] is defined as:

$$Th = k_p\sigma^2\sqrt{\frac{H}{\epsilon}}, \quad \text{(A15)}$$

which was determined empirically as the authors argued.

Appendix B. The Influence of Parameter K_p on the Edge Quality

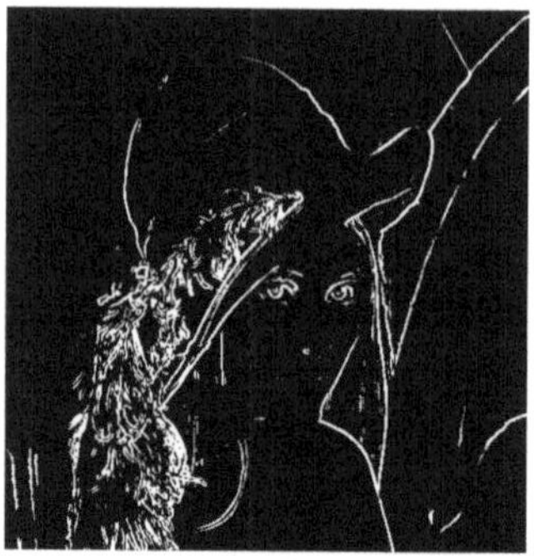

(**a**) $K_p = 0.2$

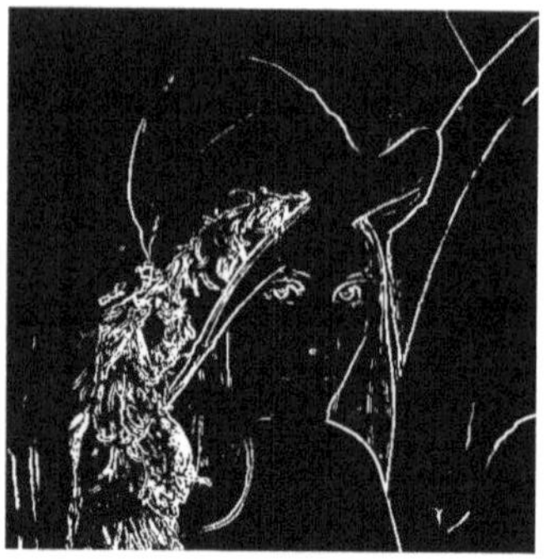

(**b**) $K_p = 0.3$

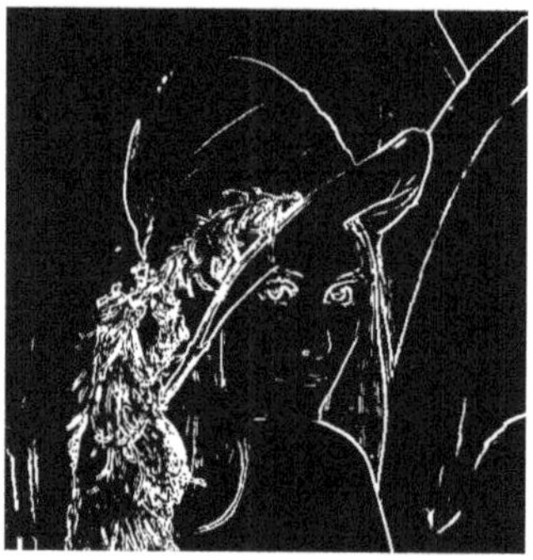

(**c**) $K_p = 0.4$

(**d**) $K_p = 0.6$

(**e**) $K_p = 0.8$

(**f**) $K_p = 0.9$

Figure A1. Resulting edge maps for several values of the parameter K_p.

Appendix C. Additional Examples of the Influence of Parameter K_P on the Resulting Edge Quality

(**a**) Original Image

(**b**) $K_p = 0.1$

(**c**) $K_p = 0.2$

(**d**) $K_p = 0.3$

(**e**) $K_p = 0.4$

(**f**) $K_p = 0.5$

(**g**) $K_p = 0.6$

(**h**) $K_p = 0.7$

Figure A2. An example of a typical case.

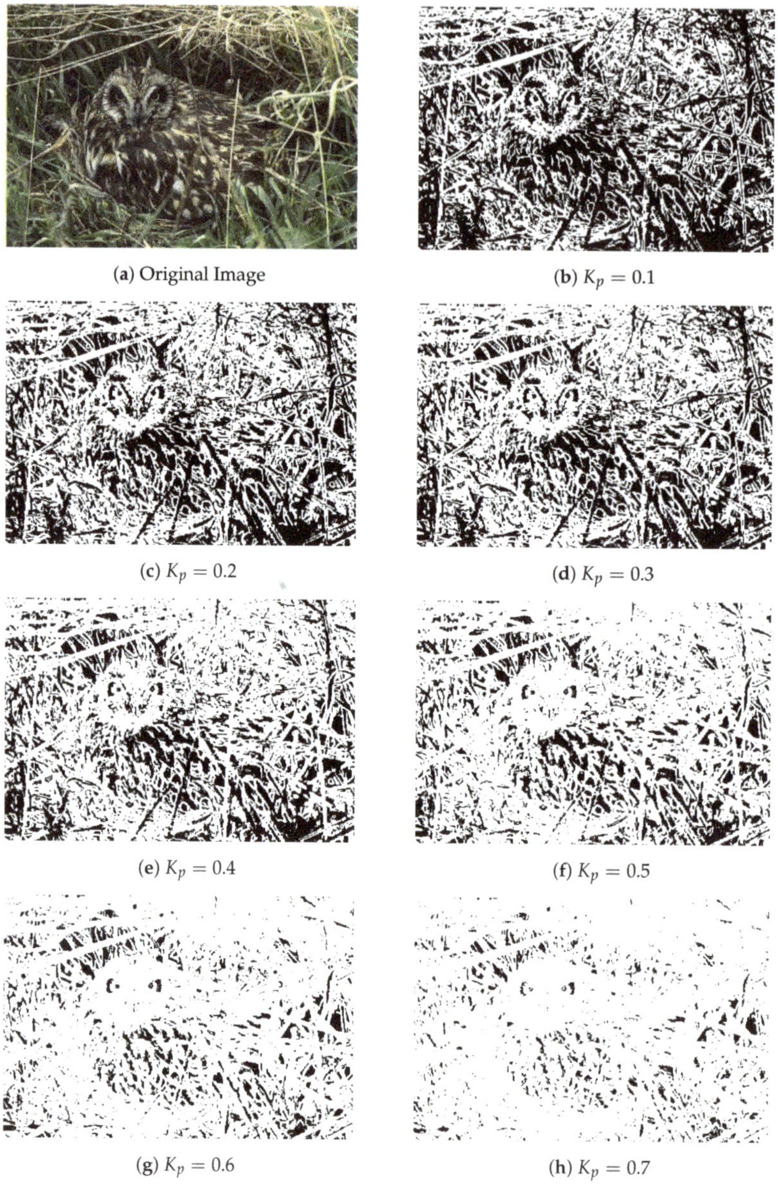

(a) Original Image (b) $K_p = 0.1$

(c) $K_p = 0.2$ (d) $K_p = 0.3$

(e) $K_p = 0.4$ (f) $K_p = 0.5$

(g) $K_p = 0.6$ (h) $K_p = 0.7$

Figure A3. An example of the filter's output for a highly textured image case.

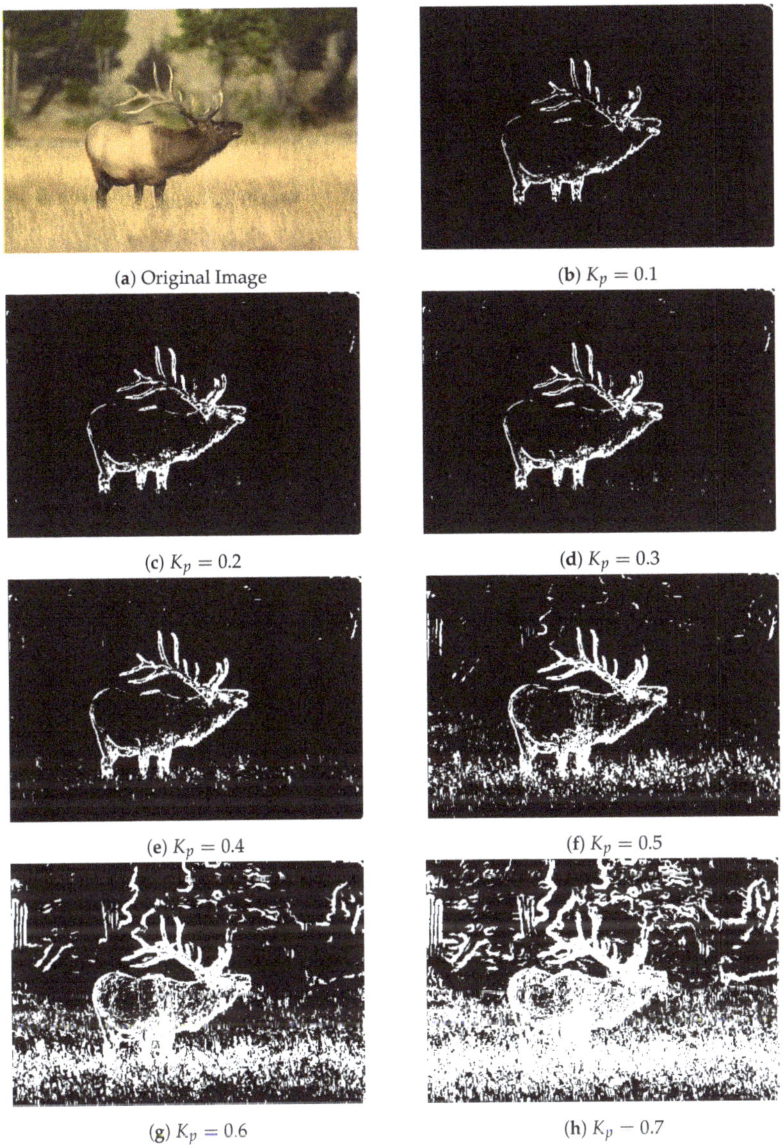

(**a**) Original Image (**b**) $K_p = 0.1$
(**c**) $K_p = 0.2$ (**d**) $K_p = 0.3$
(**e**) $K_p = 0.4$ (**f**) $K_p = 0.5$
(**g**) $K_p = 0.6$ (**h**) $K_p - 0.7$

Figure A4. Another example of a typical case.

References

1. Shao, Y.; Yuan, S.; Zhou, X.; Ye, J. Edge Detection Algorithm of MRI Medical Image Based on Artificial Neural Network. *Procedia Comput. Sci.* **2022**, *208*, 136–144. [CrossRef]
2. Ahmadian, N.; Sedaghat, A.; Mohammadi, N.; Aghdami-Nia, M. Deep-Learning-Based Edge Detection for Improving Building Footprint Extraction from Satellite Images. *Environ. Sci. Proc.* **2024**, *29*, 61. [CrossRef]
3. Chaduvula, K.; Dnvsls, I.; Markapudi, B.; Kalyanapu, S. Quantum edge detection of medical images using novel enhanced quantum representation and hill entropy approach. *Signal Image Video Process.* **2024**, *18*, 1803–1819. [CrossRef]
4. Liu, L.; Liu, Z.; Hou, A.; Qian, X.; Wang, H. Adaptive edge detection of rebar thread head image based on improved Canny operator. *IET Image Process.* **2024**, *18*, 1145–1160. [CrossRef]

5. Gonzalez-Lee, M.; Vazquez-Leal, H.; Gomez-Aguilar, J.F.; Morales-Mendoza, L.J.; Jimenez-Fernandez, V.M.; Laguna-Camacho, J.R.; Calderon-Ramon, C.M. Exploring the Cross-correlation as a Means for Detecting Digital Watermarks And its Reformulation Into The Fractional Calculus Framework. *IEEE Access* **2018**, *6*, 71699–71718. [CrossRef]
6. Gonzalez-Lee, M.; Vazquez-Leal, H.; Morales-Mendoza, L.J.; Nakano-Miyatake, M.; Perez-Meana, H.; Laguna-Camacho, J.R. Statistical Assessment of Discrimination Capabilities of a Fractional Calculus Based Image Watermarking System for Gaussian Watermarks. *Entropy* **2021**, *23*, 255. [CrossRef] [PubMed]
7. Mekideche, M.; Ferdi, Y. Edge Detection Optimization Using Fractional Order Calculus. *Int. Arab. J. Inf. Technol. (IAJIT)* **2019**, *16*, 37–42.
8. Li, D.; Zhao, C.; Jiang, M.; Huang, Y.; Li, Y. Fractional Order Edge Detection Method. In Proceedings of the 2019 IEEE 11th International Conference on Communication Software and Networks (ICCSN), Chongqing, China, 12–15 July 2019; pp. 529–534. [CrossRef]
9. Nandal, A.; Gamboa-Rosales, H.; Dhaka, A.; Celaya-Padilla, J.M.; Galvan-Tejada, J.I.; Galvan-Tejada, C.E.; Martinez-Ruiz, F.J.; Guzman-Valdivia, C. Image Edge Detection Using Fractional Calculus with Feature and Contrast Enhancement. *Circuits Syst Signal Process.* **2018**, *37*, 3946–3972. [CrossRef]
10. Ghanbari, B.; Atangana, A. Some new edge detecting techniques based on fractional derivatives with non-local and non-singular kernels. *Adv. Differ. Equ.* **2020**, *2020*, 435. [CrossRef]
11. Varga, D. Full-Reference Image Quality Assessment Based on Grünwald–Letnikov Derivative, Image Gradients, and Visual Saliency. *Electronics* **2022**, *11*, 559. [CrossRef]
12. Henriques, M.; Valério, D.; Gordo, P.; Melicio, R. Fractional-Order Colour Image Processing. *Mathematics* **2021**, *9*, 457. [CrossRef]
13. Harshavardhan, Y.; Anitha, G. Analysis of Accuracy in Identification of Bone Fracture using Canny Edge and Prewitt Edge Detection Approach. In Proceedings of the 2023 International Conference on Advances in Computing, Communication and Applied Informatics (ACCAI), Chennai, India, 25–26 May 2023. [CrossRef]
14. Zhang, J.; Zhu, Q.; Song, F.; Zhang, L.; Wang, J.; Liu, C. Multi-Scale Edge Detection of Crack in Extra-High Arch Dam Based on Orthogonal Wavelet Construction. *Trait. Signal* **2022**, *39*, 977. [CrossRef]
15. Yang, C. Evaluation of edge detection algorithm of frontal image of facial contour in plastic surgery. *Front. Phys.* **2023**, *11*, 1108393. [CrossRef]
16. Begum, J.A.; Sarmah, R. A Hybrid Image Edge Detection Approach for the Images of Tocklai Vegetative Tea Clone Series TV1, TV9, TV10 of Assam. In *International Conference on Information and Communication Technology for Intelligent Systems*; Springer Nature: Singapore, 2023; pp. 403–416.
17. Ye, Z.; Yin, H.; Ye, Y. Multiple Scale Comparative Analysis of Classical, Dynamic and Intelligent Edge Detection Schemes. In *Annual International Conference on Information Management and Big Data*; Springer Nature: Cham, Switzerland, 2022; pp. 207–221.
18. Smith, S.W. *The Scientist and Engineer's Guide to Digital Signal Processing*, 2nd ed.; California Technical Publishing: San Diego, CA, USA, 1997; ISBN 0-9660176-6-8.
19. Martin, D.; Fowlkes, C.; Tal, D.; Malik, J. The Berkeley Segmentation Dataset and Benchmark. Available online: https://www2.eecs.berkeley.edu/Research/Projects/CS/vision/bsds/ (accessed on 12 February 2024).
20. Sadykova, D.; James, A.P. Quality assessment metrics for edge detection and edge-aware filtering: A tutorial review. In Proceedings of the 2017 International Conference on Advances in Computing, Communications and Informatics (ICACCI), Udupi, India, 13–16 September 2017; pp. 2366–2369. [CrossRef]
21. Chen, G.H.; Yang, C.L.; Po, L.M.; Xie, S.L. Edge-Based Structural Similarity for Image Quality Assessment. In Proceedings of the 2006 IEEE International Conference on Acoustics Speech and Signal Processing Proceedings, Toulouse, France, 14–19 May 2006; p. II.. [CrossRef]
22. Zhai, G.; Zhang, W.; Yang, X.; Xu, Y. Image quality assessment metrics based on multi-scale edge presentation. In Proceedings of the IEEE Workshop on Signal Processing Systems Design and Implementation, Athens, Greece, 2–4 November 2005; pp. 331–336. [CrossRef]
23. López-Randulfe, J.; Veiga, C.; Rodríguez-Andina, J.J.; Fariña, J. A quantitative method for selecting denoising filters, based on a new edge-sensitive metric. In Proceedings of the 2017 IEEE International Conference on Industrial Technology (ICIT), Toronto, ON, Canada, 22–25 March 2017; pp. 974–979. [CrossRef]

applied sciences

MDPI

Article

High-Noise Grayscale Image Denoising Using an Improved Median Filter for the Adaptive Selection of a Threshold

Ning Cao * and Yupu Liu

College of Mechanical and Electrical Engineering, Zhengzhou University of Light Industry, Zhengzhou 450002, China; 332202040176@email.zzuli.edu.cn
* Correspondence: ncao@zzuli.edu.cn

Abstract: Grayscale image processing is a key research area in the field of computer vision and image analysis, where image quality and visualization effects may be seriously damaged by high-density salt and pepper noise. A traditional median filter for noise removal may result in poor detail reservation performance under strong noise and the judgment performance of different noise characteristics has strong dependence and rather weak robustness. In order to reduce the effects of high-density salt and pepper noise on image quality when processing high-noise grayscale images, an improved two-dimensional maximum Shannon entropy median filter (TSETMF) is proposed for the adaptive selection of a threshold to enhance the filter performance while stably and effectively retaining the details of the images. The framework of the proposed improved TSETMF algorithm is designed in detail. The noise in images is filtered by means of automatically partitioning a window size, the threshold value of which is adaptively calculated using two-dimensional maximum Shannon entropy. The theoretical model is verified and analyzed through comparative experiments using three kinds of classical grayscale images. The experimental results demonstrate that the proposed improved TSETMF algorithm exhibits better processing performance than that of the traditional filter, with a higher suppression of high-density noise and denoising stability. This stronger ability while processing high-density noise is demonstrated by a higher peak signal-to-noise ratio (PSNR) of 24.97 dB with a 95% noise density located in the classical Lena grayscale image. The better denoising stability, with a noise density from 5% to 95%, is demonstrated by the minor decline in the PSNR of approximately 10.78% relative to a PSNR of 23.10 dB located in the classical Cameraman grayscale image. Furthermore, it can be advanced to promote higher noise filtering and stability for processing high-density salt and pepper noise in grayscale images.

Keywords: image denoising; adaptive filters; filtering theory; image filtering; high-noise grayscale image

1. Introduction

A grayscale image is a significant representation of image information, containing black, white, and different shades of gray, which can be extensively applied in typical fields, such as medical imaging [1], computer vision [2], and image processing [3]. However, because of changes in environmental parameters and equipment accuracy, the actual image obtained always contains noise [4,5] when processed from a grayscale image, including Gaussian noise [6,7], salt and pepper noise [8], and other noise. Salt and pepper noise, as a common type of image impulse noise, can be utilized to simulate imaging sensor or signal transmission errors, resulting in isolated bright spots or dark spots in images [9]. Thus, salt and pepper noise may reduce imaging definition and visualization effects and affect the accuracy of image segmentation, edge detection, and object identification [10]. Therefore, for the sake of guaranteeing the restoration of the original details of an image and eliminating discontinuities, it is crucial to reduce the effects of noise associated with grayscale images.

At present, some methods are being used to denoise grayscale images. For instance, median filtering [11,12], deep learning [13,14], wavelet filtering [15,16], and mean filtering [17,18] are used. These methods can lower the noise effects to improve the grayscale image quality. Median filtering is commonly utilized to effectively remove salt and pepper noise. This can be accomplished by choosing an intermediate value to replace the gray pixel's value ranked inside a window [19]. For instance, Sree et al. employed a modified self-adaptive median filter to improve image quality, exhibiting superiority in terms of time complexity [20]. Toh et al. adopted a self-adaptive fuzzy switch median filter to restrain the salt and pepper noise, with a relatively fair filtering result [21]. However, assuming that high-density noise exists in a grayscale image, it is difficult to judge whether a pixel is noise by ranking median values. This may generate a poor denoising effect in the case of processing high-noise grayscale images [22].

For the sake of more effectively denoising high-density-noise images, a recursion method can be used to improve the median filter, which increases the number of non-noise pixel values in non-marginal areas to reduce the effects of noise on images [23]. However, the recursion median filter may result in replacing some normal pixel values, regardless of the damaged pixels. As a result, a threshold value can be introduced to judge the noise whose traditional selection and comparison may cause an erroneous judgment. Differences in neighboring pixels mean that calculations that are compared with the threshold value can enhance the denoising effects to some degree. In order to more precisely judge whether a pixel has been damaged in a high-density-noise grayscale image, the threshold value of the median filter can be optimized to improve the denoising effects. For example, Gupta et al. adopted a double-threshold method based on averages to detect noise, which had a higher noise detection ability and greater denoising efficiency [24]. Kuma et al., employed a dual-threshold median filter to detect and remove highly damaged images by individually calculating the median and threshold values [25]. Goyal et al., used rank mean values to calculate dual-threshold values and enhance the image denoising accuracy [26]. These filter algorithms can realize a relatively reasonable improvement for median filter threshold values; whereas, the threshold values can be mainly selected according to experience, which has a strong impact on noise detection performance. In a noise probability density function, it may result in a non-smooth approximation decreasing the image noise. Furthermore, it is insufficient and unreliable for the removal of stochastic noises.

With regard to denoising for noise distribution, it is effective to utilize maximum entropy theory to better realize denoising in high-density-noise grayscale images. Maximum entropy theory, maximizing entropy under preset constraint conditions, can acquire the most probable observed value distribution function from a statistical system [27]. Thus, it can be utilized to assess the smooth approximation degree of a probability density function with minimal deviation and maximize the Shannon entropy to estimate the data probability distributions between noise and non-noise [28]. Correspondingly, two-dimensional maximum Shannon entropy, representative of the randomness of the variable, can be adopted to explore the information of an image from the relationships between pixels. Thus, an optimal threshold can be automatically calculated using a coupled two-dimensional gray histogram with maximum entropy [29]. Two-dimensional maximum Shannon entropy can be applied in image segmentation [30,31], signal processing [32], and other areas that still lack applications in image denoising, especially in high-density-noise grayscale images.

Consequently, to achieve effective denoising for high-density grayscale images, a unique denoising approach to improve the median filter is proposed using two-dimensional maximum Shannon entropy for the adaptive selection of a threshold, taking advantage of image spatial characteristics to enhance the noise detection efficiency and denoising accuracy. Based on the two-dimensional maximum Shannon entropy of an input grayscale image, a threshold value can be calculated and a window size can be selected to replace a median value. By suppressing the effects of noise in a larger area, a detailed image can be reserved to accomplish the denoising of salt and pepper noise more efficiently and stably. In the future, by advancing a two-dimensional maximum Shannon entropy partitioning algorithm for denoising, the issue of high-density salt and pepper noise in grayscale images can be addressed.

2. Two-Dimensional Maximum Shannon Entropy

In order to conduct the digital processing of an image, it is conventional to adopt a two-dimensional matrix to represent the grayscale image [33,34]. This can effectively reflect the gray-level distributions of images [35,36], resulting in successful denoising. The location of noise should be determined before denoising occurs as the resulting threshold selection can directly influence the discriminating effects of noise [37,38]. In a single threshold system, a pixel value less or greater than the preset one can be regarded as noise [39]. The ranges of the pixel values used to identify a noise point can often be large, resulting in an increase in error detection. However, a self-adaptive dual-threshold system, with a relatively minor noise recognition range, may decrease the probability of error detection [24]. However, during the processing of high-density noise in a grayscale image, it is also unstable and difficult to handle. Hence, in order to address the poor denoising issue, it is necessary to select a better threshold value to fit with the automatic window changes.

To improve the noise detection effects during selections, a threshold value can be obtained using the gray levels of an image [40,41], which can be expressed by a gray-level histogram formed using a two-dimensional matrix [42,43]. The selection of a gray threshold may be achieved by using the valley value between two peaks in the two-dimensional histogram [44,45]. Because a common gray-level histogram cannot accurately represent the randomness of noise, the processing effects of the complex images may be limited. By contrast, two-dimensional maximum Shannon entropy can more accurately represent the randomness of noise by employing more image information. In addition, the gray level and noise distributions of image pixels also present randomness; thus, a Shannon threshold can be selected using a two-dimensional gray histogram.

In view of the Shannon threshold value method being widely used in signal processing [46,47], two-dimensional maximum Shannon entropy can be utilized to select an optimal threshold value by calculating the two-dimensional gray-level histogram of the image coupled with maximum entropy theory [48]. As a result, it can be used to obtain better image processing effects, especially for noise images. Also, a multi-dimensional histogram constructed using a grayscale image and other characteristics can be optimized, including neighborhood gradient and neighborhood variance.

For a grayscale image, the information entropy H using Shannon can be defined as follows [49]:

$$H = -\sum_{i-1}^{L} p_i \ln p_i \tag{1}$$

where L is the gray-level number for inputting an image and p is the discrete distribution probability.

In a two-dimensional gray-level histogram, the threshold point (s, t) is a division point for segmenting the image foreground and background, where s represents a threshold value using the image's gray values to segment the image and t represents a threshold value using the average gray values in the neighborhood to segment the image. Therefore, for a threshold point (s, t), two posterior probabilities, $P_0(s, t)$ and $P_1(s, t)$, of the target foreground and background can be expressed as:

$$\begin{cases} P_0(s,t) = \sum\limits_{i=0}^{s} \sum\limits_{j=0}^{t} p_{ij} \\ P_1(s,t) = \sum\limits_{i=s+1}^{L-1} \sum\limits_{j=t+1}^{L-1} p_{ij} \end{cases} \tag{2}$$

where $P_0(s, t)$ represents the posterior probabilities of the image pixel gray values and the neighborhood average gray values are less than or equal to the threshold values s and t, respectively. Also, $P_1(s, t)$ represents the posterior probabilities of the image pixel gray values and the neighborhood average gray values are greater than the threshold values s and t, respectively.

For a threshold point (s, t) in a two-dimensional image, the Shannon entropy H of the target foreground and background on a two-dimensional gray-level histogram can be represented as:

$$\begin{cases} H_0(s,t) = -\sum_{i=0}^{s}\sum_{j=0}^{t} \frac{p_{ij}}{P_0(s,t)} \ln \frac{p_{ij}}{P_0(s,t)} \\ H_1(s,t) = -\sum_{i=s+1}^{L-1}\sum_{j=t+1}^{L-1} \frac{p_{ij}}{P_1(s,t)} \ln \frac{p_{ij}}{P_1(s,t)}. \end{cases} \tag{3}$$

Hence, the criterion function threshold value T of two-dimensional maximum Shannon entropy can be defined as:

$$T = \arg \max_{0<t<L-1} |H_0(s,t) + H_1(s,t)|^2. \tag{4}$$

Here, a threshold value T can be acquired using two-dimensional maximum Shannon entropy to address the poor denoising of high-density salt and pepper noise. Compared with the entropy threshold method and the gray-level histogram threshold method, two-dimensional maximum Shannon entropy can express the image randomness and noise distribution more strongly to process complex high-density-noise images. Thus, it can automatically calculate the best threshold value and combine the median filter to realize self-adaptive denoising. Correspondingly, it may be more effective to enhance noise detection, denoising efficiency, and precision.

3. Improved TSETMF Algorithm

In order to address the balance between protecting the image detail and eliminating noise, a median filter can be improved using two-dimensional maximum Shannon entropy to realize the adaptive threshold. Under the calculated threshold, noise judgments can be achieved by using different-sized windows. A median can be replaced in a 5 × 5 window to fit the noise level for increasing the filtering effects. Hence, the proposed improved TSETMF algorithm may achieve denoising while protecting the image detail as well.

3.1. Improved Self-Adaptive Median Filter

A median filter is a common image denoising method [50] used to eliminate isolated noise by utilizing the median of each pixel value in the neighborhood area to replace the targeted pixel point. This may allow the neighborhood pixel values to be more appropriate and also enable the image detail and marginal information to be retained. Salt and pepper noise can be denoised using the median filter to acquire a satisfactory filtering effect and image edge feature [51,52].

After median filtering occurs, the image pixel value $f(x, y)$ at the coordinates (x, y) can be expressed as:

$$f(x,y) = median(l(x+i, y+j)) \tag{5}$$

where $l(x + i, y + j)$ is the neighborhood pixel values relative to the centered pixel point (x, y) and *median*() represents the median selection of the neighborhood pixel values.

During the denoising process, a two-dimensional 3 × 3 window can be employed to filter the image. Compared with the sizes of the pixel values within a certain range, a median can be selected as the new center pixel. However, the same local window size can result in conflicts between the protection of the image detail and noise elimination [53]; thus, a modified filtering method can be applied, such as the weighted median filter [54,55] or self-adaptive median filter [56]. As the weighted median filter can conduct fuzzy processing of an image, it may lose some of the image detail during the filtering of high-density noise. However, the self-adaptive median filter can select a window size that fits different noise levels, thus achieving denoising coupled with image detail protection. Moreover, the major density of salt and pepper noise can be filtered by the self-adaptive median filter to acquire clearer images [57]. Thus, the self-adaptive median filter can be utilized to change the window size according to the pixel values for different areas.

In Figure 1, denoising principle comparisons for the improved self-adaptive median filter are presented to demonstrate the effects of this more effective filtering method. Figure 1c,d represent the processing step of central pixel value ranking and replacement by adopting the self-adaptive median filter and the improved self-adaptive median filter, respectively. The improved self-adaptive median filter can be compared to the original filter to demonstrate the denoising advantage. In the self-adaptive median filtering algorithm, the processed pixel will be not employed in the following ranking, guaranteeing the independence and stability of the filtering process; however, when the noise density becomes higher, the ranked median value may be turned into a noise value. This may result in poor denoising effects, as seen in Figure 1a,b. During the partial area processing shown in Figure 1b, pixels 0 and 255 may be regarded as noise. In a 5 × 5 window, the pending pixel value in a random area is 255 and, then, the ranked pixel values are 0, 0, 0, 0, 0, 0, 0, 0, 0, 0, 0, 0, 127, 255, 255, 255, 255, 255, 255, 255, 255, 255, 255, 255, 255, and 255. Thus, the replaced central pixel value is still 255 when adopting the middle value, as seen in Figure 1c. The replaced pixel is still the noise, which may also lead to poor denoising effects. This may be interpreted by the effects of the larger-density salt and pepper noise that turn the ranked pixel values into noise values. Moreover, each ranked and replaced central pixel value can be realized based on the original noise image and will be not applied in the next processing step.

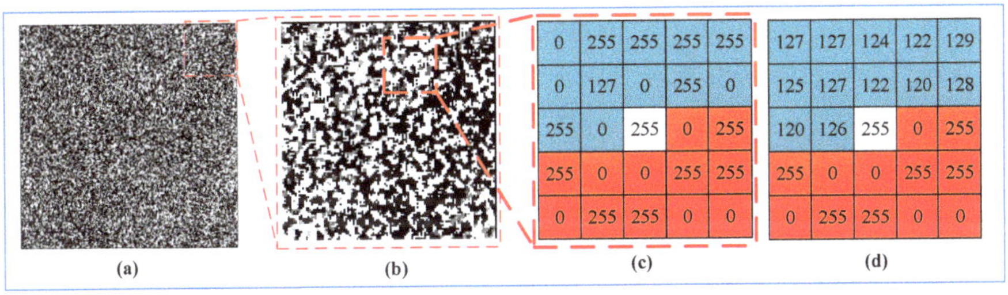

Figure 1. Denoising principle comparisons for the improved self-adaptive median filter. (**a**) A self-adaptive median filtering image after processing 95% salt and pepper noise. (**b**) Partially enlarged details. (**c**) Gray values of self-adaptive median filtering image. (**d**) Gray values of improved median filtering image using recursion method and self-adaptive window. The white central value, 255, as the original value, represents the pending processing pixel point. The blue section represents the processed pixel points. The red section represents unprocessed pixel points.

For the sake of addressing this problem, the self-adaptive median filter can be improved by utilizing the recursion method combined with a self-adaptive window. The basic principle adopts the recursion concept to filter an image. After selecting an appropriate filtering window, the median value can be regarded as the new current pixel value by comparing the current pixel value with the neighboring pixel values. At this stage, this new current pixel value, as the input of the next pixel, can proceed with the recursion operations until the filtering process has finished. Thus, this improved self-adaptive median filter may retain and deliver non-noise pixel values more effectively. Median replacement can be conducted using the improved self-adaptive median filter, whose central value represents the pending pixel value 255, as seen in Figure 1d. At this stage, after ranking the pixel values in a 5 × 5 window, the ranked pixel values are 0, 0, 0, 0, 0, 0, 120, 120, 122, 122, 124, 125, 126, 127, 127, 127, 128, 129, 255, 255, 255, 255, 255, 255, and 255. By adopting the middle value, the replaced central pixel value is 126, which may then participate in the subsequent ranking and replacement. By adopting the recursion method, the improved self-adaptive median filter window can possess larger non-noise pixel values and, thus, turn the ranked middle values into mostly non-noise pixel values. This approach can also be utilized to demonstrate the effectiveness of the denoising effects by taking advantage of the improved self-adaptive median filter.

Compared with the traditional self-adaptive median filter, the improved self-adaptive median filter, adopting the recursion method and self-adaptive window, can conduct noise judgment using different filtering windows and its ranked values include the previous pixel values after performing the median replacement. This may greatly reduce the adverse effects of high-density noise. Assuming that the signal and noise values are flipped, the accuracy of noise judgment and median replacement can be ensured to output the excellent high-noise removal effects by means of the improved self-adaptive median filter.

3.2. TSETMF Concept

The concept of the improved TSETMF algorithm can be stated as follows. After a grayscale noise image with matrix $M \times N$ is input, the initial filter window size can be set as 3×3. Firstly, taking the center of the initial filter window to coincide with the first 3×3 region center, window B can be expressed as:

$$B = \begin{pmatrix} a_{11} & a_{12} & a_{13} \\ a_{21} & a_{22} & a_{23} \\ a_{31} & a_{32} & a_{33} \end{pmatrix} \tag{6}$$

where the gray levels of nine pixels can be shown as $a_{11}, a_{12}, a_{13}, a_{21}, a_{22}, a_{23}, a_{31}, a_{32}$, and a_{33} and parameter a_{ij} represents the element at row i and column j in the 3×3 window.

Afterwards, a threshold value T_K (K represents the threshold value numbers: K = 0, 1, 2, 3, ...) can be set. At this stage, if the pixel values at a_{ij} differ from one another, the window pixel probability $P_{11} = P_{12} = \ldots P_{ij} \ldots = P_{33} = 1/9$ ($L = 9$). Assuming that the threshold values s, t can be used to realize segmentations, foreground probability P_0 and background probability P_1 can be obtained. The threshold values can be expressed as:

$$s, t \in \left(a_{ij}, s < t\right). \tag{7}$$

The Shannon entropy H_0 and H_1 of the target and background gray-level distributions can be individually calculated as:

$$\begin{cases} H_0 = -\sum\limits_{i=0}^{s}\sum\limits_{j=0}^{t} \frac{p_{ij}}{P_0} \ln \frac{p_{ij}}{P_0} \\ H_1 = -\sum\limits_{i=s+1}^{L-1}\sum\limits_{j=t+1}^{L-1} \frac{p_{ij}}{P_1} \ln \frac{p_{ij}}{P_1}. \end{cases} \tag{8}$$

Taking the image's gray-level distributions and the amount of information between different gray levels into account, the threshold value T_K can be defined based on the entropy difference calculation in the two-dimensional maximum Shannon entropy, i.e.,

$$T_k = \arg \min_{0<t<L-1} |H_0 - H_1|^2. \tag{9}$$

Then, the sum of the pixel difference D_1 between the filtering window's central values and neighboring areas can be calculated as:

$$D_1 = sum\left|a_{ij} - a_{22}\right|. \tag{10}$$

Correspondingly, the average value D of the pixel difference can be expressed as:

$$D = \frac{D_1}{9}. \tag{11}$$

Then, the average value D is taken and compared with the entropy threshold T_K. If $D > T_K$, it may be regarded as noise. Conversely, it may be regarded as non-noise. By updating each function value, the next pixel point can be calculated.

In addition, if a noise point has been identified in a 3 × 3 window, the filter window can be adjusted to 5 × 5. Each function value can be updated using the pixel values in the current filter window. Correspondingly, the gray values in the new window area can be regarded as b_{ij} $(i, j = 1, 2, 3, 4, 5)$. Assuming that $D < T_K$, this pixel value can be viewed as a normal, undamaged pixel value; otherwise, the median value is employed to replace it and the filtering process is conducted. By updating each value, the next pixel will be addressed until all pixels in the targeted image have been processed completely.

It should be noted that when making noise judgments, 3 × 3 and 5 × 5 windows may be used when processing. They also may be utilized to conduct the median replacement for a low-density-noise grayscale image. However, along with an increase in high-density noise, the probability of non-noise pixel points decreases, which may result in poor image denoising effects. Hence, in the proposed improved TSETMF algorithm, median filter pixel replacement is conducted using the 5 × 5 window.

In the proposed TSETMF algorithm, a 3 × 3 window can be used first to conduct noise judgment. If the central value of the window is judged as non-noise, it is not utilized in the subsequent filtering process with minor computational effort. On the contrary, the window size cannot be adjusted to fit the noise levels in different areas. This can result in inflexible denoising effects when processing the noise in different areas. In high-density-noise areas in particular, the smaller window is unable to adequately identify the noise; thus, the accuracy of the median replacement may be limited. However, adopting the 5 × 5 window can improve the filtering effects with relatively minor computational effort, which can also avoid the problem of misjudging details as noise. In addition, the larger window may promote the accuracy of the median replacement; however, the filtering effects present a modest improvement with the increase in the window size and, correspondingly, more computational effort is required. Consequently, in view of the filtering effects and efficiency, two filtering windows, 3 × 3 and 5 × 5, can be adopted to achieve better denoising for high-density-noise grayscale images.

3.3. TSETMF Process

According to the above-mentioned design concept, the design process of the improved TSETMF algorithm can be described as follows. Figure 2 shows a flow chart of the proposed TSETMF algorithm.

The relevant steps of the improved median filter using two-dimensional maximum Shannon entropy for use with high-noise grayscale images are as follows:

Step 1: Input a noise image $N = (N(m, n))$, composed by pixel $N(m, n)$;

Step 2: Acquire the gray-level histogram and judge the contrast ratio;

Step 3: Filter, including five substeps;

Substep 3.1: Set a filter window to 3 × 3. A threshold value T can be calculated using the two-dimensional maximum Shannon entropy threshold value method, where the entropy threshold $T_K = T$, $T = \arg\min_{0<t<L-1} |H_0(s,t) - H_1(s,t)|^2$, and the initial K value is 0, $K = K + 1$ (K represents the number of threshold values T);

Substep 3.2: Calculate the sum of the pixel difference $D_1 = sum\,|\,a_{ij} - a_{22}\,|$. If $D_1/9 < T_K$, a_{22} is non-noise, move the filter window to the next pixel point and return to Substep 3.1;

Substep 3.3: Otherwise, carry out the next step;

Substep 3.4: Adjust the filter window to 5 × 5, update the entropy threshold T_K, $K = K + 1$, and calculate $D_2 = sum\,|\,b_{ij} - b_{33}\,|$. If $D_2/25 < T_K$, b_{33} is non-noise and, therefore, the filter window can be moved to the next pixel point. Return to Substep 3.1;

Substep 3.5: Otherwise, replace b_{33} by utilizing the median and, then, reserve and deliver the replaced value to conduct the next filtering step based on the recursion method. Move the filter window to the next pixel point and return to Substep 3.1;

Step 4: The filter window traverses the whole image and finishes filtering;

Step 5: The denoised image is outputted.

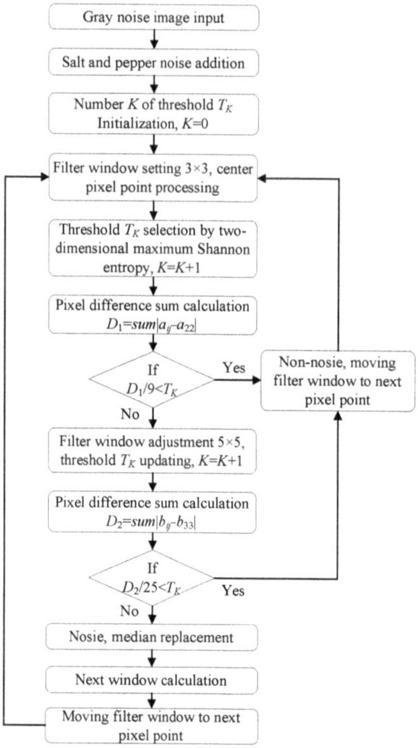

Figure 2. Flow chart of the proposed TSETMF algorithm process.

By analyzing the framework of the improved TSETMF, the two-dimensional maximum Shannon entropy of the inputted image can be calculated to reflect the abundant information degree in different zones of the image. Based on the computation results of the two-dimensional maximum Shannon entropy, it can be confirmed that the threshold values fit with the local areas of the image. Afterward, the image can be divided into different-sized windows according to the comparisons between the calculated threshold value and the pixel difference mean value. Here, 3×3 and 5×5 windows can be selected to judge the noise and, then, a median replacement can be conducted using the 5×5 window. The replaced value can be reserved and delivered using the recursion method for application in the next filtering process calculations. Therefore, the improved TSETMF can more effectively fit the noise level in different zones, thus enhancing the filtering effects of high-density-noise images.

Furthermore, it should be pointed out that window size selection may affect the noise judgment accuracy and median replacement effect of the algorithm. As for noise judgment, the image's local details may be judged as noise by mistake in a 3×3 window; thus, a 5×5 window can be selected to identify noise and non-noise values more accurately when considering more image information. As for median replacement, the ranked median values are likely to remain as noise in a 3×3 window; thus, a 5×5 window can be selected to conduct ranking and median replacement to increase the non-noise probability while processing high-density salt and pepper noise. Additionally, the computational effort may increase if a larger window size is selected. As a result, better denoising effects can be realized by adopting the appropriate window size to filter high-density salt and pepper noise in the improved TSETMF algorithm.

Compared with the traditional median filter, the proposed TSETMF algorithm can process the features in different areas by adjusting the adaptive filtering window and it can reduce the features that are misjudged as noise by comparing neighborhood pixel differences. Additionally, high-density noise can be reduced by utilizing two-dimensional maximum Shannon entropy threshold values coupled with the recursion method.

4. Experimental Results and Discussion

In order to verify the reasonability of the proposed improved TSETMF algorithm, classical grayscale images in three different scenarios were used as samples in contrast experiments. Three filtering methods relevant to high-density denoising were used to compare with the proposed improved TSETMF, including the pixel-density-based trimmed median filter (PDBTMF) [58], modified decision-based median filter (MDBMF) [59], and adaptive dual-threshold median filter (ADTMF) [25]. Additionally, two assessment methods, including the peak signal-to-noise ratio and the structural similarity index measure (SSIM), were employed to carry out the experimental comparison analysis and discussion.

4.1. Assessment Methods

To assess the performance of different image denoising methods, PSNR and SSIM indexes can be utilized to effectively evaluate denoising algorithms. The indexes consider the overall quantification and perception of image quality.

4.1.1. PSNR

Peak signal-to-noise ratio can be used to assess the distortion degree of the original image after processing. In other words, a larger PSNR represents better image quality and a larger ratio of signal and noise shows that the signal can be more easily extracted. The computational formula of PSNR can be expressed as:

$$PSNR = 10 \times \log_{10}\left(\frac{N \times MAX_I{}^2}{\sum\limits_{i=1}^{N}\left(I_{orig}(i) - I_{comp}(i)\right)^2}\right) \quad (12)$$

where MAX_I^2 represents the maximum pixel value, I_{orig} is the pixel value in the original image, I_{comp} is the pixel value in the handled image, and N is the pixel quantity.

4.1.2. SSIM

The structural similarity index measure is an evaluation index used to compare the structural similarity between two images. By calculating the index SSIM, a difference between the output image and the undistorted image can be quantified to evaluate the quality of image recovery. That is, a larger SSIM represents better image quality, which can illustrate the minor differences between the output image and the undistorted image. By comparing the brightness, contrast ratio, and structure of two images, SSIM can be used to quantify the levels of similarity [60]. The computational formula of SSIM can be expressed as:

$$SSIM(x, y) = l(x, y)^{\alpha} c(x, y)^{\beta} s(x, y)^{\gamma} \quad (13)$$

where $l(x, y)$ represents the brightness, $c(x, y)$ represents the contrast ratio, $s(x, y)$ represents the structure, x is the original image, and y is the denoised image.

The structural factor accounts for the majority of the calculation. When $\alpha = \beta = \gamma = 1$ and $c_3 = c_2/2$, the computational formula of SSIM can also be expressed as:

$$SSIM(x, y) = \frac{(2\mu_x\mu_y + C_1)(2\sigma_x\sigma_y + C_2)}{(\mu_x{}^2 + \mu_y{}^2 + C_1)(\sigma_x{}^2 + \sigma_y{}^2 + C_2)} \quad (14)$$

where μ is the corresponding mean value, C is a denominator adjustment parameter and σ^2 is the corresponding variance.

4.2. Results and Discussion

In order to assess the advantages of the proposed TSETMF denoising algorithm to improve the grayscale image quality, three kinds of standard images were selected as the denoising objects to conduct contrast verifications in MATLAB, including Lena (256 × 256 pixels) [61], Cameraman (504 × 505 pixels) [62], and COVID (1070 × 1200 pixels) [63]. Lena and Cameraman are the classical images for grayscale image processing and COVID is the grayscale micrograph. By adding different densities of salt and pepper noise, the ability of four filter algorithms to address different high-density-noise grayscale images was examined. The density was continuously increased from 5% to 95% in increments of 5%.

4.2.1. Contrastive Denoising with 95% High-Density Noise

To visually illustrate the contrastive denoising effects, salt and pepper noise at a density of 95% was artificially added to exhibit the contrastive denoising effects. This was added using the code noisy_img = imnoise(img, 'salt & pepper', 0.95) in MATLAB R2016b. As illustrated in Figures 3–5, the denoising of the Lena, Cameraman, and COVID images was conducted using the PDBTMF, MDBMF, and ADTMF algorithms and the results compared with the proposed improved TSETMF algorithm with 95% high-density noise. Figures 3a, 4a and 5a present the original Lena, Cameraman, and COVID images without noise, respectively. Figures 3b, 4b and 5b present the same images with 95% density noise, respectively. These were the input images for the denoising experiments using the various algorithms. Figure 3c–e, Figures 4c–e and 5c–e present the denoising effects of the PDBTMF, MDBMF, and ADTMF algorithms on the images, respectively. Figures 3f, 4f and 5f present the denoising effects of the proposed improved TSETMF algorithm on the three images, respectively. It should be noted that the PDBTMF algorithm removes noise by comparing the numerical relationships between the current pixel and the neighboring pixels [64]. The MDBMF algorithm is a non-linear salt and pepper filter able to maintain the signal edges [65].

Figure 3. Contrastive denoising effects of the different algorithms for the Lena image. (**a**) Original image. (**b**) Salt and pepper noise with 95% density. (**c**) PDBTMF. (**d**) MDBMF. (**e**) ADTMF. (**f**) Proposed TSETMF algorithm.

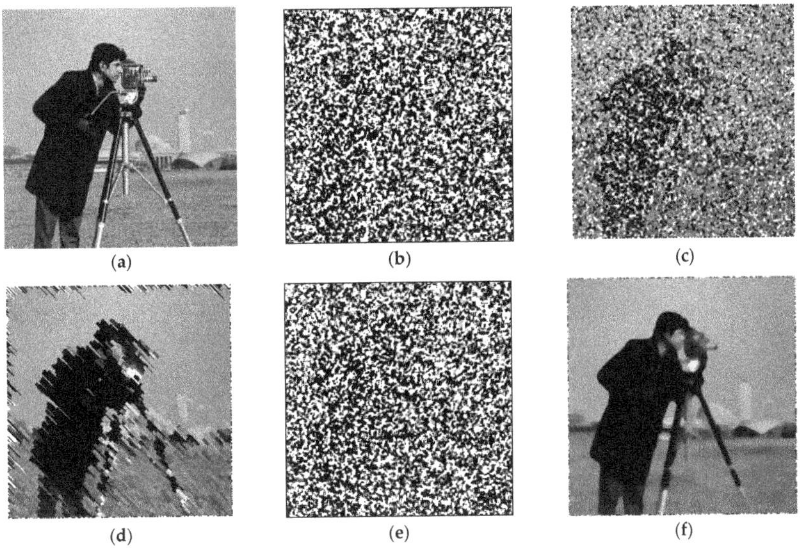

Figure 4. Contrastive denoising effects of different algorithms for the Cameraman image. (**a**) Original image. (**b**) Salt and pepper noise with 95% density. (**c**) PDBTMF. (**d**) MDBMF. (**e**) ADTMF. (**f**) Proposed TSETMF algorithm.

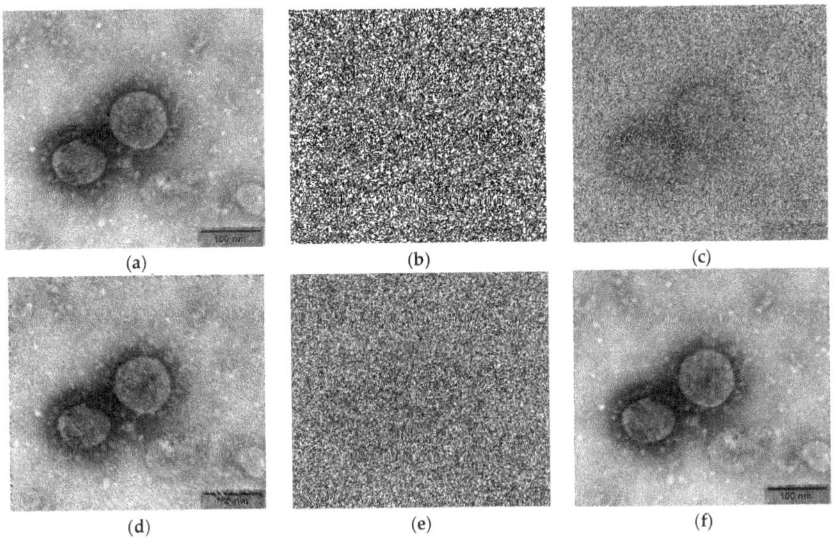

Figure 5. Contrastive denoising effects of different algorithms for the COVID image. (**a**) Original image. (**b**) Salt and pepper noise with 95% density. (**c**) PDBTMF. (**d**) MDBMF. (**e**) ADTMF. (**f**) Proposed TSETMF algorithm.

Figures 3–5 demonstrate that the PDBTMF, MDBMF, and ADTMF algorithms individually present a dramatic decline in denoising effects. For instance, the processing of the Lena image with 95% high-density salt and pepper noise displayed relatively distinct differences in the effects. Figure 3e shows the poor denoising effect achieved using ADTMF; however, the filter properties of PDBTMF with a significant amount of noise shown in Figure 3c are superior to ADTMF. Although the filter properties of MDBFM provide better denoising effects, some noise still exists, as shown in Figure 3d. By comparison, the proposed improved TSETMF algorithm exhibits little observable noise and a high degree of image smoothing and the denoising effects of this algorithm are superior to the other three. In general, the proposed improved TSETMF algorithm exhibits a relatively good filtering effect under high-density salt and pepper noise.

4.2.2. Contrastive Denoising with Continuous Increase in Noise Density

To visually illustrate the contrastive denoising effects achieved using the different algorithms, a continuous artificial increase in the noise density from 5% to 95% in increments of 5% was carried out to exhibit the denoising effects. The three classical algorithms with the parameters of PSNR and SSIM were utilized to evaluate the ability of the proposed improved TSETMF algorithm to process the first classical image, Lena. Table S1 represents PSNR comparison data from different algorithms processing Lena with increasing noise density. Figure 6 presents a change map of the PSNR with continuously increasing noise density according to the different algorithms' processing of Lena. As can be seen from Figure 6, the PSNR values of the PDBTMF algorithm when processing the Lena image begin to slowly decline after around 20% noise density and the decline accelerates rapidly after 70% noise density. The PSNR values of the MDBMF algorithm begin to slowly decline after around 20% noise density and, then, the decline accelerates after 50% noise density. The stability of MDBMF's processing effects is a little worse than that of PDBTMF. Although the PSNR values of the ADTMF algorithm show a relatively smooth declining tendency, the processing of the salt and pepper noise in the Lena image is poor. Compared with the other three filtering algorithms, the PSNR values of the proposed improved TSETMF algorithm at a 95% high-noise density reach 24.97 dB, which is much higher than that of PDBTMF at 10.63 dB, MDBMF at 18.11 dB, and ADTMF at 6.17 dB. In summary, the PSNR values of the proposed improved TSETMF algorithm always stabilize at around 25 dB and decline slowly with increasing noise density. This demonstrates that the proposed improved TSETMF algorithm can effectively enhance denoising stability when processing different noise densities.

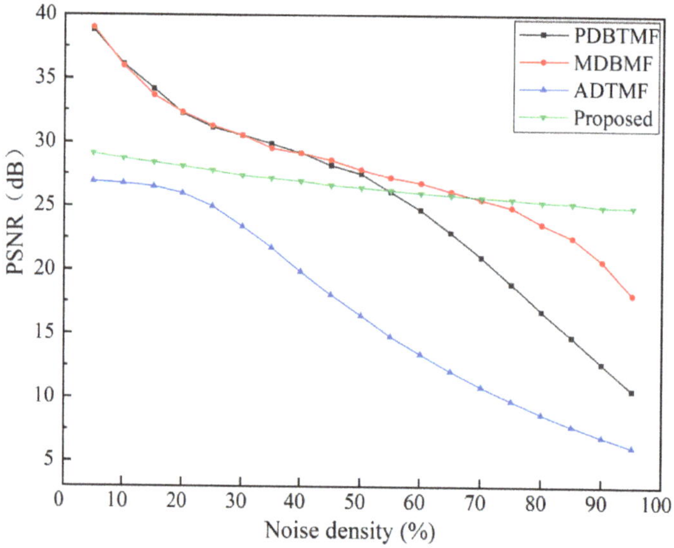

Figure 6. Change map of PSNR with continuously increasing noise density for different algorithms processing Lena.

In addition, Table S2 represents SSIM comparison data from different algorithms processing Lena with increasing noise density. Figure 7 presents the change map of the SSIM with continuously increasing noise density for the different algorithms processing Lena. For low-density noise, the PDBTMF algorithm exhibits relatively stable SSIM; however, it drops rapidly after around 40% noise density. The MDBMF algorithm obtains relatively higher SSIM but drops rapidly after around 60% noise density. The ADTMF algorithm possesses the highest SSIM under around 20% noise density. In summary, the SSIM values of the proposed improved TSETMF algorithm always stabilize above 0.81 with continuously increasing noise density. This demonstrates that the proposed improved TSETMF algorithm can effectively maintain the quality of the processed image at different noise densities, especially for high-density salt and pepper noise. It should be noted that the required running time of the proposed TSETMF algorithm is basically around 3.7 s, which is much faster than of the ADTMF algorithm. Differing from the other algorithms, although the proposed TSETMF algorithm has a relatively larger running time than that of the PDBTMF and MDBMF algorithms, it exhibits relatively stable states with increasing noise density, especially for high-density noise. Hence, this also demonstrates that the proposed TSETMF algorithm is insensitive to variable noise density.

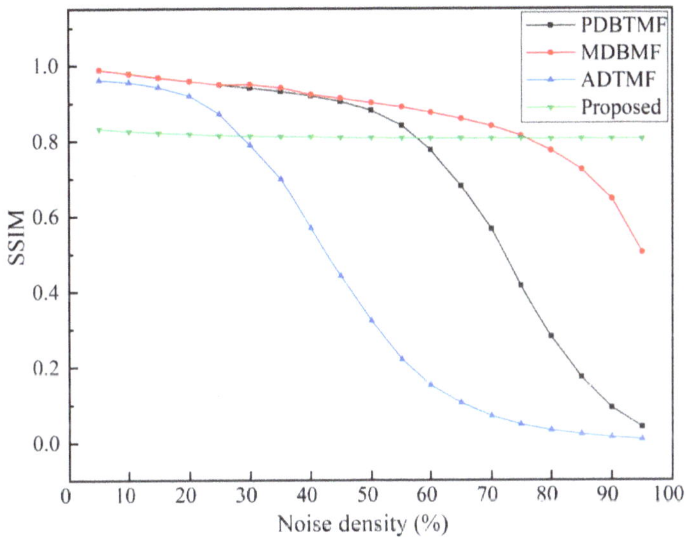

Figure 7. Change map of SSIM with continuously increasing noise density for different algorithms processing Lena.

To calculate the values of PSNR and SSIM, parameter variance is adopted. For the noise density calculations of the image, local variance in different areas, such as the noise index, can be utilized to analyze the grayscale image. Calculating the pixel value variance in each area can obtain the noise level in different areas. That is, a higher variance usually exhibits relatively stronger noise density. As a result, the noise levels of the whole grayscale image can be calculated to acquire the values of PSNR and SSIM for further comparison of the denoising effects of the algorithms.

In order to verify the advantages in image detail reservation ability using the proposed TSETMF algorithm, a partial Lena image with the addition of 95% salt and pepper noise was utilized to perform denoising, as illustrated in Figure 8. By employing two-dimensional maximum Shannon entropy coupled with pixel difference mean, an image detail can be judged to determine whether it is noise. The filtering processes for a local area in Figure 8b are presented in Figure 8c–e. Pixel 255 in Row 1 and Column 5 in Figure 8c is judged as

densities. This finding also further demonstrates that the proposed algorithm can process the Cameraman image with good high-density-noise denoising effects and excellent stable image quality.

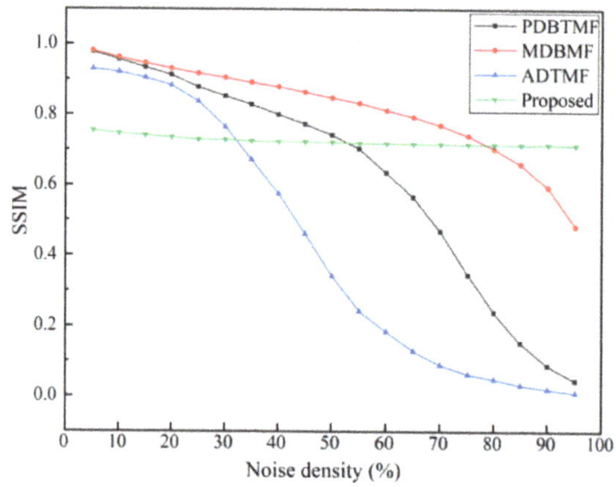

Figure 11. Change map of SSIM with continuously increasing noise density for different algorithms processing Cameraman.

By utilizing the three classical algorithms, the PSNR and SSIM parameters were utilized to evaluate the abilities of the proposed improved TSETMF algorithm when processing the third classical image, COVID. Table S5 represents PSNR comparison data from different algorithms processing COVID with increasing noise density. Figure 12 presents a change map of PSNR with continuously increasing noise density for different algorithms processing COVID. As can be seen in Figure 12, the PSNR values of the PDBTMF, MDBMF, and ADTMF algorithms when processing the COVID image decreased by approximately 20 dB. Correspondingly, the larger negative slopes show that the three algorithms cannot handle the high-density salt and pepper noise of the COVID image. However, the decrease in the PSNR values of the proposed improved TSETMF algorithm is relatively minor, from 26.22 dB to 24.78 dB, with a mere 5.49% decline ratio. In particular, as the high-density noise varied from 5% to 95%, the proposed improved TSETMF algorithm exhibited the most stable denoising properties. In other words, this TSETMF algorithm works independently of the effects of noise density and achieves the most accurate and effective processing of the high-density salt and pepper noise in the COVID image.

Table S6 represents SSIM comparison data from different algorithms processing COVID with increasing noise density. Figure 13 presents a change map of the SSIM with continuously increasing noise density for different algorithms processing COVID. The SSIM values of the PDBTMF algorithm express a declining tendency with increasing noise density but are inferior at higher-density noise. At the same time, the SSIM values of the PDBTMF algorithm decline sharply when the noise density is larger than 50%. However, the proposed improved TSETMF algorithm achieves a more stable SSIM above 0.51 at arbitrary noise densities. It should be illustrated that the SSIM is located at a relatively lower level; however, this TSETMF algorithm exhibits the most stable processing effects in terms of the denoising of high-density salt and pepper noise in the COVID image.

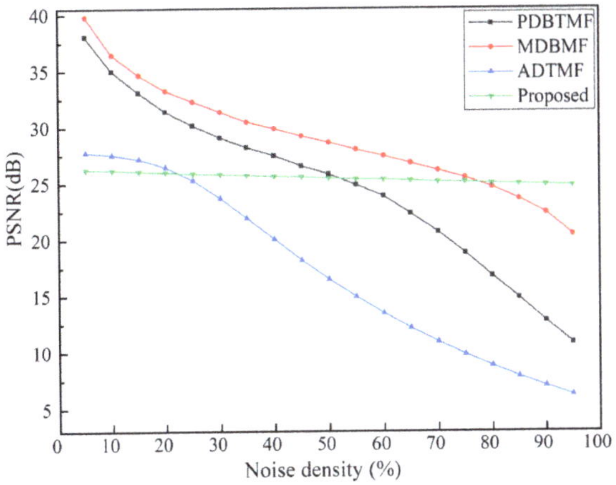

Figure 12. Change map of PSNR with continuously increasing noise density for different algorithms processing COVID.

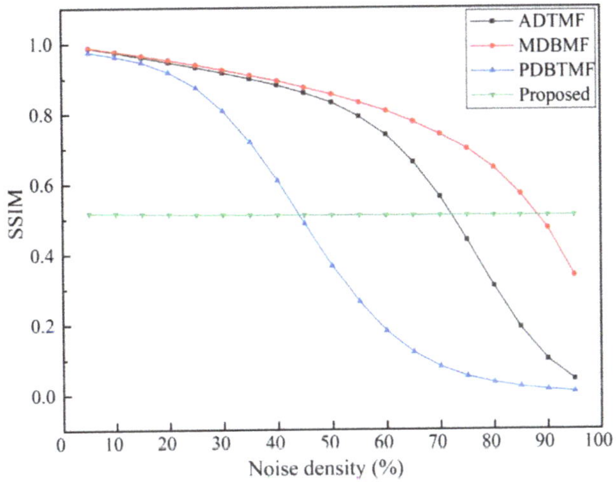

Figure 13. Change map of SSIM with continuously increasing noise density for different algorithms processing COVID.

By comparing the processing effects of the three standard images of Lena, Cameraman, and COVID presented in Figures 6, 10 and 12, the PSNR values of the PDBTMF algorithm and the MDBMF algorithm can be used to show that they have relatively better denoising effects. This is due to the specially designed filter's ability to process salt and pepper noise; whereas, it is not applicable to Gaussian noise or other noise. By contrast, the proposed improved TSETMF algorithm and the ADTMF algorithm can be utilized to address different types of noise. As can be observed from Figures 7, 11 and 13, it is obvious that the SSIM values obtained by the proposed improved TSETMF algorithm were the highest for Lena, followed by Cameraman and COVID, respectively. Additionally, with increasing pixel quantities, the level of similarity between the denoised image and the original image exhibited a minor decline; however, stability was basically maintained. Thus, the processing of more kinds of grayscale images should be conducted to explore the applicability of the proposed TSETMF algorithm and further improve the denoising performance and higher densities.

Furthermore, the minor descending PSNR values achieved by the proposed improved TSETMF algorithm demonstrate its better robustness and filtered image quality at higher-density noise levels. Also, the minor descending SSIM values achieved by TSETMF indicate that the algorithm has excellent denoising ability in the processing of higher-noise grayscale images. Moreover, this method can provide a unique approach to addressing denoising issues. Further, it can be advanced to promote high-noise filtering and stability when processing high-density salt and pepper noise in grayscale images.

Prospectively speaking, salt and pepper noise can be produced by transmission, analog-to-digital conversion, and data acquisition errors. In particular, the processing of high-density salt and pepper noise is often required for medical images, for instance, magnetic resonance images [66] and X-ray images [67]. By preliminarily analyzing the processing results for medical brain magnetic resonance images, the ability of the proposed TSETMF algorithm to produce relatively stable and excellent noise reduction effects may be demonstrated. This would also demonstrate the algorithm's strong robustness in terms of denoising high-density-noise grayscale images.

5. Conclusions

The denoising issues associated with grayscale images have become a significant area of research in the field of digital image processing. For the processing of high-noise grayscale images in particular, the denoising effects can become worse with increasing noise density. In this paper, an improved median filter algorithm, TSETMF, is proposed that utilizes two-dimensional maximum Shannon entropy to achieve the adaptive selection of thresholds to enhance the ability to process high-density noise and achieve denoising stability. The noise in images can be filtered by automatically partitioning a window size, the threshold value of which is adaptively calculated using two-dimensional maximum Shannon entropy. Three comparative experiments were conducted to verify the rationality of the TSETMF model and show its relative superiority in denoising. The experimental results demonstrated that the proposed TSETMF algorithm exhibited better processing performance with superior high-density noise suppression and denoising stability. The proposed TSETMF exhibited a stronger ability to process high-density noise, which was demonstrated by a higher PSNR value of 24.97 dB at a 95% noise density for the classical Lena grayscale image. The proposed TSETMF also exhibited better denoising stability when the noise density increased from 5% to 95%, which was demonstrated by the minor decline in the PSNR value of approximately 10.78% relative to the PSNR of 23.10 dB for the classical Cameraman grayscale image. The TSETMF algorithm is independent of the effects of noise density and achieved more accurate and effective results when processing the high-density salt and pepper noise in the COVID image. Therefore, it is clear that the proposed TSETMF can also maintain good filtering effects with excellent denoising robustness for processing high-density noise in grayscale images. This method could provide a unique approach to addressing denoising issues. Additionally, the processing of more grayscale image types should be carried out to explore the applicability of the proposed TSETMF algorithm and further improve its denoising performance and stability.

Supplementary Materials: The following supporting information can be downloaded at: https://www.mdpi.com/article/10.3390/app14020635/s1, Table S1: PSNR comparison data from different algorithms processing Lena with increasing noise density. Table S2: SSIM comparison data from different algorithms processing Lena with increasing noise density. Table S3: PSNR comparison data from different algorithms processing Cameraman with increasing noise density. Table S4: SSIM comparison data from different algorithms processing Cameraman with increasing noise density. Table S5: PSNR comparison data from different algorithms processing COVID with increasing noise density. Table S6: SSIM comparison data from different algorithms processing COVID with increasing noise density.

Author Contributions: Conceptualization, N.C.; investigation, N.C.; methodology, N.C. and Y.L.; data curation, N.C. and Y.L.; writing—original draft, N.C. and Y.L.; writing—review and editing, N.C. All authors have read and agreed to the published version of the manuscript.

Funding: This work was supported by the Key Science and Technology Research Project of Henan Province, China (Grant No. 222102220032, 212102210359), and the Doctoral Research Fund of Zhengzhou University of Light Industry (Grant No. 2019BSJJ003).

Institutional Review Board Statement: Not applicable.

Informed Consent Statement: Not applicable.

Data Availability Statement: The data presented in this study are available in the article.

Conflicts of Interest: The authors declare no conflicts of interest.

References

1. Chen, J.; Zhan, Y.; Cao, H. Adaptive sequentially weighted median filter for image highly corrupted by impulse noise. *IEEE Access* **2019**, *7*, 158545–158556. [CrossRef]
2. Kumar, S.; Singh, S.; Kumar, J. Live detection of face using machine learning with multi-feature method. *Wirel. Pers. Commun.* **2018**, *103*, 2353–2375. [CrossRef]
3. Liu, W.; Yang, S.; Ye, Z.; Huang, Q.; Huang, Y. An image segmentation method based on two-dimensional entropy and chaotic lightning attachment procedure optimization algorithm. *Int. J. Pattern Recognit. Artif. Intell.* **2020**, *34*, 2054030. [CrossRef]
4. Mahdaoui, A.E.; Ouahabi, A.; Moulay, M.S. Image denoising using a compressive sensing approach based on regularization constraints. *Sensors* **2022**, *22*, 2199. [CrossRef] [PubMed]
5. Frosio, I.; Borghese, N.A. Statistical based impulsive noise removal in digital radiography. *IEEE Trans. Med. Imaging* **2008**, *28*, 3–16. [CrossRef]
6. Goceri, E. Evaluation of denoising techniques to remove speckle and Gaussian noise from dermoscopy images. *Comput. Biol. Med.* **2022**, *152*, 106474. [CrossRef]
7. Garnett, R.; Huegerich, T.; Chui, C.; He, W. A universal noise removal algorithm with an impulse detector. *IEEE Trans. Image Process.* **2005**, *14*, 1747–1754. [CrossRef]
8. Sulaiman, S.N.; Mat Isa, N.A.; Yusoff, I.A.; Ahmad, F. Switching-based clustering algorithms for segmentation of low-level salt-and-pepper noise–corrupted images. *Signal Image Video Process.* **2015**, *9*, 387–398. [CrossRef]
9. Thanh, D.N.H.; Hai, N.H.; Prasath, V.B.S.; Hieu, L.M.; Tavares, J.M.R.S. A two-stage filter for high density salt and pepper denoising. *Multimed. Tools Appl.* **2020**, *79*, 21013–21035. [CrossRef]
10. Li, T.; Wang, W.; Xu, L.; Feng, X. Image denoising using low-rank dictionary and sparse representation. In Proceedings of the 2014 Tenth International Conference on Computational Intelligence and Security, Kunming, China, 15–16 November 2014; pp. 228–232.
11. Lin, T.C. A new adaptive center weighted median filter for suppressing impulsive noise in images. *Inf. Sci.* **2007**, *177*, 1073–1087. [CrossRef]
12. Vijayarajan, R.; Muttan, S. Iterative relaxed median filter for impulse noise removal and validation of fcm clustering using cluster error index in median filtered MR images. In Proceedings of the 4th ObCom International Conference on Recent Trends in Computing, Communication and Information Technology, Vellore, India, 9–11 December 2011; pp. 792–801.
13. Thilagavathi, M.; Deepa, P. An efficient dictionary learning algorithm for 3D Medical Image Denoising based on SADCT. In Proceedings of the 2013 International Conference on Information Communication and Embedded Systems (ICICES), Chennai, India, 21–22 February 2013; pp. 442–447.
14. Shah, Z.H.; Müller, M.; Wang, T.C.; Scheidig, P.M.; Schneider, A.; Schüttpelz, M.; Huser, T.; Schenck, W. Deep-learning based denoising and reconstruction of super-resolution structured illumination microscopy images. *Photonics Res.* **2021**, *9*, B168–B181. [CrossRef]
15. Obidin, M.V.; Serebrovski, A.P. Signal denoising with the use of the wavelet transform and the Kalman filter. *J. Commun. Technol. Electron.* **2014**, *59*, 1440–1445. [CrossRef]
16. Yu, H.; Zhao, L.; Wang, H. Image denoising using trivariate shrinkage filter in the wavelet domain and joint bilateral filter in the spatial domain. *IEEE Trans. Image Process.* **2009**, *18*, 2364–2369. [PubMed]
17. Uzan, A.; Rivenson, Y.; Stern, A. Speckle denoising in digital holography by nonlocal means filtering. *Appl. Opt.* **2013**, *52*, A195–A200. [CrossRef]
18. Teng, L.; Li, H.; Yin, S. Modified pyramid dual tree direction filter-based image denoising via curvature scale and nonlocal mean multigrade remnant filter. *Int. J. Commun. Syst.* **2018**, *31*, e3486. [CrossRef]
19. Erkan, U.; Gökrem, L.; Enginoğlu, S. Different applied median filter in salt and pepper noise. *Comput. Electr. Eng.* **2018**, *70*, 789–798. [CrossRef]
20. Sree, P.S.J.; Kumar, P.; Siddavatam, R.; Verma, R. Salt-and-pepper noise removal by adaptive median-based lifting filter using second-generation wavelets. *Signal Image Video Process.* **2013**, *7*, 111–118. [CrossRef]

21. Toh, K.K.V.; Isa, N.A.M. Noise adaptive fuzzy switching median filter for salt-and-pepper noise reduction. *IEEE Signal Process. Lett.* **2009**, *17*, 281–284. [CrossRef]
22. Shukla, A.K.; Bhateja, V.; Verma, R.L.; Alam, M.S. An Improved Directional Weighted Median Filter for Restoration of Images Corrupted with High Density Impulse Noise. In Proceedings of the 2014 International Conference on Reliability Optimization and Information Technology (ICROIT), Faridabad, India, 6–8 February 2014; pp. 506–511.
23. Peng, B.; Zhou, Y.; Li, Q.; Lin, M.; Weng, J.; Zeng, Q. FPGA Implementation of Low-Latency Recursive Median Filter. In Proceedings of the 2022 International Conference on Field-Programmable Technology (ICFPT), Hong Kong, China, 5–9 December 2022; pp. 1–7.
24. Gupta, V.; Chaurasia, V.; Shandilya, M. Random-valued impulse noise removal using adaptive dual threshold median filter. *J. Vis. Commun. Image Represent.* **2015**, *26*, 296–304. [CrossRef]
25. Kumar, S.; Raja, R.; Mahmood, M.R.; Choudhary, S. A Hybrid Method for the Removal of RVIN Using Self Organizing Migration with Adaptive Dual Threshold Median Filter. *Sens. Imaging* **2023**, *24*, 9. [CrossRef]
26. Goyal, P.; Chaurasia, V.; Meena, O.P. Impulse Noise Removal with Zero's Padding by Median Based Adaptive Filter. In Proceedings of the 2017 International Conference on Recent Innovations in Signal Processing and Embedded Systems (RISE), Bhopal, India, 27–29 October 2017; pp. 78–81.
27. Hanel, R.; Thurner, S.; Gell-Mann, M. How multiplicity determines entropy and the derivation of the maximum entropy principle for complex systems. *Proc. Natl. Acad. Sci. USA* **2014**, *111*, 6905–6910. [CrossRef] [PubMed]
28. Abramov, R. A practical computational framework for the multidimensional moment-constrained maximum entropy principle. *J. Comput. Phys.* **2006**, *211*, 198–209. [CrossRef]
29. Panda, R.; Swain, M.; Naik, M.K.; Agrawal, S.; Abraham, A. A Novel Practical Decisive Row-Class Entropy-Based Technique for Multilevel Threshold Selection Using Opposition Flow Directional Algorithm. *IEEE Access* **2022**, *10*, 110473–110484. [CrossRef]
30. Zou, Y.; Zhang, J.; Upadhyay, M.; Sun, S.; Jiang, T. Automatic image thresholding based on Shannon entropy difference and dynamic synergic entropy. *IEEE Access* **2020**, *8*, 171218–171239. [CrossRef]
31. Chiranjeevi, K.; Jena, U.R.; Harika, A. Image Compression Using Shannon Entropy-Based Image Thresholding. In Proceedings of the 3rd International Conference on Computational Intelligence in Data Mining (ICCIDM), Bhubaneswar, India, 10–11 December 2016; pp. 101–110.
32. Maleki, Y.K.; Safizadeh, M.S.; Khajavi, M.N.; Payganeh, G.; Shuruni, S. Over Hang Slant Cracked Rotor Vibration Signal Processing Based on Discrete Wavelet Transform. In Proceedings of the 2016 13th International Multi-Conference on Systems, Signals & Devices (SSD), Leipzig, Germany, 21–24 March 2016; pp. 672–676.
33. Lin, T.C.; Yu, P.T. Thresholding noise-free ordered mean filter based on Dempster-Shafer theory for image restoration. *IEEE Trans. Circuits Syst. I Regul. Pap.* **2006**, *53*, 1057–1064.
34. Duque, D.; Garzón, J.; Gharbi, T. A study of dispersion in chromatic confocal microscopy using digital image processing. *Opt. Laser Technol.* **2020**, *131*, 106414. [CrossRef]
35. Kim, D.; Kim, C. Contrast enhancement using combined 1-D and 2-D histogram-based techniques. *IEEE Signal Process. Lett.* **2017**, *24*, 804–808. [CrossRef]
36. Manda, M.P.; Kim, H.S. A fast image thresholding algorithm for infrared images based on histogram approximation and circuit theory. *Algorithms* **2020**, *13*, 207. [CrossRef]
37. Zhang, H.; Liu, H.; Shang, Z.; Li, R. Robust Image Denoising with an Improved Wavelet Threshold Method. In Proceedings of the 2015 6th IEEE International Conference on Software Engineering and Service Science (ICSESS), Beijing, China, 23–25 September 2015; pp. 301–304.
38. George, G.; Oommen, R.M.; Shelly, S.; Philipose, S.S.; Varghese, A.M. A Survey on Various Median Filtering Techniques for Removal of Impulse Noise from Digital Image. In Proceedings of the 2018 Conference on Emerging Devices and Smart Systems (ICEDSS), Tiruchengode, India, 2–3 March 2018; pp. 235–238.
39. Zhang, D.L.; Huang, D.N.; Yu, P.; Yuan, Y. Translation-invariant wavelet denoising of full-tensor gravity–gradiometer data. *Appl. Geophys.* **2017**, *14*, 606–619. [CrossRef]
40. Kubota, R.; Suetake, N. Distribution distance-based threshold auto-tuning method for switching median filter. *IEICE Electron. Expr.* **2010**, *7*, 1310–1316. [CrossRef]
41. Tan, X.; Jiang, J.; Zha, D. Threshold Switch Filter Design and Its Implementation in Image Denoising. In Proceedings of the 5th International Conference on Machine Vision (ICMV)—Computer Vision, Image Analysis and Processing, Wuhan, China, 20–21 October 2012; pp. 326–332.
42. Zhang, J.; Liao, Y.; Yan, L. An Improved Image Thresholding Method Based on Two-Dimensional Histogram. In Proceedings of the 2018 13th World Congress on Intelligent Control and Automation (WCICA), Changsha, China, 4–8 July 2018; pp. 1623–1628.
43. Sahoo, P.K.; Arora, G. A thresholding method based on two-dimensional Renyi's entropy. *Pattern Recognit.* **2004**, *37*, 1149–1161. [CrossRef]
44. Yu, C.; Dian-Ren, C.; Yang, L.; Lei, C. Otsu's Thresholding Method Based on Gray Level-Gradient Two-Dimensional Histogram. In Proceedings of the 2010 2nd International Asia Conference on Informatics in Control, Automation and Robotics (CAR 2010), Wuhan, China, 6–7 March 2010; pp. 282–285.
45. Celik, T. Two-dimensional histogram equalization and contrast enhancement. *Pattern Recognit.* **2012**, *45*, 3810–3824. [CrossRef]

46. Kharazmi, O.; Contreras-Reyes, J.E.; Balakrishnan, N. Jensen–Fisher information and Jensen–Shannon entropy measures based on complementary discrete distributions with an application to Conway's game of life. *Physica D* **2023**, *453*, 133822. [CrossRef]
47. Kumar, R.; Singh, J.; Sharma, S.; Li, C.; Królczyk, G.; Eldin, E.M.T.; Wojciechowski, S. Identification of localized defects and fault size estimation of taper roller bearing (NBC_30205) with signal processing using the Shannon entropy method in MATLAB for automobile industries applications. *Heliyon* **2022**, *8*, e12053. [CrossRef] [PubMed]
48. Yang, W.; Cai, L.; Wu, F. Image segmentation based on gray level and local relative entropy two-dimensional histogram. *PLoS ONE* **2020**, *15*, e0229651. [CrossRef]
49. Saraiva, P. On Shannon entropy and its applications. *Kuwait J. Sci.* **2023**, *50*, 194–199. [CrossRef]
50. Tsai, H.H.; Chang, B.M.; Lin, X.P. Using decision tree, particle swarm optimization, and support vector regression to design a median-type filter with a 2-level impulse detector for image enhancement. *Inf. Sci.* **2012**, *195*, 103–123. [CrossRef]
51. Chen, B.; Cui, J.; Xu, Q.; Shu, T.; Liu, H. Coupling denoising algorithm based on discrete wavelet transform and modified median filter for medical image. *J. Central South Univ.* **2019**, *26*, 120–131. [CrossRef]
52. Sinha, P.K.; Hong, Q.H. An improved median filter. *IEEE Trans. Med. Imaging* **1990**, *9*, 345–346. [CrossRef]
53. Erkan, U.; Enginoğlu, S.; Thanh, D.N.H.; Hieu, L.M. Adaptive frequency median filter for the salt and pepper denoising problem. *IET Image Process.* **2020**, *14*, 1291–1302. [CrossRef]
54. Ganesh, M.S.R.; Kadali, K.S.; Bhukya, R.; Palleswari, Y.T.R.; Siva, A.; Pragaspathy, S. Design of Decision Based Recursive Weighted Median Filter with Exponential Weights. In Proceedings of the 1st International Conference on Applied Mathematics, Modeling and Simulation in Engineering (AMSE), Virtual, 15–16 September 2021; p. 12016.
55. Guo, S.; Wang, G.; Han, L.; Song, X.; Yang, W. COVID-19 CT image denoising algorithm based on adaptive threshold and optimized weighted median filter. *Biomed. Signal Process. Control* **2022**, *75*, 103552. [CrossRef] [PubMed]
56. Xie, Y.; Zhu, Z.; Zhang, X.; Wang, Q. An Adaptive Median Filter Using Local Texture Information in Images. In Proceedings of the 2014 IEEE/ACIS 13th International Conference on Computer and Information Science (ICIS), Taiyuan, China, 4–6 June 2014; pp. 177–180.
57. Nalli, P.K.; Kadali, K.S.; Bhukya, R.; Palleswari, Y.T.R.; Siva, A.; Pragaspathy, S. Design of Exponentially Weighted Median Filter Cascaded with Adaptive Median Filter. In Proceedings of the 1st International Conference on Applied Mathematics, Modeling and Simulation in Engineering (AMSE), Virtual, 15–16 September 2021; p. 12020.
58. Jana, B.R.; Thotakura, H.; Baliyan, A.; Sankararao, M.; Deshmukh, R.G.; Karanam, S.R. Pixel density based trimmed median filter for removal of noise from surface image. *Appl. Nanosci.* **2023**, *13*, 1017–1028. [CrossRef]
59. Kunsoth, R.; Biswas, M. Modified Decision Based Median Filter for Impulse Noise Removal. In Proceedings of the 2016 International Conference on Wireless Communications, Signal Processing and Networking (WiSPNET), Chennai, India, 23–25 March 2016; pp. 1316–1319.
60. Meng, Y.; Zhang, J. A Novel Gray Image Denoising Method Using Convolutional Neural Network. *IEEE Access* **2022**, *10*, 49657–49676. [CrossRef]
61. Kodak Lossless True Color Image Suite. Available online: http://r0k.us/graphics/kodak/ (accessed on 1 July 2023).
62. TEST IMAGES. Available online: https://ccia.ugr.es/cvg/dbimagenes/ (accessed on 1 July 2023).
63. National Microbiology Data Center. Available online: http://nmdc.cn/nCov/en/ (accessed on 1 July 2023).
64. Qi, H.; Tan, S.; Li, Z. Anisotropic Weighted Total Variation Feature Fusion Network for Remote Sensing Image Denoising. *Remote Sens.* **2022**, *14*, 6300. [CrossRef]
65. Wang, L.; Shi, Y.; Li, H. Anti-EMI noise digital filter design for a 60-kW five-level SiC inverter without fiber isolation. *IEEE Trans. Power Electron.* **2017**, *33*, 13–17. [CrossRef]
66. Alanazi, T.M.; Berriri, K.; Albekairi, M.; Ben Atitallah, A.; Sahbani, A.; Kaaniche, K. New Real-Time High-Density Impulsive Noise Removal Method Applied to Medical Images. *Diagnostics* **2023**, *13*, 1709. [CrossRef]
67. Garg, B. An adaptive minimum-maximum value-based weighted median filter for removing high density salt and pepper noise in medical images. *Int. J. Ad Hoc Ubiquitous Comput.* **2020**, *35*, 84–95. [CrossRef]

applied sciences

MDPI

Article

Genetic Programming to Remove Impulse Noise in Color Images

Daniel Fajardo-Delgado [1], Ansel Y. Rodríguez-González [2], Sergio Sandoval-Pérez [1], Jesús Ezequiel Molinar-Solís [1] and María Guadalupe Sánchez-Cervantes [1,*]

1 Department of Systems and Computation, Tecnológico Nacional de México/Instituto Tecnológico de Ciudad Guzmán, Ciudad Guzmán 49100, Mexico; daniel.fd@cdguzman.tecnm.mx (D.F.-D.); sergio.sp@cdguzman.tecnm.mx (S.S.-P.); jesus.ms@cdguzman.tecnm.mx (J.E.M.-S.)

2 CICESE-UT3, Tepic 63155, Mexico; ansel@cicese.edu.mx

* Correspondence: maria.sc1@cdguzman.tecnm.mx; Tel.: +52-341-575-2050

Abstract: This paper presents a new filter to remove impulse noise in digital color images. The filter is adaptive in the sense that it uses a detection stage to only correct noisy pixels. Detecting noisy pixels is performed by a binary classification model generated via genetic programming, a paradigm of evolutionary computing based on natural biological selection. The classification model training considers three impulse noise models in color images: salt and pepper, uniform, and correlated. This is the first filter generated by genetic programming exploiting the correlation among the color image channels. The correction stage consists of a vector median filter version that modifies color channel values if some are noisy. An experimental study was performed to compare the proposed filter with others in the state-of-the-art related to color image denoising. Their performance was measured objectively through the image quality metrics PSNR, MAE, SSIM, and FSIM. Experimental findings reveal substantial variability among filters based on noise model and image characteristics. The findings also indicate that, on average, the proposed filter consistently exhibited top-tier performance values for the three impulse noise models, surpassed only by a filter employing a deep learning-based approach. Unlike deep learning filters, which are black boxes with internal workings invisible to the user, the proposed filter has a high interpretability with a performance close to an equilibrium point for all images and noise models used in the experiment.

Keywords: digital image processing; color image denoising; genetic programming; impulse noise; adaptive filters

1. Introduction

Recently, the notion of color has played a relevant role in a large number of computer vision applications. Color information provides features that are invariant to scale, translation, and rotation changes, which are suitable for image segmentation [1], image classification [2,3], or image retrieval [4,5]. One of the most critical tasks in computer vision applications is image denoising, which involves recovering an image from a degraded noisy version. Various types of noise can affect digital color images, particularly impulse noise [6].

Impulse noise in digital images is a random variation in the intensity of pixels caused by short-duration pulses of high energy. This type of noise can significantly degrade the quality of images and poses various challenges in real-world applications. For example, the impulse noise in dashboard camera footage under low-light conditions [7] can lead to the misinterpretation of videos, making it challenging to accurately identify vehicles involved in incidents. Additionally, impulse noise is a kind of ordinary noise in medical imaging (X-rays, MRIs, and CT scans) [8] that can result in the misinterpretation or disappearance of critical details important in diagnosis.

Impulse noise commonly occurs during the acquisition or transmission of an image caused by imperfections on the device lens, malfunctioning camera photosensors, the aging of the storage material, errors during the compression process, and the electronic instability of the image signal [9]. Addressing impulse noise in real-world applications often involves the use of various image processing techniques to restore the integrity of images. Impulse noise affects color digital images in such a way that the perturbed pixels differ significantly from their local neighborhood in the image domain.

Nature-inspired optimization algorithms have been widely applied in the image processing literature to address various challenges, including optimizing image quality evaluation [10], feature selection [11], and image reconstruction [12]. Of particular note is genetic programming [13], an evolutionary computing technique based on the principle of natural selection, which offers a flexible and adaptive methodology for addressing image processing problems. Like other evolutionary algorithms, the main idea is to transform a population of individuals (programs) by applying natural genetic operations such as reproduction, mutation, and selection [14]. The adaptability and robustness of genetic programming make it well suited for addressing the challenges associated with impulse noise removal, particularly for color digital images.

Outline and Contribution

This paper proposes a novel adaptive filter to remove impulse noise in color images. The contribution of this work is twofold. First, this is the first filter to remove noise in color images by exploiting the correlation among the image channels through the genetic programming paradigm. The filter consists of a two-stage solution comprising detection and correction processes. The detection stage decomposes the input color image into its red-green-blue channels; then, it uses a binary classification model to identify which channel values for each image pixel are perturbed by noise. The correction stage modifies each pixel identified as noisy according to its perturbed channels and neighborhood. Second, the detection stage of the proposed filter is an interpretable model that performs very well under different conditions by considering three impulse noise models: salt and pepper, uniform, and correlated. Experimental results show that the filter is the second closest to an equilibrium point in terms of the performance balance, outperformed only by a filter using a black-box deep learning-based approach.

The remainder of this paper is organized as follows. Section 2 presents the related works on color image denoising methods for impulse noise. Section 3 introduces some preliminary concepts for the problem of color image denoising. Section 4 describes the proposed adaptive filter and the evolutionary process used for its training. Section 5 shows the experimental results obtained from a comparison of the proposed filter with other methods for filtering. Finally, Section 6 presents some concluding remarks.

2. Related Works

A large number of filters for impulse noise removal from color images have been proposed in the literature, e.g., [15]. Two types of filters, robust and adaptive, stand out in scenarios where images are degraded by complex noise patterns or variations in lighting and contrast. Robust filters deal with noisy pixels as a violation of the spatial coherence of the image intensities. The most well-known robust filter is the vector median filter (VMF) [16], a non-linear method that is still a reference in the field. The VMF orders the color input vectors based on their relative magnitude differences in a predefined sliding window. However, robust filters apply a correction procedure to every image pixel, even if the pixels are not noisy. Therefore, filtered images commonly present too much smoothing and extensive blurring [9]. Other methods exploit the sparsity of the image in some transform domains, formulating noise removal as an optimization problem. For example, the generalized synthesis and analysis prior algorithm (GSAPA) proposed in [17] uses the split-Bregman technique to break down the optimization problem with multiple regularization parameters into relatively easy-to-solve subproblems. In [18], an extension of the mean-shift technique was introduced to effectively reduce Gaussian and impulsive noise in color digital images; utilizing a novel similarity measure between pixels and a patch at the block's center, the technique demonstrates efficiency in restoring heavily disturbed images.

On the other hand, adaptive filters assume that only some image pixels are perturbed by noise. These filters adapt to various image characteristics and noise statistics using different approaches. One of these approaches is the fuzzy peer-group concept, which associates a set of neighboring pixels whose distance to a central pixel does not exceed a threshold founded on fuzzy logic (see, for example, [19]). Under this approach, the fuzzy modified peer-group filter (FMPGF) [20] stands out due to its efficiency. Other approaches use fuzzy logic tools to measure magnitude differences, providing an adaptive framework to distinguish between noise and data. For example, the adaptive fuzzy filter proposed in [21] uses a noise-detection mechanism to select a small portion of input image pixels and convolves them with a set of weighted kernels to create a layer of convolved feature vectors. The feature vectors are then fed into a fuzzy inference system, where fuzzy membership degrees and a reduced set of fuzzy rules play a crucial role in categorizing pixels as either noise-free, associated with edges, or noisy. Another fuzzy inference rule-based filter for impulse noise is the noise adaptive fuzzy switching median (NAFSM) filter [22]. The NAFSM filter uses two-stage processing specialized for salt-and-pepper noise detection and removal, preserving strong edges through spatial averaging. A recent contribution in a similar vein is the adaptive fuzzy filter based on histogram estimation (AFHE) [23]. The AFHE filter dynamically adjusts the window size based on local noise densities using fuzzy-based criteria. Additionally, it incorporates an iterative procedure based on the Gaussian mean for further processing. Another recent development presented in [24] introduces a spatio-temporal filter designed to eliminate impulse noise from videos through the application of fuzzy logic. The distinctive feature of this filter is its ability to leverage both spatial and temporal correlations and color components in a sequential process, allowing it to effectively handle high impulse noise levels, even up to 70%. Other adaptive approaches are based on more straightforward decisions, such as the decision-based algorithm for the removal of impulse noise (DBAIN) [25]. The DBAIN filter processes a noisy image by first detecting salt-and-pepper noise (as its major decision) and then replacing the noisy pixel values with the median of their neighboring pixels. Some comprehensive studies of adaptive filters for impulse noise removal from color images are presented in [15,26].

Machine learning-based techniques have also been applied to remove impulse noise from color images. For example, a support vector machine (SVM)-based filtering technique was proposed in [27]. Later, fuzzy c-means (FCM) clustering combined with a fuzzy-support vector machine (FSVM) was introduced in [28]. Additionally, multiple neuro-fuzzy filters were trained with an artificial bee colony algorithm and combined with a decision tree algorithm in [29] to denoise corrupted images. Also, neural network-based denoising methods are another popular approach. For instance, a convolutional neural network-based denoising method mainly composed of a sparse block, a feature enhancement block, an attention block, and a reconstruction block was described in [30]. Also, a convolutional autoencoder-based feature map domain was combined with low-rank models to improve denoising quality in [31]. Recently, a novel denoising network called DeQCANet was introduced in [32] for removing color random-valued impulse noise. This work implements a quaternion convolutional neural network, incorporating a novel quaternion map construction strategy to enhance color features across channels. The proposed denoising technique exhibits competitive performance compared to other well-established methods for denoising color images. Another recent development is the impulse detection convolutional neural network (IDCNN) introduced in [33], which utilizes a switching filtering technique consisting of a deep neural network architecture to detect noisy pixels, followed by a restoration stage of these pixels through the fast adaptive mean filter. In [34], a neural network architecture was introduced to recognize images affected by random-valued impulse noise, comprising a preprocessing stage and incorporating a pixel distortion detector, a cleaning mechanism, and a neural network complex for image recognition. An overview of deep learning techniques on image denoising can be found in [35]. While convolutional neural networks and deep learning-based approaches excel in performance, they are complex and opaque. Their intricate architectures and complex hierarchical representations in these techniques make it challenging to decipher the exact decision-making process, limiting the transparency and understanding of how the denoising outcomes are achieved. Achieving transparency is crucial for various reasons, especially in applications where interpretability is essential for user trust, accountability, and ethical considerations.

Alternative filtering techniques tackle the challenge of image denoising through an evolutionary computing approach. For instance, in [36], Toledo et al. introduced a denoising method employing a genetic algorithm. In their method, an input noisy image is represented as an individual, and the individuals of the initial population are represented as mutated versions of the image. The evolutionary process applied to the population allows for the continuous refinement and adaptation of the original noisy individual until an enhanced image is found. In a similar vein, in [37], we addressed image denoising by merging output images of robust and adaptive filters to integrate them as an evolving population for a genetic algorithm. Genetic algorithms, in this context, are frequently employed to fine-tune specific filter parameters, essentially framing them as an optimization task. On the other hand, genetic programming has emerged as a highly promising field for the creation of adaptive filters aimed at noise reduction; however, no filters use genetic programming to remove impulse noise from color digital images. Nevertheless, there are a few works that have addressed impulse noise removal for grayscale images, the most relevant being [38–40].

Petrovic and Crnojevic [38] used genetic programming to produce two binary classification models for identifying noisy pixels in grayscale images following a cascade approach. While the first model identifies the majority of noisy pixels located within homogeneous regions of the image, the second is trained to specialize in identifying complex cases of noisy pixels (e.g., those with amplitudes close to their local neighborhood). The classification models were trained using test images contaminated with a mixture of two impulse noise models: salt and pepper and uniform. Once the noisy pixels are detected, they are corrected using a conventional α-trimmed mean method as part of a two-stage filter. On the other hand, Majid et al. [39] used genetic programming to estimate the optimal value of every noisy pixel in a grayscale image. The estimation combines the useful information of local clean pixels within a small neighborhood with arithmetic operators. In their approach, Majid et al. used the directional derivative to detect pixels perturbed by salt-and-pepper and uniform noise. Their filter was tested using standard images perturbed with a noise density from 10 to 90%. Their experimental results showed that, compared to other approaches, their filter can restore noisy images while preserving edges and fine details, especially in the presence of high impulse noise density. Khmag et al. [40] presented a filter based on a two-step switching scheme to remove both salt-and-pepper and additive white Gaussian noises. Their filter uses a patch-based approach, which decomposes a noisy image into a group of patches and then applies a clustering process to gather all patches with the same features and textures. They use genetic programming to generate an adaptive local filter to denoise each singular class of patches with different textural forms. The restoration process of these filters is performed by applying second-generation wavelet thresholding to the clustered patches. Other applications of genetic programming in image processing can be found in [41]. It is important to emphasize that although many of the techniques developed for monochrome images can be directly applied to color image denoising, the independent processing of color image channels is commonly inappropriate, leading to the generation of strong artifacts. To address this challenge, developing methodologies that effectively exploit the inherent correlation among color channels becomes imperative, ensuring more accurate and artifact-free denoising results in the realm of color image processing.

3. Preliminaries: Color Image Denoising

Let I be an image with red-green-blue (RGB) color space with values from 0 to 255. The image I is represented by a two-dimensional matrix consisting of N pixels. Each color pixel $\vec{x}_i$ is a three-dimensional vector, with one dimension for each color primary or channel, where $i = 1 \ldots N$ indicates the pixel location on the image domain.

3.1. Impulse Noise Models

There are three impulse noise models used for color images in the contemporary literature [42]. These models differ according to the noise correlation of the image channels and how the noise affects the pixels. Let x_i^q be a random variable whose output represents a value corrupted by noise in the q-th channel of pixel $\vec{x}_i$. Then, x_i^q behaves according to the following models:

(a) Salt-and-pepper noise. The value of x_i^q can only be 0 or 255 with the same probability.
(b) Uniform impulse noise. The value of x_i^q is chosen independently and uniformly at random from the range $[0, 255]$.
(c) Correlated impulse noise. The value of x_i^q is any number uniformly distributed between 0 and 255 for all $q \in \{1, 2, 3\}$.

Let p be the probability of the appearance of noise in any pixel $\vec{x}_i$. Then, the amount of noise (or noise density) is distributed randomly over approximately $p \times 100\%$ pixels of the image.

3.2. Image Quality Metrics

In this work, the following metrics are used to objectively measure the quality of the output images after the filtering process: the peak signal-to-noise ratio (PSNR), mean absolute error (MAE), structural similarity index measure (SSIM), and feature similarity index measure (FSIM). These metrics provide quantitative values of how close or far a filtered image I_F is from its original reference image I_O.

The PSNR and MAE are the most widely used and straightforward full-reference quality metrics. The advantages of these metrics are that they are simple to calculate, transparent in physical meaning, and independent of visual conditions. The PSNR measures the effectiveness of a filter in removing noise, whereas the MAE evaluates the performance of a filter in preserving the details of an image. The PSNR measure is defined via the mean-square error (MSE) as follows:

$$\text{PSNR} = 20 \log_{10}\left(\frac{255}{\sqrt{\text{MSE}}}\right), \tag{1}$$

$$\text{MSE} = \frac{1}{3N}\sum_{i=1}^{N}\sum_{q=1}^{3}(I_O(x_i^q) - I_F(x_i^q))^2. \tag{2}$$

The MAE measure is expressed in the following form:

$$\text{MAE} = \frac{1}{3N}\sum_{i=1}^{N}\sum_{q=1}^{3}\left|I_O(x_i^q) - I_F(x_i^q)\right|. \tag{3}$$

Note that a high PSNR value means a higher amount of noise removed from the image. Conversely, a low MAE value means fewer lost details in the image. The computational complexity of these two metrics is $O(N)$ for any color image I.

On the other hand, the SSIM and FSIM are metrics that compute the similarity between restored and original images based on human visual perception. The SSIM compares local patterns of pixel intensities normalized for luminance and contrast, whereas the FSIM makes the comparison based on two low-level features: phase congruency and gradient magnitude. The SSIM is defined as

$$\mathrm{SSIM}(I_O, I_F) = \frac{2\mu_{I_O}\mu_{I_F} + C_1}{\mu_{I_O}^2 + \mu_{I_F}^2 + C_1} \cdot \frac{2\sigma_{I_O}\sigma_{I_F} + C_2}{\sigma_{I_O}^2 + \sigma_{I_F}^2 + C_2} \cdot \frac{\sigma_{I_O I_F} + C_3}{\sigma_{I_O}\sigma_{I_F} + C_3}, \tag{4}$$

where the first term signifies the luminance comparison function, assessing the proximity of the mean luminance in both images (μ_{I_O} and μ_{I_F}). The second term represents the contrast comparison function, gauging the similarity in contrast between the two images, as measured by their standard deviations (σ_{I_O} and σ_{I_F}). The third term indicates the structure comparison function, quantifying the correlation coefficient between the images I_O and I_F. The positive constants C_1, C_2, and C_3 are introduced to prevent division by zero.

On the other hand, the FSIM is defined as

$$\mathrm{FSIM}(I_O, I_F) = \frac{1}{N} \sum_{x,y} F(I_O(x,y), I_F(x,y)), \tag{5}$$

where $F(I_O(x,y), I_F(x,y))$ is a function that measures the similarity between the corresponding pixel values (x,y) in the two images. This function typically takes into account the luminance, contrast, and structure comparisons. The formulation and mathematical details of the SSIM and FSIM can be found in [43] and [44], respectively. Unlike the PSNR and MAE metrics, the SSIM and FSIM are normalized between 0 and 1, with 1 being the best possible result. However, the SSIM and FSIM have a higher computational complexity compared to the PSNR and MAE.

4. Methodology

The proposed adaptive filter consists of two main stages for color image denoising: detection and correction. The detection stage takes a color image I_N perturbed by impulse noise as input. In this stage, the color image is split into R, G, and B channels to separately evaluate each pixel in a binary classification model. For each channel, the model produces a binary mask representing the set of pixels classified as noisy.

The correction stage uses a version of a vector median filter applied only to the identified noisy pixels. The correction process of any pixel $\vec{x}_i$ consists of modifying one or more of its RGB channel values according to the pixel intensity values of its neighbors. In this context, the set of neighboring pixels of $\vec{x}_i$, denoted as $\mathcal{N}(\vec{x}_i)$, represents a 3×3 square window centered on $\vec{x}_i$ in the spatial domain of the image. Modifying the pixel value of $\vec{x}_i$ requires computing the sum of the absolute differences of the pixel intensities between $\vec{x}_i$ and its neighborhood. These differences among pixel intensities around $\vec{x}_i$ are denoted as $d_i^{\mathcal{N}(\vec{x}_i)}$ such that

$$d_i^{\mathcal{N}(\vec{x}_i)} = \sum_{\forall \vec{x}_j \in \mathcal{N}(\vec{x}_i)} ||\vec{x}_i - \vec{x}_j||_1. \tag{6}$$

Let $D(\vec{x}_i)$ be the set of the pixel intensity differences between every pair of pixels considering $\vec{x}_i$ and its neighborhood, i.e., $D(\vec{x}_i) = \{d_j^{\mathcal{N}(\vec{x}_i)} | \forall \vec{x}_j \in \mathcal{N}(\vec{x}_i)\}$. Then, a noisy pixel $\vec{x}_i$ is replaced (in one or more of its channels) with the element with the minimum values from $D(\vec{x}_i)$. If only one channel of pixel $\vec{x}_i$ is identified as noisy (and the other two are not), only the perturbed value of this channel is replaced. On the other hand, if at least two channels are noisy in $\vec{x}_i$, then the pixel is replaced entirely. Since building the set $D(\vec{x}_i)$ requires $O(1)$ time given a fixed 3×3 window, the correction of the noisy pixels takes $O(N)$ time to complete. After the correction process, a new color image I_F is generated. Figure 1 illustrates the two stages of the adaptive filter.

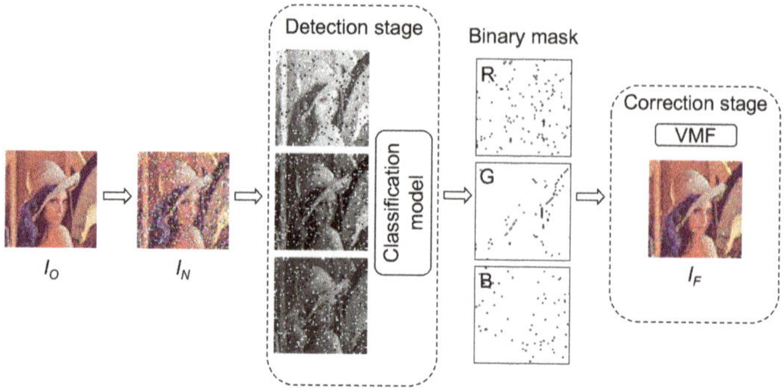

Figure 1. The sequence of the adaptive filter's stages: the detection stage takes as input a noised image I_N, splitting it into its color channels, and then it uses a classification model to detect noisy pixels; the correction stage uses a vector median filter to repair only the detected noisy pixels.

4.1. Genetic Programming Design

We use genetic programming to generate the binary classification model for detecting noisy pixels in a color image. In a typical machine learning workflow, the training stage involves using a dataset to produce the classification model, whereas only a single image is required in the proposed evolutionary approach. This approach leverages the versatility and adaptability of the genetic programming design, allowing it to effectively learn and adapt to complex noise patterns using only a single training instance. This training image I has a noised version I_N perturbed by the impulse noise models described in Section 3.1.

In this context, an individual is a classification model used to evaluate any pixel $\vec{x}_i$ of an image I to decide whether $\vec{x}_i$ is noisy. An individual is represented by a parse tree structure with $O(m)$ nodes selected from a set of primitives consisting of functions and terminals. The internal nodes of the tree consist of a set of functions $F = \{$`add(x,y)`, `sub(x,y)`, `mul(x,y)`, `mydiv(x,y)`, `mysigmoid(x)`$\}$. Four elements of the set of functions denote the basic arithmetic operations of addition, subtraction, multiplication, and division. In particular, the division operator `mydiv(x,y)` is protected in the sense that it does not signal "division by zero". The sigmoid function `mysigmoid(x)` $= \frac{1}{1+e^{-x}}$ guarantees that the results range between 0 and 1.

Additionally, the leaves of the tree consist of a set of terminals $T = \{$`pc_dist`, `mu_dist`, `median_dist`, `sd_dist`, `pxc`$\}$ that apply statistics operations to the set of neighboring pixels $\mathcal{N}(\vec{x}_i)$ of pixel $\vec{x}_i$ in image I. Given a fixed 3×3 window size, the computations of these statistics take $O(1)$ time. Table 1 describes the set of terminals. It should be noted that the selection of the set of primitives (functions and terminals) was mainly carried out through some preliminary experimental tests.

Table 1. Description of the set of terminal primitives T representing the different features of neighboring pixels.

Primitive	Description
`pc_dist`	The differences among pixel intensities around $\vec{x}_i$, i.e., $d_i^{\mathcal{N}(\vec{x}_i)}$.
`mu_dist`	Average of the set $D(\vec{x}_i)$.
`median_dist`	Median of the set $D(\vec{x}_i)$.
`sd_dist`	Standard deviation of the set $D(\vec{x}_i)$.
`pxc`	The RGB values of pixel $\vec{x}_i$.
$[-1 \ldots 1]$	Random values within the range of -1 to 1.

On the other hand, an individual's fitness represents its ability to correctly detect noisy pixels in an image. For this aim, an image I_O is perturbed using the three impulse noise models, each with a density of 10%, as described in Section 3.1. The produced noisy image

I_N is used as input for each individual of the initial population. Each individual of the population independently evaluates each pixel $\vec{x}_i$ of I_N to decide whether $\vec{x}_i$ is perturbed by noise. Evaluating any pixel requires $O(m)$ time for any individual; therefore, the detection process requires $O(mN)$ time to complete. The output generated by each individual is a binary mask indicating which pixels are identified as noisy in I_N. This binary mask is used in the correction stage to produce the filtered image I_F, which is compared to I_O via the image quality metrics PSNR and MAE described in Section 3.2. The results of these metrics are used to compute the individual's fitness in the detection stage. It is worth noting that only these two metrics were chosen due to their low computational complexity. Figure 2 illustrates this procedure.

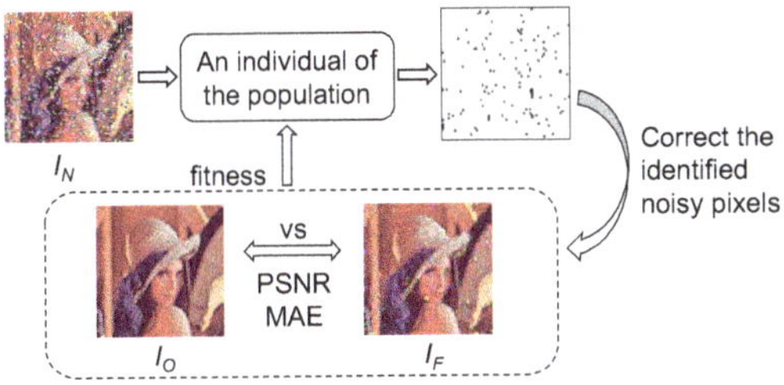

Figure 2. The fitness computation process for an individual I_F of the population by comparing I_F to an original reference image I_O.

4.2. The Proposed Evolutionary Algorithm

As part of the evolutionary process (also called training), the population of individuals produces offspring through crossover and mutation operators. The offspring have their fitness evaluated and compete for a place in the next generation. This process iterates until a certain number of generations is reached. This evolutionary process is described in Algorithm 1.

Algorithm 1: The evolutionary process of the detection stage

Input: A color image I_N perturbed by impulse noise.
Output: A classification model trained to identify the noisy pixels of I_N.
1: (Initialization) Generates a set of μ individuals from the initial population.
2: (Evaluation) Evaluates the fitness of each individual of the initial population.
3: **repeat**
  4: (Selection of parents) Builds a group of $\lambda = P_c\mu$ individuals based on their fitness.
  5: (Crossover) Recombines the pairs of selected parents to generate a set of λ offspring.
  6: (Mutation) Mutates the offspring with a probability of P_m through the correction of the image.
  7: (Evaluation) Evaluates the fitness of each individual of the λ offspring.
  8: (Survivor selection) Builds a new generation of μ individuals using deterministic fitness-based replacement.
until *it completes* τ *generations*;
9: **return** the fittest individual of the last generation.

Line 1 of Algorithm 1 generates an initial population of μ random individuals. To generate this population, we use the simplest and most popular `full` method to produce complete random trees. Each tree is generated recursively by randomly selecting primitives from the sets of functions and terminals. Primitives from the set of functions F are selected as the internal nodes of the tree, whereas those from the set of terminals T are selected as the leaves. The maximum depth of each of the initial trees is constrained to three. Considering random trees of size $O(m)$, the initial population generation requires $O(\mu m)$ time.

Lines 2 and 7 of Algorithm 1 perform the fitness evaluation of each individual of the population. The quality metrics MAE and PSNR, described in Section 3.2, are used for this aim. These metrics compare a filtered image I_F, produced by the detection and correction stages according to each individual, with its noiseless version I_O (see Figure 2). The MAE indicates a better filter performance with a lower value, and the PSNR does the same with a higher value. Then, maximizing fitness is equivalent to maximizing the ratio between the MAE and PSNR. The fitness evaluation for all the μ individuals of the population takes $O(\mu m N)$ time. Note that the SSIM and FSIM are not considered in the fitness evaluation due to their higher computational complexity.

Line 4 of Algorithm 1 performs a random selection of pairs of individuals with replacement until it generates a group of $\lambda = P_c\mu$ individuals, where P_c denotes the crossover ratio. The tournament selection is used to randomly select three individuals from the population and then select the fittest two. Implementing the tournament selection requires $O(\mu)$ time.

Line 5 of Algorithm 1 recombines pairs of individuals from the group selected by Line 4. A one-point crossover is used, where a random vertex is chosen within two copies of parent individuals, and then they exchange the subtrees rooted at the selected vertices between them. Recombining the entire population requires $O(\mu)$ time.

Line 6 of Algorithm 1 implements the uniform mutation operator to introduce diversity in the population. This operator takes as input an individual with probability P_m, and then it randomly selects a vertex of the tree to replace it with a new random subtree. Each subtree is generated using the `full` method in $O(m)$ time. Thus, uniform mutation applied to the $P_m\lambda$ offspring takes $O(\mu m)$ time.

Line 8 of Algorithm 1 generates a new population through the union of the μ individuals from the last population and their λ offspring. A fitness-based replacement (implemented with a sorting algorithm) is used, guaranteeing the survival of the fittest individuals. The execution time of this step is $O(\mu \log \mu)$.

Finally, Algorithm 1 iterates Lines 4–8 until they complete τ generations. Then, the algorithm returns the fittest individual of the last generation (Line 9). The overall execution time of Algorithm 1 is $O(\tau\mu(mN + \log \mu))$.

5. Experimental Results

Experiments were conducted to evaluate the performance of the proposed adaptive filter. The filter was implemented using scikit-image 0.18.3, a Python module that includes a collection of algorithms designed for image processing. Additionally, the evolutionary process (described in Algorithm 1) and its variation operations were implemented using DEAP 1.2.2, an open source evolutionary computation framework. The experiments were carried out on a 3.6 GHz Intel Core i7 (Mac) with four cores, 8 GB of RAM, and OS X 11.5.2.

5.1. Determination of Parameters

The classification model's training process was performed using a 24-bit color version of the popular image of Lena. This training image, denoted as I_N in Section 4, was simultaneously contaminated by the three impulse noise models with a total density of 30%, i.e., 10% for each of the models described in Section 3.1. Combining the impulse noise models into a single image provides insights into the algorithm's ability to handle various noise types and densities by evaluating the proposed method's robustness, generalization capabilities, and potential practical utility in image processing applications.

On the other hand, Table 2 shows the evolutionary settings used by the genetic program during the training process. These settings were estimated via experimentation and validation. A set of preliminary trials was conducted to find the best parameters of Algorithm 1 by considering the tradeoff between time and efficiency; however, similar to other evolutionary techniques, this approach has the limitations expressed in the NFL (no free lunch) by considering that there is no single set of evolutionary settings that will perform optimally on all possible color digital images.

Table 2. Configuration settings of the proposed genetic programming algorithm related to its behavior and performance during the training process.

Parameter	Value
Population size, μ	100
Crossover rate, P_c	0.9
Mutation rate, P_m	0.1
Parent selection	Tournament ($k = 3$)
Survivor selection	Fitness-based ($\mu + \lambda$)
Completion criteria	When the algorithm reaches $\tau = 100$ generations

After model training, a set of trees (representing the individuals of the last generation) was produced. Each of these trees comprises the set of primitives (functions and terminals) described in Section 4.1. The tree identified as the fittest individual is available in a PDF, which can be downloaded from https://bitbucket.org/dfajardod/impulse_noise_gpfilter/src/ (accessed on 20 October 2023).

5.2. Benchmarks

Thirty benchmarking color images were used as test images for the proposed adaptive filter (GP). Each of these images was perturbed by the three impulse noise models with four different densities (5%, 10%, 15%, and 20%), i.e., a total of 360 test color images. These noise densities were selected to ensure a more equitable comparison among the different comparison filters. This decision stems from the recognition that certain filters have been specifically designed for higher noise densities, whereas others may perform more effectively in scenarios with lower noise levels. By evaluating the filters across an intersecting range of noise densities, we aim to conduct a comprehensive and balanced assessment. In this vein, the comparison of filters encompassed a diversity of robust and adaptive filters, some of which are widely used in digital image processing, whereas others use advanced adaptive methods. Filters using fuzzy logic tools to provide adaptiveness to local features were used, such as the fuzzy metric peer-group filter (FMPGF) and the noise adaptive fuzzy switching median (NASFM). Additionally, the decision-based algorithm for removing impulse noise (DBAIN) was also used, a filter designed for highly corrupted color images. Given their performance, the vector median filter (VMF) and the generalized synthesis and analysis prior algorithm (GSAPA) were also considered. Finally, a deep learning approach, the impulse detection convolutional neural network (IDCNN), was also used. The performance metrics used to compare the quality of the resulting images of these filters were the MAE, PSNR, SSIM, and FSIM (described in Section 3.2).

5.3. Performance of the Detection Stage

Experiments were conducted to measure the performance of the binary classification model implemented in the detection stage of the proposed GP filter. To this end, prior information about noisy pixel locations was stored by comparing the 360 test noisy images with their noiseless original counterparts. Later, the detection stage of the proposed GP was applied by classifying pixels as noisy or not noisy. Finally, a comparison of the model predictions with the stored prior information enabled the generation of a confusion matrix containing true positive (tp), true negative (tn), false positive (fp), and false negative (fn) predictions. The performance metrics applied to these predictions were the following: accuracy, precision, recall, specificity, and F1 score.

Accuracy (Acc.) indicates the extent to which the predictions about the condition of the pixels differed from the real conditions, i.e., Acc = (tp + tn)/(tp + tn + fp + fn). Precision (Prec.) indicates how well the classifier performed concerning each pixel's noisy or noiseless status, computed by tp/(tp + fp). On the other hand, recall (or sensitivity) is the percentage of noisy pixels that were correctly identified, calculated by tp/(tp + fn). Similarly, regarding the noiseless pixels, specificity (Spec.) is calculated by tn/(tn + fp). Finally, the F1 score represents the harmonic mean of precision and recall, i.e., F1 = (Prec·Recall)/(Prec + Recall).

Table 3 shows the average results of the performance metrics regarding the proposed binary classification model. As can be observed, in general, the model increased the accuracy, precision, and F1 score according to the increase in the image's noise density, whereas the sensibility and specificity decreased in this respect. Note that the model is highly efficient in detecting noisy rather than noiseless pixels. Finally, although the model achieved a better balance between precision and recall in terms of salt-and-pepper noise, better accuracy was obtained in terms of uniform and correlated noise.

Table 3. Average performance of the binary classification model applied to the test images perturbed by salt-and-pepper, uniform, or correlated noise.

		$p = 0.05$	$p = 0.10$	$p = 0.15$	$p = 0.20$
Salt and pepper	Acc.	0.7558	0.7462	0.7696	0.7906
	Prec.	0.3668	0.5107	0.6192	0.6963
	Recall	0.9981	0.9939	0.9853	0.9702
	Spec.	0.7191	0.6635	0.6495	0.6412
	F1	0.5306	0.6697	0.7570	0.8086
Uniform	Acc.	0.8217	0.7852	0.7776	0.7826
	Prec.	0.3559	0.4647	0.5479	0.6163
	Recall	0.9829	0.9796	0.9740	0.9667
	Spec.	0.8053	0.7427	0.7081	0.6890
	F1	0.5175	0.6271	0.6991	0.7514
Correlated	Acc.	0.8676	0.8428	0.8354	0.8409
	Prec.	0.3009	0.4139	0.4994	0.5773
	Recall	0.9948	0.9934	0.9909	0.9873
	Spec.	0.8611	0.8266	0.8088	0.8054
	F1	0.4515	0.5738	0.6547	0.7209

Since the correction stage of the proposed GP filter consists of a modified version of the VMF (see Section 4), the average performance comparisons shown in the following section allow us to determine the influence of the detection stage on the efficiency of the GP filter.

5.4. Performance of the Proposed Filter

Tables 4 and 5 show the average results of the quality metrics obtained after filtering the test images to remove each of the impulse noise models: salt and pepper, uniform, and correlated. Table 4 presents the average values of the MAE and PSNR, whereas Table 5 shows those corresponding to the SSIM and FSIM.

As observed in Tables 4 and 5, in general, the proposed GP filter ranked second in average values across all quality metrics (MAE, PSNR, SSIM, and FSIM) for the uniform and correlated noise models, closely following the IDCNN filter. This suggests that the GP filter performed well overall compared to the other filters, particularly in conjunction with these noise models. Regarding salt-and-pepper noise, the DBAIN filter excelled across all quality metrics, closely paralleled by the NAFSM and IDCNN filters. This behavior was due to their specialization in detecting and removing this noise model. However, the competitiveness of the NAFSM and DBAIN filters declined for the uniform and correlated noise. Furthermore, the difference in magnitude of their average values for these noise models was significant, becoming more pronounced as the noise became more prevalent, showcasing a specialization that might not generalize well to other noise types. The IDCNN filter, based on a deep learning model, exhibited robustness to variations in the scale, orientation, and lighting conditions of color images, demonstrating its adaptability to different image textures and noise models. VMF, on the other hand, notably produced images with lower-quality values. This is because it did not differentiate between pixels based on their noise levels or the type of noise they exhibited, resulting in excessive blurring in images with large contrasting regions. Finally, the proposed GP filter generally outperformed the GSAPA and FMPGF filters across all noise models, demonstrating competitive performance across different noise models and ranking consistently well compared to other filters.

Table 4. Performance comparison of the average MAE and PSNR values of the filters applied to the test images perturbed by salt-and-pepper, uniform, and correlated noise. The best, second-best, and third-best values are indicated in purple, teal, and brown, respectively.

	Filter	$p = 0.05$		$p = 0.10$		$p = 0.15$		$p = 0.20$	
		MAE	PSNR	MAE	PSNR	MAE	PSNR	MAE	PSNR
Salt and pepper	IDCNN [33]	0.7903	38.1716	1.4747	34.4618	2.4699	29.4046	4.9519	23.0100
	GP	1.0939	35.0095	1.5978	31.5771	2.5213	27.6317	4.1993	23.6414
	DBAIN [25]	0.4772	38.4290	0.7630	36.0019	1.1004	34.0328	1.5002	32.3204
	NAFSM [22]	0.6070	36.1685	0.9462	34.2428	1.2883	32.9280	1.6345	31.8994
	GSAPA [17]	2.6156	31.7966	2.9833	31.0663	3.5351	30.1346	4.2661	29.2487
	FMPGF [20]	2.2195	28.8003	3.8605	24.0488	6.5878	20.4174	10.4068	17.8075
	VMF [16]	3.1961	30.5483	3.8062	27.4112	5.1515	23.2530	8.0343	19.2650
Uniform	IDCNN [33]	0.7684	38.3377	1.3842	35.3368	2.0003	33.3050	2.7118	31.1671
	GP	1.0140	34.4532	1.3874	32.1703	1.9043	30.1309	2.6113	28.2127
	DBAIN [25]	4.8939	20.3859	9.1438	17.5642	13.3550	15.8917	17.5735	14.6853
	NAFSM [22]	4.8221	20.4132	9.2765	17.5368	13.6620	15.8390	18.0242	14.6200
	GSAPA [17]	2.6536	31.7040	2.9988	31.0339	3.4723	30.2954	4.2545	29.2325
	FMPGF [20]	2.2267	29.4335	3.2508	27.5745	4.3313	26.0814	5.5097	24.7540
	VMF [16]	3.1275	31.6515	3.4545	30.3364	3.8811	28.9711	4.4963	27.3815
Correlated	IDCNN [33]	0.3695	42.2402	0.6119	39.4709	0.8544	37.7503	1.0627	36.6582
	GP	0.9586	34.9322	1.2799	32.9630	1.7195	30.9907	2.3007	29.0910
	DBAIN [25]	4.8995	20.3836	9.1560	17.5635	13.3640	15.8837	17.6076	14.6789
	NAFSM [22]	4.8599	20.3924	9.2837	17.5376	13.6712	15.8314	18.0630	14.6114
	GSAPA [17]	2.6684	31.6861	3.0830	30.9442	3.7525	29.8858	4.7601	28.4749
	FMPGF [20]	1.5161	31.8201	1.8178	31.0714	2.1347	30.3423	2.4708	29.6420
	VMF [16]	3.1635	31.5580	3.4802	30.3551	3.8537	29.1292	4.3345	27.7417

Table 5. Performance comparison of the average SSIM and FSIM values of the filters applied to the test images perturbed by salt-and-pepper, uniform, and correlated noise. The best, second-best, and third-best values are indicated in purple, teal, and brown, respectively.

	Filter	$p = 0.05$		$p = 0.10$		$p = 0.15$		$p = 0.20$	
		SSIM	**FSIM**	**SSIM**	**FSIM**	**SSIM**	**FSIM**	**SSIM**	**FSIM**
Salt and pepper	IDCNN [33]	0.9902	0.9928	0.9788	0.9846	0.9461	0.9659	0.8297	0.9056
	GP	0.9792	0.9872	0.9681	0.9819	0.9365	0.9682	0.8642	0.9360
	DBAIN [25]	0.9919	0.9957	0.9875	0.9935	0.9819	0.9905	0.9745	0.9864
	NAFSM [22]	0.9888	0.9938	0.9828	0.9908	0.9770	0.9874	0.9712	0.9836
	GSAPA [17]	0.9681	0.9710	0.9610	0.9656	0.9476	0.9576	0.9256	0.9485
	FMPGF [20]	0.9475	0.9647	0.8679	0.9244	0.7452	0.8589	0.6209	0.7855
	VMF [16]	0.9472	0.9680	0.9146	0.9566	0.8162	0.9227	0.6514	0.8505
Uniform	IDCNN [33]	0.9907	0.9930	0.9829	0.9866	0.9729	0.9795	0.9537	0.9693
	GP	0.9748	0.9866	0.9609	0.9824	0.9371	0.9753	0.9010	0.9633
	DBAIN [25]	0.6042	0.8595	0.4702	0.7747	0.3899	0.7143	0.3318	0.6689
	NAFSM [22]	0.6036	0.8591	0.4693	0.7734	0.3888	0.7127	0.3307	0.6674
	GSAPA [17]	0.9672	0.9701	0.9602	0.9651	0.9478	0.9581	0.9195	0.9468
	FMPGF [20]	0.9305	0.9646	0.8891	0.9464	0.8493	0.9265	0.8108	0.9031
	VMF [16]	0.9519	0.9693	0.9413	0.9654	0.9219	0.9587	0.8857	0.9463
Correlated	IDCNN [33]	0.9951	0.9967	0.9923	0.9943	0.9894	0.9919	0.9868	0.9891
	GP	0.9780	0.9864	0.9706	0.9828	0.9563	0.9765	0.9313	0.9665
	DBAIN [25]	0.6352	0.8648	0.4885	0.7770	0.4017	0.7107	0.3399	0.6585
	NAFSM [22]	0.6348	0.8643	0.4876	0.7757	0.4007	0.7089	0.3386	0.6569
	GSAPA [17]	0.9663	0.9692	0.9545	0.9612	0.9278	0.9460	0.8818	0.9218
	FMPGF [20]	0.9728	0.9785	0.9680	0.9748	0.9628	0.9707	0.9572	0.9663
	VMF [16]	0.9533	0.9683	0.9446	0.9637	0.9313	0.9570	0.9080	0.9463

The average results presented in Tables 4 and 5 encompass a diverse set of 360 test color images with different features such as size, shape, color texture, light conditions, edge characteristics, etc. The complete set of resulting filtered images, along with their original sizes and denoised versions, is available in the Supplementary Materials. However, four test images with different distinguishable characteristics were selected for illustrative purposes to visually analyze the filters' efficiency: Baboon, Goldhill, Pepper, and Caps.

Figure 3 shows the visual results of some of the comparison filters applied to the Baboon image, considering the salt-and-pepper, uniform, and correlated noise models from top to bottom, respectively. Since the Baboon image has more profound and larger textured areas compared to the other test images, robust filters such as the VMF exhibited lower performance. Because of this, the resulting images of this filter were visually omitted. Among the filtered images, Figure 3a closely resembles the version of the image before adding noise. On the other hand, some filtered images show additional artifacts, e.g., Figure 3g. The ICDNN filter (Figure 3j–l) and the proposed GP filter (Figure 3m–o) excelled in noise removal while preserving the details of the images across the three different noise models.

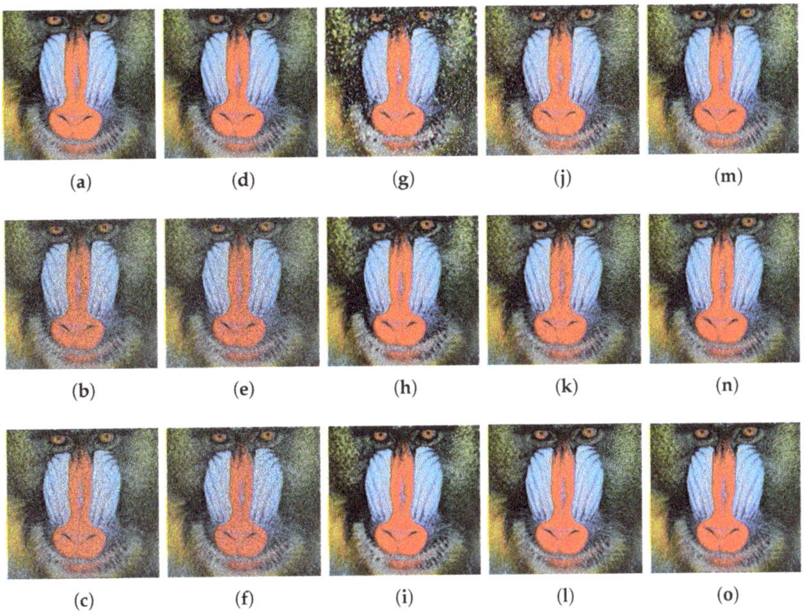

Figure 3. Output images of the five best filters considering the Baboon image perturbed by salt-and-pepper, uniform, and correlated noise, with a noise density of $p = 0.20$: (**a–c**) NAFSM; (**d–f**) DBAIN; (**g–i**) FMPGF; (**j–l**) IDCNN; (**m–o**) GP.

Figure 4 shows the resulting images produced by some of the comparison filters applied to the Goldhill image, arranged according to the three noise models from top to bottom. The Goldhill image has similar color tonalities to the Baboon image but has a few smooth areas and complex geometric patterns, resulting in significant contrast differences. For this reason, the filtered images shown here exhibit similar visual behavior to the filtered Baboon images. As observed in the filtered images, the NAFSM filter performed the best for salt-and-pepper noise (very close to the version of the image before adding noise). Although the IDCNN filter (Figure 4j–l) excelled in noise removal while preserving the details of the images for uniform and correlated noise, the proposed GP (Figure 4m–o) filter maintained consistent performance across the three different noise models. In general, the proposed GP filter ranked second for uniform noise and achieved some of the best MAE values for correlated noise.

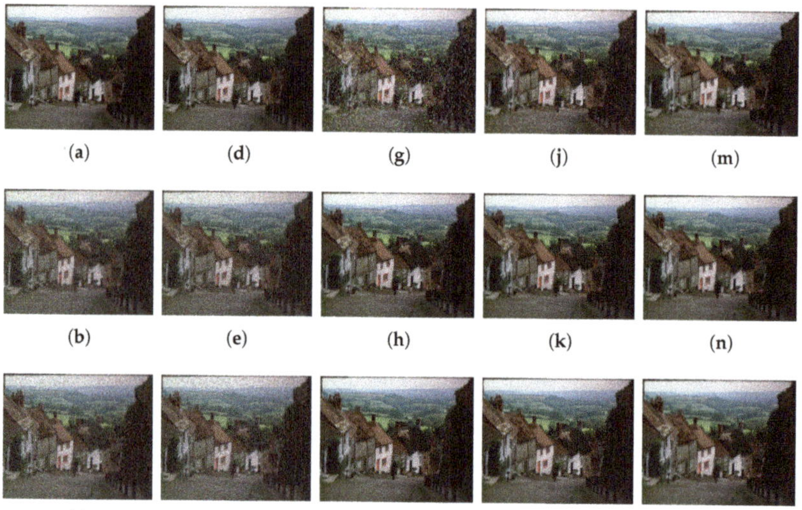

(a) (d) (g) (j) (m)
(b) (e) (h) (k) (n)
(c) (f) (i) (l) (o)

Figure 4. Output images of the five best filters considering the Goldhill image perturbed by salt-and-pepper, uniform, and correlated noise, with a noise density of $p = 0.20$: (**a–c**) NAFSM; (**d–f**) DBAIN; (**g–i**) FMPGF; (**j–l**) IDCNN; (**m–o**) GP.

Figures 5 and 6 show the filtered images produced by some of the filters applied to the images of the Peppers and Caps, respectively, including the VMF (which does not appear in Figures 3 and 4). Unlike the previous images, in these images, the VMF demonstrates very competitive results across the three noise models, even producing some of the best images considering uniform and correlated noise. This is because these images have large, smooth regions with more contrast information. The VMF, IDCNN, and the proposed GP filters were generally competitive in these test images for both the uniform and correlated noise models.

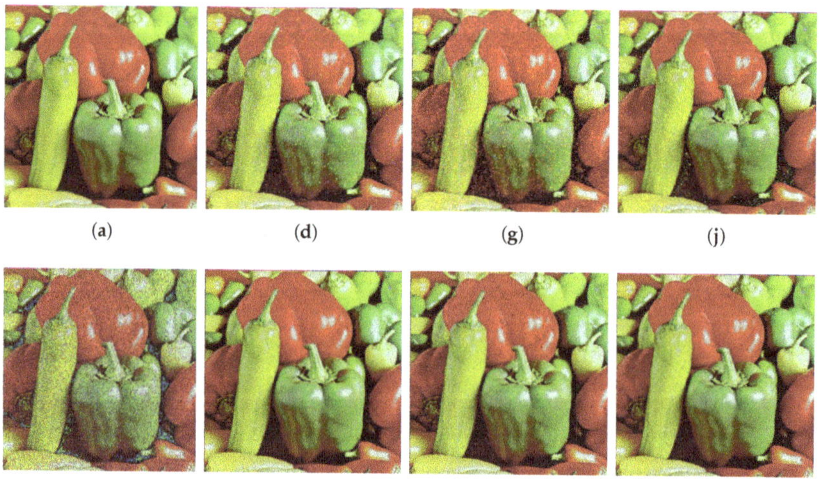

(a) (d) (g) (j)
(b) (e) (h) (k)

Figure 5. *Cont.*

(c) (f) (i) (l)

Figure 5. Output images of the five best filters considering the Peppers image perturbed by salt-and-pepper, uniform, and correlated noise, with a noise density of $p = 0.20$: (**a**–**c**) NAFSM; (**d**–**f**) VMF; (**g**–**i**) IDCNN; (**j**–**l**) GP.

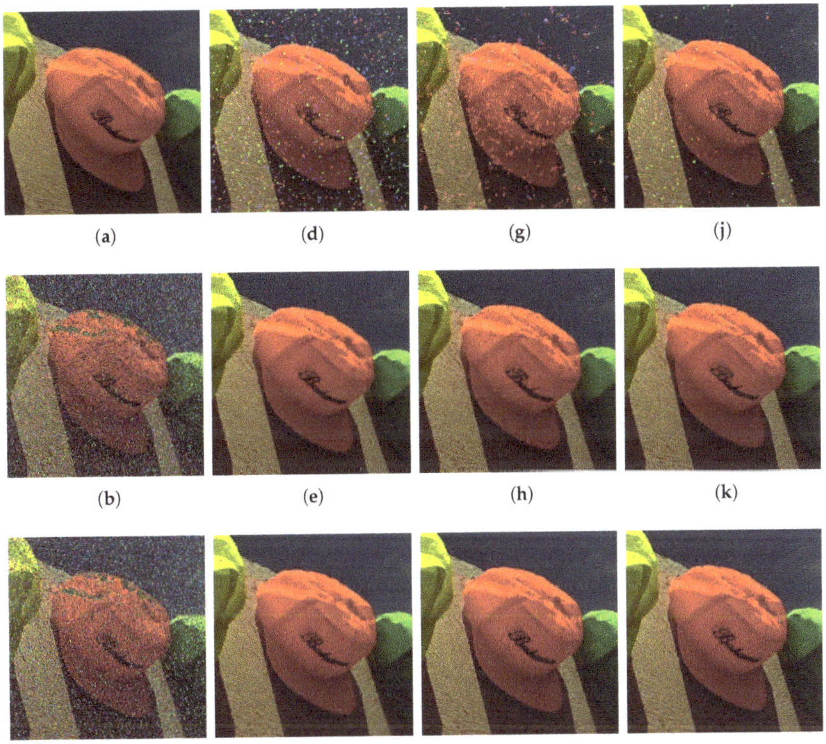

(a) (d) (g) (j)

(b) (e) (h) (k)

(c) (f) (i) (l)

Figure 6. Output images of the five best filters considering the Caps image perturbed by salt-and-pepper, uniform, and correlated noise, with a noise density of $p = 0.20$: (**a**–**c**) NAFSM; (**d**–**f**) VMF; (**g**–**i**) IDCNN; (**j**–**l**) GP.

5.5. Discussion

In this context, overall performance relies on the capacity of a filter to simultaneously detect and remove any impulse noise model (salt and pepper, uniform, or correlated) without a preference or specialization. Therefore, the filtering process for each noise model can be seen as an objective function for a multi-objective problem. Each objective function depends on the image quality metrics used. Since a lower MAE value means fewer lost details in the image, searching for the optimum performance considering the MAE can be seen as a minimization multi-objective problem. Conversely, the cases for the PSNR, SSIM, and FSIM all represent maximization multi-objective problems (see Section 3.2). Figures 7–10 illustrate the extent to which the performance of the comparison filters deviates with respect to a hypothetical optimum, also known as an equilibrium point in the context of multi-objective optimization [45]. In this work, the equilibrium point represents the best values obtained simultaneously for each corresponding noise model.

Figure 7 presents a three-dimensional Pareto front for the MAE average values, considering the complete set of test images with noise densities $p = 0.05, 0.10, 0.15,$ and 0.20. As can be observed, the MAE average values of the proposed GP filter (indicated by a red diamond) are among the closest to the equilibrium point for all noise densities, on par with the IDCNN and GSAPA filters. Given their specialization in salt-and-pepper noise, the NAFSM and DBAIN move away from the equilibrium point as the noise density level increases for the other two noise models. The average values of these two filters are located in a two-dimensional opposite extreme point at $p = 0.20$. Consistent with the results of Table 4, the NAFSM and DBAIN are the furthest from the optimum.

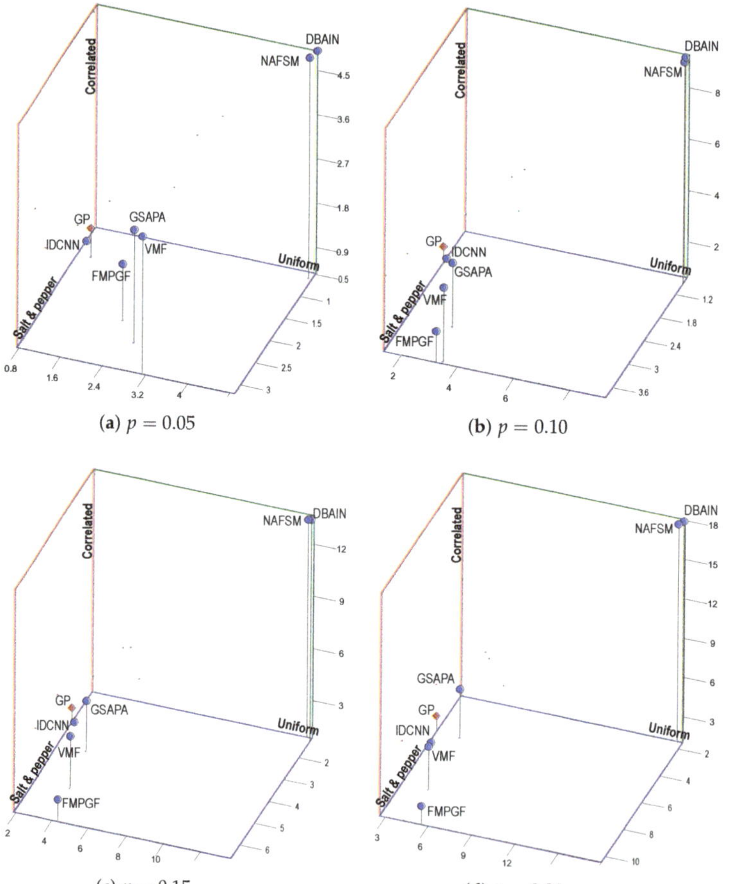

(**a**) $p = 0.05$ (**b**) $p = 0.10$

(**c**) $p = 0.15$ (**d**) $p = 0.20$

Figure 7. Three-dimensional Pareto front for MAE average values by considering the whole set of test images with noise densities $p = 0.05, 0.10, 0.15,$ and 0.20.

Similar to the behaviors shown in Figure 7 but oriented in the opposite direction, Figure 8 depicts the three-dimensional Pareto front for the PSNR average values. In this metric, the IDCNN filter demonstrates the best average values for the maximization multi-objective problem, followed by the GP filter, for $p = 0.05$ and 0.10. However, it is unclear which one of the average values of the IDCNN, GP, or GSAPA filters is the second closest to equilibrium for $p = 0.15$ and 0.20. It is also hard to determine which of the filters yields the furthest average values from the optimum. Unlike in Figure 7, the DBAIN is in a two-dimensional extreme point concerning the equilibrium point across all noise densities, followed by the NAFSM. Similarly to Figure 8, but with normalized values, Figures 9 and 10 present the three-dimensional Pareto fronts for the SSIM and FSIM average values, respectively.

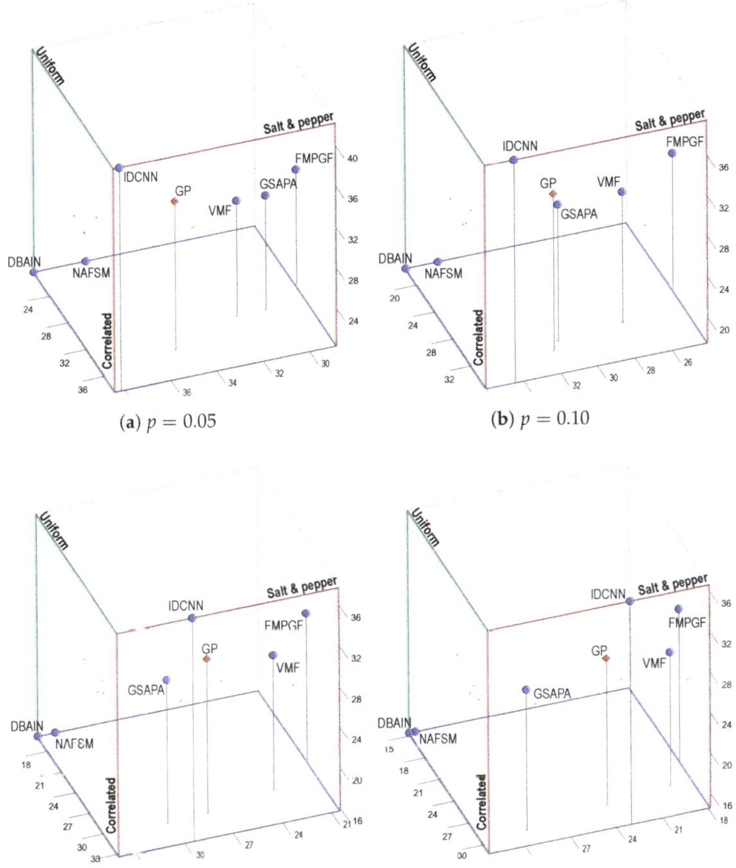

(**a**) $p = 0.05$ (**b**) $p = 0.10$

(**c**) $p = 0.15$ (**d**) $p = 0.20$

Figure 8. Three-dimensional Pareto front for PSNR average values by considering the whole set of test images with noise densities $p = 0.05, 0.10, 0.15,$ and 0.20.

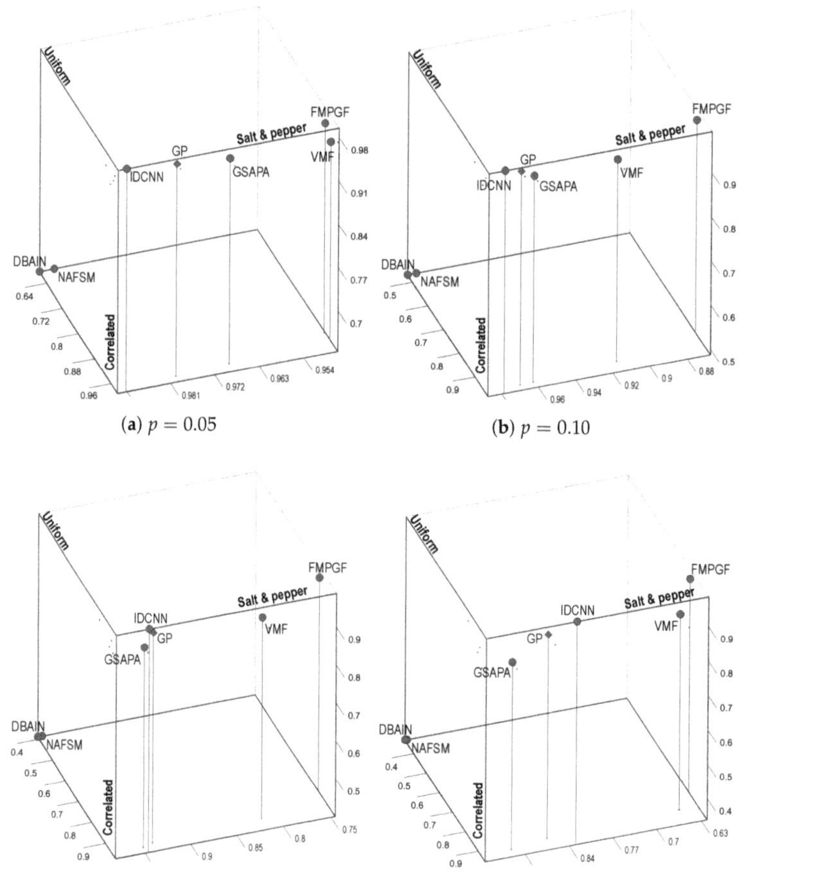

(**a**) $p = 0.05$ (**b**) $p = 0.10$

(**c**) $p = 0.15$ (**d**) $p = 0.20$

Figure 9. Three-dimensional Pareto front for SSIM average values by considering the whole set of test images with noise densities $p = 0.05, 0.10, 0.15,$ and 0.20.

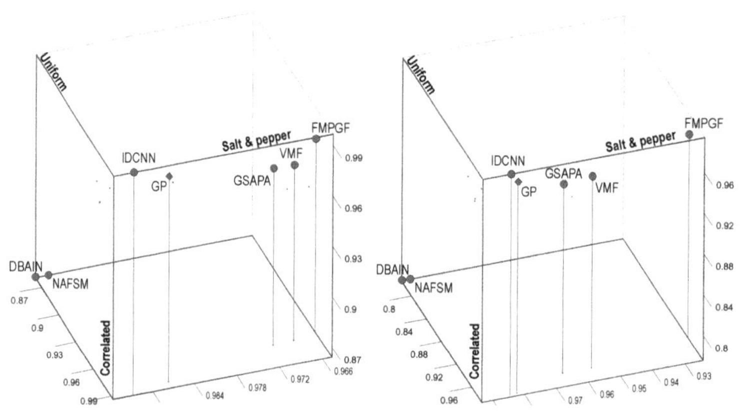

(**a**) $p = 0.05$ (**b**) $p = 0.10$

Figure 10. *Cont.*

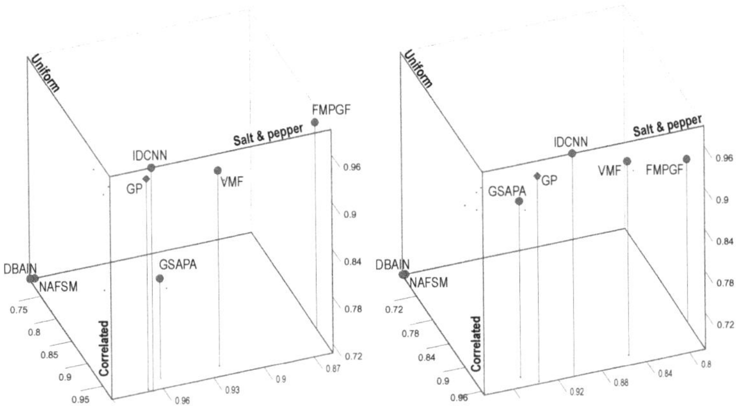

(**c**) $p = 0.15$ (**d**) $p = 0.20$

Figure 10. Three-dimensional Pareto front for FSIM average values by considering the whole set of test images with noise densities $p = 0.05, 0.10, 0.15$, and 0.20.

6. Conclusions and Future Work

This work presents an adaptive filter designed for the removal of three prevalent types of impulse noise, namely salt and pepper, uniform, and correlated noise, in color digital images. The proposed filter employs a two-step process, leveraging a binary classification model to identify noisy pixels within the image, followed by a correction step tailored to the specific color channels. What sets this proposed filter apart from the majority of filters utilizing classification models for noise removal is its high level of interpretability. This interpretability is a result of the evolutionary approach taken during model training—a process rooted in the principles of the genetic programming paradigm. By evolving the model through an iterative genetic programming framework, the resulting filter not only achieves effective noise reduction but also provides insights into the decision-making process of the classification model. Another distinctive feature of the training is that it only required a single image purposefully contaminated by the impulse noise models. Using a unique training image was particularly useful in reducing the computational complexity.

An experimental study was conducted to evaluate the performance of the proposed adaptive filter. A comparison with other filters was performed via the four image quality metrics (PSNR, MAE, SSIM, and FSIM). The experimental results show that most comparison filters present variability in the values of their quality metrics depending on the noise model and the image characteristics. In this vein, the proposed filter, called GP in Tables 4 and 5, consistently obtained good performance values, second only to the ICDNN, which uses a deep learning-based approach. When measuring efficiency as a minimizing/maximizing multi-objective problem, as shown in Figures 7–10, the proposed filter is one of the closest to an equilibrium point across all images and noise models used in the experiment, on par with the ICDNN and GSAPA filters.

Future work will focus on the integration of alternative machine learning techniques for the identification and correction of noisy pixels in color digital images. An intriguing avenue of exploration would be predicting the correlation of color channels to facilitate improved pixel replacement strategies within the image. This innovative approach holds promise for further enhancing the robustness and adaptability of the proposed adaptive filter in diverse real-world scenarios. It would also be interesting to explore how the genetic programming algorithm can be fine-tuned or adapted according to user preferences and specific requirements for noise removal in color images. Finally, optimizing the evolutionary settings of the genetic programming algorithm by employing other metaheuristic algorithms or ensemble approaches is also a topic left for future research.

Supplementary Materials: The following supporting information can be downloaded at: https://bitbucket.org/dfajardod/impulse_noise_gpfilter/src/.

Author Contributions: Conceptualization, D.F.-D. and M.G.S.-C.; methodology, D.F.-D., M.G.S.-C. and A.Y.R.-G.; software, D.F.-D. and M.G.S.-C.; validation, A.Y.R.-G., S.S.-P. and J.E.M.-S.; writing—original draft preparation, D.F.-D. and M.G.S.-C.; supervision, A.Y.R.-G., S.S.-P. and J.E.M.-S.; project administration, D.F.-D. and M.G.S.-C. All authors have read and agreed to the published version of the manuscript.

Funding: This research was funded by the Tecnológico Nacional de México under grant number 18205.23-P.

Institutional Review Board Statement: Not applicable.

Informed Consent Statement: Not applicable.

Data Availability Statement: For benchmarking purposes, the complete set of filtered resulting images is available as supplementary materials with their original sizes and denoised versions. We also include a PDF with additional experimental results.

Acknowledgments: The authors are thankful to Dulce C. Cruz-Ramírez and Isabel G. Vázquez-Gómez for their technical help in the early stages of this work.

Conflicts of Interest: The authors declare no conflict of interest.

Abbreviations

The following abbreviations are used in this manuscript:

GP	Genetic programming
PSNR	Peak signal-to-noise ratio
MAE	Mean absolute error
SSIM	Structured similarity index measure
FSIM	Feature similarity index measure
NAFSM	Noise adaptive fuzzy switching media
DBAIN	Decision-based algorithm for the removal of impulse noise
FMPGF	Fuzzy modified peer-group filter
VMF	Vector median filter
GSAPA	Generalized synthesis and analysis prior algorithm
IDCNN	Impulse detection convolutional neural network

References

1. Garcia-Lamont, F.; Cervantes, J.; López, A.; Rodriguez, L. Segmentation of images by color features: A survey. *Neurocomputing* **2018**, *292*, 1–27. [CrossRef]
2. Pawlak, T.; Pilarska, A.A.; Przybył, K.; Stangierski, J.; Ryniecki, A.; Cais-Sokolińska, D.; Pilarski, K.; Peplińska, B. Application of Machine Learning Using Color and Texture Analysis to Recognize Microwave Vacuum Puffed Pork Snacks. *Appl. Sci.* **2022**, *12*, 5071. [CrossRef]
3. Gowda, S.N.; Yuan, C. ColorNet: Investigating the Importance of Color Spaces for Image Classification. In *Proceedings of the Lecture Notes in Computer Science*; Jawahar, C., Li, H., Mori, G., Schindler, K., Eds.; Springer International Publishing: Cham, Switzerland, 2019; pp. 581–596.
4. Lin, C.J.; Dewan, J.H.; Thepade, S.D. Image Retrieval Using Low Level and Local Features Contents: A Comprehensive Review. *Appl. Comput. Intell. Soft Comput.* **2020**, *2020*, 8851931. [CrossRef]
5. Khwildi, R.; Ouled Zaid, A. HDR image retrieval by using color-based descriptor and tone mapping operator. *Vis. Comput.* **2020**, *36*, 1111–1126. [CrossRef]
6. Goyal, B.; Dogra, A.; Agrawal, S.; Sohi, B.; Sharma, A. Image denoising review: From classical to state-of-the-art approaches. *Inform. Fusion* **2020**, *55*, 220–244. [CrossRef]
7. Yu, C.; Hou, L.Z. Realization of a Real-Time Image Denoising System for Dashboard Camera Applications. *IEEE Trans. Consum. Electron.* **2022**, *68*, 181–190. [CrossRef]
8. Li, C.; Li, J.; Luo, Z. An impulse noise removal model algorithm based on logarithmic image prior for medical image. *Signal Image Video Process.* **2021**, *15*, 1145–1152. [CrossRef]
9. Smolka, B. Efficient Technique of Impulsive Noise Detection and Replacement in Color Digital Images. In *Proceedings of the Sensor Networks and Signal Processing*; Peng, S.L., Favorskaya, M.N., Chao, H.C., Eds.; Springer: Singapore, 2021; pp. 171–185.

10. Varga, D. Full-Reference Image Quality Assessment Based on an Optimal Linear Combination of Quality Measures Selected by Simulated Annealing. *J. Imaging* **2022**, *8*, 224. [CrossRef]
11. Geem, Z.W.; Fong, S.; Zhuang, Y.; Tang, R.; Yang, X.S.; Deb, S. Selecting Optimal Feature Set in High-Dimensional Data by Swarm Search. *J. Appl. Math.* **2013**, *2013*, 590614. [CrossRef]
12. Mirjalili, S.; Song Dong, J.; Sadiq, A.S.; Faris, H. Genetic Algorithm: Theory, Literature Review, and Application in Image Reconstruction. In *Nature-Inspired Optimizers: Theories, Literature Reviews and Applications*; Mirjalili, S., Song Dong, J., Lewis, A., Eds.; Springer International Publishing: Cham, Switzerland, 2020; pp. 69–85. [CrossRef]
13. Koza, J.R. *Genetic Programming: On the Programming of Computers by Means of Natural Selection*; MIT Press: Cambridge, MA, USA, 1992.
14. Mirjalili, S. *Evolutionary Algorithms and Neural Networks*; Springer: Cham, Switzerland, 2019.
15. Mafi, M.; Martin, H.; Cabrerizo, M.; Andrian, J.; Barreto, A.; Adjouadi, M. A comprehensive survey on impulse and Gaussian denoising filters for digital images. *Signal Process.* **2019**, *157*, 236–260. [CrossRef]
16. Astola, J.; Haavisto, P.; Neuvo, Y. Vector median filters. *Proc. IEEE* **1990**, *78*, 678–689. [CrossRef]
17. Aggarwal, H.K.; Majumdar, A. Generalized Synthesis and Analysis Prior Algorithms with Application to Impulse Denoising. In Proceedings of the 2014 Indian Conference on Computer Vision Graphics and Image Processing, Bangalore, India, 14–18 December 2014; Association for Computing Machinery: New York, NY, USA, 2014; ICVGIP '14. [CrossRef]
18. Kusnik, D.; Smolka, B. Robust mean shift filter for mixed Gaussian and impulsive noise reduction in color digital images. *Sci. Rep.* **2022**, *12*, 14951. [CrossRef] [PubMed]
19. Arnal, J.; Súcar, L. Fast Method Based on Fuzzy Logic for Gaussian-Impulsive Noise Reduction in CT Medical Images. *Mathematics* **2022**, *10*, 3652. [CrossRef]
20. Camarena, J.G.; Gregori, V.; Morillas, S.; Sapena, A. Fast detection and removal of impulsive noise using peer groups and fuzzy metrics. *J. Vis. Commun. Image Represent.* **2008**, *19*, 20–29. [CrossRef]
21. Habib, M.; Hussain, A.; Rehman, E.; Muzammal, S.M.; Cheng, B.; Aslam, M.; Jilani, S.F. Convolved Feature Vector Based Adaptive Fuzzy Filter for Image De-Noising. *Appl. Sci.* **2023**, *13*, 4861. [CrossRef]
22. Toh, K.K.V.; Mat Isa, N.A. Noise Adaptive Fuzzy Switching Median Filter for Salt-and-Pepper Noise Reduction. *IEEE Signal Process. Lett.* **2010**, *17*, 281–284. [CrossRef]
23. Roy, A.; Manam, L.; Laskar, R.H. Removal of 'Salt & Pepper' noise from color images using adaptive fuzzy technique based on histogram estimation. *Multimed. Tools Appl.* **2020**, *79*, 34851–34873. [CrossRef]
24. Singh, I.; Verma, O.P. Impulse noise removal in color image sequences using fuzzy logic. *Multimed. Tools Appl.* **2021**, *80*, 18279–18300. [CrossRef]
25. Srinivasan, K.S.; Ebenezer, D. A New Fast and Efficient Decision-Based Algorithm for Removal of High-Density Impulse Noises. *IEEE Signal Process. Lett.* **2007**, *14*, 189–192. [CrossRef]
26. Morillas, S.; Gregori, V.; Sapena, A.; Camarena, J.G.; Roig, B. Impulsive Noise Filters for Colour Images. In *Color Image and Video Enhancement*; Springer International Publishing: Cham, Switzerland, 2015; pp. 81–129. [CrossRef].
27. Roy, A.; Laskar, R.H. Multiclass SVM based adaptive filter for removal of high density impulse noise from color images. *Appl. Soft Comput.* **2016**, *46*, 816–826. [CrossRef]
28. Roy, A.; Laskar, R.H. Fuzzy SVM based fuzzy adaptive filter for denoising impulse noise from color images. *Multimed. Tools Appl.* **2019**, *78*, 1785–1804. [CrossRef]
29. Caliskan, A.; Cil, Z.A.; Badem, H.; Karaboga, D. Regression-based neuro-fuzzy network trained by ABC algorithm for high-density impulse noise elimination. *IEEE Trans. Fuzzy Syst.* **2020**, *28*, 1084–1095. [CrossRef]
30. Tian, C.; Xu, Y.; Li, Z.; Zuo, W.; Fei, L.; Liu, H. Attention-guided CNN for image denoising. *Neural Netw.* **2020**, *124*, 117–129. [CrossRef] [PubMed]
31. Luo, Q.; Liu, B.; Zhang, Y.; Han, Z.; Tang, Y. Low-rank decomposition on transformed feature maps domain for image denoising. *Vis. Comput.* **2021**, *37*, 1899–1915. [CrossRef]
32. Cao, Y.; Fu, Y.; Zhu, Z.; Rao, Z. Color Random Valued Impulse Noise Removal Based on Quaternion Convolutional Attention Denoising Network. *IEEE Signal Process. Lett.* **2022**, *29*, 369–373. [CrossRef]
33. Radlak, K.; Malinski, L.; Smolka, B. Deep Learning Based Switching Filter for Impulsive Noise Removal in Color Images. *Sensors* **2020**, *20*, 2782. [CrossRef] [PubMed]
34. Orazaev, A.; Lyakhov, P.; Baboshina, V.; Kalita, D. Neural Network System for Recognizing Images Affected by Random-Valued Impulse Noise. *Appl. Sci.* **2023**, *13*, 1585. [CrossRef]
35. Tian, C.; Fei, L.; Zheng, W.; Xu, Y.; Zuo, W.; Lin, C.W. Deep learning on image denoising: An overview. *Neural Netw.* **2020**, *131*, 251–275. [CrossRef]
36. Toledo, C.F.M.; de Oliveira, L.; da Silva, R.D.; Pedrini, H. Image denoising based on genetic algorithm. In Proceedings of the 2013 IEEE Congress on Evolutionary Computation, Cancun, Mexico, 20–23 June 2013; pp. 1294–1301. [CrossRef]
37. Fajardo-Delgado, D.; Sánchez, M.G.; Molinar-Solis, J.E.; Fernandez-Zepeda, J.A.; Vidal, V.; Verdiú, G. A hybrid genetic algorithm for color image denoising. In Proceedings of the 2016 IEEE Congress on Evolutionary Computation (CEC), Vancouver, BC, Canada, 24–29 July 2016; pp. 3879–3886. [CrossRef]
38. Petrovic, N.I.; Crnojevic, V. Universal Impulse Noise Filter Based on Genetic Programming. *IEEE Trans. Image Process.* **2008**, *17*, 1109–1120. [CrossRef]

39. Majid, A.; Lee, C.H.; Mahmood, M.T.; Choi, T.S. Impulse noise filtering based on noise-free pixels using genetic programming. *Knowl. Inf. Syst.* **2012**, *32*, 505–526. [CrossRef]
40. Khmag, A.; Ramli, A.R.; Al-Haddad, S.; Yusoff, S.; Kamarudin, N. Denoising of natural images through robust wavelet thresholding and genetic programming. *Vis. Comput.* **2017**, *33*, 1141–1154. [CrossRef]
41. Khan, A.; Qureshi, A.S.; Wahab, N.; Hussain, M.; Hamza, M.Y. A recent survey on the applications of genetic programming in image processing. *Comput. Intell.* **2021**, *37*, 1745–1778. [CrossRef]
42. Chanu, T.R.; Singh, T.R.; Singh, K.M. A survey on impulse noise removal from color image. *Turk. J. Comput. Math. Educ. (TURCOMAT)* **2021**, *12*, 4274–4295.
43. Wang, Z.; Bovik, A.; Sheikh, H.; Simoncelli, E. Image quality assessment: From error visibility to structural similarity. *IEEE Trans. Image Process.* **2004**, *13*, 600–612. [CrossRef] [PubMed]
44. Zhang, L.; Zhang, L.; Mou, X.; Zhang, D. FSIM: A Feature Similarity Index for Image Quality Assessment. *IEEE Trans. Image Process.* **2011**, *20*, 2378–2386. [CrossRef] [PubMed]
45. Jiang, R.; Yin, H.; Peng, K.; Xu, Y. Multi-objective optimization, design and performance analysis of an advanced trigenerative micro compressed air energy storage system. *Energy Convers. Manag.* **2019**, *186*, 323–333. [CrossRef]

applied sciences

MDPI

Article

Optimum Multilevel Thresholding for Medical Brain Images Based on Tsallis Entropy, Incorporating Bayesian Estimation and the Cauchy Distribution

Xianwen Wang [1,2], Yingyuan Yang [1,2], Minhang Nan [1,3], Guanjun Bao [4] and Guoyuan Liang [1,5,*]

1 Shenzhen Institutes of Advanced Technology, Chinese Academy of Sciences, Shenzhen 518055, China; xw.wang1@siat.ac.cn (X.W.); yy.yang3@siat.ac.cn (Y.Y.); mh.nan@siat.ac.cn (M.N.)
2 University of Chinese Academy of Sciences, Beijing 100049, China
3 Department of Biomedical Engineering, Southern University of Science and Technology, Shenzhen 510085, China
4 College of Mechanical Engineering, Zhejiang University of Technology, Hangzhou 310023, China; gjbao@zjut.edu.cn
5 Guangdong Provincial Key Laboratory of Robotics and Intelligent System, Shenzhen Institutes of Advanced Technology, Chinese Academy of Sciences, Shenzhen 518055, China
* Correspondence: gy.liang@siat.ac.cn

Abstract

Entropy-based thresholding is a widely used technique for medical image segmentation. Its principle is to determine the optimal threshold by maximizing or minimizing the image's entropy, dividing the image into different regions or categories. The intensity distributions of objects and backgrounds often overlap and contain many outliers, making segmentation extremely difficult. In this paper, we introduce a novel thresholding method that incorporates the Cauchy distribution into the Tsallis entropy framework based on Bayesian estimation. By introducing Bayesian prior probability estimation to address the overlap in intensity distributions between the two classes, we enhance the estimation of the probability that a pixel belongs to either class. Additionally, we utilize the Cauchy distribution, known for its heavy-tailed characteristics, to fit grayscale pixel distributions with outliers, enhancing tolerance to extreme values. The optimal threshold is derived through the optimization of an information measure formulated using updated Tsallis entropy. Experimental results demonstrate that the proposed method, called Cauchy-TB, achieves significant superiority to existing approaches on two public medical brain image datasets.

Keywords: brain image analysis; image segmentation; Tsallis entropy; Bayesian estimation; Cauchy distribution; multilevel thresholding

1. Introduction

In the past decade, medical image segmentation technologies have become increasingly critical for clinical applications. The compilation of medical images enables intuitive and objective patient assessments. In addition to thresholding, various other image segmentation methods are widely used in the field. These include region-based segmentation, contour-detection-based segmentation, graph-based segmentation pixel clustering algorithms, watershed algorithms, machine learning-based approaches, and deep learning techniques. Each method's suitability depends on the requirements and characteristics of the specific medical image segmentation task.

Region-based segmentation [1,2] directly finds regions in images by using methods such as region growing and global cutting. Edge-based methods [3,4], which detect edges using operators such as Roberts, Sobel, and Laplace, are often combined with other algorithms. Popular clustering methods for segmentation include K-Means and Fuzzy C-Means, as noted in [5,6]. Graph-based methods [7,8] leverage graph theory for segmentation, while watershed segmentation [9] separates overlapping objects based on pixel similarities.

Classical machine learning methods such as PCA [10], LDA [11], LBP [12], HOG [13], GLCM [14], and frequency domain analysis [15] are employed to extract shape, texture, and structural features from images. These features are utilized with classifiers such as SVM [16] and K-means [14] in tasks such as classification or clustering. Deep learning methods, especially CNNs [17] such as U-Net [18], are highly effective in medical image segmentation. U-Net uses data augmentation to expand datasets and improve the model's generalization capability. However, CNNs encounter difficulties in capturing global dependencies. To address this, researchers apply Transformer architectures [19], known for their self-attention mechanism, to various image processing tasks. Recently, SAM [20], a universal model for image segmentation, has shown promising results spanning various image types.

Due to significant grayscale differences among various biological tissues and organs in medical images, thresholding has therefore become a popular technique for object segmentation that balances efficiency and accuracy. The key difficulty is to find the optimal threshold that distinguishes the foreground from the background in the image. Entropy measures the amount of information in images. The higher the entropy is, the more information the image has. Essentially, the goal of the maximum entropy algorithm is to find an optimal threshold that maximizes the sum of entropy between the background and foreground regions.

Kapur's maximum entropy method [21] can achieve good results even when the image histogram is not bimodal. However, similar to the Otsu method [22], it does not consider spatial information and is susceptible to noises. Saha [23] developed a class-uncertainty-based framework called minimum homogeneity- and uncertainty-based energy (MHUE) for optimum threshold selection. Liu [24] further improved the MHUE algorithm by integrating the histogram-based feature with the spatial contextual feature, which demonstrates excellent performance in medical image segmentation. In 2004, Albuquerque [25] first proposed a method based on Tsallis entropy. Subsequently, Sarkar [26] employed 2D Tsallis entropy for a multi-thresholding algorithm. More recently, methods such as Masi entropy [27] have been continuously introduced.

Entropy-based thresholding methods are widely used due to their simplicity and applicability in various scenarios. However, they face challenges when dealing with pixel intensity distributions that contain overlapping components and outliers, as illustrated in Figure 1. This study introduces a novel method, called Cauchy-TB, to address these challenges. By integrating Bayesian prior probability estimation and the Cauchy distribution into the classical Tsallis entropy framework (Figure 2), we aim at improving the robustness and accuracy of segmentation results. Experimental results demonstrate the significant advantages of Cauchy-TB on two publicly available medical brain image datasets.

The contributions of this paper to the literature can be summarized as follows:

1. We introduce a novel Tsallis-entropy-based thresholding method for medical image segmentation by incorporating Bayesian prior probability estimation to effectively handle overlaps in intensity distributions between two classes;
2. We integrate the Cauchy distribution, recognized for its heavy-tailed properties, to improve the framework's robustness to outliers;

3. We further develop this approach for multi-class segmentation and determine the optimal threshold by optimizing the information measure function.

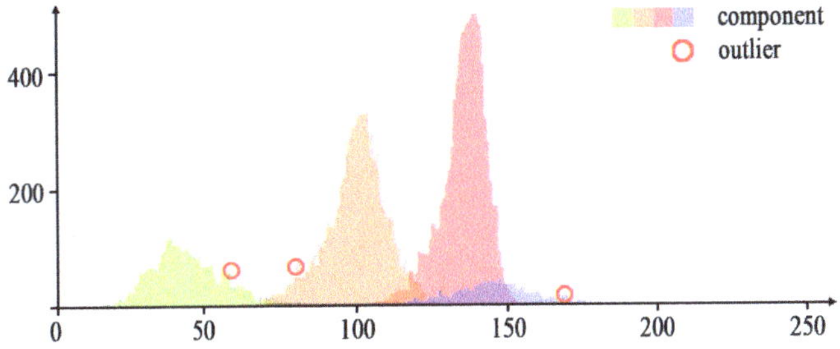

Figure 1. The histogram of medical images consists of histograms of different components, whose distributions overlap and contain many outliers.

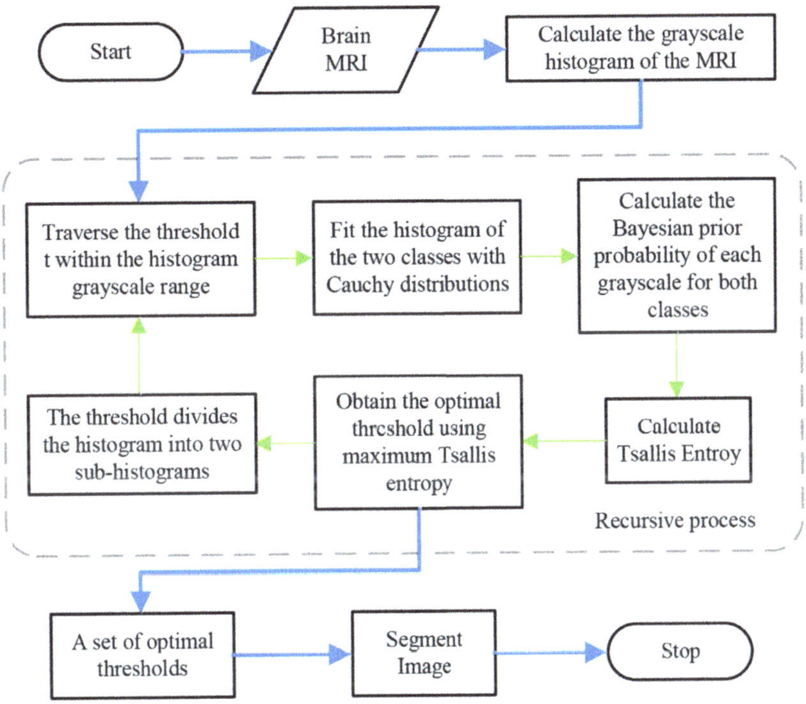

Figure 2. The major steps of the proposed method, Cauchy-TB. The green arrow indicates the direction of flow in the recursive process.

The structure of this paper is outlined as follows: Section 2 provides a review of related work, and Section 3 explains the principles of our method in detail. Experimental results are presented in Section 4. Section 5 discusses them in depth. Finally, Section 6 concludes the study with remarks summarizing the key findings.

2. Related Work

Many thresholding methods have been proposed, including global methods based on intensity histograms, global methods based on local properties, and adaptive thresholding.

2.1. Global Thresholding Based on Intensity Histograms

Otsu's method [22] is a classic non-parametric unsupervised algorithm for automatic image thresholding, calculating the optimal threshold by maximizing the between-class variance of the image. Several improvements have been proposed to enhance its performance. Abutaleb [28] introduced a two-dimensional histogram to consider pixel neighborhood information, improving the Otsu method's performance in noise handling. Bindu [29] improved the algorithm by using image histograms and global thresholding techniques, reducing computation time and improving segmentation quality. Yuan [30] weighted cumulative probability parameters to improve segmentation for single-peaked histograms. Feng [31] proposed a method combining 3D Otsu and multi-scale image representation, demonstrating stable results and robustness to noise.

The entropy-based algorithm is also widely utilized, finding the optimal threshold through entropy. Kapur [21] proposed the maximum entropy method, achieving good results even for non-ideal bimodal histograms. However, it lacks consideration of spatial information, leading to poor noise robustness. Li [32] used the Cuckoo Search Algorithm to enhance the Maximum Entropy method, improving both its accuracy and its efficiency. The MHUE method [23] integrates grayscale class uncertainty and spatial uniformity into an energy function. It shows excellent performance in segmenting fuzzy images and medical images. Liu [33] proposed a segmentation method based on fuzzy entropy that considered inter-class and intra-class differences, and in 2012, they improved the method with a new energy function [24]. Albuquerque [25] introduced a Tsallis entropy-based method, while Sarkar [26] applied 2D Tsallis entropy to multi-threshold problems. Zou [34] developed a Tsallis-entropy-based threshold segmentation method that utilizes multi-scale and multi-directional Gabor transformations. Recently, new methods such as Masi entropy [27] have been utilized. Prabaharan [35] compared the performance of eight thresholding methods on microscopic medical images and found that Kapur's entropy threshold performed the best. Naik [36] introduced a multilevel thresholding method based on non-entropy maximization, utilizing threshold scores. They used the AO-PSO optimizer to reduce computational costs for multi-class segmentation. Li [37] proposed an enhanced version of the Barnacle Mating Optimizer, which made substantial advancements in both precision and efficiency.

Recently, Venugopal [38] proposed a deep learning model called the Deep Threshold Prediction Network (DTP-Net) for threshold prediction. The model takes grayscale images as input, with the goal of determining the optimal grayscale threshold by maximizing the Dice similarity index (DSI) between the segmented image and the ground truth.

2.2. Global Methods Based on Local Attributes

Johnson [39] proposed a semi-automatic boundary detection algorithm for 3D MRI images that calculates thresholds by analyzing the pixel intensity distribution in circular regions surrounding the selected object pixels and background pixels, enabling accurate and efficient measurement of ventricular volume. Yadav [40] introduced a novel algorithm that combines thresholding and morphological techniques to enhance image features and reduce noise. It has been validated on brain MRI and CT angiography images. Kalyani [41] proposed an algorithm based on robust Teaching–Learning-Based Optimization (TLBO) to address the issue of increased computation time in multilevel thresholding. The algorithm achieves precise segmentation of medical images, such as images of irises, psoriasis, and cancer cells. They also introduced the concept of the Exchange Market Algorithm (EMA) [42] to balance exploration and exploitation, with the Otsu-based EMA technique demonstrating superior segmentation accuracy and computation time compared to other methods. Chandra De [5] applied Particle Swarm Optimization (PSO) with the Kapur entropy criterion for segmenting MRI brain tumor images. Nyo [43] employed multiple Otsu thresholds and morphological operations for accurate brain tumor segmentation. Both methods showed promising results in segmenting brain tumors from MRI images. A hybrid fitness function was developed by Ibrahim [44] through the combination of Otsu's method and Kapur's entropy method, which was integrated with the Electric Eel Foraging Optimization (EEFO) method for multilevel thresholding to identify optimal thresholds. Sowmiya [45] proposed a multilevel thresholding hybrid Leader Coronavirus Optimization method combined with a kernel-based Bayesian Fuzzy Clustering (kernel-BFC) method for foreground and background image segmentation.

2.3. Adaptive Thresholding

An adaptive method usually assigns different threshold values to different regions or pixels based on local pixel statistics, which is useful for extracting small and sparse regions. Common methods include local-statistics-based, local-variance-based, and local-mean-based methods, but they require more computational resources. Classical methods include the Niblack method [46], which calculates the local threshold using the pixel mean and variance in a neighborhood. This method has good robustness against noise, but the choice of processing template window size has a significant impact on the results. The Sauvola method [47] uses the local grayscale mean of the template window as a reference, divides the image into different categories based on the standard deviation, and calculates multiple thresholds based on image categories. These methods adaptively select thresholds based on local image characteristics, leading to more accurate segmentation results. Hemachander [48] proposed an algorithm for local adaptive thresholds that maintains segmentation result continuity. Chaira [49] introduced a local method based on intuitionistic fuzzy set theory, achieving good segmentation results in low-contrast samples. Tarkhaneh [50] introduced a Differential Evolution-based algorithm that balances local and global search for improved efficiency. Recently, Khalid [51] employed a grid search method to segment Regions of Interest (ROIs) in ultrasound medical images, improving segmentation results by calculating overlapping regions between automatically and manually extracted ROIs. Ariyanfar [52] developed an adaptive thresholding technique with boundary curvature and tortuosity control. Li [53] introduced a center point selection method to address foreground deviation and used continuity detection to improve segmentation accuracy and the method's capacity for generalization. Gharehchopogh [54] proposed an enhanced version of the African Vulture Optimization Algorithm (AVOA), which integrates three binarization thresholding algorithms—Kapur entropy, Tsallis entropy, and the Otsu method—for multi-threshold image segmentation. Li [55] combined the Arithmetic Optimization Algorithm (AOA) with the Harris Hawks Optimizer (HHO) to improve the AOA's exploitation phase, thereby achieving an optimal threshold vector for multilevel thresholding image segmentation.

3. Theory and Methodology

In this section, we first prove that the optimal segmentation boundary can always be found near the ground truth boundary. Then, we describe the proposed Cauchy-TB method and its extension to multilevel segmentation.

3.1. The Optimal Segmentation Boundary

In Figure 3, we can see that the boundary in the bottom right around the white matter stays stable when threshold changes from 100 to 105, but those around the gray matter (GM, shown in the cyan bounding box) change significantly. Furthermore, when the threshold changes from 105 to 110, the boundaries inside the GM change significantly. Both the situations show that those boundaries near the truth of tissue boundaries may possess higher stability as the thresholds change.

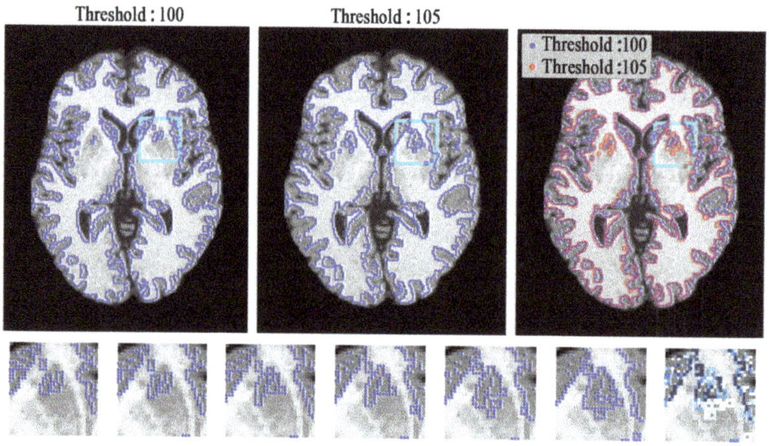

(a)

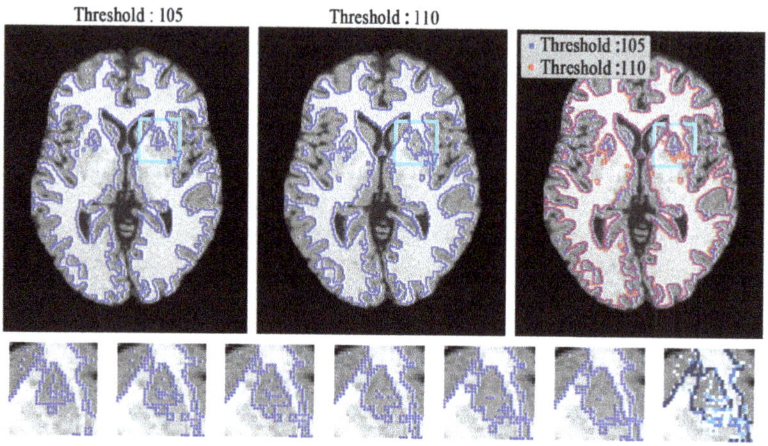

(b)

Figure 3. Edges of the thresholding result. (**a**) Top left: 100; top middle: 105; top right: 100 (blue), 105 (red); bottom: local thresholding result of the region in the cyan box with 100–105 and the heatmap at the rightmost; (**b**) top left: 105; top middle: 110; top right: 105 (blue), 110 (red); bottom: local thresholding result of the region in cyan box with 105–110 and the heatmap at the rightmost. (The heatmap was generated as follows: As the threshold varies, superimpose the boundary pixels and increase the pixel count by one each time. The pixel with the highest count is set to the darkest blue. Thus, the darker a boundary pixel is, the more stable it is).

We designed an experiment to test for a significant difference in stability between pixels around the true boundaries and the rest. In our experiment, we randomly selected 3000 samples from the image to form a set S and filtered out those in the background. The samples were labeled as positive if their distance to the edge was less than 1 or labeled as negative if was greater than 1. As Figure 4 shows, for each pixel $s \in S$, we recorded the lower segmentation threshold bound $L(s)$ and the upper segmentation threshold bound $U(s)$ when it appeared near the edges. By measuring the range $\Delta(s)$ of the two thresholds, we could compare the distributions of Δ in the positive and negative groups to see if there existed a certain tendency.

$$\Delta(s) = U(s) - L(s) \tag{1}$$

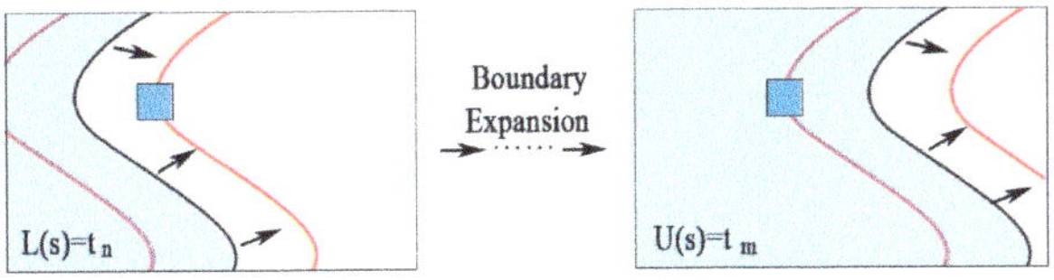

Figure 4. Definitions of $L(s)$ and $U(s)$.

Figure 5 illustrates the $\Delta(s)$ distribution statistics for positive samples (blue dots) and negative samples (red dots) across two slices used in the experiment, highlighting that positive samples exhibit a larger average Δ than negative samples. To assess the difference in central tendency between these two populations, we conducted a Mann–Whitney test. The null hypothesis (H_0) is that the population X and Y have the same distribution; the alternative hypothesis (H_1) is that they have different distributions.

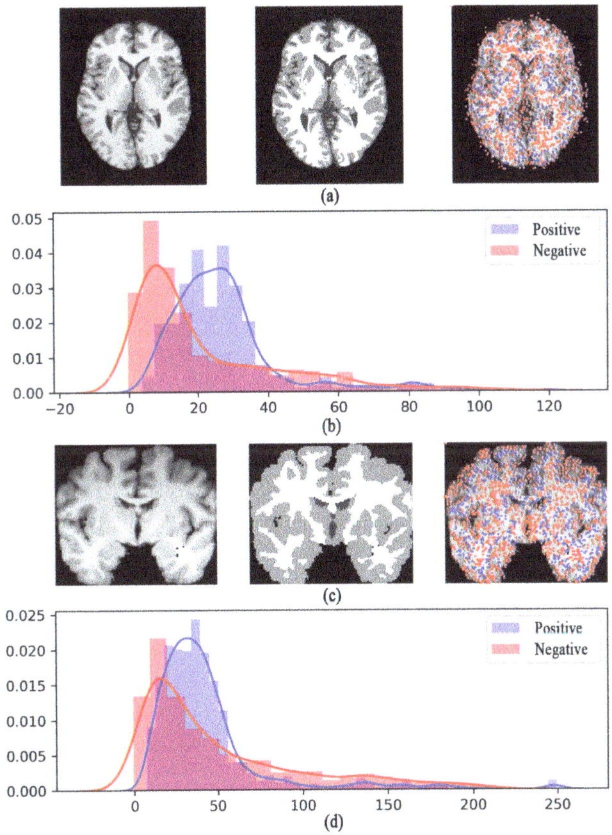

Figure 5. Threshold range $\Delta(s)$ distribution statistics, the blue and red lines represent the fittings of the positive and negative distributions, respectively. (**a**) displays the original experimental image; the ground truth segmentation of gray matter, white matter, and cerebrospinal fluid; and the selected points for positive and negative samples. (**b**) shows the $\Delta(s)$ distribution statistics of the positive and negative samples from (**a**), where the horizontal axis represents delta and the vertical axis indicates its frequency. (**c**,**d**) are the results from a different slice.

The Mann–Whitney U statistic is defined as

$$U = \sum_{i=1}^{n} \sum_{j=1}^{m} S(X_i, Y_j), \tag{2}$$

where

$$S = \begin{cases} 1 & X < Y \\ \frac{1}{2} & X = Y \\ 0 & X > Y \end{cases} \tag{3}$$

The statistics for some slices in the BrainWeb dataset are calculated. As shown in Table 1, if we select a confidence level of $1 - \alpha = 0.95$, we can conclude that the Δ values from these two groups are from different distributions.

Table 1. Mann–Whitney test results.

Slice	U Statistic	p-Value
45	28,878.5	5.852×10^{-49}
60	16,829.5	9.648×10^{-67}
75	46,223.0	3.902×10^{-14}
90	10,089.5	7.101×10^{-77}
105	6505.5	3.320×10^{-63}
120	9205.5	4.634×10^{-71}

To the best of our knowledge, there are few intensity-based methods that consider pixel-wise edge stability. Li [56] evaluated shape stability with the region expanding rate (RER) and selected a threshold with a low RER; Serena [57] considered the area-stable elongation to find the stable region. All of the above methods measured an overall stability pattern between boundaries. In fact, pixels on the edge possess different stability values, as Figure 3 shows. Therefore, we can conclude that pixels on the edge possess stronger stability.

As the threshold varies continuously, a stable boundary remains consistent and is typically closer to the ground truth boundary. As previously mentioned, Tsallis entropy introduces an adjustable parameter q, giving it an advantage when processing images with complex structures and noise. By leveraging the characteristics of Tsallis entropy, we can calculate the entropy values of the image at different thresholds and find the one with as many stable boundaries as possible corresponding to flat regions or special inflection points on the entropy curve. By adjusting the parameter q, the sensitivity of Tsallis entropy to probability distributions can be modulated, thereby highlighting the features of stable boundaries. Consequently, exploring the representation of Tsallis entropy based on a certain probability distribution model will help to determine the optimum threshold for segmentation, therefore improving the accuracy and robustness of image segmentation.

3.2. The Proposed Tsallis-Entropy-Based Method

Our previous work [58] incorporates Bayesian posterior probability estimation into the traditional Tsallis entropy framework and dramatically improves the estimation of the optimal threshold. Unfortunately, the intensity distributions of the pixels from objects and the background are assumed to be Gaussian, which is not quite accurate and is susceptible to noise in most cases. To address this problem, we introduce the Cauchy distribution as a replacement; this distribution has a higher tolerance for outliers. In addition, we further extend the segmentation method to multiple classes to achieve effective multilevel thresholding.

3.2.1. Definition of Classical Tsallis Entropy

The mathematical form of classical Tsallis entropy in image thresholding was initially introduced in [25]. For an image **I** with **L** gray levels, the entropy can be defined as follows:

$$S_q = \frac{1 - \sum_{i=0}^{L-1} p_i^q}{q-1} \tag{4}$$

where q in the formula represents the entropy exponent, which indicates the degree of non-additivity. When $q > 1$, it represents stronger interdependence or collective behavior among the system's components. p_i represents the probability of intensity i.

The pseudo-additivity principle applies to Tsallis entropy in independent statistical models:

$$S_q(X+Y) = S_q(X) + S_q(Y) + (1-q)S_q(X)S_q(Y) \tag{5}$$

For a given threshold t, the image is segmented into object and background regions, corresponding to the gray-level intervals 0, 1, 2, 3, ..., t and t + 1, t + 2, ..., L − 2, L − 1, respectively. Assuming that $p_i = p_0, p_1, \ldots, p_{L-1}$ represents the gray-level probability distribution, the background and object distributions can be expressed as

$$P_B = \frac{p_0}{p_b}, \frac{p_1}{p_b}, \ldots, \frac{p_t}{p_b} \tag{6}$$

$$P_O = \frac{p_{t+1}}{p_o}, \ldots, \frac{p_{L-1}}{p_o} \tag{7}$$

where $p_b = \sum_{i=0}^{t} p_i$ and $p_o = \sum_{i=t+1}^{L-1} p_i$. The Tsallis entropy can be formulated as

$$S_q^B(t) = \frac{1 - \sum_{i=0}^{t} (\frac{p_i}{p_b})^q}{q-1} \tag{8}$$

$$S_q^O(t) = \frac{1 - \sum_{i=t+1}^{L-1} (\frac{p_i}{p_o})^q}{q-1} \tag{9}$$

The objective function for determining the optimal threshold seeks to maximize the information measure between the two classes of gray levels:

$$t_{opt} = \arg\max_t \, [S_q^B(t) + S_q^O(t) + (1-q)S_q^B(t)S_q^O(t)] \tag{10}$$

3.2.2. The Proposed Cauchy-TB Method

The classical Tsallis entropy is defined under the assumption that the intensity distributions of the object and background classes are independent of each other. For each intensity i, after being classified as object or background, it is represented by a single probability in its corresponding class distribution. This probability is then used in the calculation of Tsallis entropy, as illustrated in Equations (8)–(10).

In classical information theory, entropy measures the level of uncertainty in a system [59]. However, Figure 6a illustrates that the intensity distributions of objects and the background often overlap. This means that pixels classified as part of the background may actually belong to objects, and vice versa. Essentially, the intensity distributions of objects and backgrounds influence each other. As a result, independently calculating the probabilities of pixels belonging to either the object or background, as shown in Equations (8) and (9), is suboptimal. A better approach is to compute these probabilities using the combined intensity distributions over the entire intensity space. Considering that the intensity distributions of background and objects in medical images often contain many outliers, fitting the intensity distribution with a Gaussian distribution may not be suitable.

Therefore, we propose replacing the Gaussian distribution with a long-tailed distribution, for example, the Cauchy distribution, as shown in Figure 6b. A long-tailed distribution in statistics is typically characterized by a highly imbalanced distribution, where the majority of observations are concentrated in the front (i.e., the short tail) of the distribution, while the tail part (the long tail) contains relatively few but highly significant observations.

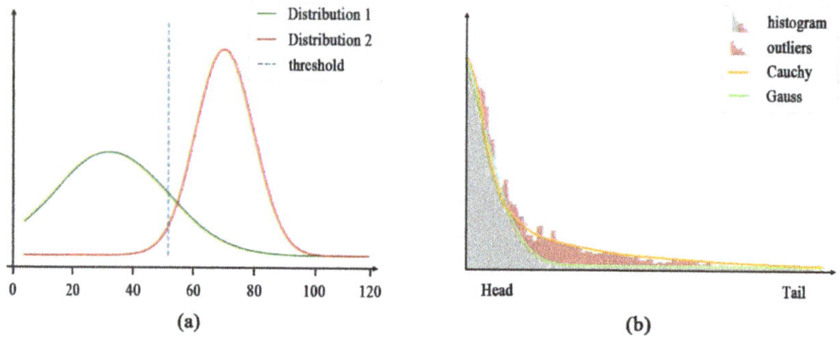

Figure 6. (**a**) The histogram shows two alternating Gaussian distribution curves, with a vertical line indicating a partition at a threshold of t = 50. (**b**) In the tail (orange) of the distribution, the red points represent outliers, which are typically not handled well by a Gaussian distribution (green line).

The tail of a long-tailed distribution decays more gradually than that of the Gaussian distribution. A defining feature of any long-tailed distribution is that its tail is significantly longer than that of a Gaussian distribution, and the total volume of the tail data may be quite substantial. As a result, outliers in the tail of the distribution can have a significant impact on the overall distribution. This characteristic allows a long-tailed distribution to better accommodate outliers, providing a more robust fit to the intensity of both objects and background.

Long-tailed distributions have been widely utilized in previous studies, with one notable application being the t-SNE algorithm proposed by Hinton [60]. t-SNE employs Student's t-distribution, which is referred to as the Cauchy distribution when having 1 degree of freedom, to measure the similarity between data points, as opposed to the traditional Gaussian distribution. This choice enables t-SNE to effectively handle rare points or outliers in a long-tailed distribution, thereby preserving the clustering structure of the dataset while appropriately distributing the rare points in the tail. t-SNE performs particularly well in datasets containing a large number of common patterns and a few rare events, making it highly suitable for handling data with long-tailed distributions.

Based on the above observation, we propose a new method that combines Tsallis entropy, Bayesian prior probability, and the long-tailed Cauchy distribution; this proposed method is called Cauchy–Tsallis Bayesian Estimation (Cauchy-TB).

Let $p_{o,t}(i)$ and $p_{b,t}(i)$ describe the probability density functions of pixels classified as part of objects or the background, with intensity i at threshold t, as given by

$$p_{o,t}(i) = P[\mathcal{F}(s) = i | s \in S_{o,t}] \tag{11}$$

$$p_{b,t}(i) = P[\mathcal{F}(s) = i | s \in S_{b,t}] \tag{12}$$

$$S = S_{o,t} \cup S_{b,t} \tag{13}$$

where S represents the total set of pixels within the image, while $\mathcal{F}(s)$ denotes the gray-level intensity of a pixel s belonging to S. The sets $S_{o,t}$ and $S_{b,t}$ represent the sets of object and background pixels defined by threshold t.

Assume that the object and background pixel distributions follow Cauchy distributions, denoted by $C(\theta o(t), x0, o(t))$ and $C(\theta b(t), x0, b(t))$, respectively, where $\theta o(t)$, $\theta b(t)$, $x0, o(t)$, and $x0, b(t)$ are the scale and location parameters for object and background pixels, respectively, formulated as

$$p_{o,t}(i) = \frac{1}{\pi}\left[\frac{\theta_o}{(x - x_{0,o})^2 + \theta_o^2}\right] \tag{14}$$

$$p_{o,b}(i) = \frac{1}{\pi}\left[\frac{\theta_b}{(x - x_{0,b})^2 + \theta_b^2}\right] \tag{15}$$

At threshold t, the prior probability of a pixel being part of the object is $\gamma(t)$, with $1 - \gamma(t)$ indicating the probability of belonging to the background. $\gamma(t)$ is estimated as follows:

$$\gamma(t) = \frac{|S_{o,t}|}{|S|} \tag{16}$$

where $|X|$ represents the number of elements in the set X. Therefore, applying Bayes' rule, we can formulate the posterior probability for a pixel of intensity i being part of the object or background:

$$P_t[s \in S_o | \mathcal{F}(s) = i] = \frac{\gamma(t)p_{o,t}(i)}{p_t(i)} \tag{17}$$

$$P_t[s \in S_b | \mathcal{F}(s) = i] = \frac{(1 - \gamma(t))p_{b,t}(i)}{p_t(i)} \tag{18}$$

where $p_t(i)$ is calculated by

$$p_t(i) = \gamma(t)p_{o,t}(i) + (1 - \gamma(t))p_{b,t}(i) \tag{19}$$

Therefore, the Tsallis entropy expressions for both object and background classes presented in Equations (8) and (9) are reformulated

$$C_q^B(t) = \frac{1 - \sum_{i=0}^{L-1}\left(\frac{(1-\gamma(t))p_{b,t}(i)}{p_t(i)}\right)^q}{q - 1} \tag{20}$$

$$C_q^O(t) = \frac{1 - \sum_{i=0}^{L-1}\left(\frac{\gamma(t)p_{o,t}(i)}{p_t(i)}\right)^q}{q - 1} \tag{21}$$

The information measure function is then updated and expressed as

$$t_{opt} = \arg\max_t \left(C_q^B(t) + C_q^O(t) + (1 - q)C_q^B(t)C_q^O(t)\right) \tag{22}$$

and the optimal threshold t_{opt} can be estimated using common optimization algorithms.

3.2.3. The Multilevel Thresholding Method

The histograms of real medical images often exhibit complex distributions with more than two distinct peaks, reflecting the diverse nature of tissues and structures in the images. To achieve accurate segmentation in such cases, it is essential to employ advanced methods that can handle multilevel thresholding.

Cauchy-TB can accurately identify one of the valleys in the histogram, segmenting the image into category 1, representing one type of tissue or structure, and a region to be further segmented, containing categories 2 and 3, which represent other types of tissues or structures. Within this region, the method can be applied recursively for binary segmentation to separate categories 2 and 3 as shown in Figure 7.

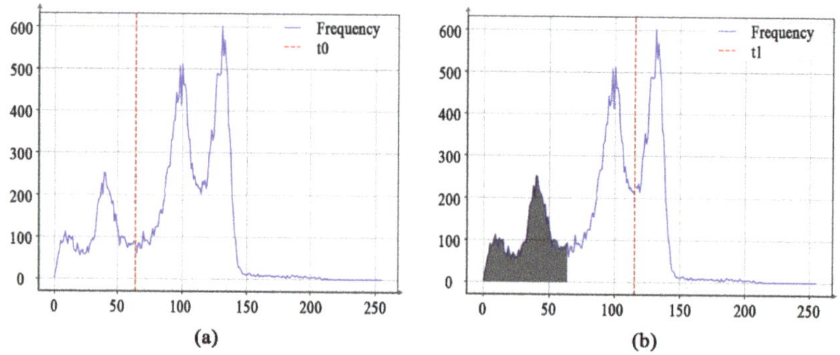

Figure 7. (**a**) The threshold obtained using Cauchy-TB based on the entire histogram. (**b**) The threshold obtained using Cauchy-TB based on the remaining histogram after removing one category from the original histogram.

By applying this recursive method, it is possible to extend the segmentation to four or more levels, enabling the identification and extraction of multiple regions of interest within the image. This approach enhances the segmentation effectiveness, particularly in complex medical images with diverse tissue types and structures. The pseudocode Algorithm 1 of our algorithm is as follows.

Algorithm 1 Cauchy-TB for Multi-Thresholding Image Segmentation

Input: Brain MRI grayscale image, number of thresholds n
Compute the grayscale histogram of the input image
for $i = 1$ **to** n **do,**
  Initialize the maximum Tsallis entropy (denoted as TE), the corresponding optimal threshold t_i, and the current histogram grayscale range $[L_{\min}, L_{\max}]$
  for $t = L_{\min}$ **to** $L_{\max}$ **do**
    Compute the Cauchy distribution parameters x and μ for the regions on both sides of the threshold t
    Calculate the posterior probabilities for each grayscale level between the left and right classes
    Compute the Tsallis entropy E based on the posterior probabilities
    if $E > TE$ **then**
      Update $TE = E$ and set the optimal threshold $t_i = t$
    end if
  end for
  The threshold t_i found at this step is the i-th optimal threshold, and the histogram is divided for further processing in the subsequent iterations
end for
Output: A set of optimal thresholds

4. Experimental Results and Analysis

4.1. Datasets

1. BrainWeb: BrainWeb is a well-known benchmark dataset that simulates a brain database and offers phantom images accompanied by ground truth labels [61]. In our

experiments, we utilized phantom brain MRI images generated with the following parameters: modality (pulse sequences) = T1, slice thickness (in-plane pixel size is always 1 × 1 mm) = 1 mm, noise (calculated relative to the brightest tissue) = 3%, intensity non-uniformity ("RF") = 20%. We obtained two sets of data from the dataset for our experiments. The first set consists of 120 slices numbered from 30 to 119, and the second set consists of eight Z-plane-cut brain slices (Z1, Z2, Z5, Z10, Z36, Z72, Z108, and Z144).

2. MRBrainS13: MRBrainS13 [62] is another well-recognized benchmark dataset that primarily provides three types of multi-modal MRI brain images for segmenting gray matter, white matter, and cerebrospinal fluid: T1-weighted images, T1-weighted inversion recovery images, and FLAIR images. The sequence we used is a 3D T1-weighted scan registered to T2 FLAIR (voxel size: 0.958 mm × 0.958 mm × 3.0 mm).

4.2. Parameter Selection

The parameter q, which reflects the degree of non-extension in the system, plays a significant role in image segmentation and warrants discussion. Typically, the selection of q depends on the characteristics of the image being segmented. However, there is no explicit relationship between the value of q and specific image categories. When $q > 1$, it represents stronger interdependence or collective behavior among the system's components. Consequently, in the following experiments, q is treated as a manually tuned hyperparameter, with a value of 4 assigned for the BrainWeb dataset and 5 for the MRBrainS13 dataset. After experimental validation Figure A1, these values yielded the best results.

4.3. System Environment

We conducted all experiments using Python (v.3.9) on a setup equipped with a standard CPU. The essential libraries installed included opencv-python (v.4.10.0), matplotlib (v.3.8.4), numpy (v.1.23.5), and scipy (v.1.13.1), along with parallel processing libraries such as numba (v.0.60.0) and scikit-learn (v.1.5.1). Additionally, we utilized the SimpleITK (v.2.4.1) library for medical image processing and functools for advanced functional programming.

4.4. Evaluation Metrics

To quantitatively assess the performance of the proposed Cauchy-TB algorithm, we utilized statistical metrics such as sensitivity, specificity, precision, and accuracy to study the relationship between the segmentation outcomes and the ground truth. The Jaccard coefficient (JC) and the Dice similarity coefficient (DSC) are utilized to measure the overlap of the segmented region with ground truth. The formulas for calculating these metrics are as follows:

$$Sensitivity = T_P/(T_P + F_N) \tag{23}$$

$$Specificity = T_N/(T_N + F_P) \tag{24}$$

$$Precision = T_P/(T_P + F_P) \tag{25}$$

$$Accuracy = (T_P + T_N)/(T_P + T_N + F_P + F_N) \tag{26}$$

$$JC = |I_g \cap I_t|/|I_g \cup I_t| \tag{27}$$

$$DSC = 2|I_g \cap I_t|/|I_g| \cup |I_t| \tag{28}$$

In the formulas, I_g represents the ground truth. T_N, T_P, F_N, and F_P denote true negative, true positive, false negative, and false positive, respectively. Higher values of T_N, T_P, F_N, and F_P indicate better performance.

We also introduced three new metrics for algorithm performance evaluation. The Peak Signal-to-Noise Ratio (PSNR) is employed to evaluate the quality of reconstructed or compressed images, with higher values indicating better quality. The Structural Similarity Index (SSIM) compares the similarity in structure between two images, ranging from -1 to 1, where 1 indicates perfect similarity. The Feature Similarity Index (FSIM) assesses image similarity, ranging from 0 to 1, where 1 indicates perfect similarity. The original image and the segmented image are used as inputs. The formulas are defined as follows:

$$PSNR = 10\log_{10}\left(\frac{{Max_I}^2}{MSE}\right) \tag{29}$$

where MSE is the Mean Squared Error and Max_I represents the maximum pixel intensity of image I.

$$SSIM(I_a, I_b) = \frac{(2\mu_{I_a}\mu_{I_b} + c_1) * (2\sigma_{I_a I_b})}{(\mu_{I_a}^2 + \mu_{I_b}^2 + c_1) * (\sigma_{I_a}^2 + \sigma_{I_b}^2 + c_2)} \tag{30}$$

Let I_a and I_b represent the two input images, where μ and σ represent the average and standard deviation of pixel intensities in the images, respectively. $\sigma_{I_a I_b}$ denotes the covariance between I_a and I_b, with c_1 and c_2 being constants used to stabilize the denominator.

$$FSIM = \frac{\sum_{x\in\Omega} S_L(X) * PC_m(X)}{\sum_{x\in\Omega} PC_m(X)} \tag{31}$$

$S_L(x)$ represents the overall similarity between two images, I_a and I_b. PC denotes the phase consistency between images, and Ω represents the full spatial domain of the images.

4.5. Comparative Experiments and Analysis

4.5.1. General Assessment

(A) Binary segmentation

Two coommonly performed binary segmentation methods (the Otsu and Tsallis-BE methods) were selected to be compared with the proposed Cauchy-TB to demonstrate its advantages. We selected 90 slice images numbered 30–119 from the BrainWeb dataset and grouped them into nine groups, with each group containing 10 images in sequential order. Additionally, we selected 15 images from the MRBrainS13 dataset and divided them evenly into three groups.

Tables 2 and 3 show the comparative experimental results for 13 groups of slices. We present the average results for each group of images. Obviously, Cauchy-TB outperformed all other methods in terms of the metrics JC, DSC, SSIM. On the BrainWeb dataset, our average accuracy, JC, and DSC reached 98.62%, 98.36%, and 98.17%, respectively. Compared to the Tsallis-BE method, our method performed better by 0.3%, 0.4%, and 0.2%, respectively. On the MRBrainS13 dataset, our average accuracy, JC, and DSC reached 91.71%, 88.30%, and 93.69%, respectively. Compared to the Tsallis-BE method, our method performed better by 0.6%, 0.96%, and 0.55%, respectively. In the MRBrainS13-3 group alone, there was a very small difference in accuracy compared to the Tsallis-BE method, with a reduction of only 0.03%. Similar superiority was also reflected in the PSNR, FSIM, and SSIM metrics, where our method showed an average performance improvement across both datasets. Only in the Group BrainWeb-3 and MRBrainS13-2 groups did our PSNR and FSIM scores slightly lag behind those of Tsallis-BE. Overall, across the six proposed metrics, our method demonstrated outstanding overall performance.

Table 2. Accuracy, JC, and DSC in comparative experiments for binary segmentation.

Group	Otsu			Tsallis-BE			Cauchy-TB		
	Accuracy	JC	DSC	Accuracy	JC	DSC	Accuracy	JC	DSC
BrainWeb-1	0.9749	0.9683	0.9839	0.9843	0.9802	0.9900	**0.9844**	**0.9805**	**0.9902**
BrainWeb-2	0.9700	0.9611	0.9802	0.9729	0.9647	0.9820	**0.9816**	**0.9764**	**0.9880**
BrainWeb-3	0.9516	0.9415	0.9698	0.9752	0.9698	0.9847	**0.9808**	**0.9769**	**0.9883**
BrainWeb-4	0.9440	0.9359	0.9669	0.9856	0.9836	0.9917	**0.9881**	**0.9865**	**0.9932**
BrainWeb-5	0.9578	0.9506	0.9747	0.9873	0.9851	0.9925	**0.9879**	**0.9861**	**0.9930**
BrainWeb-6	0.9476	0.9388	0.9684	0.9872	0.9851	0.9925	**0.9875**	**0.9856**	**0.9927**
BrainWeb-7	0.8991	0.8831	0.9347	0.9877	0.9856	0.9927	**0.9894**	**0.9878**	**0.9938**
BrainWeb-8	0.6792	0.6392	0.7798	0.9839	0.9819	0.9909	**0.9888**	**0.9875**	**0.9937**
BrainWeb-9	0.8660	0.8453	0.9097	0.9836	0.9808	0.9903	**0.9874**	**0.9854**	**0.9927**
BW-Average	0.9100	0.8960	0.9409	0.9831	0.9796	0.9897	**0.9862**	**0.9836**	**0.9917**
MRBrainS13-1	0.8919	0.8497	0.9185	0.9206	0.8890	0.9409	**0.9292**	**0.9018**	**0.9480**
MRBrainS13-2	0.9024	0.8623	0.9255	0.8987	0.8561	0.9216	**0.9087**	**0.8710**	**0.9303**
MRBrainS13-3	0.8959	0.8494	0.9176	**0.9137**	0.8750	0.9318	0.9134	**0.8761**	**0.9325**
MRB-Average	0.8967	0.8538	0.9205	0.9110	0.8734	0.9314	**0.9171**	**0.8830**	**0.9369**

The accuracy, JC, and DSC were computed for sliced images from the BrainWeb and MRBrainS13 datasets using three methods for binary segmentation. The best result is indicated by the bold number.

Table 3. PSNR, FSIM, and SSIM of comparative experiments for binary segmentation.

Group	Otsu			Tsallis-BE			Cauchy-TB		
	PSNR	FSIM	SSIM	PSNR	FSIM	SSIM	PSNR	FSIM	SSIM
BrainWeb-1	28.1767	0.5917	0.7539	28.1642	0.6001	0.7557	**28.1861**	**0.6084**	**0.7571**
BrainWeb-2	27.1518	0.5933	0.6722	27.1487	0.6049	0.6729	**27.1526**	**0.607**	**0.6761**
BrainWeb-3	26.4694	0.5958	0.5881	**26.4842**	0.6055	0.5935	26.476	**0.6183**	**0.5965**
BrainWeb-4	26.799	0.6329	0.5766	26.8078	0.6382	0.5835	**26.8108**	**0.6571**	**0.5836**
BrainWeb-5	26.781	0.6489	0.5801	26.7844	0.6539	0.5851	**26.7893**	**0.6682**	**0.5852**
BrainWeb-6	26.7898	0.6595	0.5887	26.7968	0.6647	0.5952	**26.7991**	**0.6843**	**0.5957**
BrainWeb-7	27.0001	0.6856	0.6207	26.9822	0.6904	0.6316	**27.0209**	**0.7341**	**0.6331**
BrainWeb-8	27.2866	0.6861	0.62	27.2857	0.6917	0.6571	**27.2884**	**0.8449**	**0.6573**
BrainWeb-9	27.782	0.6805	0.6607	27.7611	0.6873	0.673	**27.7838**	**0.7499**	**0.6739**
BW-Average	27.4731	0.6304	0.6366	27.4762	0.6408	0.6411	**27.4868**	**0.6631**	**0.6547**
MRBrainS13-1	33.1807	0.9605	0.8018	33.1734	0.9669	0.8052	**33.1857**	**0.9755**	**0.8062**
MRBrainS13-2	32.5183	0.8931	0.7882	**32.5239**	**0.9028**	0.787	32.5226	0.8977	**0.7884**
MRBrainS13-3	33.3294	0.9753	0.8032	33.3227	0.9793	0.8071	**33.3323**	**0.9888**	**0.8079**
MRB-Average	32.6761	0.9423	0.7974	32.6733	0.9497	0.7998	**32.6802**	**0.9607**	**0.8008**

The PSNR, FSIM, and SSIM were computed for sliced images from the BrainWeb and MRBrainS13 datasets using three methods for binary segmentation. The best result is indicated by the bold number.

Table 4 presents the average runtime of the three methods across the two datasets. The Otsu method was implemented using the existing cv2 library, and due to issues with code development and optimization, its average runtime is relatively short. Both Tsallis-BE and Cauchy-TB are self-implemented methods, and it can be observed that their average runtimes were similar, both within the order of seconds. This runtime is acceptable for the segmentation of a relatively small number of brain MRI images.

As shown in Figure 8, Cauchy-TB also demonstrated superior performance on the metrics of sensitivity and precision, with average values reaching over 97%, slightly better than the Tsallis-BE method. However, our method lagged slightly behind in specificity, although the results were still satisfactory. The Tsallis-BE method performed well in all three metrics. Otsu's performance in sensitivity was the most unstable, showing significant fluctuations in values. Overall, our method performed the best, showing significantly improved results in all metrics except specificity.

Table 4. Average time performance comparison.

Dataset	Otsu	Tsallis-BE	Cauchy-TB
BrainWeb	6.7194×10^{-5}	4.7576	5.1973
MRBrainS13	5.129×10^{-5}	6.4871	6.5095

Figure 9 shows a magnified view of the segmentation results of slice 90 of the BrainWeb dataset, compared with the ground truth image. It can be observed that for complex edge areas, both Cauchy-TB and the Tsallis-BE method outperformed the Otsu method. They could clearly and accurately delineate the target region with fewer misclassifications. However, the Tsallis-BE method showed over-segmentation in edge details, where some background pixels were erroneously classified as foreground, leading to differences from the ground truth in the edge contours. Cauchy-TB represented an obvious improvement in this aspect.

Figure 10 demonstrates the results of image thresholding on some slices taken from the BrainWeb and MRBrainS13 datasets. A comparison revealed that the segmentation achieved by the Otsu method was the worst, showing poor stability in the results. Cauchy-TB and Tsallis-BE were more similar to the ground truth, with the Tsallis-BE method performing well but being slightly inferior to ours in some perceptible details.

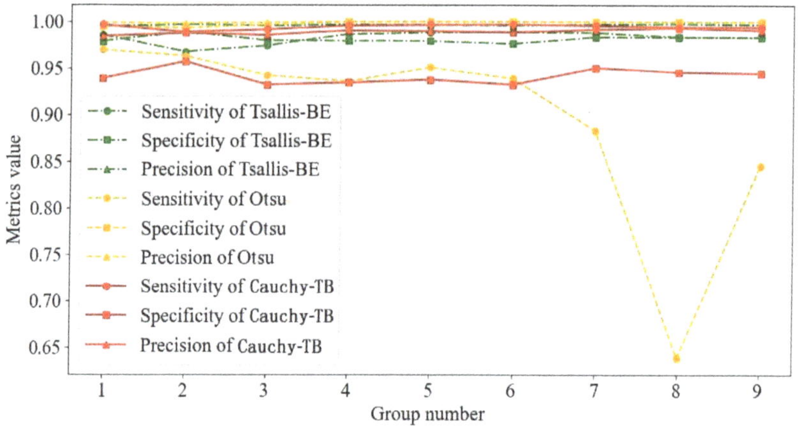

Figure 8. The sensitivity, specificity and precision curves of image thresholding results obtained by using the Cauchy-TB, Tsallis-BE, and Otsu method on nine groups from the BrainWeb dataset.

(B) Ternary segmentation

We compared the results of three-class thresholding between the Tsallis-BE and Cauchy-TB methods on nine groups of images from the BrainWeb dataset. Table 5 shows the comparative experimental results, with average results presented for each group of images. Our method outperformed Tsallis-BE significantly on the metrics of JC and DSC for all groups of images except the first group. On the BrainWeb dataset, our method achieved average accuracy, JC, and DSC of 97.09%, 95.08%, and 97.44%, respectively. Compared to the Tsallis-BE method, these metrics were improved by 0.5%, 0.8%, and 0.4%, respectively. The possible reason why Tsallis-BE performed slightly better in the first group of images is that the pixels of each part of the brain in the low-index slices were relatively few, and the fit obtained using the Cauchy distribution is slightly less appropriate than that obtained using the Gaussian distribution.

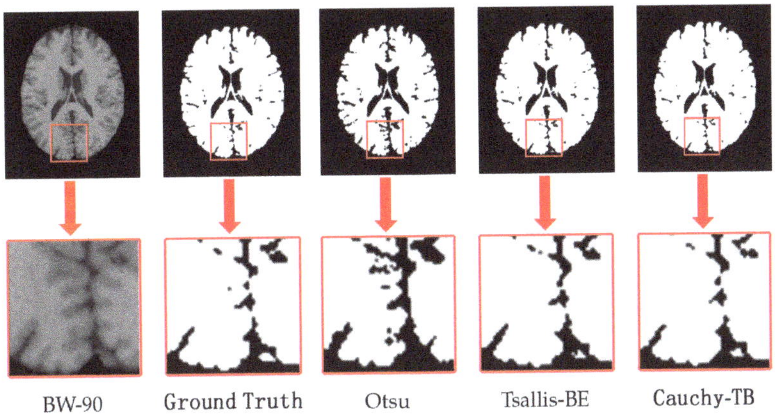

Figure 9. Enlarged images of the segmentation results of slice 90 in BrainWeb with three methods.

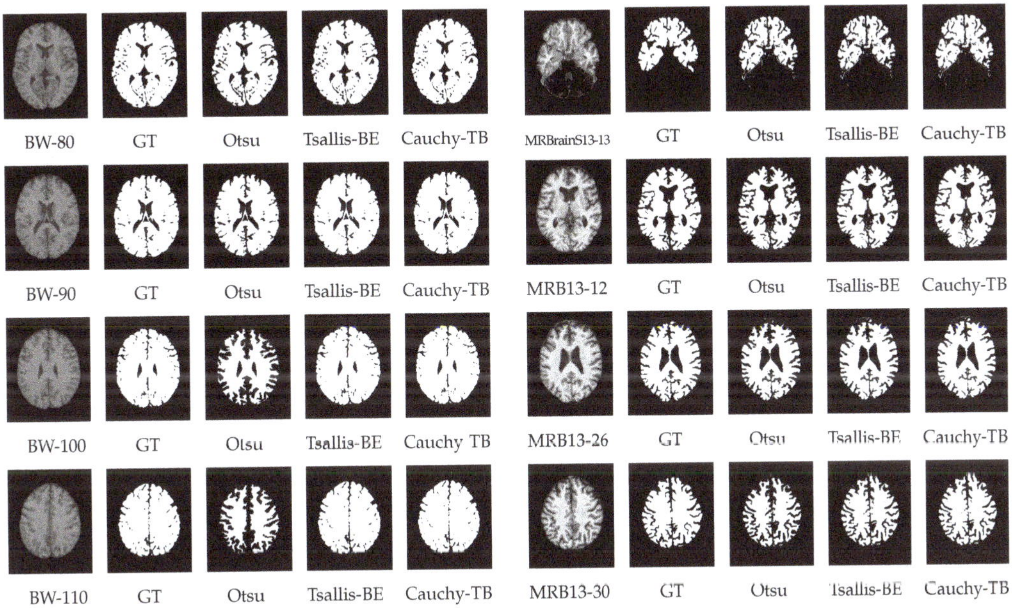

Figure 10. The results of image thresholding by the Cauchy-TB, Otsu, and Tsallis-BE methods. For both the left (BrainWeb) and right (MRBrainS13) groups, the columns from left to right represent the original slice; the ground truth (GT); and the results of Otsu, Cauchy-TB and Tsallis-BE, respectively.

Table 8. Segmented images obtained by applying Cauchy-TB with various numbers of thresholds on the BrainWeb dataset.

Slice		**Two Thresholds**	**Three Thresholds**
	Original Image	Thresholded Image	
	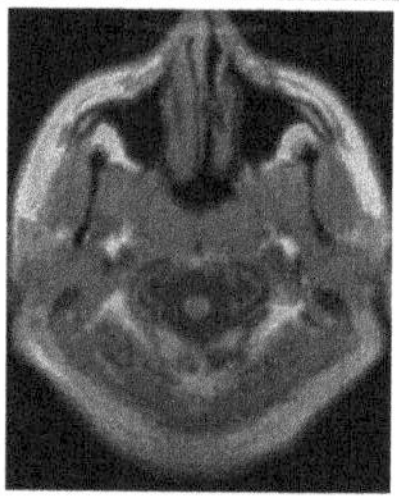	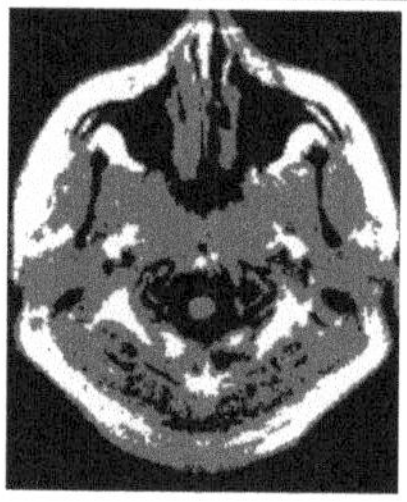	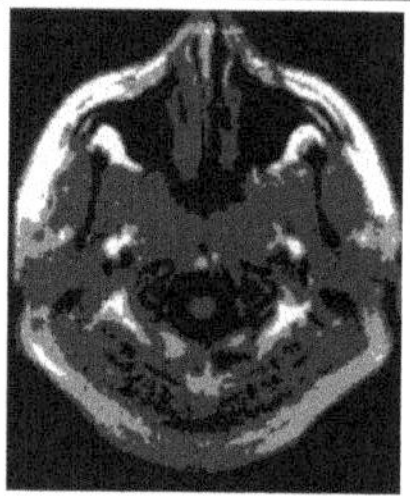
Z1	Ground Truth	Histogram	
	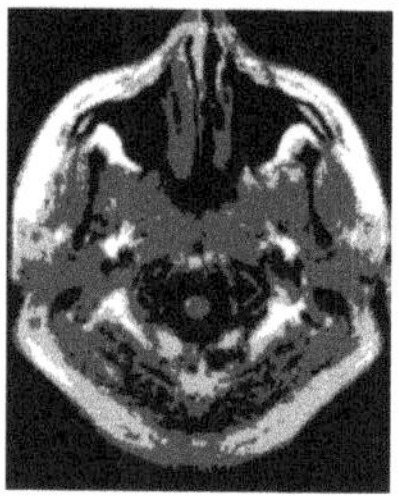	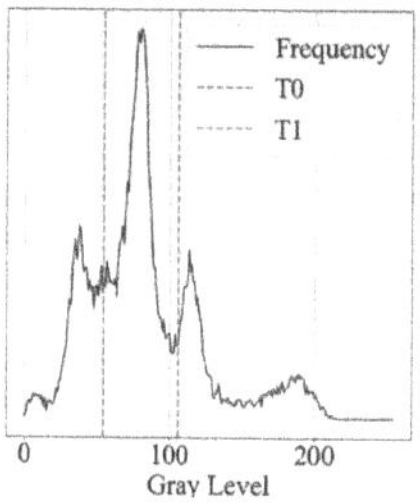	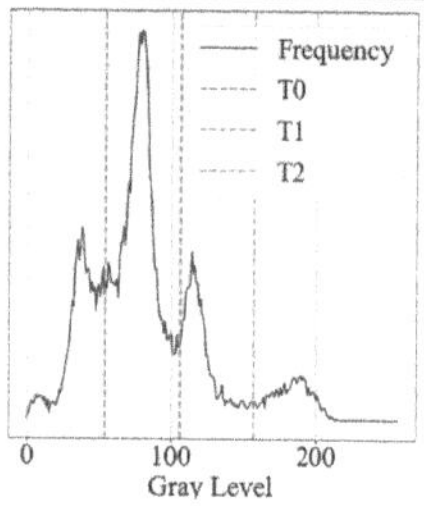
	Original Image	Thresholded Image	
	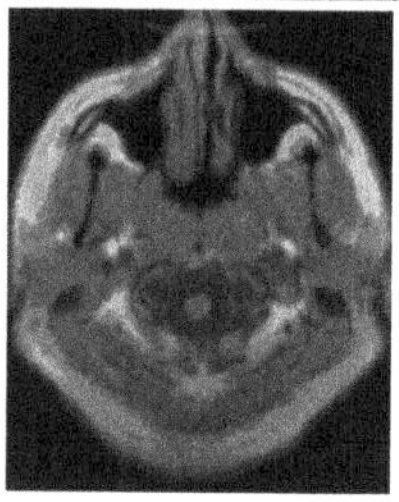	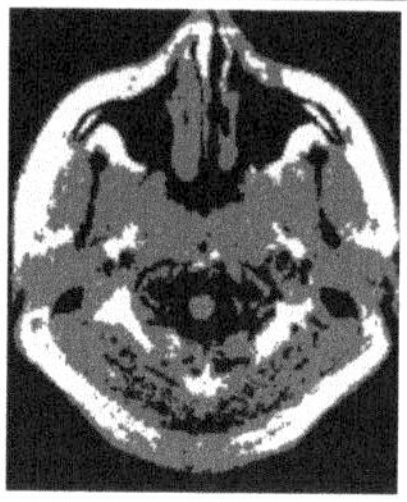	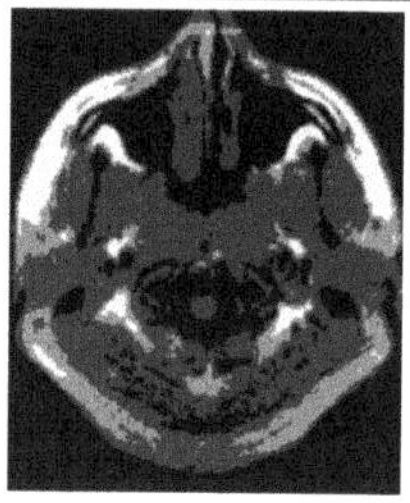
Z2	Ground Truth	Histogram	
	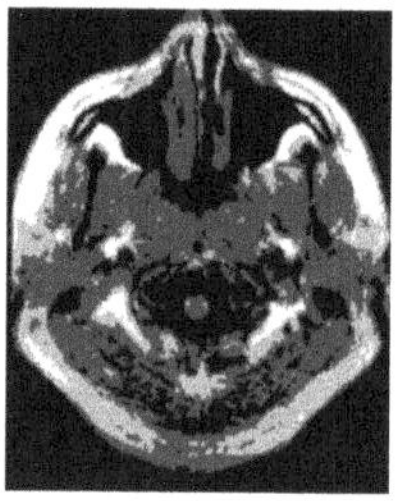	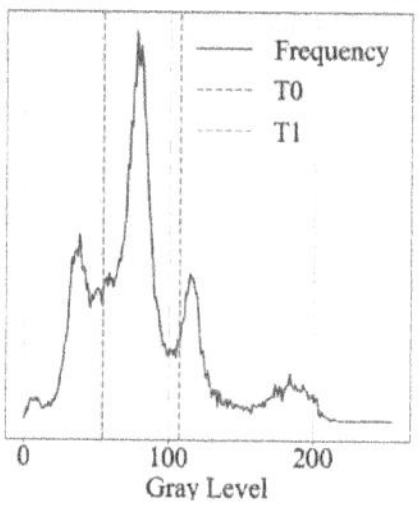	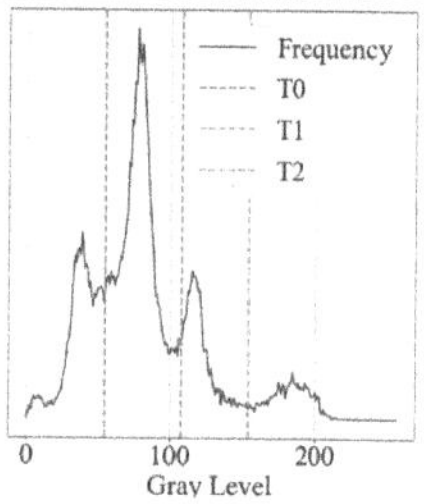

Table 8. *Cont.*

Slice		2 Thresholds	3 Thresholds
	Original Image	Thresholded Image	
Z5	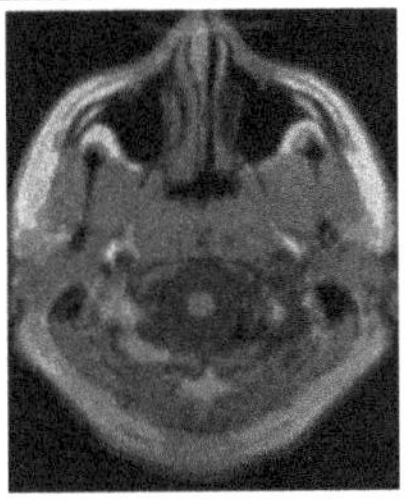	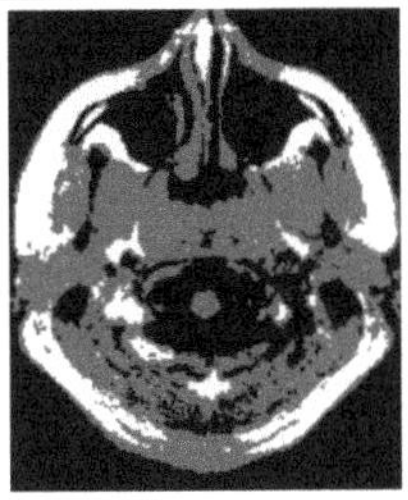	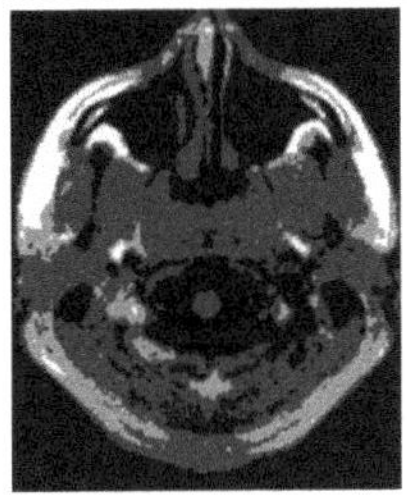
	Ground Truth	Histogram	
	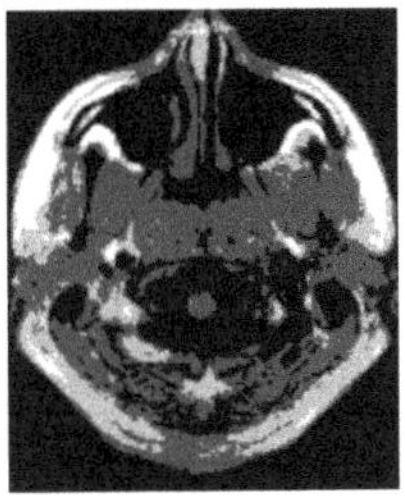	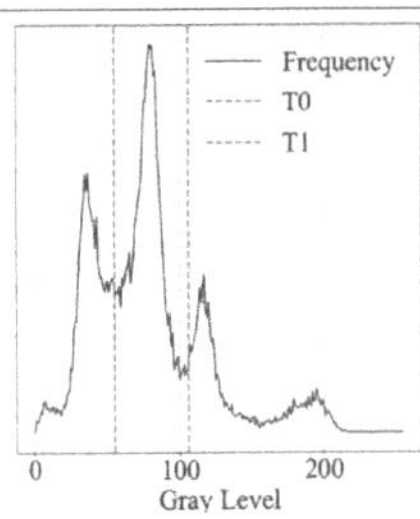	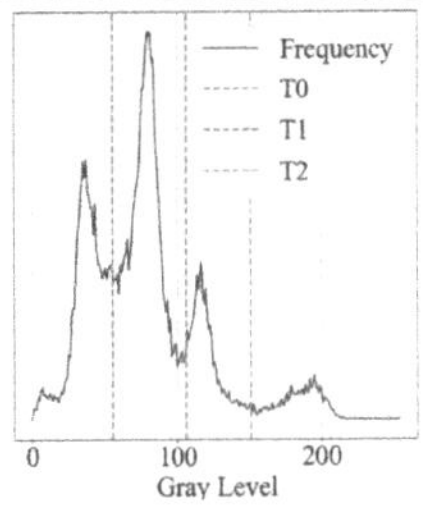
	Original Image	Thresholded Image	
Z10	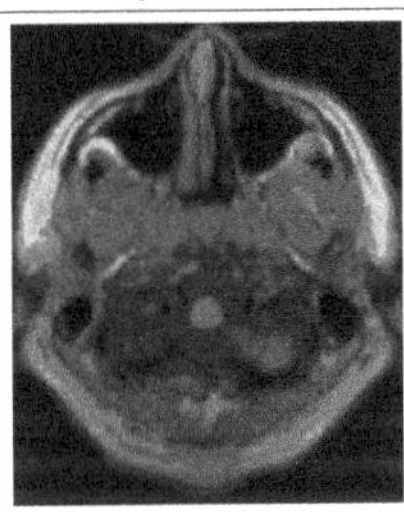	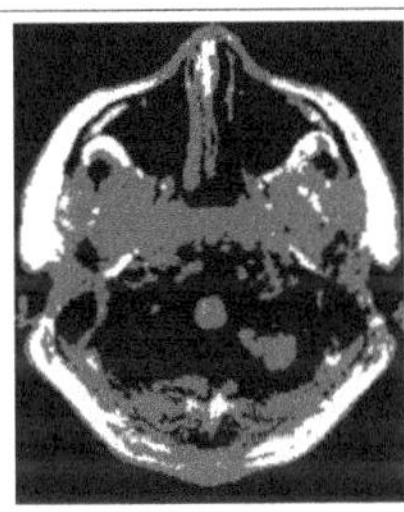	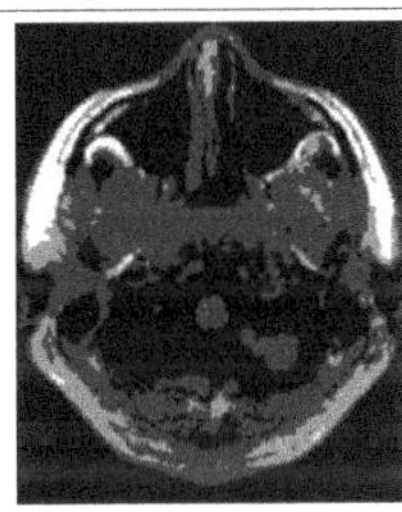
	Ground Truth	Histogram	
	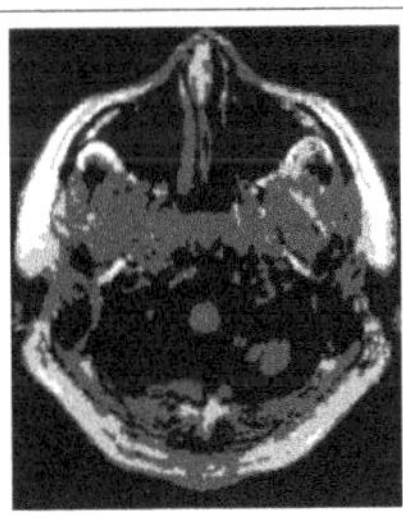	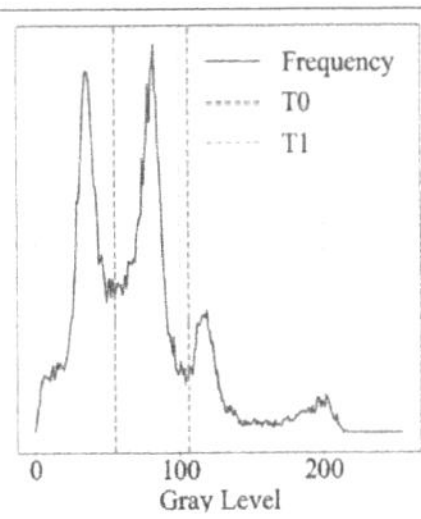	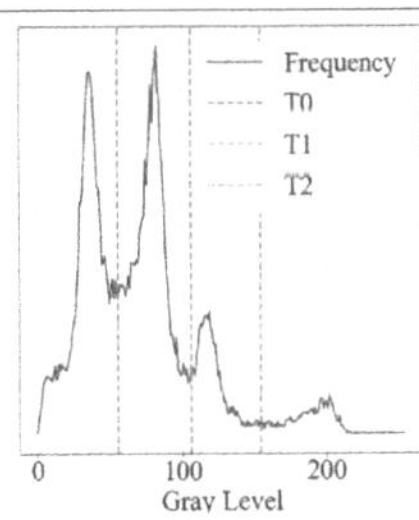

Table 8. *Cont.*

Slice		**2 Thresholds**	**3 Thresholds**
	Original Image	Thresholded Image	
Z36	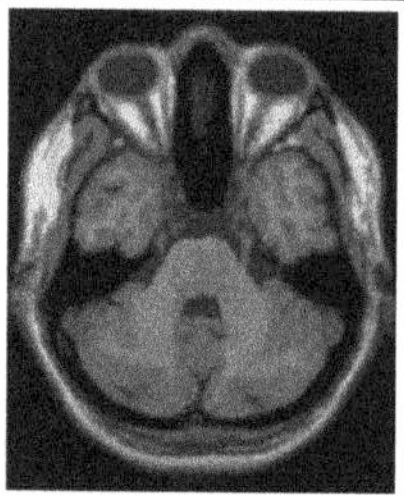	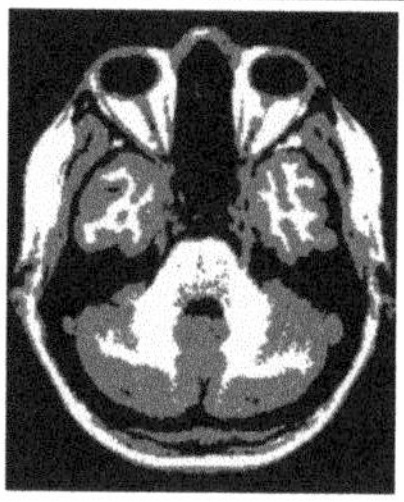	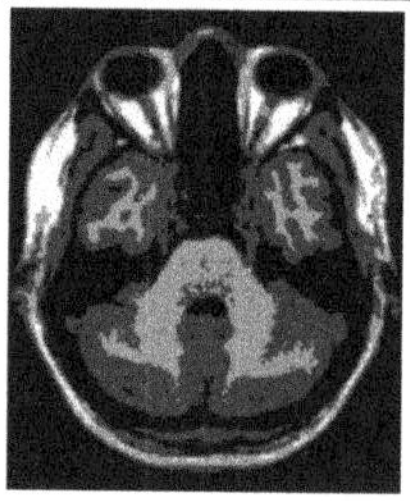
	Ground Truth	Histogram	
	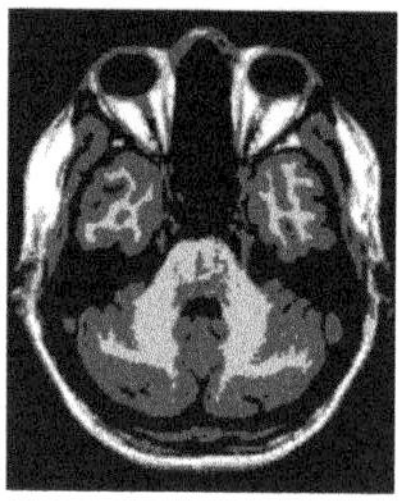	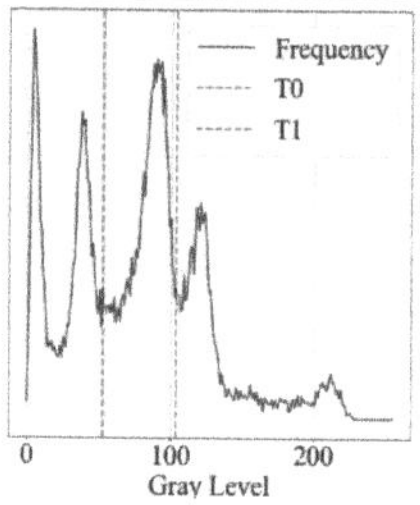	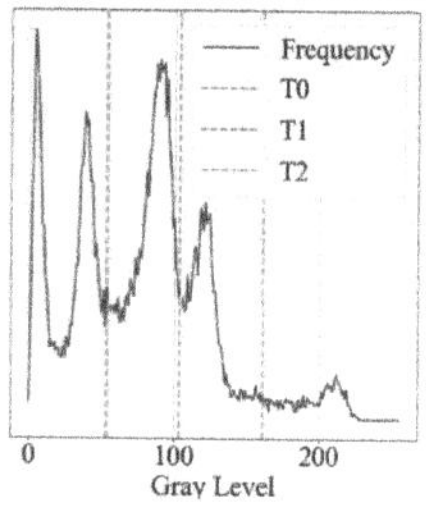
	Original Image	Thresholded Image	
Z72	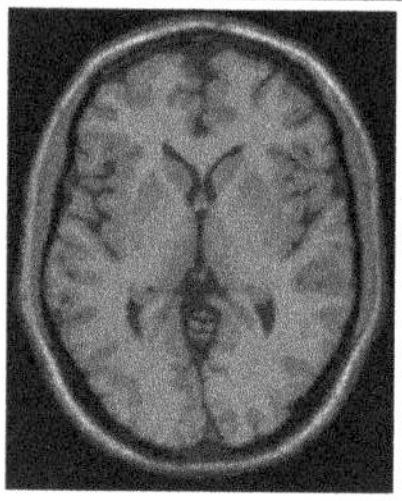	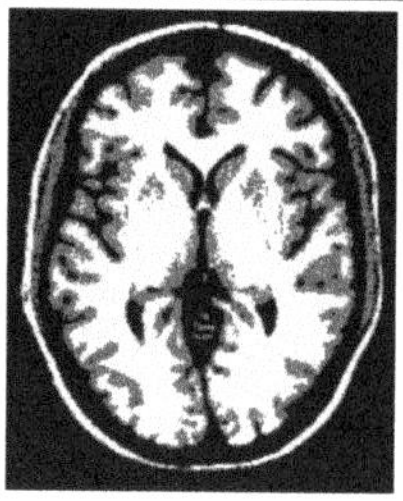	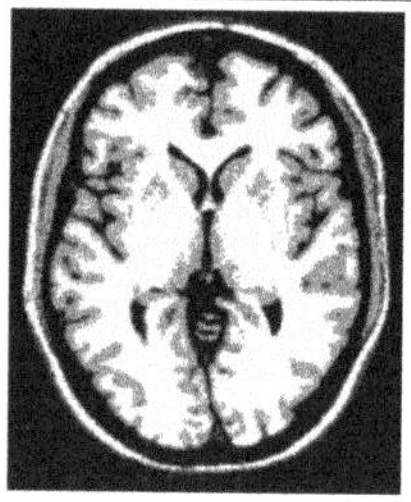
	Ground Truth	Histogram	
	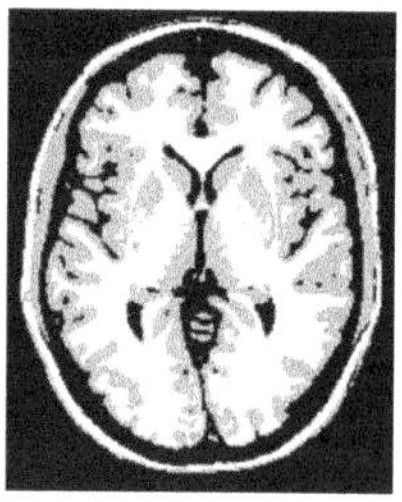	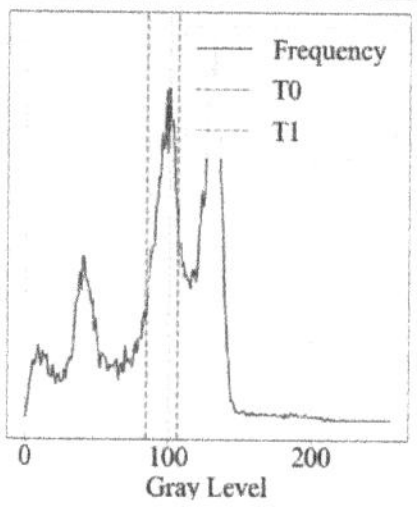	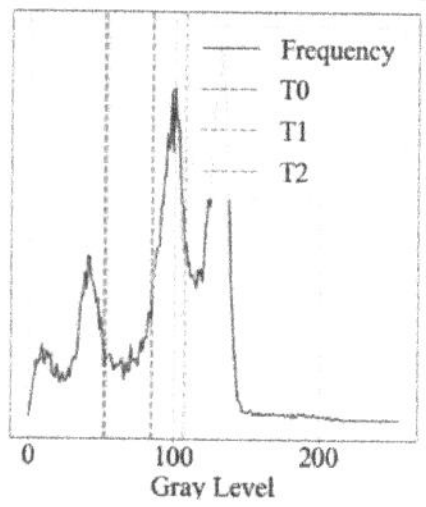

Table 8. *Cont.*

Slice		2 Thresholds	3 Thresholds
	Original Image	Thresholded Image	
Z108	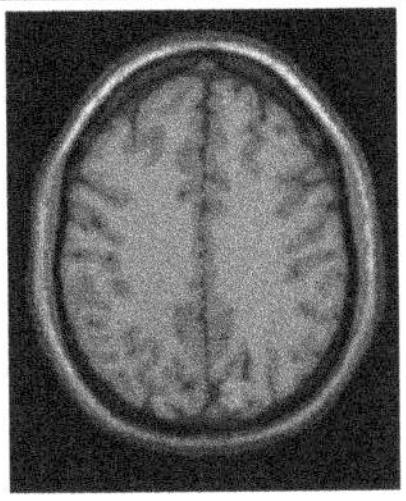	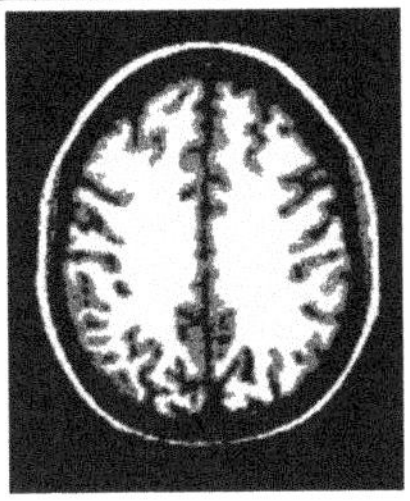	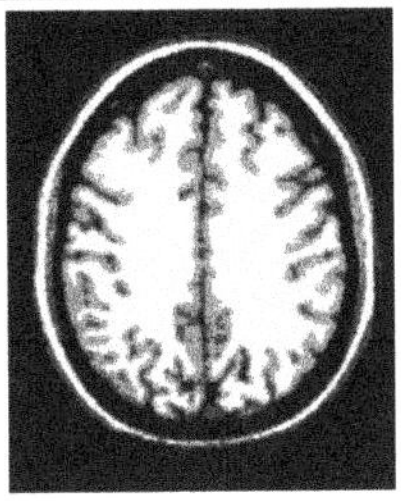
	Ground Truth	Histogram	
	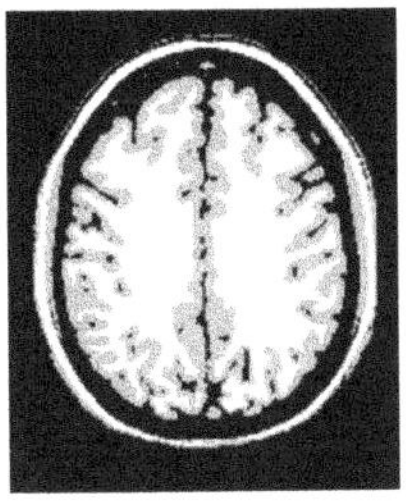	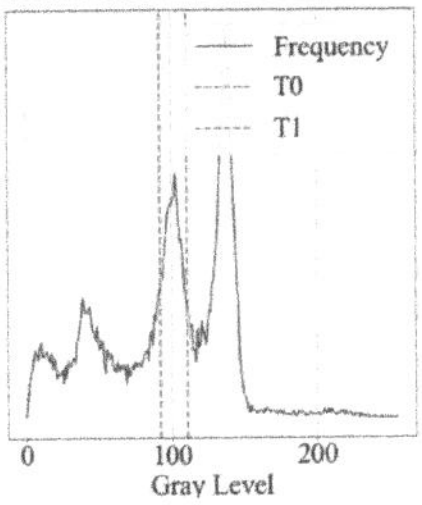	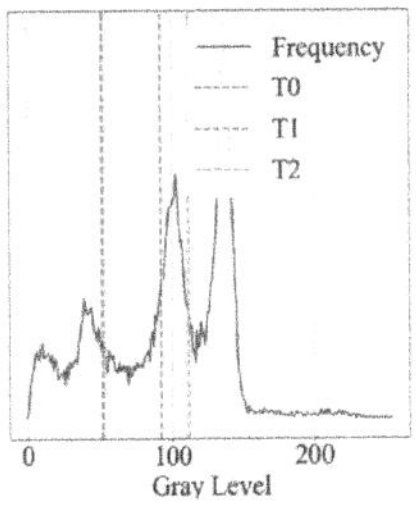
	Original Image	Thresholded Image	
Z144	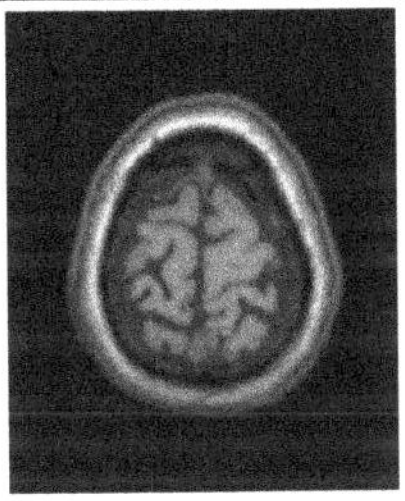	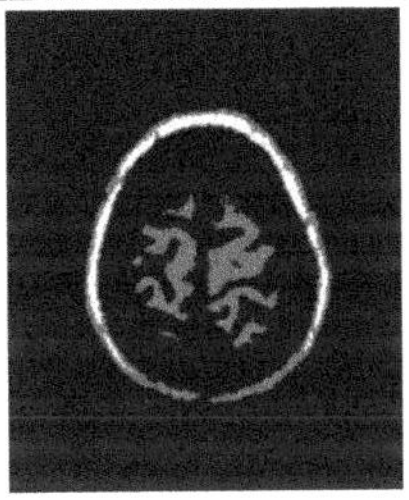	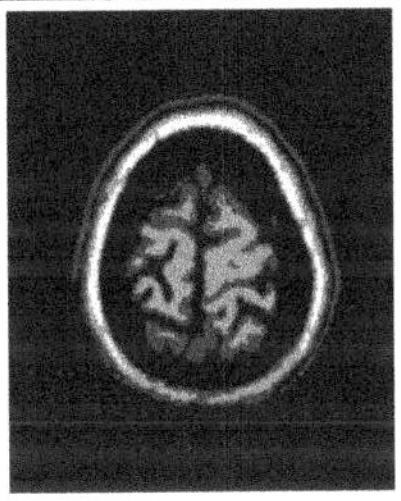
	Ground Truth	Histogram	
	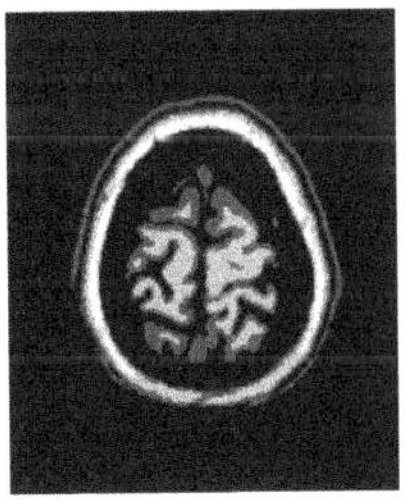	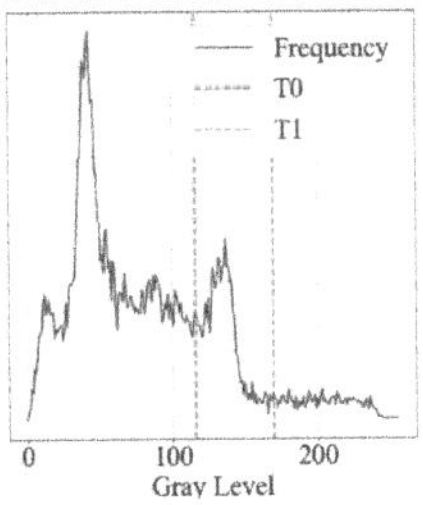	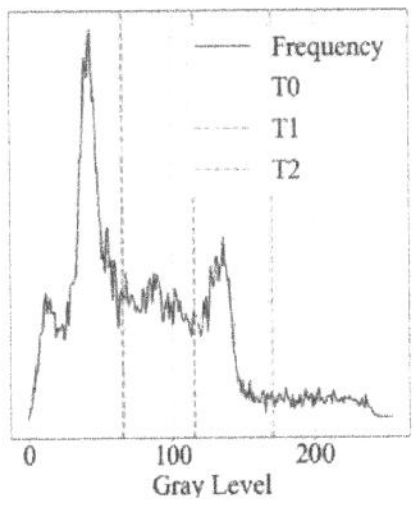

5. Discussion

Compared to previous binary segmentation methods, our proposed Cauchy-TB demonstrates comprehensive superiority on the metrics of accuracy, JC, and DSC, while performing comparably in sensitivity and specificity. When extended to solve the multilevel image segmentation problem, similar superiority can be observed. Overall, our method exhibits the best performance. We selected eight popular methods in the field as a standard and compared their performance on eight images from the BrainWeb dataset. Our method showed significant improvements on PSNR and FSIM metrics. The advantages of

Tsallis entropy mainly lie in its flexibility and adaptability. By adjusting the parameter q, Tsallis entropy can handle more complex, nonlinear images that are significantly affected by noise, providing more accurate segmentation results. The strength of Bayesian posterior probability lies in its ability to address the issue of two distributions becoming isolated during thresholding. By offering a more accurate probability distribution, it enhances the overall segmentation performance. The Cauchy distribution we introduced has better tolerance for outliers, which becomes more pronounced as image noise increases. Additionally, by extending our method to multilevel segmentation tasks based on a recursive approach, we greatly reduce the computational resources and time required.

In the case of multi-class problems with complex tissue structures, as the number of required categories increases, our method may show certain limitations. This is due to the higher uncertainty in estimating parameters when the pixel count for certain categories is low in the ground truth distribution, which could lead to significant estimation errors. To address this issue, non-parametric methods, such as kernel density estimation, can be used to avoid making strong assumptions about the distribution, thereby providing more robust and accurate results in such situations. In practical medical applications, automated brain imaging segmentation tools can significantly reduce the time and effort required by doctors. With automated segmentation, doctors can focus more on analysis and decision-making, rather than spending extensive time manually segmenting images. Although our method does not show a clear advantage in terms of time efficiency, we have achieved improvements in segmentation accuracy. Furthermore, it is evident that there is a limit to the effectiveness of global thresholds for image segmentation. In future research, our focus will be on improving time efficiency and finding local thresholds for regions prone to misclassification.

6. Conclusions

This paper integrates the advantage of entropy-based image thresholding methods with the properties of MRI image intensity probability distributions, proposing a new method for image thresholding based on the Cauchy distribution and Tsallis entropy. We introduce Bayesian posterior probability within the traditional Tsallis entropy framework and use the Cauchy distribution to fit the grayscale distribution. Furthermore, we generalize the method to solve the problem of multilevel thresholding. Comparative experiments on the BrainWeb and MRBrainS13 datasets demonstrate that Cauchy-TB achieves superior performance compared to other existing methods. Future work will include extending the idea to improve the estimation of local optimum thresholds and enhancing time efficiency.

Author Contributions: X.W.: methodology, software, validation, formal analysis, investigation, resources, data curation, writing—original draft preparation, writing—review and editing. Y.Y.: methodology, software, validation, formal analysis, investigation, resources. M.N.: investigation, resources, data curation. G.B.: methodology, writing—review and editing. G.L.: conceptualization, methodology, formal analysis, investigation, writing—original draft preparation, writing—review and editing. All authors have read and agreed to the published version of the manuscript.

Funding: This work is supported in part by the Huangpu Special Program of the Science and Technology Service Network Initiative of the Chinese Academy of Sciences under grant No. STS-HP-202201 and in part by the Fundamental and Applied Fundamental Research Fund of Guangdong Province under grant No. 2023B1515250007.

Institutional Review Board Statement: Ethical review and approval were waived for this study due to reason that both datasets we used are simulated and do not contain any real personal information.

Informed Consent Statement: Not applicable

Data Availability Statement: [BrainWeb: Simulated Brain Database] [http://www.bic.mni.mcgill.ca/brainweb/ (accessed on 19 May 2024)]; [MR Brain Segmentation Challenge 2013 Data] [https://mrbrains13.isi.uu.nl/ (accessed on 19 May 2024)] .

Acknowledgments: The authors would like to thank Sijin Luo and Yuqi Yan for their contributions to the early version of this paper.

Conflicts of Interest: The authors declare no conflicts of interest. The funders had no role in the design of the study; in the collection, analyses, or interpretation of data; in the writing of the manuscript; or in the decision to publish the results.

Abbreviations

Cauchy-TB	Cauchy–Tsallis Bayesian Estimation Method
MHUE	Minimum Homogeneity- and Uncertainty-Based Energy
MRI	Magnetic Resonance Imaging
GM	Grey Matter
t-SNE	t-Distributed Stochastic Neighbor Embedding
JC	Jaccard Coefficient
DSC	Dice Similarity Coefficient
PSNR	Peak Signal-to-Noise Ratio
SSIM	Structural Similarity Index
FSIM	Feature Similarity Index
Tsallis-BE	Tsallis–Bayesian Estimation Method
BW	BrainWeb Dataset
MRB	MRBrainS13 Dataset
GT	Ground Truth

Appendix A. Justification for the Choice of the Parameter q

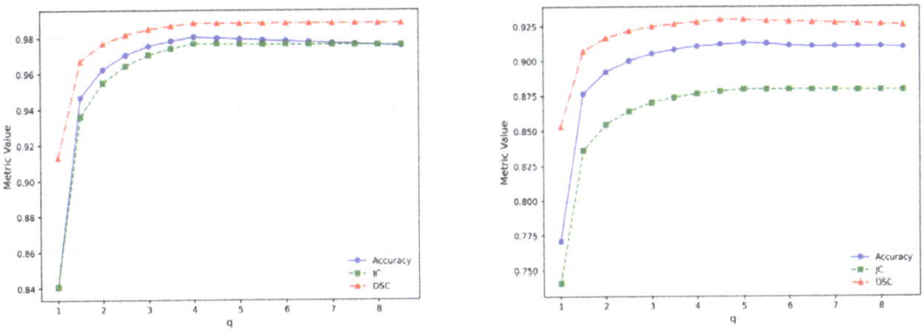

Figure A1. We started with $q = 1$ and incremented the value by 0.5, traversing up to 8.5, while recording the changes in the ACC, JC, and DSC metrics on the BrainWeb and MRBrainS13 datasets as q varied. It can be observed that the best overall performance occurs at $q = 4$ for the BrainWeb dataset and $q = 5$ for the MRBrainS13 dataset. (**Left**) Performance on the BrainWeb dataset. (**Right**) Performance on the MRBrainS13 dataset.

References

1. Nock, R.; Nielsen, F. Statistical region merging. *IEEE Trans. Pattern Anal. Mach. Intell.* **2004**, *26*, 1452–1458. [CrossRef]
2. Kashyap, R.; Gautam, P. Modified region based segmentation of medical images. In Proceedings of the 2015 International Conference on Communication Networks (ICCN), Gwalior, India, 19–21 November 2015; pp. 209–216.
3. Canny, J. A computational approach to edge detection. *IEEE Trans. Pattern Anal. Mach. Intell.* **1986**, *6*, 679–698. [CrossRef]
4. Gupta, D.; Anand, R.S. A hybrid edge-based segmentation approach for ultrasound medical images. *Biomed. Signal Process. Control* **2017**, *31*, 116–126. [CrossRef]
5. Dhanachandra, N.; Manglem, K.; Chanu, Y.J. Image segmentation using K-means clustering algorithm and subtractive clustering algorithm. *Procedia Comput. Sci.* **2015**, *54*, 764–771. [CrossRef]

6. Abdel-Maksoud, E.; Elmogy, M.; Al-Awadi, R. Brain tumor segmentation based on a hybrid clustering technique. *Egypt. Inform. J.* **2015**, *16*, 71–81. [CrossRef]
7. Boykov, Y.; Kolmogorov, V. An experimental comparison of min-cut/max-flow algorithms for energy minimization in vision. *IEEE Trans. Pattern Anal. Mach. Intell.* **2004**, *26*, 1124–1137. [CrossRef] [PubMed]
8. Chen, X.; Pan, L. A survey of graph cuts/graph search based medical image segmentation. *IEEE Rev. Biomed. Eng.* **2018**, *11*, 112–124. [CrossRef]
9. Vincent, L.; Soille, P. Watersheds in digital spaces: An efficient algorithm based on immersion simulations. *IEEE Trans. Pattern Anal. Mach. Intell.* **1991**, *13*, 583–598. [CrossRef]
10. Nandi, D.; Ashour, A.S.; Samanta, S.; Chakraborty, S.; Salem, M.A.; Dey, N. Principal component analysis in medical image processing: A study. *Int. J. Image Min.* **2015**, *1*, 65–86. [CrossRef]
11. Rathi, V.P.; Palani, S. Brain tumor MRI image classification with feature selection and extraction using linear discriminant analysis. *arXiv* **2012**, arXiv:1208.2128.
12. Nanni, L.; Lumini, A.; Brahnam, S. Local binary patterns variants as texture descriptors for medical image analysis. *Artif. Intell. Med.* **2010**, *49*, 117–125. [CrossRef]
13. Abbasi, S.; Tajeripour, F. Detection of brain tumor in 3D MRI images using local binary patterns and histogram orientation gradient. *Neurocomputing* **2017**, *219*, 526–535. [CrossRef]
14. Ramamurthy, B.; Chandran, K. Content based medical image retrieval with texture content using gray level co-occurrence matrix and k-means clustering algorithms. *J. Comput. Sci.* **2012**, *8*, 1070.
15. Vasilache, S.; Ward, K.; Cockrell, C.; Ha, J.; Najarian, K. Unified wavelet and gaussian filtering for segmentation of CT images; application in segmentation of bone in pelvic CT images. *BMC Med. Inform. Decis. Mak.* **2009**, *9*, S8. [CrossRef]
16. Ayachi, R.; Ben Amor, N. Brain tumor segmentation using support vector machines. In Proceedings of the European Conference on Symbolic and Quantitative Approaches to Reasoning and Uncertainty (ECSQARU), Verona, Italy, 1–3 July 2009; pp. 736–747.
17. Kayalibay, B.; Jensen, G.; van der Smagt, P. CNN-based segmentation of medical imaging data. *arXiv* **2017**, arXiv:1701.03056 .
18. Ronneberger, O.; Fischer, P.; Brox, T. U-net: Convolutional networks for biomedical image segmentation. In *Proceedings of the Medical Image Computing and Computer-Assisted Intervention–MICCAI 2015: 18th International Conference, Munich, Germany, 5–9 October 2015, Proceedings, Part III 18*; Springer: Berlin/Heidelberg, Germany, 2015; pp. 234–241.
19. Qian, Z.; Li, K.; Lai, M.; Chang, E.I.C.; Wei, B.; Fan, Y.; Xu, Y. Transformer based multiple instance learning for weakly supervised histopathology image segmentation. In Proceedings of the International Conference on Medical Image Computing and Computer-Assisted Intervention (MICCAI), Singapore, 18–22 September 2022; pp. 160–170.
20. Kirillov, A.; Mintun, E.; Ravi, N.; Mao, H.; Rolland, C.; Gustafson, L.; Xiao, T.; Whitehead, S.; Berg, A.C.; Lo, W.; et al. Segment anything. In Proceedings of the IEEE/CVF International Conference on Computer Vision(ICCV), Paris, France, 2–3 October 2023; pp. 4015–4026.
21. Kapur, J.N.; Sahoo, P.K.; Wong, A.K. A new method for gray-level picture thresholding using the entropy of the histogram. *Comput. Vis. Graph. Image Process.* **1985**, *29*, 273–285. [CrossRef]
22. Otsu, N. A threshold selection method from gray-level histograms. *Automatica* **1975**, *11*, 23–27. [CrossRef]
23. Saha, P.; Udupa, J. Optimum image thresholding via class uncertainty and region homogeneity. *IEEE Trans. Pattern Anal. Mach. Intell.* **2001**, *23*, 689–706. [CrossRef]
24. Liu, Y.; Liang, G.; Saha, P.K. A new multi-object image thresholding method based on correlation between object class uncertainty and intensity gradient. *Med. Phys.* **2012**, *39*, 514–532. [CrossRef]
25. De Albuquerque, M.P.; Esquef, I.A.; Mello, A.G. Image thresholding using Tsallis entropy. *Pattern Recognit. Lett.* **2004**, *25*, 1059–1065. [CrossRef]
26. Sarkar, S.; Das, S. Multilevel image thresholding based on 2D histogram and maximum Tsallis entropy—A differential evolution approach. *IEEE Trans. Image Process.* **2013**, *22*, 4788–4797. [CrossRef] [PubMed]
27. Shubham, S.; Bhandari, A.K. A generalized Masi entropy based efficient multilevel thresholding method for color image segmentation. *Multimed. Tools Appl.* **2019**, *78*, 17197–17238. [CrossRef]
28. Abutaleb, A.S. Automatic thresholding of gray-level pictures using two-dimensional entropy. *Comput. Vis. Graph. Image Process.* **1989**, *47*, 22–32. [CrossRef]
29. Bindu, C.H.; Prasad, K.S. An efficient medical image segmentation using conventional OTSU method. *Int. J. Adv. Sci. Technol.* **2012**, *38*, 67–74.
30. Yuan, X.c.; Wu, L.s.; Peng, Q. An improved Otsu method using the weighted object variance for defect detection. *Appl. Surf. Sci.* **2015**, *349*, 472–484. [CrossRef]
31. Feng, Y.; Zhao, H.; Li, X.; Zhang, X.; Li, H. A multi-scale 3D Otsu thresholding algorithm for medical image segmentation. *Digit. Signal Process.* **2017**, *60*, 186–199. [CrossRef]

32. Li, A.; Li, Y.; Wang, T.; Niu, W. Medical image segmentation based on maximum entropy multi-threshold segmentation optimized by improved cuckoo search algorithm. In Proceedings of the 2015 8th International Congress on Image and Signal Processing (CISP), Shenyang, China, 14–16 October 2015; pp. 470–475.
33. Liu, D.; Jiang, Z.; Feng, H. A novel fuzzy classification entropy approach to image thresholding. *Pattern Recognit. Lett.* **2006**, *27*, 1968–1975. [CrossRef]
34. Zou, Y.; Zhang, J.; Zhou, H.; Sun, S.; Xia, P. Tsallis Entropy Thresholding Based on Multi-scale and Multi-direction Gabor Transform. *J. Electron. Inf. Technol.* **2023**, *45*, 707–717.
35. Prabaharan, L.; Raghunathan, A. Segmentation of human spermatozoa using improved Havrda-Chavrat entropy-based thresholding method. *J. Intell. Fuzzy Syst.* **2022**, *43*, 5279–5292. [CrossRef]
36. Naik, M.K.; Panda, R.; Samantaray, L.; Abraham, A. A novel threshold score based multiclass segmentation technique for brain magnetic resonance images using adaptive opposition slime mold algorithm. *Int. J. Imaging Syst. Technol.* **2022**, *32*, 1397–1413. [CrossRef]
37. Li, H.; Zheng, G.; Sun, K.; Jiang, Z.; Li, Y.; Jia, H. A logistic chaotic barnacles mating optimizer with Masi entropy for color image multilevel thresholding segmentation. *IEEE Access* **2020**, *8*, 213130–213153. [CrossRef]
38. Venugopal, V.; Joseph, J.; Das, M.V.; Nath, M.K. DTP-Net: A convolutional neural network model to predict threshold for localizing the lesions on dermatological macro-images. *Comput. Biol. Med.* **2022**, *148*, 105852. [CrossRef] [PubMed]
39. Johnson, L.; Pearlman, J.; Miller, C.; Young, T.I.; Thulborn, K.R. MR quantification of cerebral ventricular volume using a semiautomated algorithm. *Am. J. Neuroradiol.* **1993**, *14*, 1373–1378.
40. Yadav, A.K.; Roy, R.; Somwanshi, D. Thresholding and morphological based segmentation techniques for medical images. In Proceedings of the 2016 International Conference on Recent Advances and Innovations in Engineering (ICRAIE), Jaipur, India, 23–25 December 2016; pp. 1–5.
41. Kalyani, R.; Sathya, P.D.; Sakthivel, V.P. Multilevel thresholding for medical image segmentation using teaching-learning based optimization algorithm. *Int. J. Intell. Eng. Syst.* **2021**, *14*, 11–21.
42. Ghorbani, N.; Babaei, E. Exchange market algorithm. *Appl. Soft Comput.* **2014**, *19*, 177–187. [CrossRef]
43. Nyo, M.T.; Mebarek-Oudina, F.; Hlaing, S.S.; Khan, N.A. Otsu's thresholding technique for MRI image brain tumor segmentation. *Multimed. Tools Appl.* **2022**, *81*, 43837–43849. [CrossRef]
44. Ibrahim, N.A.; Mohamed, E.R.; Hamza, H.M.; Alsahafi, Y.S.; Hosny, K.M. Masked face image segmentation using a multilevel threshold with a hybrid fitness function. *Intell. Syst. Appl.* **2024**, *24*, 200445. [CrossRef]
45. Sowmiya, R. Hybrid leader corona virus herd optimizer with multilevel thresholding techniques for foreground and background image segmentation. *Comput. Electr. Eng.* **2024**, *120*, 109569.
46. Niblack, W. *An Introduction to Digital Image Processing*; Strandberg Publishing Company: Copenhagen, Denmark, 1985.
47. Sauvola, J.; Pietikäinen , M. Adaptive document image binarization. *Pattern Recognit.* **2000**, *33*, 225–236. [CrossRef]
48. Hemachander, S.; Verma, A.; Arora, S.; Panigrahi, P.K. Locally adaptive block thresholding method with continuity constraint. *Pattern Recognit. Lett.* **2007**, *28*, 119–124. [CrossRef]
49. Chaira, T. Intuitionistic fuzzy segmentation of medical images. *IEEE Trans. Biomed. Eng.* **2010**, *57*, 1430–1436. [CrossRef] [PubMed]
50. Tarkhaneh, O.; Shen, H. An adaptive differential evolution algorithm to optimal multi-level thresholding for MRI brain image segmentation. *Expert Syst. Appl.* **2019**, *138*, 112820. [CrossRef]
51. Khalid, S.; Zhu, H.; Yang, T. Improved adaptive threshold segmentation of ultrasound medical images. In Proceedings of the 2021 3rd International Conference on Intelligent Medicine and Image Processing (IMIP), Tianjin, China, 23–26 April 2021; pp. 1–6.
52. Ariyanfar, A.; Klein, K.; von Rechenberg, B.; Darwiche, S.; Dailey, H.L. Adaptive image segmentation reveals substantial cortical bone remodelling during early fracture repair. *Comput. Methods Biomech. Biomed. Eng. Imaging Vis.* **2024**, *12*, 2345165. [CrossRef] [PubMed]
53. Li, J.; Gui, X. Fully Automatic Grayscale Image Segmentation: Dynamic Thresholding for Background Adaptation, Improved Image Center Point Selection, and Noise-Resilient Start/End Point Determination. *Appl. Sci.* **2024**, *14*, 9303. [CrossRef]
54. Gharehchopogh, F.S.; Ibrikci, T. An improved African vultures optimization algorithm using different fitness functions for multi-level thresholding image segmentation. *Multimed. Tools Appl.* **2024**, *83*, 16929–16975. [CrossRef]
55. Qiao, L.; Liu, K.; Xue, Y.; Tang, W.; Salehnia, T. A multi-level thresholding image segmentation method using hybrid Arithmetic Optimization and Harris Hawks Optimizer algorithms. *Expert Syst. Appl.* **2024**, *241*, 122316. [CrossRef]
56. Li, Z.; Najarian, K. Biomedical Image Segmentation Based on Shape Stability. In Proceedings of the 2007 IEEE International Conference on Image Processing, San Antonio, TX, USA, 16 September–19 October 2007; Volume 6, pp. VI-281–VI-284.
57. Serna, A.; Marcotegui, B.; Decenciere, E.; Baldeweck, T.; Pena, A.M.; Brizion, S. Segmentation of elongated objects using attribute profiles and area stability: Application to melanocyte segmentation in engineered skin. *Pattern Recognit. Lett.* **2014**, *47*, 172–182. [CrossRef]

58. Luo, S.; Luo, Z.; Zhan, Z.; Liang, G. Optimum Thresholding for Medical Brain Images Based on Tsallis Entropy and Bayesian Estimation. In Proceedings of the 2022 IEEE 35th International Symposium on Computer-Based Medical Systems (CBMS), Shenzhen, China, 21–22 July 2022; pp. 360–365.
59. Shannon, C.E. A mathematical theory of communication. *Bell Syst. Tech. J.* **1948**, *27*, 379–423. [CrossRef]
60. Van der Maaten, L.; Hinton, G. Visualizing data using t-SNE. *J. Mach. Learn. Res.* **2008**, *9*, 11.
61. Cocosco, C.A.; Kollokian, V.; Remi, K.; Pike, G.; Evans, A. BrainWeb: Online Interface to a 3D MRI Simulated Brain Database. *NeuroImage* **1997**, *5*, 425.
62. Mendrik, A.; Vincken, K.; Kuijf, H.; Breeuwer, M.; Bouvy, W.H.; Bresser, J.D.; Alansary, A.; de Bruijne, M.; Carass, A.; El-Baz, A.; et al. MRBrainS Challenge: Online Evaluation Framework for Brain Image Segmentation in 3T MRI Scans. *Comput. Intell. Neurosci.* **2015**, *2015*, 813696. [CrossRef]
63. Bandyopadhyay, R.; Kundu, R.; Oliva, D.; Sarka, R. Segmentation of brain MRI using an altruistic Harris Hawks' Optimization algorithm. *Knowl.-Based Syst.* **2021**, *232*, 107468. [CrossRef]
64. Aranguren, I.; Valdivia, A.; Morales-Castañeda, B.; Oliva, D.; Elaziz, M.A.; Perez-Cisneros, M. Improving the segmentation of magnetic resonance brain images using the LSHADE optimization algorithm. *Biomed. Signal Process. Control* **2021**, *64*, 102259. [CrossRef]
65. Mishra, D.; Bose, I.; De, U.C.; Das, M. Medical image thresholding using particle swarm optimization. In Proceedings of the Intelligent Computing, Communication and Devices: Proceedings of ICCD 2014, Seoul, Republic of Korea, 19–22 October 2014; Volume 1, pp. 379–383.
66. Mirjalili, S.; Mirjalili, S.M.; Lewis, A. Grey wolf optimizer. *Adv. Eng. Softw.* **2014**, *69*, 46–61. [CrossRef]
67. Erukala Mahender, D.C.R.B.; Kumar, K.S. Multi-level thresholding for image segmentation on medical images using multi otsu and sine cosine optimization algorithm. *Ann. Rom. Soc. Cell Biol.* **2021**, *25*, 12305–12316.
68. Anitha, J.; Pandian, S.I.A.; Agnes, S.A. An efficient multilevel color image thresholding based on modified whale optimization algorithm. *Expert Syst. Appl.* **2021**, *178*, 115003. [CrossRef]
69. Wang, S.; Sun, K.; Zhang, W.; Jia, H. Multilevel thresholding using a modified ant lion optimizer with opposition-based learning for color image segmentation. *Math. Biosci. Eng.* **2021**, *18*, 3092–3143. [CrossRef] [PubMed]
70. WangNo, N.; Chiewchanwattana, S.; Sunat, K. An efficient adaptive thresholding function optimized by a cuckoo search algorithm for a despeckling filter of medical ultrasound images. *J. Ambient. Intell. Humaniz. Comput.* **2023**, 14, 15429–15454. [CrossRef]

applied sciences

MDPI

Article

Development of Automated Image Processing for High-Throughput Screening of Potential Anti-Chikungunya Virus Compounds

Pathaphon Wiriwithya [1], Siwaporn Boonyasuppayakorn [2,3], Pattadon Sawetpiyakul [4], Duangpron Peypala [5] and Gridsada Phanomchoeng [1,3,*]

1 Department of Mechanical Engineering, Faculty of Engineering, Chulalongkorn University, Bangkok 10330, Thailand; pathaphon.w@gmail.com
2 Department of Microbiology, Faculty of Medicine, Chulalongkorn University, Bangkok 10330, Thailand
3 Applied Medical Virology Research Unit, Chulalongkorn University, Bangkok 10330, Thailand
4 Department of Biology, Faculty of Science, Chulalongkorn University, Bangkok 10330, Thailand
5 Department of Microbiology, Faculty of Science, Chulalongkorn University, Bangkok 10330, Thailand
* Correspondence: gridsada.phanomchoeng@gmail.com or gridsada.p@chula.ac.th

Abstract

Chikungunya virus, a member of the Alphavirus genus, continues to present a global health challenge due to its widespread occurrence and the absence of specific antiviral therapies. Accurate detection of viral infections, such as chikungunya, is critical for antiviral research, yet traditional methods are time-consuming and prone to error. This study presents the development and validation of an automated image processing algorithm designed to improve the accuracy and speed of high-throughput screening for potential anti-chikungunya virus compounds. Using MvTec Halcon software (Version 22.11), the algorithm was developed to detect and classify infected and uninfected cells in viral assays, and its performance was validated against manual counts conducted by virology experts, showing a strong correlation with Pearson correlation coefficients of 0.9807 for cell detection and 0.9886 for virus detection. These values indicate a high correlation between the algorithm and manual counts performed by three virology experts, demonstrating that the algorithm's accuracy closely matches expert manual evaluations. Following statistical validation, the algorithm was applied to screen antiviral compounds, demonstrating its effectiveness in enhancing the throughput and accuracy of drug discovery workflows. This technology can be seamlessly integrated into existing virological research pipelines, offering a scalable and efficient tool to accelerate drug discovery and improve diagnostic workflows for vector-borne and emerging viral diseases. By addressing critical bottlenecks in speed and accuracy, it holds promise for tackling global virology challenges and advancing research into other viral infections.

Keywords: automated image processing; high-throughput screening; biomedical imaging; image analysis in virology; image analysis

1. Introduction

The chikungunya virus (Chick V), a member of the Alphavirus genus and Togaviridae family [1], has been a global health concern since it was first identified in the United Republic of Tanzania in 1952 [2]. Over the past several decades, outbreaks have predominantly occurred in Africa and Asia, with the virus spreading to over 60 countries, leading to

 https://doi.org/10.3390/app15010385

millions of infectious cases [2,3]. In subsequent years, there were signs of a wider spread of infections [4], with reports in early 2000s of cases in Europe and the Americas, demonstrating the virus's adaptability [5]. Currently, according to reports, the chikungunya virus can be found in both tropical and subtropical regions [6]. The most found strains include the East Central South Africa (ECSA) strain and the Indian Ocean Lineage (IOL) strain [7,8].

Chikungunya virus is primarily transmitted through the bites of Aedes aegypti and Aedes albopictus mosquitoes [9]. Upon infection, individuals typically develop chikungunya fever, a condition characterized by high fever, headaches, muscle pain, and severe joint inflammation [10] that can persist for weeks or even months, leading to joint deformities in severe cases [11]. Although chikungunya fever is rarely fatal, it can lead to significant morbidity, and in some instances, organ failure has been observed as a rare but severe complication [12]. Despite extensive research efforts over the years, no specific vaccine or antiviral therapy for chikungunya virus is currently available [13], and treatment remains limited to symptomatic relief [14]. This makes the development of new treatments and diagnostic methods an urgent priority as the number of cases continues to rise globally [15,16].

Recent advancements in artificial intelligence and machine learning have shown great potential in the field of virology, especially in the detection of respiratory infections through medical imaging. For instance, the PulmoNet model demonstrated the potential of artificial intelligence in analyzing medical images for respiratory viral infections [17]. These advancements, while focused on respiratory viruses, suggest the potential for adaptation to other viral infections. For vector-borne diseases like chikungunya, innovative approaches combining Internet of Things (IoT) and machine learning technologies are being developed. A notable example is the MosquIoT system, which uses AI and image processing to monitor Aedes aegypti mosquitoes, the primary vectors for chikungunya and other viruses [18]. Although MosquIoT does not directly analyze viral particles, its integration of AI into entomological surveillance represents a crucial step toward improved disease control efforts. In addition, nanoparticle-based biosensors are being developed to detect chikungunya, marking another frontier in diagnostic technology that could be combined with image-based detection methods [19].

While these technologies show potential, a significant gap remains in the direct application of image processing techniques for chikungunya virus detection. Current efforts, such as the development of magnetic bead-based sample extraction coupled with polymerase spiral reaction, emphasize the need for rapid and accurate on-site diagnostic methods [20]. However, these approaches are not yet widely integrated with image processing technologies, leaving considerable room for further research into automated systems targeting chikungunya.

In the biomedical field, image processing techniques have already made substantial contributions, particularly in viral infection detection [21]. High-throughput image analysis has become invaluable for screening large datasets, enabling rapid identification of infected cells in viral assays [22]. For viruses like dengue and Zika, automated image processing offers considerable advantages in speed and accuracy over traditional manual methods [23]. These improvements are particularly critical in drug discovery, where large libraries of compounds must be screened with high precision. Machine learning algorithms, in tandem with image segmentation techniques, have become indispensable for distinguishing infected cells from healthy ones, greatly enhancing the reliability of viral assays [24,25]. However, despite the success of these technologies in other viral research, they remain underutilized in chikungunya virus studies. Traditional methods, such as immunofluorescence assays, still rely on manual counting, which is both time-consuming and prone to error [26,27].

Recent advancements in AI-driven imaging, such as viral plaque counting [28] and ELISPOT assays [29], have demonstrated the potential for automated analysis in virology. While these studies focus on generalized virus detection or plaque formation, the current study specifically targets the Chikungunya virus, addressing unique challenges associated with detecting infected cells and viral particles in high-throughput workflows. By focusing on this specific pathogen, the algorithm offers a tailored approach that builds on and advances the capabilities of existing methodologies.

Automated systems that integrate machine learning into image analysis workflows have the potential to accelerate antiviral compound screening while improving accuracy. Yet, there remains a notable research gap in applying these technologies specifically to chikungunya virus studies [30]. This study addresses this gap by developing an automated image processing methodology designed to detect and classify infected and uninfected cells in high-throughput chikungunya virus assays. By utilizing MvTec Halcon software, an automated algorithm was created to optimize cell counting, segmentation, and feature extraction in viral assays.

Manual screening of viral assays requires significant time and concentration, particularly when processing large numbers of cells and viruses. This workload can cause fatigue, increasing the likelihood of human error and reducing the reliability of results. Furthermore, manual methods are inherently limited in scalability, making them unsuitable for high-throughput workflows. These challenges highlight the critical need for automated solutions to improve accuracy, consistency, and efficiency in virology research, particularly for vector-borne diseases like Chikungunya.

To validate the accuracy of this approach, the algorithm's performance was rigorously compared against manual analyses conducted by three virology experts. Following validation, the algorithm was applied to screen antiviral compounds in chikungunya virus experiments, demonstrating its potential to transform drug discovery workflows. This research highlights the importance of integrating advanced image processing technologies into biomedical applications, particularly in addressing emerging infectious diseases. By improving the speed and accuracy of antiviral screening, this study represents a significant advancement in chikungunya virus research and emphasizes the critical role of technological innovation in modern virology.

2. Materials and Methods

This research focused on developing an automated cell counting program capable of distinguishing between two cell types: normal (uninfected) cells, which appear round and blue, and infected cells, which are identifiable by their blue color with yellow inclusions. Due to the differing characteristics of these cell types, separate counting methods were implemented for each. Images of the cells were captured using the Immunospot CTL machine (Cellular Technology Limited, Shaker Heights, OH, USA) and subsequently analyzed with MvTec Halcon software. The software processed the images, detecting and classifying cells based on their color and morphological features. The resulting data were further analyzed to quantify the differences between the infected and uninfected cells.

2.1. Image Processing Software for Cell and Virus Counting

MvTec Halcon is a comprehensive set of pre-built machine vision algorithms capable of analyzing various types of data, including image processing, deep learning, and machine learning. It was developed by MVtec, a company based in Germany, and is widely applicable for the development of machine vision software. Halcon helps to reduce production costs and development time, making it convenient for rapid software development. For image analysis, Halcon is known for its speed, completeness, accuracy, and robustness [31]. As shown in Figure 1, an example of the MvTec Halcon program performs the detection.

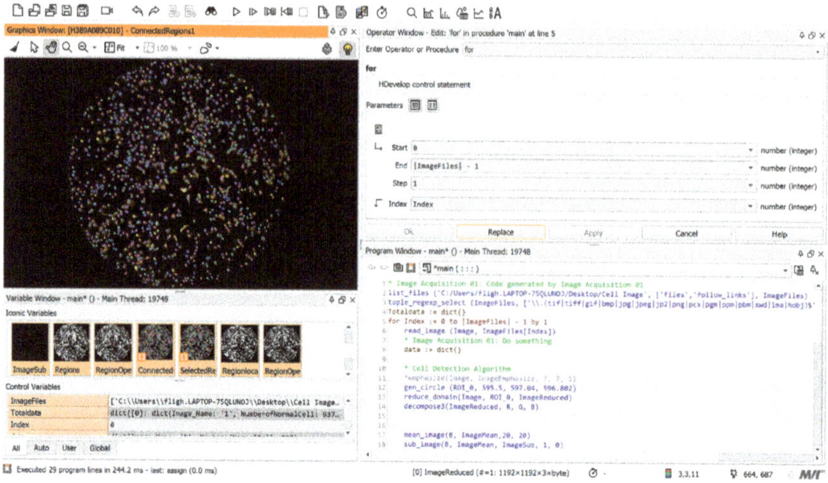

Figure 1. Screenshot of MvTec Halcon software showing the cell detection algorithm, with segmented cell regions and program code for image acquisition and analysis.

2.2. Cell Culture

The cell culture and viral infection experiments were conducted at the Medical Virology Research Center of Chulalongkorn University, Thailand. Initially, cells were cultured in sterile flasks using M199 medium, which provides essential nutrients for cell growth and maintenance [32]. The cells were incubated under controlled conditions at 37 °C in a humidified environment with 5% CO_2 for 24 to 30 h, allowing them to adhere to the flask's surface and form a stable monolayer. Ensuring proper adhesion at this stage is critical for uniform cell distribution in downstream applications, such as infection assays.

Once the cells reached the appropriate confluence, they were prepared for transfer to a 96-well plate for further experimental procedures. The detachment of cells from the flask surface was achieved using 0.05% trypsin, a proteolytic enzyme that cleaves cell-surface proteins and facilitates cell release while maintaining cell viability. Prior to trypsin application, the medium containing fetal bovine serum (FBS), which inhibits trypsin activity, was removed, and the cells were rinsed with sterile phosphate-buffered saline (PBS) to enhance the detachment process. The flask was then incubated with the trypsin solution at 37 °C and 5% CO_2 for a few minutes, until cell rounding, and detachment was visually confirmed under a microscope.

To stop the enzymatic action of trypsin and prevent excessive cell damage, fresh M199 medium supplemented with 10% FBS was added to the flask. The FBS contains protease inhibitors that neutralize trypsin, allowing the cells to be resuspended in a nutrient-rich medium. Once resuspended, the cells were gently agitated to ensure an even distribution.

Cell concentration was measured using a hemocytometer, a tool for counting both viable and non-viable cells. A trypan blue viability assay was employed, where the dye selectively penetrates dead cells, allowing for easy distinction between live (unstained) and dead (blue-stained) cells. The goal was to achieve a target concentration of approximately 10,000 cells per well to ensure consistency across all experimental wells.

2.3. Viral Infection

After the cells were seeded into the 96-well plate, the experimental infection process began. Each well was treated with 100 μL of the virus solution, followed by the addition of 1 μL of a specific viral inhibitor to assess its potential effects on viral replication. The plates were incubated under conditions optimal for viral entry and replication, with periodic gentle shaking to ensure the even distribution of the virus and inhibitor throughout the wells.

After an appropriate incubation period, which allowed for viral attachment and entry into the cells, the excess viral solution was carefully removed to avoid over-infection. Fresh maintenance media, supplemented with an additional 2 μL of the inhibitor, was then added to each well to support ongoing cell viability and viral replication for time-course studies. The plates were incubated for the required duration, after which imaging techniques were used to visualize and quantify the effects of both the viral infection and the inhibitor treatment on the cultured cells.

2.4. Image System and Setup

The imaging process was conducted using the ImmunoSpot S6 Ultra system from Cellular Technology Limited (CTL), Shaker Heights, OH, USA, a platform commonly used in high-throughput assays. This system is equipped with a Digital Area Scan camera capable of capturing images with a resolution of up to 10 million pixels, providing the detailed visual data necessary for accurate analysis. To ensure consistent illumination across all wells of the 96-well plate, the system employed a ring of 96 high-intensity LED lights. This uniform lighting minimized shadows and ensured clear visibility of the cells, which was critical for reliable data capture [33].

For fluorescence detection, the system was outfitted with specialized optical filters tailored to the assay's requirements. A 440 nm filter was used to detect the blue signal, representing uninfected cells, while a 600 nm filter captured the yellow signal emitted by infected cells. These wavelength-specific filters allowed for precise separation of the blue and yellow signals, reducing the risk of signal overlap. This ensured accurate differentiation between the two cell types, allowing for reliable identification and quantification during analysis. The combination of these optical filters with the high-resolution imaging capabilities provided a solid foundation for distinguishing between normal and infected cells, supporting further analysis [33].

2.5. Cell Image Acquisition

The ImmunoSpot device was configured to capture images at a 2.0508× zoom level, determined through experimentation as the most effective setting for this study. This adjustment was necessary because, at the original un-zoomed resolution, the cells appeared too small for accurate analysis, making it difficult to distinguish them from the background or potential image noise. The selected zoom level provided enhanced clarity and resolution, minimizing blurring and color diffusion, which significantly improved the accuracy of subsequent analyses. As shown in Figure 2, images were captured from a 96-well plate, with (a) presenting the entire well, (b) showing a zoomed-in portion of the well, and (c) highlighting individual cells for detailed visualization.

At this optimized zoom level, the cells appeared round and blue, as detected by the 440 nm filter. Although slight variations in cell size and shape were observed, these differences were minimal, allowing for consistent identification across the images. This consistency was crucial for differentiating actual cells from potential image artifacts or noise, ensuring accurate cell counting. Due to the improved detail provided by the zoomed setting, all subsequent analyses were performed using these zoomed images rather than the standard, lower-magnification images, to maintain accuracy and reliability. In the cell counting program, every visible cell within the field was counted, and the total cell count was systematically recorded for further analysis.

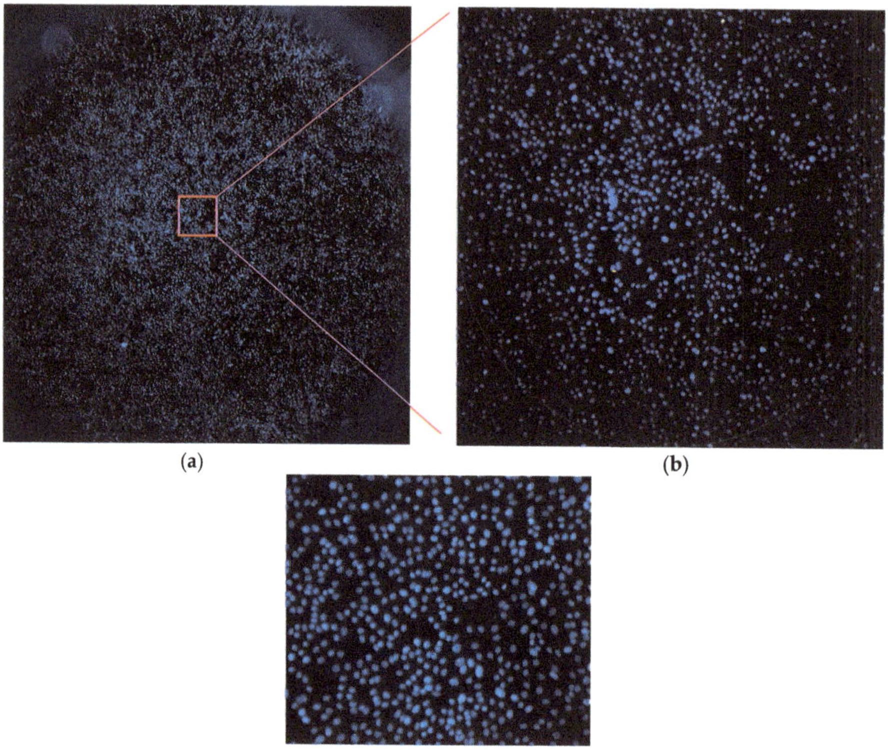

(a) (b) (c)

Figure 2. An image captured from a 96-well plate. (**a**) shows the entire well, providing a view of the overall cell distribution. (**b**) is a zoomed-in portion of the well, offering a closer look at the cellular arrangement. (**c**) presents a cropped section from the zoomed image, highlighting the detailed structure of individual cells for enhanced visualization.

2.6. Virus Image Acquisition

Infected cells were distinctly identified by their blue cell bodies surrounded by yellow inclusions or borders, as shown in the attached figure. This characteristic coloration, resulting from the specific imaging settings and filters applied, created a clear contrast between infected and uninfected cells. The blue central region represented the uninfected cell body, while the surrounding yellow areas indicated viral infection or activity. Although the yellow inclusions varied slightly in size and shape, they remained distinct enough to differentiate infected cells from background noise or image artifacts.

The optimized imaging settings allowed for clear visualization of both the cell shapes and the yellow inclusions, facilitating accurate identification and counting of infected cells. This distinct separation of the blue and yellow areas was crucial in ensuring that only infected cells were counted during analysis. The ability to clearly see these details in the images greatly improved the reliability and precision of the cell-counting process for viral infection.

3. Experiment

Initially, images captured by the ImmunoSpot machine were set to cover the entire well at the default zoom level specified by the manufacturer. However, when these un-zoomed images were processed using the Halcon program, it became evident that the cells appeared too small, resulting in unclear visibility and noticeable color blurring. This greatly reduced the effectiveness of image analysis and made it difficult to accurately differentiate between cells and background noise. To address this issue, the ImmunoSpot machine's settings were adjusted to capture images at a zoom level of 2.0508× as shown in Figure 3, which provided clearer and more distinct images suitable for accurate cell analysis.

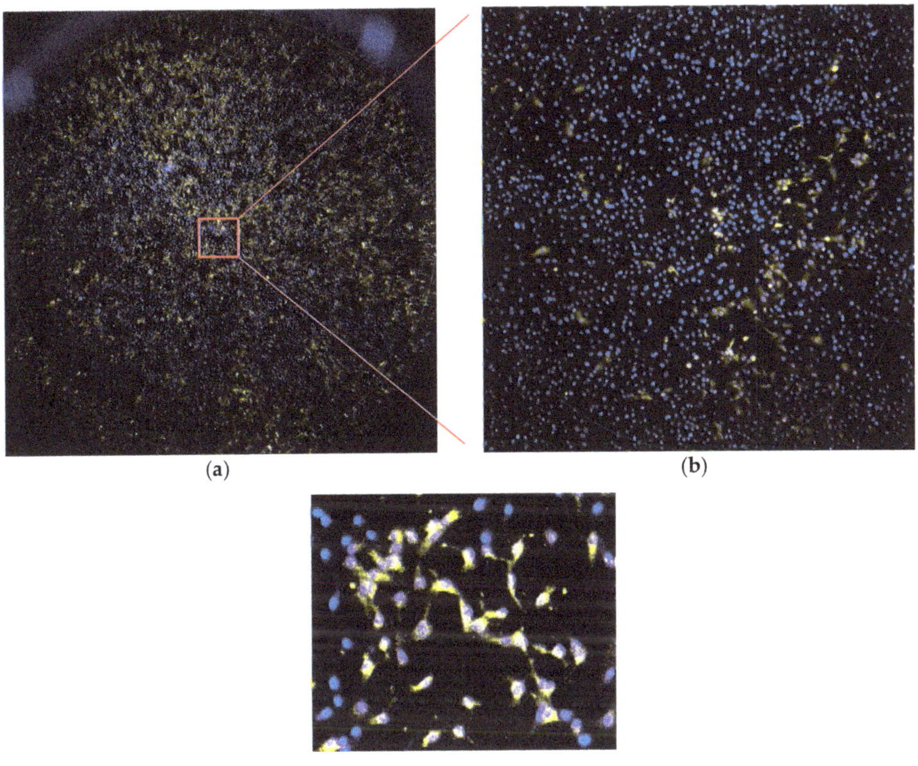

Figure 3. An image captured from a 96-well plate. (**a**) shows the entire well, providing a view of the overall infected cell distribution. (**b**) is a zoomed-in portion of the well, offering a closer look at the virus arrangement. (**c**) presents a cropped section from the zoomed image, highlighting the detailed structure of individual virus for enhanced visualization.

3.1. Cell Detection Algorithm

The cell detection algorithm is designed to process and analyze images for identifying and counting cells, and its implementation is outlined both through a flowchart and pseudocode. While both representations describe the same core process, the flowchart provides a high-level visual overview, and the pseudocode offers a detailed step-by-step breakdown of the algorithm's operations.

The flowchart shown in Figure 4 begins with image acquisition, where relevant images are listed, filtered, and loaded into the system, ensuring that only necessary data are processed. The algorithm then proceeds to the pre-processing phase, where the focus is on enhancing image quality and isolating regions of interest (ROI). Here, the image is decomposed into RGB channels, with the B channel being selected to capture the color range most representative of the cells. This step is followed by applying a mean filter to reduce noise and subtracting the mean to enhance contrast and highlight significant features for further analysis.

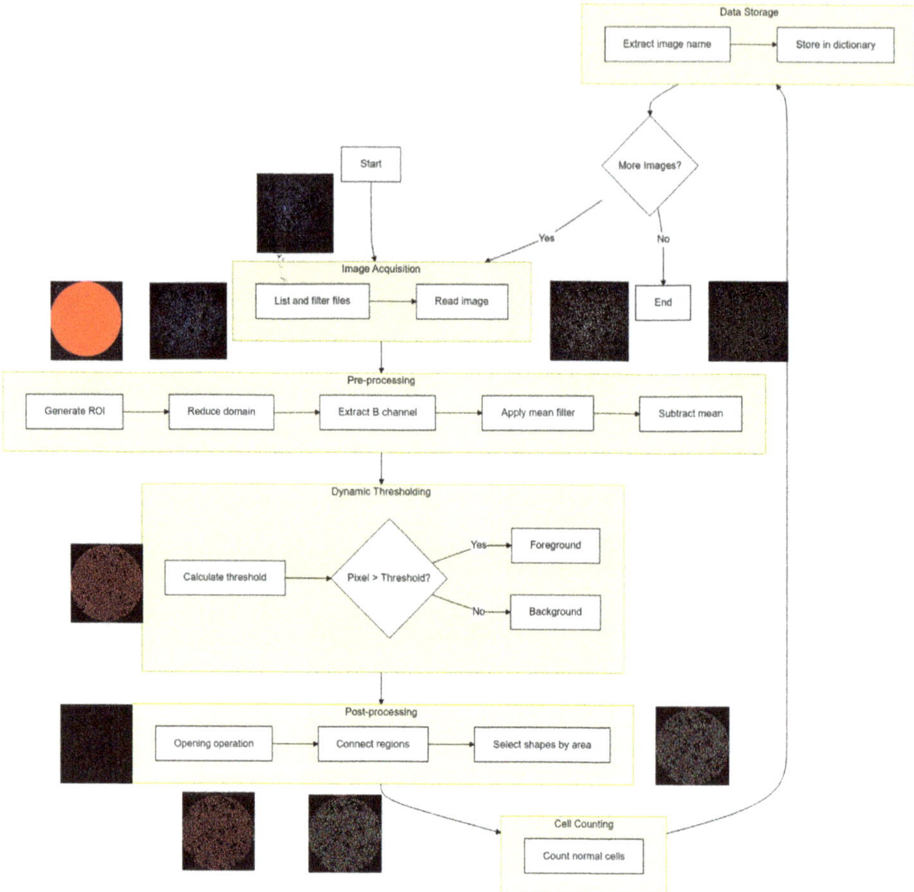

Figure 4. Flowchart illustrating the steps of the cell detection algorithm.

Next is the Dynamic Thresholding stage, which plays a critical role in distinguishing between foreground (potential cells) and background pixels. A dynamic threshold is calculated based on the local image characteristics, enabling the algorithm to classify pixels as either part of the cell (foreground) or background [34].

The post-processing phase involves morphological operations, such as opening, which removes small noise while preserving larger structures. Regions are connected to form coherent cell shapes, and shape selection is applied based on area, isolating likely cells for further analysis. In the final steps, the algorithm enters the cell counting phase, quantifying cells based on predefined criteria, and then moves into data storage, where image names and cell counts are systematically stored for easy retrieval.

The pseudocode in Algorithm 1 for the cell detection algorithm outlines a structured approach to process images and gather relevant data. The algorithm begins by reading and filtering images, enhancing important features through preprocessing techniques to improve accuracy. It then focuses on isolating specific color channels for optimal cell identification and applies noise reduction and thresholding to distinguish cell regions from the background. Morphological operations are used to refine these regions, ensuring that only relevant cells are counted. Finally, the algorithm compiles the results' image names and cell count into a structured JSON file, streamlining data storage and retrieval for further analysis.

Algorithm 1. Cell Detection and Data Collection.

```
Input: directory ← {path to image directory}
Input: supportedExtensions ← {list of supported image file extensions}
Output: jsonFile ← {file containing image names and normal cell counts}
imageFiles ← {d_1, ..., d_n} ← ListFilesInDirectory(directory)
imageFiles ← FilterFiles(imageFiles, supportedExtensions)
totalData ← {} (empty dictionary)
for i = 1 to |imageFiles| do
    image ← ReadImage(imageFiles[i])
    data ← {} (initialize dictionary for each image)
    imageEmphasize ← EmphasizeImage(image, kernelSize = 7 × 7, factor = 1)
    (R, G, B) ← DecomposeToRGB(image)
    imageMean ← CalculateMeanImage(B, kernelSize = 30 × 30)
    imageSub ← SubtractImages(B, imageMean)
    regions ← ThresholdImage(imageSub, thresholdValues = [40, 199])
    regionOpening ← PerformOpeningCircle(regions, radius = 2)
    connectedRegions ← ConnectRegions(regionOpening)
    selectedRegions ← SelectShapesByArea(connectedRegions,areaRange = [30, 500])
    normalCellCount ← CountObjects(selectedRegions)
    imageName ← ExtractImageName(imageFiles[i])
    data["Image_Name"] ← imageName
    data["NumberofNormalCell"] ← normalCellCount
    totalData[i] ← data
end for
WriteToJSON(totalData, jsonFile)
```

3.2. Virus Detection Algorithm

The virus detection flowchart in Figure 5 proceeds with HSV Conversion and Thresholding, where the RGB image is transformed into the HSV color space. This conversion simplifies the detection of color-based regions, particularly focusing on the yellow regions that indicate infected areas. The pre-processing steps, similar to those used in the cell counting algorithm, involve listing and filtering image files, generating the region of interest (ROI), and decomposing the image into RGB channels. To isolate the infected regions, thresholds are applied to both the H (Hue) and V (Value) channels, specifically targeting yellow hues associated with infection. The resulting regions are then refined by intersecting the thresholded areas, excluding non-relevant regions and noise to ensure only potential infected areas remain.

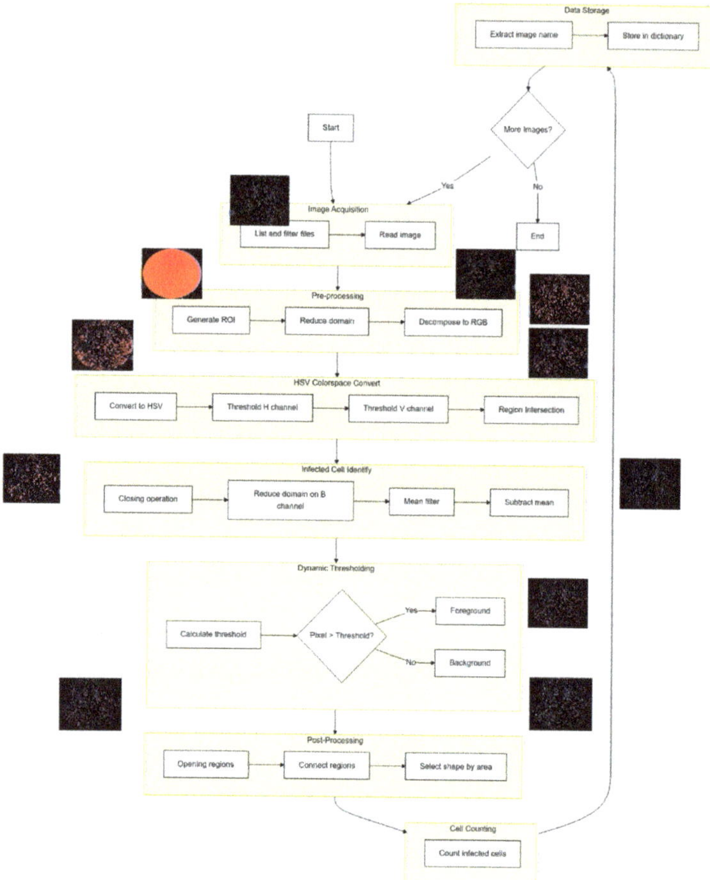

Figure 5. Flowchart illustrating the steps of the Virus detection algorithm.

In the infected cell identification phase, additional operations are applied to enhance the detected regions. A closing operation is used to smooth the boundaries of these regions and eliminate small gaps or holes. The domain is further reduced on the B (Blue) channel to focus the analysis on the yellow regions, which represent infected cells. A mean filter is applied to the B channel, followed by subtracting the mean to enhance contrast, making it easier to distinguish infected areas from background noise.

The Dynamic Thresholding step is critical in classifying pixels based on intensity. A calculated threshold differentiates between the foreground (infected areas) and the background (non-infected areas). Pixels with intensity above the threshold are classified as part of the foreground, signaling infection, while those below are classified as background, refining the detection process.

In the post-processing stage, the algorithm cleans up detected regions using an opening operation to remove small noise or artifacts that might have been incorrectly identified as infected cells. The regions are then connected to form larger, continuous areas, representing infected cells. Based on their size, regions are filtered to exclude those that do not meet the criteria for infected cells.

In the final phase, cell counting, the algorithm counts the connected regions identified as infected cells and records these counts along with the corresponding image name. During the data storage phase, the image names and infected cell counts are stored in a dictionary for future analysis. A decision point ensures efficient batch processing by checking for any additional images to process.

The pseudocode of the virus detection algorithm in Algorithm 2 begins by reading and filtering image files from a specified directory. The RGB image is converted into the HSV color space, where thresholding is applied to both the Hue and Value channels to isolate the yellow regions representing viral infection. After intersecting these thresholded regions to remove noise, morphological operations such as closing and domain reduction are performed to refine the infected areas. The algorithm enhances contrast using mean subtraction, followed by further thresholding and morphological operations to accurately isolate infected regions. Finally, the connected regions are counted as infected cells, and the results—image names and virus-infected cell counts—are stored in a JSON file for easy access.

Algorithm 2. Virus Detection and Data Collection.

```
Input: directory ← {path to image directory}
Input: supportedExtensions ← {list of supported image file extensions}
Output: jsonFile ← {file containing image names and normal cell counts}
imageFiles ← {d1, ..., dn} ← ListFilesInDirectory(directory)
imageFiles ← FilterFiles(imageFiles, supportedExtensions)
totalData ← {} (empty dictionary)
for i = 1 to |imageFiles| do
    image ← ReadImage(imageFiles[i])
    data ← {} (initialize dictionary for each image)
    (R, G, B) ← DecomposeToRGB(image)
    (H, S, V) ← TransformRGBToHSV(R, G, B)
    regions1 ← ThresholdImage(V, thresholdValuesV = [100, 255])
    regions2 ← ThresholdImage(S, thresholdValuesS = [0, 160])
    regionIntersection ← Intersection(regions1, regions2)
    regionClosing ← PerformClosingCircle(regionIntersection, radius = 9)
    imageReduced ← ReduceDomain(B, regionClosing)
    imageMean ← CalculateMeanImage(imageReduced, kernelSize = 30 × 30)
    imageSub ← SubtractImages(imageReduced, imageMean)
    regions3 ← ThresholdImage(imageSub, thresholdValuesSub = [30, 191])
    regionsOpened ← PerformOpeningCircle(regions3, radius = 3)
    connectedRegions ← ConnectRegions(regionsOpened)
    selectedRegions ← SelectShapesByArea(connectedRegions, areaRange = [13.53,
    1000])
    virusCellCount ← CountObjects(selectedRegions)
    imageName ← ExtractImageName(imageFiles[i])
    data["Image_Name"] ← imageName
    data["NumberofInfectedCell"] ← virusCellCount
    totalData[i] ← data
end for
WriteToJSON(totalData, jsonFile)
```

4. Results

4.1. Algorithm Validation

To assess the performance of the developed cell and virus detection algorithms, 150 images containing both cells and viruses were selected for comparison against manual counts conducted by three experts. Each expert manually counted the cells and viruses within the images, providing a benchmark for evaluating the algorithm's ability to distinguish and classify the two types separately. The comparison between the manual counts and the algorithm-generated results was visualized through various statistical methods. Linear regression was employed to analyze the relationship between the manual and algorithmic counts, while a Bland–Altman plot provided insight into any potential biases or discrepancies between the two methods. Additionally, a box plot was used to illustrate the distribution and variance in the count data, offering a comprehensive view of the algorithm's performance in comparison to expert assessment. These visualizations help demonstrate the effectiveness of the algorithm in detecting cells and viruses.

The manual counting process shown in Figure 6a was conducted by three independent experts who analyzed the same set of images using pre-defined criteria to distinguish between infected and uninfected cells. Infected cells were identified by their blue cell bodies surrounded by distinct yellow inclusions, while uninfected cells exhibited a uniform blue color. To address inter-observer variability, the mean or median of the counts from the three experts was calculated and used as the ground truth for algorithm evaluation, ensuring consistency and minimizing discrepancies.

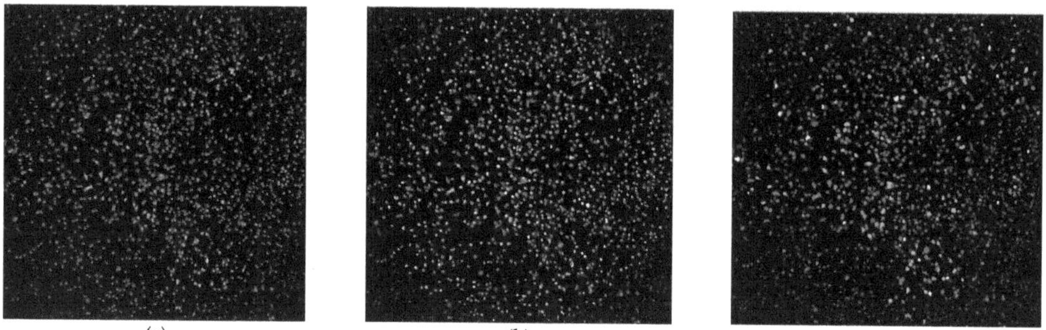

(a) (b) (c)

Figure 6. (**a**) Manual counting by expert, (**b**) algorithm cell counting, (**c**) algorithm virus counting.

4.1.1. Linear Regression

The linear regression graph in Figure 7a illustrates the comparison between the cell counts from 150 images manually counted by experts (x-axis) and the counts generated by the cell counting algorithm (y-axis). The data points, marked as purple crosses, represent individual image counts, ranging from 400 to 1900 cells per image. The blue line with a slope of 1 represents the reference line, which signifies perfect agreement between the expert and algorithm counts. The red dashed line is the linear fit line that highlights the trend of the algorithm's performance. Based on the regression analysis, the linear equation derived is $y = 0.96x$, indicating that the algorithm slightly underestimates the cell count in comparison to the expert counts. The coefficient of determination R^2 is calculated to be 0.9618, reflecting a strong correlation between the algorithm's output and the expert counts, suggesting that the algorithm performs consistently across different cell counts [35].

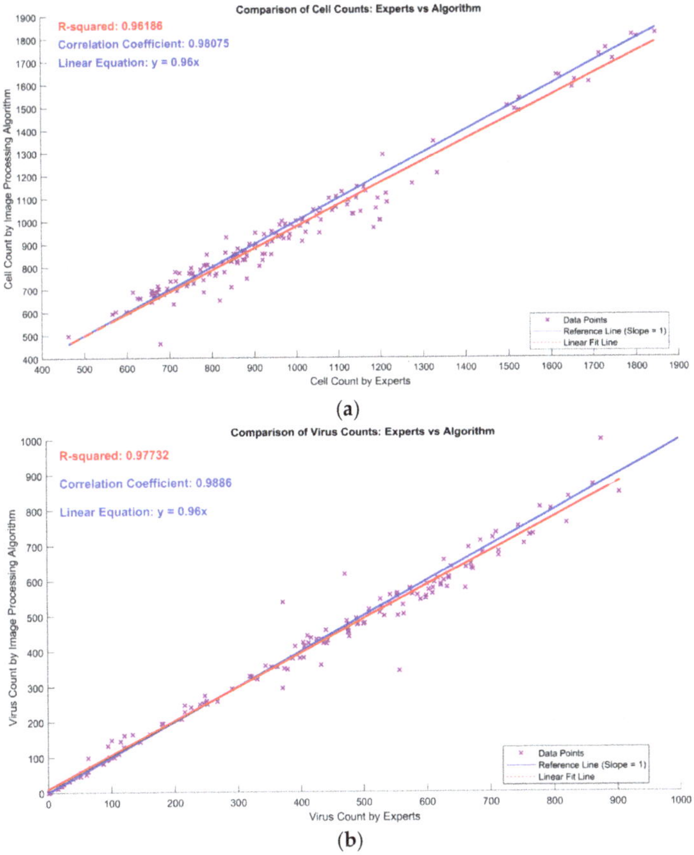

Figure 7. Linear regression graphs show the results of the linearity, correlation coefficient, and R-squared values. (**a**) Linear regression graph comparing the cell counting algorithm with expert manual counts, and (**b**) linear regression graph comparing the virus counting algorithm with expert manual counts.

Similarly, Figure 7b presents the virus detection algorithm, which shows a comparable trend of strong correlation with expert counts. The linear regression analysis produces a linear equation of $y = 0.96x$, indicating a slight underestimation of virus counts by the algorithm. Nevertheless, the higher coefficient of determination, $R^2 = 0.9773$, indicates an even stronger correlation between the algorithm's output and expert counts, surpassing the performance of the cell counting algorithm.

Moreover, to assess the correlation between the expert and machine counting, Pearson's correlation coefficient method was employed to measure the strength of the linear relationship between the two variables [36]. Pearson's coefficient of the cell counting algorithm was found to be 0.9807, indicating a very strong positive correlation between the manual counts by the experts and the machine's output, compared to similar studies, such as one using an algorithm for viral plaque assays (Pearson coefficient of 0.9221) [27]; this study demonstrates superior performance with coefficients of 0.9807 and 0.9886 for cell and virus detection, respectively. These results highlight the improved accuracy and robustness of the proposed approach, supporting its potential for broader application in virology research. To further confirm the significance of this correlation, a p-value was calculated. In this case, the p-value was less than 0.05, suggesting that the correlation between the expert and machine counts is statistically significant [37], meaning the observed relationship is unlikely to be due to random chance. This reinforces the reliability of the algorithm in replicating expert-level performance. Similarly, the virus detection algorithm exhibited an even stronger correlation, with a Pearson's coefficient of 0.9886, further underscoring the accuracy and reliability of the algorithm in detecting viral counts.

4.1.2. Bland–Altman Plot

A Bland–Altman plot is a statistical method used to evaluate the agreement between two measurement techniques [38]. In this case, the Bland–Altman plot was applied to compare the expert manual counts and the cell counting algorithm's performance, as shown in Figure 8a. The plot visualizes the differences between the two measurements (expert and algorithm) against their averages. The mean bias is −21.51, indicating that the algorithm slightly underestimates cell counts compared to the expert counts. The limits of agreement, which range from −133.28 to 90.26, represent the boundaries within which 95% of the differences are expected to fall. Most of the data points lie within these limits, suggesting that the algorithm's discrepancies are within acceptable boundaries (±2 standard deviations). Therefore, the Bland–Altman analysis confirms that the algorithm performs with reasonable accuracy and consistency.

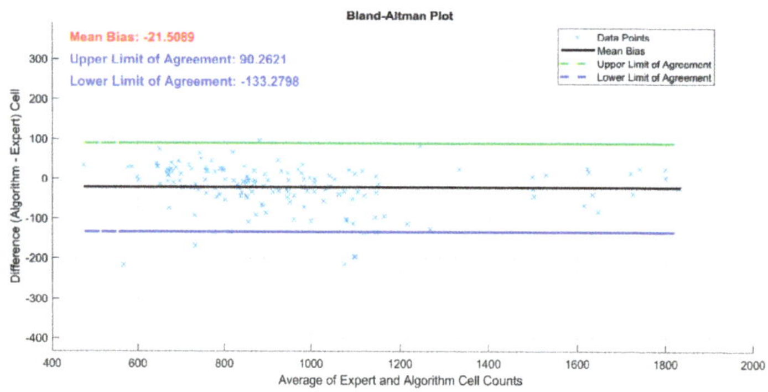

(a)

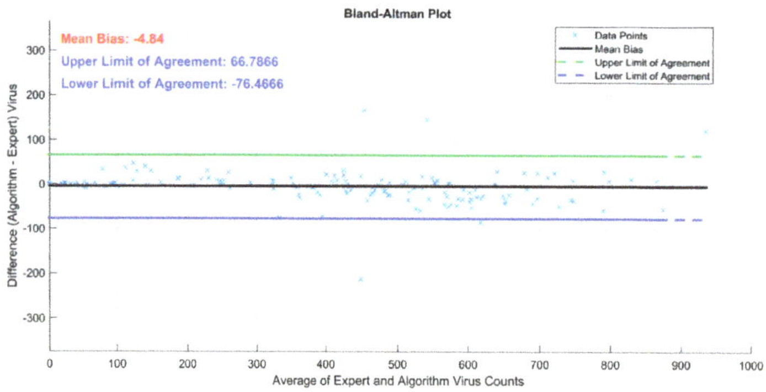

(b)

Figure 8. (**a**) Bland–Altman plot for the cell counting algorithm, and (**b**) Bland–Altman plot for the virus counting algorithm, illustrating the agreement between the algorithm and expert counts.

Similarly, the Bland–Altman plot for the virus detection algorithm in Figure 8b shows a mean bias of −4.84, indicating a slight underestimation of virus counts. The limits of agreement for this algorithm are narrower, ranging from −76.47 to 66.79, demonstrating less variability compared to the cell counting algorithm. As with the cell counting algorithm, most of the data points fall within these limits, reinforcing the precision and reliability of the virus detection algorithm in replicating expert-level performance. Together, these Bland–Altman analyses confirm that both algorithms perform with high accuracy and consistency across a range of cell and virus counts.

4.1.3. Box Plot

The box plot for the cell counting algorithm, shown in Figure 9a, provides a visual summary of the distribution of cell counts as measured by three experts, with the algorithm's performance overlaid to assess its alignment with expert counts. The box plot is constructed using key statistical measures, including the 1st quartile (25th percentile) and 3rd quartile (75th percentile), which represent the middle 50% of the expert data. The box itself covers this interquartile range (IQR), while the whiskers extend to values within two times the IQR, capturing most of the data's spread. Any points outside this range are considered outliers [39].

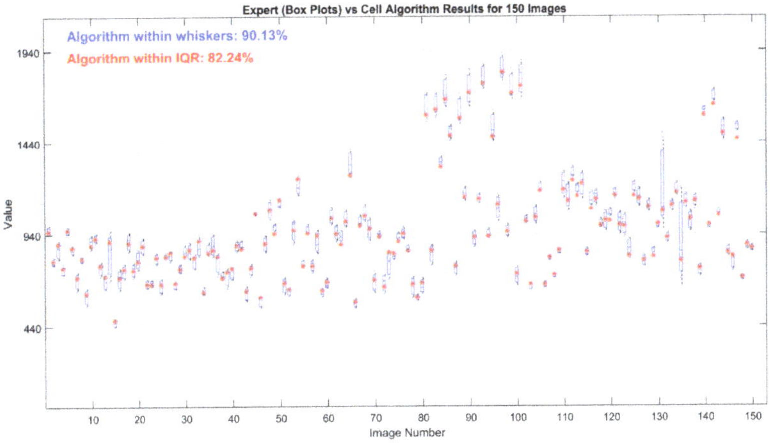

(a)

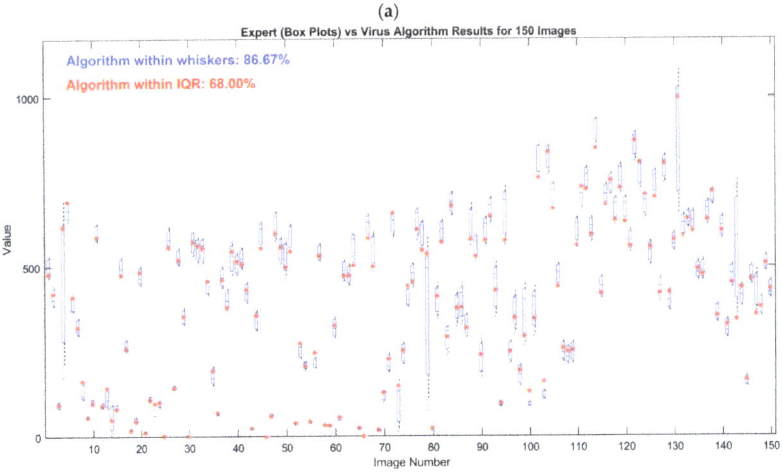

(b)

Figure 9. Box plots comparing the algorithm performance to expert counts. (**a**) Box plot for the cell counting algorithm, and (**b**) box plot for the virus counting algorithm, assessing whether the algorithms fall within the range of expert counts.

To evaluate how well the algorithm performs in comparison to expert counts, the percentage of algorithm-generated cell counts that fall within these ranges was calculated. The results indicate that 90.13% of the algorithm's data fall within the whiskers, demonstrating that the algorithm's output is generally in line with expert assessments, with only a small proportion of outliers. Additionally, 82.24% of the algorithm's data lie within the IQR, which highlights that most of the algorithm's results are consistent with the central tendency of the expert counts. This suggests that the algorithm performs with a high degree of accuracy and consistency, as its results largely overlap with the expert-derived quartiles.

The box plot for the virus detection algorithm, shown in Figure 9b, highlights the distribution of virus counts based on expert assessments, with a focus on evaluating how the algorithm's results align with the experts' counts. In this analysis, 86.67% of the algorithm's data fall within the whiskers, indicating a high degree of consistency with the experts' results. Additionally, 68.0% of the algorithm's data are within the interquartile range (IQR), suggesting a slightly wider spread compared to the cell counting algorithm. Despite the broader range within the IQR, the algorithm's performance remains robust, with most data points aligning closely with expert evaluation.

5. Discussion

After validating the performance of the cell and virus detection algorithms, these tools were applied in a laboratory setting to evaluate how different inhibitors affect the Chikungunya virus. In the experimental setup, as shown in the image in Figure 10, several inhibitors were tested across multiple wells, along with key control groups: cell + viruses (positive control), cell + DMSO, and cells (negative control).

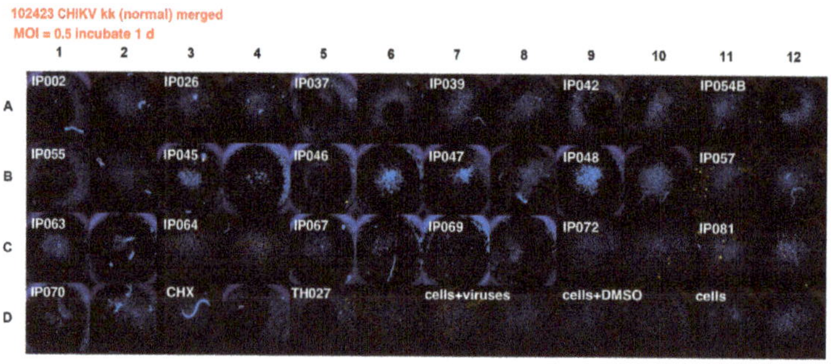

Figure 10. Merged fluorescence images of cells infected with the chikungunya virus (CHIKV) at an MOI of 0.5, incubated for 1 day. Rows (A–D) and columns (1–12) represent different sample wells, with specific conditions or treatments labeled above the wells.

For each well, the cell detection algorithm was used to count the number of cells, and the virus detection algorithm quantified the number of viral particles. The positive control, cell + viruses, served as a reference for maximum viral presence, while the negative control, cells, indicated the baseline where no virus was present, confirming normal cell growth. The cell + DMSO wells were included to account for any potential effects of the solvent (DMSO) used to dissolve the inhibitors.

Each inhibitor was tested in duplicate wells to ensure accurate measurements, and the cell and virus counts from each well were averaged to improve reliability. The averaged data were then used to calculate the percentage of cell viability, which reflects how well the cells survive in the presence of the inhibitor. The percentage of viral inhibition measures the inhibitor's effectiveness in reducing viral presence compared to the positive control.

The results from these calculations are plotted to show the percentage of viral inhibition and cell viability for each inhibitor. The controls play an essential role in interpreting these results. The cell + viruses control represents the maximum viral activity, serving as a baseline for comparing inhibitor effectiveness. The cell + DMSO control ensures that any reduction in viral counts is due to the inhibitor and not the solvent, while the cell control shows the normal cell count in the absence of the virus, confirming the health of the cell culture. This approach enables the identification of inhibitors that effectively reduce viral counts without significantly impacting cell viability, which is crucial for selecting candidates for further experimentation.

5.1. *Compared to Negative Control*

For comparison with the negative control, which contains no virus, the data from the normal cell count are used as a baseline. If the percentage of normal cells in the experimental well exceeds 100%, it suggests that the experimental conditions may promote cell growth or enhance survival compared to the negative control. Conversely, a percentage below 100% indicates fewer normal cells relative to the negative control, suggesting that the experimental conditions may inhibit cell growth or lead to cell loss.

5.2. *Compared to Positive Control*

For comparison with the positive control, data from the infected cell count are used, as the positive control contains the highest viral load. A percentage greater than 100% indicates more infected cells in the experimental well compared to the positive control, suggesting that the inhibitor may be ineffective or could even exacerbate the infection. Conversely, a percentage below 100% indicates fewer infected cells, suggesting that the inhibitor is effective in reducing viral infection. The lower the percentage, the more effective the inhibitor is at reducing infection.

The scatter plot in Figure 11 illustrates the % viability and % remaining virus for each inhibitor. The x-axis represents the various inhibitor names, while the y-axis shows the percentage values. Blue dots represent the % viability, indicating how many cells survived in the presence of the inhibitor. Red dots represent the % remaining virus, which shows the viral presence after applying the inhibitor.

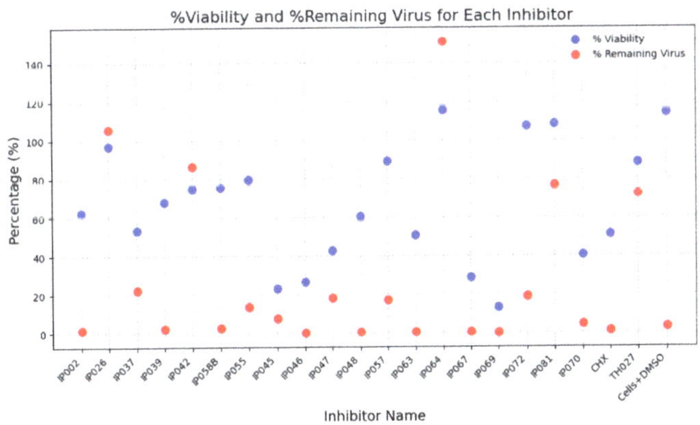

Figure 11. Scatter plot illustrating the relationship between % cell viability and % remaining virus for each inhibitor substance, showing the impact of various inhibitors on both cell survival and virus presence.

For most inhibitors, a balance between viability and remaining virus is observed. Higher blue dots paired with lower red dots indicate that the inhibitor is effective at reducing viral infection while maintaining cell survival. For instance, inhibitors like IP072 and IP057 show high cell viability (blue) with low remaining virus (red), making them potentially effective candidates. On the other hand, inhibitors like IP0 show relatively low cell viability, suggesting potential cytotoxic effects or less favorable conditions for cell survival.

In some cases, red dots are higher than blue dots, such as IP042, suggesting that the inhibitor may not be very effective in reducing viral presence. Similarly, substances like cells + DMSO serve as the control, showing expected high cell viability with minimal viral presence, helping to validate the performance of the other inhibitors.

5.3. Cost and Feasibility Analysis

The cost of implementing the proposed automated image processing system primarily involves software licensing for MVTec Halcon. The standard license for MVTec Halcon is estimated at $3000. Unlike manual evaluation, which requires ongoing labor costs, the automated system minimizes recurring expenses after the initial investment.

In terms of time efficiency, the manual counting method typically takes around 5 min per sample, equating to over 83 h to process 1000 samples. In comparison, the automated algorithm completes the same task in less than 1 s per sample, requiring only 17 min for 1000 samples. This represents a reduction of over 99% in processing time, significantly increasing throughput for high-volume applications.

When evaluating long-term costs, manual evaluation can result in personnel expenses exceeding $2000 for 1000 samples at a rate of $20/hour. Over time, the automated system becomes more cost-effective due to its negligible processing time and labor independence.

5.4. Broader Applications and Future Perspectives

The proposed image processing algorithm, while tailored for detecting chikungunya virus-infected cells, can be adapted to analyze samples for other viral infections with minimal modifications. By adjusting the imaging parameters, such as fluorescence detection wavelengths and morphological feature thresholds, the algorithm could be applied to infections like dengue, Zika, or influenza, where distinct cellular changes or specific markers are present. This flexibility is inherent in the design of the image segmentation and feature extraction processes, which rely on adaptable parameters.

The system also holds potential for broader drug discovery applications. Its capability to analyze cellular morphology and quantify specific features can facilitate the screening of drug candidates targeting bacterial or parasitic infections. Furthermore, toxicological studies, which require accurate assessment of cellular damage or viability, could benefit from this high-throughput, accurate, and reproducible method.

Future enhancements could involve expanding the imaging setup to accommodate multiplexed staining protocols, enabling the simultaneous detection of multiple cellular markers. These improvements would further broaden the algorithm's utility across a wider range of biomedical research fields.

6. Conclusions

This study presents the development and validation of an automated image processing algorithm for high-throughput screening of potential anti-chikungunya virus compounds. The algorithm, created using MvTec Halcon software, demonstrated high accuracy in detecting and classifying infected and uninfected cells in viral assays, with strong agreement compared to manual counts conducted by three virology experts. Statistical validation through Pearson correlation, linear regression, Bland–Altman analyses, and box plots confirmed the algorithm's reliability.

In addition to validation, the algorithm was applied to screen various antiviral compounds, showcasing its potential to significantly enhance the speed and accuracy of drug discovery workflows. By automating labor-intensive and error-prone processes, this approach offers a more efficient means of screening antiviral compounds, which is crucial in the context of increasing chikungunya virus infections. This methodology holds promise for broader applications in virological research, particularly in studying other vector-borne diseases, and emphasizes the importance of integrating image processing technologies in modern biomedical research.

Future work could focus on using deep learning models to train and recognize the specific shapes and characteristics of cells, viruses, and noise commonly found in well plates. This approach could improve segmentation and classification accuracy, especially in challenging cases. Additionally, integrating these advancements with optimized imaging workflows and adapting the system for low-resource environments could further expand its accessibility and utility in various research and clinical settings.

Author Contributions: Conceptualization, S.B. and G.P.; Data curation, P.W., S.B., P.S. and D.P.; Formal analysis, P.W., S.B. and G.P.; Funding acquisition, G.P.; Methodology, P.W. and S.B.; Project administration, P.W. and G.P.; Resources, S.B. and G.P.; Software, P.W. and G.P.; Supervision, S.B. and G.P.; Validation, P.W., P.S. and D.P.; Visualization, P.W., S.B., P.S. and D.P.; Writing—original draft, P.W. and G.P.; Writing—review and editing, P.W., S.B., P.S., D.P. and G.P. All authors have read and agreed to the published version of the manuscript.

Funding: This research project is supported by the Ratchadaphiseksomphot Endowment Fund of Chulalongkorn University, grant number CU_GI_67_004_2100_001.

Institutional Review Board Statement: Not applicable.

Informed Consent Statement: Not applicable.

Data Availability Statement: Any inquiry can be directly sent to the corresponding author.

Conflicts of Interest: The authors declare no conflicts of interest.

References

1. Lumsden, W. An epidemic of virus disease in Southern Province, Tanganyika territory, in 1952–1953 II. General description and epidemiology. *Trans. R. Soc. Trop. Med. Hyg.* **1955**, *49*, 33–57. [CrossRef] [PubMed]
2. Constant, L.E.C.; Rajsfus, B.F.; Carneiro, P.H.; Sisnande, T.; Mohana-Borges, R.; Allonso, D. Overview on chikungunya virus infection: From epidemiology to state-of-the-art experimental models. *Front. Microbiol.* **2021**, *12*, 744164.
3. Njenga, M.K.; Nderitu, L.; Ledermann, J.P.; Ndirangu, A.; Logue, C.H.; Kelly, C.H.L.; Sang, R.; Sergon, K.; Breiman, R.; Powers, A.M. Tracking epidemic chikungunya virus into the Indian Ocean from East Africa. *J. General. Virol.* **2008**, *89*, 2754–2760. [CrossRef]
4. Rezza, G.; Nicoletti, L.; Angelini, R.; Romi, R.; Finarelli, A.; Panning, M.; Cordioli, P.; Fortuna, C.; Boros, S.; Magurano, F.; et al. Infection with chikungunya virus in Italy: An outbreak in a temperate region. *Lancet* **2007**, *370*, 1840–1846. [CrossRef]
5. Yactayo, S.; Staples, J.E.; Millot, V.; Cibrelus, L.; Ramon-Pardo, P. Epidemiology of Chikungunya in the Americas. *J. Infect. Infect. Dis.* **2016**, *214* (Suppl. S5), S441–S445. [CrossRef]
6. Hucke, F.I.L.; Bugert, J.J. Current and promising antivirals against chikungunya virus. *Front. Public Health* **2020**, *8*, 618624. [CrossRef] [PubMed]
7. Phadungsombat, J.; Imad, H.A.; Nakayama, E.E.; Leaungwutiwong, P.; Ramasoota, P.; Nguitragool, W.; Matsee, W.; Piyaphanee, W.; Shioda, T. Spread of a novel Indian Ocean Lineage carrying E1-K211e/E2-V264A of chikungunya virus east/central/South African genotype across the Indian subcontinent, Southeast Asia, and eastern Africa. *Microorganisms* **2022**, *10*, 354. [CrossRef] [PubMed]
8. Deeba, F.; Haider, M.S.H.; Ahmed, A.; Tazeen, A.; Faizan, M.I.; Salam, N.; Hussain, T.; Alamery, S.F.; Parveen, S. Global transmission and evolutionary dynamics of the Chikungunya virus. *Epidemiol. Infect.* **2020**, *148*, e63. [CrossRef] [PubMed]
9. Cunze, S.; Kochmann, J.; Koch, L.K.; Klimpel, S. Niche conservatism of Aedes albopictus and Aedes aegypti-two mosquito species with different invasion histories. *Sci. Rep.* **2018**, *8*, 7733. [CrossRef] [PubMed]

10. Burt, F.J.; Chen, W.; Miner, J.J.; Lenschow, D.J.; Merits, A.; Schnettler, E.; Kohl, A.; Rudd, P.A.; Taylor, A.; Herrero, L.; et al. Chikungunya virus: An update on the biology and pathogenesis of this emerging pathogen. *Lancet Infect. Dis.* **2017**, *17*, e107–e117. [CrossRef] [PubMed]
11. Halstead, S.B. Reappearance of chikungunya, formerly called dengue, in the Americas. *Emerg. Infect. Infect. Dis.* **2015**, *21*, 557–561. [CrossRef] [PubMed]
12. Koeltz, A.; Lastere, S.; Jean-Baptiste, S. Intensive care admissions for severe chikungunya virus infection, French Polynesia. *Emerg. Infect. Dis.* **2018**, *24*, 794–796. [CrossRef]
13. Amaral, J.K.; Bilsborrow, J.B.; Schoen, R.T. Chronic chikungunya arthritis and rheumatoid arthritis: What they have in common. *Am. J. Med.* **2020**, *133*, e91–e97. [CrossRef]
14. Ganesan, V.K.; Duan, B.; Reid, S.P. Chikungunya virus: Pathophysiology, mechanism, and modeling. *Viruses* **2017**, *9*, 368. [CrossRef]
15. Garg, M.; Kumar, S.; Garg, C.; Kaushik, S.; Buttar, H. Demystifying therapeutic potential of medicinal plants against chikungunya virus. *Indian. J. Pharmacol.* **2021**, *53*, 403–411. [CrossRef] [PubMed]
16. Radtke, R.; Jesser, A. Rapid Analysis of Thorax Images for the Detection of Viral Infections. *J. Image Graph.* **2023**, *11*, 115–120. [CrossRef]
17. Abdulahi, A.T.; Ogundokun, R.O.; Adenike, A.R.; Shah, M.A.; Ahmed, Y.K. PulmoNet: A novel deep learning based pulmonary diseases detection model. *BMC Med. Imaging* **2024**, *24*, 51. [CrossRef] [PubMed]
18. Aira, J.; Olivares, T.; Delicado, F.M.; Vezzani, D. MosquIoT: A system based on IoT and machine learning for the monitoring of Aedes aegypti (Diptera: Culicidae). *IEEE Trans. Instrum. Meas.* **2023**, *72*, 2509613. [CrossRef]
19. Shahrtash, S.A.; Ghnim, Z.S.; Ghaheri, M.; Adabi, J.; Hassanzadeh, M.A.; Yasamineh, S.; Afkhami, H.; Kheirkhah, A.H.; Gholizadeh, O.; Moghadam, H.Z. Recent advances in the role of different nanoparticles in the various biosensors for the detection of the chikungunya virus. *Mol. Biotechnol.* **2024**, 1–26. [CrossRef]
20. Sharma, S.; Pardasani, D.; Dash, P.K.; Parida, M.; Dubey, D.K. Development of magnetic bead based sample extraction coupled polymerase spiral reaction for rapid on-site detection of Chikungunya virus. *Sci. Rep.* **2020**, *10*, 11651. [CrossRef]
21. Bharathisindhu, P. Deep Convolutional Neural Network with Image Processing Techniques and Resnet252v2 for Detection of Covid19 from X-Ray Images. *Mapana J. Sci.* **2023**, *22*, 129–145.
22. Cruz, D.J.M.; Bonotto, R.M.; Gomes, R.G.B.; da Silva, C.T.; Taniguchi, J.B.; No, J.H.; Lombardot, B.; Schwartz, O.; Hansen, M.A.E.; Freitas-Junior, L.H. Identification of novel compounds inhibiting chikungunya virus-induced cell death by high throughput screening of a kinase inhibitor library. *PLoS Neglected Trop. Dis.* **2013**, *7*, e2471. [CrossRef]
23. Bolívar-Marin, S.; Bosch, I.; Narváez, C.F. Combination of the Focus-Forming Assay and Digital Automated Imaging Analysis for the Detection of Dengue and Zika Viral Loads in Cultures and Acute Disease. *J. Trop. Med.* **2022**, *2022*, 2177183. [CrossRef]
24. Cardona-Ospina, J.A.; Stittleburg, V.; Millan-Benavidez, N.; Restrepo-Chica, J.; Key, A.; Rojas-Gallardo, D.M.; Piantadosi, A.; Collins, M.H.; Waggoner, J.J. Sensitive and stable molecular detection of dengue, chikungunya, and Zika viruses from dried blood spots. *Am. J. Trop. Med. Hyg.* **2022**, *107*, 296–299. [CrossRef]
25. Gou, T.; Hu, J.; Zhou, S.; Wu, W.; Fang, W.; Sun, J.; Hu, Z.; Shen, H.; Mu, Y. A new method using machine learning for automated image analysis applied to chip-based digital assays. *Analyst* **2019**, *144*, 3274–3281. [CrossRef] [PubMed]
26. Poornima, J.; Krishnaveni, K. Detection of dengue fever with platelets count using image processing techniques. *Indian. J. Sci. Technol.* **2016**, *9*, 1–7. [CrossRef]
27. Phanomchoeng, G.; Kukiattikoon, C.; Plengkham, S.; Boonyasuppayakorn, S.; Salakij, S.; Poomrittigul, S.; Wuttisittikulkij, L. Machine-learning-based automated quantification machine for virus plaque assay counting. *PeerJ Comput. Sci.* **2022**, *8*, e878. [CrossRef] [PubMed]
28. Plengkham, S.; Kukiattikoon, C.; Phanomchoeng, G.; Boonyasuppayalorn, S. Development of an Automated Viral Plaque Assay Program and ELISpot Counting Program on 96-Well Plate Platform. In Proceedings of the 2022 International Conference on Electrical, Computer and Energy Technologies (ICECET), Prague, Czech Republic, 20–22 July 2022; IEEE: Piscataway, NJ, USA, 2022; pp. 1–8.
29. Kukiattikoon, C.; Vongsoasup, N.; Ajavakom, N.; Phanomchoeng, G. Automate platform for capturing and counting ELISpot on 96-Well plate. In Proceedings of the 2021 International Conference on Engineering and Emerging Technologies (ICEET), Istanbul, Turkey, 27–28 October 2021; IEEE: Piscataway, NJ, USA, 2021; pp. 1–5.
30. Coimbra, L.D.; Borin, A.; Fontoura, M.; Gravina, H.D.; Nagai, A.; Shimizu, J.F.; Bispo-dos-Santos, K.; Granja, F.; Oliveira, P.S.; Franchini, K.G.; et al. Identification of compounds with antiviral activity against SARS-CoV-2 in the MMV pathogen box using a phenotypic high-throughput screening assay. *Front. Virol.* **2022**, *2*, 854363. [CrossRef]
31. Huang, B.; Liu, J.; Chen, M.; Fan, Q. Recognition of blurring alphabet character on timing pulley drawing based on HALCON image processing technology. In *Journal of Physics: Conference Series, Proceedings of the 2021 International Conference on Information Technology and Big Data Engineering (ITBDE 2021), Wuhan, China, 25–27 April 2021*; IOP Publishing: Bristol, UK, 2021; p. 012015.

32. Engelmann, K.; Friedl, P. Growth of human corneal endothelial cells in a serum-reduced medium. *Cornea* **1995**, *14*, 62–70. [CrossRef]
33. ImmunoSpot. S6 Ultra M2. Available online: https://immunospot.com/immunospot-s6-ultra-m2.html (accessed on 4 October 2024).
34. Sundararajan, D. *Digital Image Processing: A Signal Processing and Algorithmic Approach*; Springer: Berlin/Heidelberg, Germany, 2017.
35. Zhang, G.; Zhang, J.; Chen, P.; Wang, B. Cell Counting in Image Based on Ridge Regression. In Proceedings of the 2018 IEEE 9th International Conference on Software Engineering and Service Science (ICSESS), Beijing, China, 23–25 November 2018; IEEE: Piscataway, NJ, USA, 2018; pp. 1074–1078.
36. Huang, Y.; Bell, J.; Kuksin, D.; Sarkar, S.; Pierce, L.T.; Newton, D.; Qiu, J.; Chan, L.L.-Y. Practical application of cell counting method performance evaluation and comparison derived from the ISO Cell Counting Standards Part 1 and 2. *Cell Gene Ther. Insights* **2021**, *7*, 937–960. [CrossRef]
37. Di Leo, G.; Sardanelli, F. Statistical significance: *P* value, 0.05 threshold, and applications to radiomics—Reasons for a conservative approach. *Eur. Radiol. Exp.* **2020**, *4*, 1–8. [CrossRef] [PubMed]
38. Bland, J.M.; Altman, D. Statistical methods for assessing agreement between two methods of clinical measurement. *Int. J. Nurs. Stud.* **2010**, *47*, 931–936. [CrossRef]
39. Wickham, H.; Stryjewski, L. 40 years of boxplots. *Am. Stat.* **2011**, *2011*.

MDPI AG
Grosspeteranlage 5
4052 Basel
Switzerland
Tel.: +41 61 683 77 34

Applied Sciences Editorial Office
E-mail: applsci@mdpi.com
www.mdpi.com/journal/applsci

www.ingramcontent.com/pod-product-compliance
Lightning Source LLC
Chambersburg PA
CBHW061550210926
51850CB00009B/2064
* 9 7 8 3 7 2 5 8 6 4 5 4 6 *